Sig   ı

Anglo-Saxon Paganism Revisited

Signals of Belief in Early England

Anglo-Saxon Paganism Revisited

edited by
Martin Carver, Alex Sanmark and Sarah Semple

Oxbow Books
Oxford and Oakville

Published by
Oxbow Books, Oxford, UK

© Oxbow Books and the individual authors, 2010

ISBN 978-1-84217-395-4

This book is available direct from:

Oxbow Books, Oxford, UK
(Phone: 01865-241249; Fax: 01865-794449)

and

The David Brown Book Company
PO Box 511, Oakville, CT 06779, USA
(Phone: 860-945-9329; Fax: 860-945-9468)

or from our website

www.oxbowbooks.com

A CIP record of this book is available from the British library

Library of Congress Cataloging-in-Publication Data

Signals of belief in early England : Anglo-Saxon paganism revisited / edited by Martin Carver, Alex Sanmark, and Sarah Semple.
      p. cm.
  Based on 2 conferences held 2005-2006 at Oxford University.
  ISBN 978-1-84217-395-4
  1. Anglo-Saxons--Religion--Congresses. 2. Civilization, Anglo-Saxon--Congresses. 3. England--Religious life and customs--Congresses. 4. Paganism--England--History--To 1500--Congresses. 5. England--Church history--449-1066--Congresses. I. Carver, M. O. H. II. Sanmark, Alexandra. III. Semple, Sarah, 1973-
  BL980.G7S54 2010
  293.0942'09021--dc22

                    2010017469

Printed and bound in Great Britain by
Hobbs the Printers, Totton, Hampshire

We offer this collection to Audrey Meaney
in appreciation of her studies of Anglo-Saxon paganism.

Contents

Preface

Our aim in this book is to throw new light on the intellect of the earliest English – the way they thought, the way they viewed the world, and the way they viewed worlds other than this. Previous understanding of the topic, well rooted in the ideas of its time, regarded the English as adherents of two consecutive religions: Paganism governed the settlers of the 4th–6th century, but was superseded in the 7th–10th century by Christianity. Of the two, Christianity, a religion of the book, documented itself thoroughly, while in failing to do so Paganism laid itself open to centuries of abuse, conjecture or mindless admiration.

In developing new objectives, our premise is threefold: firstly, that our true quarry is a set of beliefs that varied from place to place. Secondly, that what people believed, whether pure reason or intellectual mish-mash, was expressed in their material culture – so that, thirdly, archaeology can rediscover them. We here align with the modern advocates of cognitive approaches, for whom the study of early thinking holds no terrors. However we know that even the best archaeology provides no open access to the mind. We begin from the material culture: landscapes, sites and objects, and extract from them those non-functional aspects that we ascribe to expressions of the imagination – but know that we cannot necessarily enter that imagination itself. We record, and study, *signals of belief* rather than what was believed. We know that this is only the beginning, although it is a new beginning. Since every community is likely to have its own take on cosmoslogy, there will be many hundreds of communities to study before an underlying system – if there was one – is to emerge.

Our premise is therefore that paganism was not a religion with supraregional rules and institutions but a loose term for a variety of local intellectual world views (Martin Carver). More controversially, we extend the same courtesy to Christianity. Although insisting on its universality, Christianisation too hides a multiplicity of locally negotiated positions, that probably did not amount to a religion (in the orthodox sense) until the 8th century or later. Neither paganism nor Christianity are treated here as independent agents, out to confront and better each other. They are sources on which people, local people – the true agents of Anglo-Saxon England – eclectically drew.

Those sources were themselves widely spread: on the shores of the Baltic, the North Sea and the Mediterranean. In seeking to discover and define signals of belief, we roam widely across the range of material culture and widely too over Northern Europe. Our chapters explore signals from the landscape (Sarah Semple), water cults (Julie Lund), burial rites (Howard Williams), the hall (Jenny Walker), animals in life and art (Pluskowski) and the horse in particular, king of animals (Chris Fern). In the final chapters, Alex Sanmark digs for the character of the Anglo-Saxon soul and Sue

Content and Howard Williams review antiquarian and archaeological construction of Anglo-Saxon paganism from the sixteenth century to the present day. To these of course, we here add constructs of our own. Each of our authors looks across the sea to Scandinavia, as well as to the woods and fields, mires and mounds of Old England. The result, we hope, is a new appreciation of the intellectual preoccupations and anxieties of a crucial age.

   The idea for this book first arose from a conference on Paganism and Popular Practice organised at Oxford in 2005 by Sarah Semple and Alex Sanmark. Two subsequent conferences, on Paganism and the Hall, hosted by the Sutton Hoo Society, gave it a renewed impetus. We are very grateful to those who organised the conferences and to their numerous speakers, who, even where they have not contributed to the book in its final form have helped to inspire its contents. We are particularly grateful to Neil Price and Ronald Hutton for their Foreword and Afterword, each of which lends our collection additional wisdom and authority.

NOTE: In this book, early medieval in England means the 4th–10th century AD and the Late Iron Age is this same period in Scandinavia.

Martin Carver, Alex Sanmark and Sarah Semple

List of Contributors

MARTIN CARVER is Emeritus Professor of Archaeology at the University of York and current editor of *Antiquity*. *martincarver@yahoo.co.uk*

SUE CONTENT is a doctoral student at the Department of History and Archaeology, University of Chester where she is pursuing research into the history of Anglo-Saxon archaeology. *sue.content@hotmail.co.uk*

CHRIS FERN is a free-lance archaeologist and Research Associate of the University of York, specialising in the early medieval period in Britain. He is particularly interested in the art and funerary customs of the Anglo-Saxons and other northern European cultures, as well as the study of animal–human relations in the period. *cjrf100@aol.com*

RONALD HUTTON is Professor of History at the University of Bristol and author of the highly influential works *The Pagan Religions of the Ancient British Isles* and *The Stations of the Sun*. *R.Hutton@bristol.ac.uk*

JULIE LUND is a Senior Lecturer in archaeology at the University of Oslo and has written on the cognitive landscape of Viking Age Scandinavia, making a special study of the symbolism of bridges and crossing points in the early Middle Ages. *julie.lund@hf.uio.no*

ALEKS PLUSKOWSKI is Lecturer in Archaeology at the University of Reading. His research embraces the exploitation of animals and attitudes to animals in medieval Europe. *a.g.pluskowski@reading.ac.uk*

NEIL PRICE is Professor of Archaeology at the University of Aberdeen, and author of *The Viking Way*. *neil.price@abdn.ac.uk*

ALEXANDRA SANMARK is a Post Doctoral Research Associate at the Millenium Institute Centre for Nordic Studies and adjunct Lecturer at the Department of History, University of Western Australia. She is the author of *Power and Conversion*. *alexandra.sanmark@orkney.uhi.ac.uk*

SARAH SEMPLE, is Senior Lecturer in Archaeology at the Durham University and has written extensively on the wider functions and meaning of landscape in the early medieval period. *s.j.semple@durham.ac.uk*

JENNY WALKER is a recent graduate of the Department of Archaeology, University of York, studying the function and meaning of the hall in north-west Europe. *jennywalker@swift-mail.com*

HOWARD WILLIAMS is Professor of Archaeology in the Department of History and Archaeology at the University of Chester. His research interests include mortuary archaeology and the history and theory of early medieval archaeology. He is the author of *Death and Memory in Early Medieval Britain*. *howard.williams@chester.ac.uk*

Acknowledgements

This book has its origin in two conferences, on Paganism and Popular Practice in Anglo-Saxon England (at Oxford University in 2005) and Anglo-Saxon Paganism (hosted by the Sutton Hoo Society in 2006). A further Sutton Hoo Society conference in 2008 on Life in the Anglo-Saxon Hall proved equally stimulating. From the many speakers on these occasions, the present authors have, by their perseverance and passion for the subject, largely selected themselves.

Foreword

Heathen Songs and Devil's Games

Neil Price

Sometime around the year 1014, the pulpits of Anglo-Saxon England resounded to the words of the caustic homily known as *Sermo lupi ad anglos*, 'The Sermon of the Wolf to the English'. The author of the piece was almost certainly Archbishop Wulfstan of York, one of the nation's leading clergymen, and he was writing as the reign of Æþelræd drew to its turbulent close in a wave of Viking invasions. Wulfstan had little doubt as to where the blame lay for the collapse of society that he saw all around – clearly with the English themselves, punished for straying from God's path and therefore deservedly quaking in their congregations as priests passed on the message up and down the land. What concerns us here is the detail of what Wulfstan was throwing in the faces of his flock. He sees "everywhere despisers of divine laws and Christian customs", and in a long list of those bearing "the stains of sin" we find the interesting pairing of *wiccan 7 wælcyrian*. Modern translators usually render this as something like 'sorcerers and witches', but in the present context we should stick closer to the original and talk of wiccans and valkyries.

The meaning of the former is not to be confused with its modern Pagan appropriation, but clearly refers to some kind of person with powers beyond the ordinary. The latter is equally clearly related to the Old Norse *valkyrja*, one of the 'choosers of the slain' who – among their many duties, some better-known than others – brought the spirits of the warrior dead to new homes in the next world. So what were they doing in Anglo-Saxon England nearly four centuries after the supposed Christian conversion, in a context that was sufficiently widespread as to worry the highest officers of the Church?

A few years previously, so late as 959, something even farther from the light was troubling enough to be worth addressing at length in the ecclesiastical canons of King Edgar:

> "We enjoin, that every priest zealously promote Christianity, and totally extinguish every heathenism; and forbid well worshippings, and necromancies, and divinations, and enchantments, and man worshippings, and the vain practices which are carried on with various spells, and with sanctuaries, and with elders, and also with various other trees, and with stones, and with many various delusions, with which men do much of what they should not. [...] And we enjoin, that every Christian man zealously accustom his children to Christianity, and teach them the Paternoster and the Creed. And we enjoin, that on feast days heathen songs and devil's games be abstained from."

These are only two examples, and this book contains many more. The late Saxon advocations to keep to a Christian path are also echoed in similar Continental texts, some of them even more explicit in what they imply about indigenous practices (Burchard of Worms, for example, writing in the tenth century, reprimands "dancing, wearing masks, singing and drinking in the graveyard"[1]). These texts represent the clear persistence of ancient customs over many generations into the period when, if we follow the smooth assurances of clerical propaganda, we might believe that they ought to have disappeared. And if this was the shape of *Christian* England, it raises the obvious question as to what the thought-world of the Anglo-Saxons looked like *before* the advent of the new faith.

The problem of paganism

Despite an enormous amount of archaeological evidence, the general (and, in a largely non-literate society, obvious) dearth of written sources that directly deal with the pre- and proto-Christian period has meant that these fundamental questions have been frequently neglected in academic studies in favour of economic, social and political perspectives. Over the last couple of decades it is true that we have seen important and stimulating works on specific elements of the Anglo-Saxon mind, shining welcome light on at least some of its darker corners. Most of them are referenced in these pages, but alongside these studies of charms, elves, plantlore, witches, magic and a possible Anglo-Saxon shamanism, it is the funerary evidence that has received most attention. Much of this work has natural links to the monumental output of Audrey Meaney, whose years spent patiently excavating Anglo-Saxon attitudes this collection honours.

Nonetheless, it is remarkable that the present book represents the first attempt for nearly two decades to present an overall survey of early English beliefs that cannot be firmly situated within a Christian frame. The problem perhaps lies primarily in terminology, about which redundant arguments are the bane of much archaeological research the world over. The disquieting fact is that almost every single noun or adjective arising in this debate can be viably dismantled as soon as it appears. The 'religion' of the Anglo-Saxons appears to have been no such thing. 'Paganism' is a largely empty concept defined by what it is not (Christianity), and the notion of 'tradition' hardly describes ideas that were dynamic in the extreme. Indeed, it is hard to trace consistency or rules of any kind: regional variation and change over time are keywords here. In the sense of identity and ethnicity, we are not even sure exactly who it is whose beliefs are under discussion. Above all, anyone wishing to address the intricacies of early English mentality soon succumbs to a form of 'mission creep' that sees the subject matter bleed relentlessly out into almost every aspect of society and culture – which should tell us something.

What sets this volume apart (and there are many things that do so) is the editorial sensibilities exemplified in the preface and Martin Carver's agenda-setting paper. With refreshing vigour, Martin and his co-authors aim to "throw light on the intellect of the earliest English", to explore not some kind of pagan orthodoxy but the patterns left by

---

[1] My thanks to Christina Lee for this reference.

local world-views. In this, as the contributors here clearly understand, the book matches the agendas current in the study of early Scandinavian mental landscapes – what Jens Peter Schjødt has evocatively called a 'discursive space', describing a swathe of cognitive terrain in which many things could be encountered by the inhabitants of the early medieval North. This is a place within which they also left an individual mark, sometimes a material one, and thus makes perfect territory for students of tangible culture to explore.

One of the major contributions of this book is to map out, in detail, how far we have come in this task – the byways taken and the trails left unblazed. It also acknowledges the broader context of English beliefs set against those of the contemporary Scandinavians and Germans, these being similarly diverse, unorthodox and regionally variable over time. We learn here that these kinds of comparisons were being made as early as the 1700s by antiquaries like James Douglas, and even included links to the spiritual ideas of circumpolar peoples such as the Sámi. The cross-cultural resonances are indeed striking. I mentioned above the *wælcyrian* of Wulfstan, and in linking it to Old Norse I was careful not to refer (as many others have done) to a loan-word, for we have no real way of telling whether the pre-Christian Saxons also had 'proper' valkyries in the Scandinavian sense of the term. Perhaps they did, and they would hardly have been out of place beside Woden and the rest. Nearly four hundred years separate Wulfstan's homily and the spear-carrying figure on the Finglesham buckle, and the implications of that alone bear thinking about.

In passing we can note that Anglo-Saxon world-views similarly need to be considered not just against what tried to supplant them, but also in relation to what came before. It is surprising how little work has been devoted to the fate of late Romano-British religion – an equally confusing hybrid of early Christianity and indigenous practices – in the light of whatever happened when the Saxons arrived in Britannia.

The list of crucial issues tackled here is very long, and very encouraging. In these pages we wander through referential, numinous landscapes, imbued with the power of place and forming part of the technology of remembrance. We perceive arenas of performance and poetry, for both the living and the dead. The relationship between these latter categories – which may be ours rather than theirs – has been long neglected in Anglo-Saxon studies despite the focus on funerary archaeology, and it is revived here as a serious concern. The border between humans and animals is seen to be hazier than we have earlier admitted, and this has interesting links with beliefs concerning the nature of personhood and the soul. We are also starting to seriously explore the apparently dominant role of women as agents and mediators of supernatural power, with particularly fruitful connections to work along these lines in Scandinavia. Materials and media too come in for greater scrutiny: what did it mean to the early English to live among trees and work with stone, what did they see in water and the liminal zones of the tides and marshes? Not only the importance of the elements in Anglo-Saxon belief is addressed, but also the most fleeting of effects – were burials made by moonlight, and if so, why? Lastly we are learning to see the archaeological data in their most basic form, the artefacts themselves, with new eyes. We can now talk of objects not just in terms of their cultural biography but as agents in their own right.

One observation that also emerges from this book concerns the cyclical nature of academic interpretation. In these pages, for example, we read of the rather elaborate attempts that were made in the nineteenth century to deconstruct (as we would put it now) the pagan concept as applied to the pre-Christian English. We would do well to remember that past scholarship – sometimes several centuries back – contains serious ideas every bit as radical as those we view in that light today. In the same vein we should also see to it that even the most well-worn paths are still kept clear, a case in point being the study of Anglo-Saxon funerary urns. Despite immense amounts of research on the cemetery data, we sometimes need to remind ourselves what an extraordinary resource they represent for the symbolic repertoire of early English mortuary behaviour.

This book is also crucially self-critical, especially in the Afterword prepared by Professor Hutton. Archaeologists write constantly of identity, ideology, ethnicity, and yet frequently forget that we ourselves possess all of these things. As I have mentioned, relations with the ancestral dead make a welcome return in this volume, and I think it is also appropriate to acknowledge that ancestry lasts a long time: these 'pagan' Anglo-Saxons are part of the authors' North European heritage too.

In short, *Signals of Belief* quite simply represents the state of the art, with supporting references to the work on which it builds, and summarises with admirable caution and sensitivity most of what we currently know about the intricate mental world of the pre-Christian English. All future journeys through this difficult terrain must necessarily start here, and they could not have a better guide.

Chapter 1

Agency, Intellect and the Archaeological Agenda

Martin Carver

Introduction

On the battlefield, the valkyries have arrived, their horses gallop across the sky with a light rain falling as they shake the sweat from their flanks. Sorcerers send spells and counter-spells across the field; they change form, their spirits fighting in the sky in constantly shifting animal shapes. On the ground below berserker and ulfhetnar echo the bestial theme. They run howling and foaming through the groups of fighting men. Some wear animal skins, some are naked and some have thrown away shield and armour and rely on their consuming frenzy alone. Perhaps a pale man in a broad-brimmed hat can be seen walking here and there in the field. He carries a staff and two ravens fly above his head. None of this can be seen by the ordinary Viking of course; but what else could explain that lucky spear cast, that man's amazing survival after such a blow, the incredible accuracy of that arrow? It's a good thing that your side has its own sorcerers, lucky you remembered to bring your amulets and charms. That jackdaw's leg has never failed you yet. But there is always the chance that today you will be among the chosen slain; that you will quench the thirst of battle with the horn of mead and hear yourself welcomed into the hall of the gods.

This passage is paraphrased from Neil Price's remarkable book *The Viking Way* (2002) which offered a well-argued evocation of Viking spirituality, and has done much to make the study of non-Christian religion once more respectable among archaeologists. His method was multidisciplinary, putting anthropological observation, early literature and archaeological discoveries into discourse with each other, and letting each source of evidence complement and support and patch up the holes in the others. He uses the observations of anthropologists studying Siberian, Canadian and Sámi shamans to provide analogies for spiritual specialists, arguing in turn for Viking shamans both male and female, whose task, like that of their later analogues, is to heal and prophesy. The Siberian shaman encountered in the 19th century takes intoxicating drink, beats a drum and waves it in the air to conjure up spirits with chanting. He foams at the mouth and emits high pitched noises, before being guided back to the world by a girl who makes copulating gestures (Price 2002: 266). The Sámi shaman had a belt hung with a needle case, knife, brass rings, bird claws and the penis bone of a bear (*ibid.* 269). Some of these items survive and have been collected – for example there are about 80 Siberian ritual drums – so that in addition to observations of contemporary ritual performance, we have some of the stage props.

Taking a step back in time, Price reviews literature of the Medieval and later periods that record the comments of writers thought to have been in touch with non-Christian beliefs and practices. He collects 51 descriptions of valkyries and 204 of Odin. He sketches an eccentric community of divine players (irresistibly reminiscent of the members of an archaeology department): the 'silent one', 'the wind man', 'the thunderer', 'the ancestral mother' and 'the old one in furs'. He draws attention particularly to the shamanistic woman, as here in Eriks' saga: *When she arrived in the evening, together with the man who had been sent to escort her, she was wearing a blue or black cloak fitted with straps, decorated with stones right down to the hem. She wore a string of glass beads around her neck. On her head she wore a black lambskin hood lined with white catskin. She had hairy calfskin shoes, with long sturdy laces, and they had great knobs of tin on the end. On her hands she wore catskin gloves which were white and furry inside.* And then we are introduced to some of the tools of her trade: *Around her waist she had a belt of tinder wood, on which was a large leather pouch. In this she kept the charms that she used for her sorcery. And she carried a staff with a knob at the top (ibid. 168).*

Equipped with such images we are then ready to go back still further – to Viking times – and see whether such spiritual specialists have been captured within the archaeological record. Neil Price finds them waiting for us, particularly the women, in their graves. For example the lady buried in a wagon body in Fyrkat 4, with her silver toe-rings, knife and whetstone, numerous silver pendants, bronze bowl and miniature chair. By her side, a meat spit, a wooden staff and an oak box containing a pig's jaw bone, seeds of henbane and owl pellets. Here surely is the once famous and powerful female shaman, source of wisdom and reassurance, mistress of life and death, whose authority was to be challenged and eventually expunged by institutionalised Christianity.

This hypothetical female specialist has been glimpsed in earlier centuries too. Tania Dickinson's "cunning woman" buried in the 6th century at Bidford-on-Avon (Wa.), was equipped with brooches, a knife, glass and amber beads, bronze tubes and a dozen tiny pendants shape like miniature buckets. These buckets had been worn on a kind of bib beneath the chin, and the assemblage as a whole led even the sober and logical Dickinson to suggest that this was "the grave of someone with special powers" (1993). For Helen Geake (2003) the cunning woman was not only an agent of healing, no doubt of quarrels as well as wounds, but the supervisor and caretaker of the Anglo-Saxon cemetery. This idea, while tentative, is attractive, since it credits women with the psychosomatic expertise of seeing people out of the world as well as bringing them into it.

A number of recent studies have proposed a new model for what happened to these specialists at Christianisation, by looking at graves of the relevant period and noting that it is women who are the leaders in symbolic innovation. Bierbrauer (2003) maps the arrival of crosses and peacocks on brooches and ear-rings south of the Alps between the 5th and 7th centuries, and suggests that it implies an adoption of Christianity independent of social structure. By implication, it is an adoption led by women, since they were the bearers of the symbols concerned. North of the Alps, the Alamans and Bavarians sewed gold foil crosses onto tunics, but the adoption of cruciform brooches is otherwise delayed, because, according to Bierbrauer, "in the sixth and seventh century ... the Germanic world north of the Alps was still deep in syncretism" (2003: 442). From the 8th century Jörn Staecker (2003) finds the symbolic repertoire expressive of a varied and changing ideological allegiance, and it is the female graves that carry the main investment: Thor's hammer pendants and crucifix pendants. Female leadership in the adaptation of Christianity was also discovered by Anne-Sofie Gräslund (2003) on the rune-stones of eastern Sweden; and Linn Lager (2003) proposes that the rune-stones show a geographically varied and drawn-out conversion process. Here we have a picture of Christianisation in Scandinavia, in which women, key spiritual agents in the pagan period, remained in charge during the conversion process. Only when Christianity became institutionalised within the political process of nation-building did women all over Europe surrender their spiritual authority (Carver 2001; 2003; *cf.* Hutton 1991: 250; and compare his 1991: 324: "the victory of the new faith was relatively swift and absolute").

What was it then, this 'paganism' that was abandoned so definitively at the beginning of the Middle Ages? We are used to seeing paganism only as the dead ghost behind Christianity, as the philosophy of 'not-Christ'; Christian writers have made sure of that. The pagan is an intellectual cave-man, a spiritual half-wit, a manic depressive amazed to hear about heaven, a mindless practitioner of ancestral rites, looking for meaning in trees and pondweed. The message is clear – don't go there: it is only for the weird, the witches and the irredeemably wicked.

Is there another road back that navigates between the prurient and the judgemental? It is a tough assignment, not only because of the misconceptions and wishful thinking of modern pagans, hedonists and Christian historians, but because we are not sure where we are going. Even when we think we can argue from graves and sculpture that pre-Christian religion had a high intellectual content and was just as interested in virtue as its successor, we have only opened the steel door of propaganda a chink onto the pagan garden. We are aware that the pagan world deserves our sense of equality and diversity, but can we give it? How can we compete with the relentless rhetoric of Christian salvation and its inheritance? Archaeology offers one way forward, but as we will see, there is no ready-made archaeological toolbox. The theoretical kit is broadly cognitive, but we will need a lot more tools than that (see Hutton 1993).

We do however have an advantage over previous scholars who delved into old religion and thankfully saved much of the evidence for us. In the last twenty years, early medieval archaeologists have explored religion as politics, religion as process, religion as symbolic language, as the architect of landscape, as multi-vocal and reflexive, and designed the archaeological protocols to go with these new approaches. It may also be that in our period of interest, the chances of understanding paganism are greatly increased, precisely because its oppressor was so well recorded: Christianity becomes the protector of the pre-Christian. We are also better equipped in that triad of disciplines that, as Neil Price showed, are the most effective way of opening the chink still further. In this we have yet another advantage over any who pursued the pagans in the Europe of the 19th and 20th centuries: a wholly new order of archaeological investigation.

Detecting, deducing and defining

David Lewis-Williams' stimulating book *The Mind in the Cave* (2002) has redefined the world of early spirituality for archaeologists and can be used as a hypothetical underpinning of every thing that was to come later. He argues that cave art is a record of dreams, and offers a persuasive case that the shaman became a religious specialist through a facility to interpret dreams or to enter the world of dreams (and return with inspiring messages) through self-induced trance. He also demonstrates how, in times of social stress, such people can transmogrify into politicians, and raises in the mind of the reader the startling implication that every leader from the Palaeolithic to the present has successfully professed guidance from the spirit world. Such an apparently indestructible delusion could not have been possible unless the propensity was embedded in most human beings.

There may also be a connection between the degree to which spiritual dependence operates and the physical deprivation experienced by its protagonists – deprivation that we now encounter relatively infrequently in the western world. Price mentions for example the anthropological observation of "arctic hysteria", the tendency of very tired and hungry people to hallucinate. Whatever scepticism may be felt at such generalities, I can personally vouch for the truth of it: in situations of prolonged fatigue you do see rocks move, dead people reappear and animals talk. Not only fatigue and drugs, but starvation and fear can deprive the brain of oxygen so that it plays its tricks. It is not difficult to see why certain peoples sought entrance to the spirit world from those about to die, or by inflicting persistent torture on themselves like the early Christian monks.

This is only to suggest that *if* the pagan Anglo-Saxons had shamans and believed in a spirit world entered occasionally through pain or ecstasy, they would be conforming to a global norm, active as long as there had been humans (Hutton 1991: 109; Sanmark, this vol.). Furthermore, in this respect at least (the need to contact and propitiate the 'other') Christianity was a no less enthusiastic champion of the irrational delusion than paganism. With its sins and relics, its devotions and penances, angels and saints, cherubim and seraphim, heaven, hell and purgatory, its transubstantiation of bread and wine into flesh and its fondness for ritual killing, especially of religious deviants, Christianity was simply much the same, only more so.

The kind of research that seeks to penetrate the ancient mind is archaeology's current frontier and involves a new kind of discourse between the different media. David Lewis-Williams is not reticent about using art, anthropology, psychology, ethnology, drug experience and 19th century politics to support his argument. Francis Thackeray (2005) recently connected three figures in a Lesotho cave with a photograph taken in 1934 at the edge of the Kalahari desert of a man dancing in an animal skin. The scenes, suggesting the enactment of a dying roan antelope striped with wounds, implied sympathetic magic to aid hunting and seemed to be endorsed by surviving linguistic connections between words for wounds, stripes and need. Such multi-disciplinary inquiries require us to open different windows on to the past and put the different vistas presented by each into discourse. We can stop believing theorists who maintain that the human being is helplessly partial, the past is an illusion and that all observation is contradictory. Instead we can believe, if we are brave enough, that humans are irredeemably inquisitive, the world is diverse and that all observations are complementary (Carver 2002). In the Viking period we have ethnological observation, sagas and graves – which can be woven together to give an evocative vision of the non-Christian mind, as Price has shown. And in the pre-Viking period we have at least that, and perhaps more: a broader range of sites, literature, and if we allow ourselves to roam more freely, more ethnological analogy.

However before we embark on an exploration of *The Saxon Way*, it might be worth confronting some of the epistemological problems. The first of these lies in making equations with the very old, the very new and the not-so-new's version of the not-so-old. *Ethnography* provides detailed information for the observer, but it is 1000 years too late and not untainted by the agenda of the performer, as demonstrated by Derrida's critique of the Nambikwara "writing lesson" which gave reflexivity its impetus (Carver 2002: 469–470). The *literature* is inspiring, evocative and imprecise, but 200 years out of date. And the *archaeological evidence* is contemporary, but partial, allusive, coded and equivocal. Cross-referencing between these three sources, with their three different contexts can certainly provide a measure of comfort, but each link between them – the rod of office for example, may acquire spurious ritual airs.

A second problem is that we cannot see ritual, religion or magic archaeologically unless it is the subject of some material investment. Logically, the ordinary cannot of itself imply the extraordinary, or the normal imply the para-normal, without special pleading. Therefore we tend to be confined in archaeology to the high investment sector, rich burials and buildings that are well-dated and associated with distinctive finds, since it is only there that the unusual is evident. But by the same token this is a theatre in which political interference is almost guaranteed. In other words the evidence from graves and monuments, while embracing belief, does so in a context of political purpose. And in most cases we can expect to get more politics than paganism. We are left wondering whether Price's shamanistic woman (above) might not have been a queen, just as rich male warrior graves are seen as leaders rather than shamans.

A third problem, in Anglo-Saxon England at least, has been the study of pagan belief as though it belonged sui generis to the 5–8th century and to the island. This may be our period and place of interest, but no people on earth has ever lived in a timeless vacuum. Anglo-Saxon England did not then exist, nor did Christian institutions; what did exist was a variety of peoples on the east side of Britain who were constructing a variety of beliefs fuelled by their ancestral memories, the prehistoric landscapes they could see or remember, and their contacts with adjacent territories, perhaps most importantly Scandinavia. It would be more productive, it seems to me, to move the whole study of Anglo-Saxon paganism, or indeed the whole study of Anglo-Saxon archaeology, into a region defined by the Northern Seas, and give it a strong prehistoric dimension. To do otherwise would be like trying to study Christianity in Britain without Rome, though we shall need Rome with us here too.

If we take the well-known site of Sutton Hoo, it is easy to see that it is high investment that gives it archaeological visibility. High investment also qualifies it to express the numinous and the religious and their public messages; the ideological and the political. The burial chambers of Sutton Hoo are illuminated by texts, such as Beowulf, but are not explained or even given a context by them. Nor are texts provided with an anchor of reality by the chambers. This is because a burial chamber is itself a text, laden with *topos* and *intertextuality* (Carver 2000). Although there are suggestive links between the burial and the text, to compare the two is only to compare competitors in rhetoric. The barrows and the chambers make allusions to local prehistory and to Roman and German ideas, including eclectic samples of intellectual constructs relating to virtue, death and resurrection that we group crudely and inaccurately as 'pagan' or 'Christian'. It is highly unlikely that the burial parties were trying to conform to, or combine, orthodox Christianity and paganism, because neither existed; or, if they existed, neither was sufficiently institutionalised to command uniformity of practice. Whatever the contemporary documents may claim (and few are contemporary), during the period 5–8th century in north-west Europe no monolithic paganism, and no monolithic Christianity is asserted in the material record. What is asserted, in sites and cemeteries and metalwork, is an astonishing variety of intellectual and metaphysical ideas, which made this truly one of the great periods for thinking people to be alive: it is an age of the unorthodox, although orthodoxy would triumph before the millennium was out.

Cognitive approaches, as developed by Colin Renfrew for non-literate societies (1985a, b), have taken us a long way towards a belief that we can recognise examples of reified cult and even the ethos and theocracy implied. The arguments hinge on the observation of the non-functional, of strangeness, of exaggeration: ceremonial geography, repeated symbols, unnecessary slaughter, and conspicuous waste. For this reason, barrows and henges must signify cult. But there is also a feeling that we need to situate such findings in belief systems, as opposed to mindless megalomania: to avoid the conclusion that people were just bad or mad. Religion may be irrational but at least it gives a reason for its irrationality. In historic periods (and by extension, in prehistoric periods too) we can justify the alignment of religion with strangeness, because we have behavioural analogies recorded in texts (Carver 1993). However, we are also bound to admit that, if we went hunting for our analogies in a different place, virtually all the physical trappings ascribed to religion – special dress, the staff of office, feasting, sacrifice, portentous buildings, fatuous ornamentation – can be ascribed to power-mad earthly leaders too. Who is to say whether the witnesses to a hanging are muttering "receive, O Woden, this gift of thy people" or "that'll teach him a lesson".

It is certainly possible that people communed with the supernatural in their own invented way, but *ipso facto*, archaeology will find it hard to recognise verifiable examples. Tim Insoll (2004: 8) makes a division between 'primal' and 'world' religions, where the world religions always subsume the primal. He also explains the territory to which archaeology is confined by its dependence of material culture, using a Yoruba case study. Here a 'shrine' is a place imbued with multiple and overlapping references of sight, sound and smell. The shrine of Ogunladin, the blacksmith of Oduduna in the ruler's palace of Ife is a place where "complex chains of meaning are created between iron and Ogun, and between Ogun and his role as circumciser, scarifier, carver, excisor and body decoration for example.......... Ogun creates order by transforming, by means of iron tools, the forest into farms and cities. Ogun links can be further extended into the domain of colour symbolism; he is linked with white and red, the extremes through which the iron goes in being created from iron ore. Moreover, Ogun is fiery; he is cooled by snail fluid [which heals scars], but also through the sacrifice of dogs, the dog being a carnivorous animal" (Insoll 2004: 118, citing Pemberton 1997: 130 and Drewal 1997: 255). These symbolic chains (as Insoll calls them) do leave archaeological traces, and Howard Williams shows here how they may have operated in Anglo-Saxon cemeteries; but we have no guide or explanation of where the chains lead.

That intellectual destination can be inferred by analogy. Analogy, however, often reassigns the past into the narrow, over-classified boxes provided by the present. The thinkers of the past, at least at certain periods, and the early middle ages was one of them, could be pluralist and inventive. Religious specialists, if not otherwise constrained by secular forces, will follow their ideas and imaginations and compose their own prescriptions for the supernatural. Note that this is not a question of labelling a religious practice as 'syncretic', a word which carries the opprobrium of confusion or contamination. As Insoll points out, syncretism is an inadequate term of interpretation because it is assumed that two 'givens' are being blended to make a third (2004: 131–4). Thus in our period the players are assumed to be pagans and Christians, even though neither the components nor their product are homogenous. Paganism is itself a rich blend of prehistoric and imported ideas that varies with the landscape, and arguably within the landscape.

In Africa, terms such as *paganism*, *animism* and *magic* have been abandoned and replaced with "African traditional religion" (Insoll 2004: 139). In early medieval Europe we should think of new terminology too, but neither "traditional" nor "religion" seems appropriate to me. 'Traditional' is inappropriate, since in the 5th–8th century we are patently investigating a world of new ideas; 'religion' suggests common practice, but we are starting from an observation of inventive variety. Moreover, in the early middle ages we are probably well on in the process whereby the world of the gods has become part of the local, national or universal power base. By narrowing the study of paganism to high investment sites and objects, we inevitably align it with the exercise of power. For this reason, I assume that what we mainly infer from archaeological evidence is not religion, or even belief, but politics, and its intellectual substrate, ideology. I do not believe we can see religion, so I fear I cannot contribute to the topic of 'paganism'. The stalemate in the recognition of religion in archaeological evidence, well chronicled by Content and Williams (this vol.), was caused by the belief that all the evidence must converge on a normative set of beliefs that could be defined as Pagan or Christian. We can change the agenda simply by assuming that no such normative behaviour existed, and that the monumentality of the 5th–8th century is not convergent but divergent.

It might be possible to distinguish, within the ideological programme that drives monumentality, some of the sense of the non-human that we could label spirituality. Perhaps more safely, the way people chose to make a monument or design a burial should be owed to a dominant or consensual intellect: that is, the way the occupants of Anglo-Saxon England thought in that place, in that context, at that moment of history. We may study this by deconstructing the monument into the many 'references' that it makes. We will find that they are numerous and eclectic and the emphasis is always different. In this lies the originality of each one, and it explains our dissatisfaction with the labels of historiographical tradition. With this focus, I want to try shedding the baggage of decades.

A programme for investigating Anglo-Saxon spirituality

Studying early medieval sites in the field, first Sutton Hoo, in a pagan hinterland, and then Portmahomack, in a Christian one, has been like climbing two different sides of the same mountain. In each case, there were highly developed paradigms, intricate lines of reasoning but contained within a narrow field of view. Paganism v. Christianity has been maintained as a persistent dichotomy, as immovable structuralist opposites. At the summit, one can easily see how restricted the vision was of each team of climbers, roped together and struggling up their particular slopes. Each type of archaeology, the 'pagan' and the 'Christian,' is studied in England by a different exclusive group of scholars and excavators, and each has maintained a resolute ignorance of the other. And those other factions of the modern archaeology department, the prehistorians and the early medieval archaeologists have also managed to get along fine without benefit of mutual discourse. I would suggest that if we are to make progress in the understanding of the early Anglo-Saxon mind we should exercise three principles: first we must study the period as a continuum with prehistory, since there is little doubt the Anglo-Saxons could see prehistory all about them; second we should adopt the premise that monumentality was the result of agency – showing us what local people were thinking and where their allegiance lay; and thirdly, perhaps most important, we are never entitled to assume, in the 5th–8th century, that this monumentality refers to an institutionalised religion, either pagan or Christian in persuasion, since we have no reliable evidence that there was one. A profitable approach may therefore be to listen to the variety of thinking that is implied by the monuments and to treasure its originality.

With these terms and conditions, caveats and abridgements in mind, we could go on a short voyage of exploration to see where such a programme of inquiry might lead. Since I view the terms 'pagan' and 'Christian' as imprecise and anachronistic generalisations, I shall try not to use them, but where I do so in a particular discussion, it is because they were already embedded there. In seeking the materiality of otherness, I shall focus on burials and mounds in particular, and temples and churches – places of assembly. In the new perspective we shall be concerned less with what things meant to worshippers, or even which gods and goddesses were being hailed. We are engaged instead with the changing contexts of belief – why that, why there, why then; and as a consequence, the shifts in the intellectual map of NW Europe that these changes imply.

Burial

The territory to be explored is the Northern seas, but just like any other voyage we cannot go everywhere, so will pick and choose. It is axiomatic to the study that people crossed these waters regularly in the early Middle Ages, allowing us to assume that there was an ideological discourse from coast to coast. This means that people in England or Scotland or Scandinavia did not need to wait for a particular idea to arrive; the monuments rather report the moment that an idea was chosen, adapted and reified by the local community concerned. Distribution maps raise a whole lot of interesting questions in this regard, long before we get to our first barrow. For example, the distribution of pottery imported from the Mediterranean in the 5–6th century (*A ware*) and from south-west France in the 6–7th century (*D, E ware*) is extremely eccentric. It is focused on an expanding territory centred on the Irish Sea. While it would not have been hard for sailors who had made it through the Bay of Biscay to do the extra few leagues to London or York, nevertheless, apparently they did not; this pottery did not arrive in Kent or Northumbria, even when the latter became nominally Christian. Similarly, claw beakers and reticella glass, made in Kent, are finding their way to east Scandinavia, but not to Scotland – why not? Something irrational, or at least non-economical, is controlling voyages and structuring the seaways.

In the late 6th century, people were building burial mounds over cremations at Gamla Uppsala, boat burials at Slusegård on Bornholm, symbol stones on Gotland, square-ditched barrows (also with symbol stones) in Pictland, stone churches with *porticus* in Kent, Type 1 megalithic churches in SW Ireland and new kinds of 'monastic' settlements on Iona and in the NE Scottish firthlands. This is not intellectual anarchy, it has regional integrity; the pattern has structure but is the structure of a debate, in which the participants experience shifting viewpoints. Böhme's mapping of princely graves and founder churches in the Rhineland, shows that the churches follow the graves up the Rhine between the 5th century and the 8th. This does not look like migration or a change in social structure. It can, however, be equated with a response to a political movement which travels from the area of the Rhinemouth up in to the Swiss Alps. If this is so, then the first response is to build burial mounds, and the second to build a church. Monumentality here is therefore subject to a kind of 'bow-wave effect' in which monument-building responds to forces that are approaching but have yet to arrive (Carver 2001 for references).

I employed this model in the interpretation of the burial mounds constructed at Sutton Hoo and elsewhere (1986: 1992) calling them "reactive" and citing them as examples of "defiant paganism". The idea was later enthusiastically taken up by Robert van de Noort, who published a map of early medieval barrows in North West Europe, and interpreted their appearance as responses to Christianity (van de Noort 1993; see also Lutovsky 1996 for inclusion of the Slavic examples). I still think the idea of reactive monumentality has some value, but it cannot always imply reaction to the same threat. For example, Mound 2 at Högom in Medelpad is a splendid monument commemorating a warrior lying on a bed, but dated to the 5th century – not a period in which the northern Baltic would be likely to feel itself under much pressure from Christian missionaries (Ramqvist 1992).

Thus if burial mounds relate to belief, the belief belongs to a historical context: a unique expression constructed from a common vocabulary. Listing grave goods, like making dictionaries, does not tell us what people were thinking; we have to listen to every grave. For example, Mads Ravn (2003: 134) identifies a group of young men dedicated to board games, drinking, horses and hairdressing; but such objects are found all over Europe and do not require a religious gloss. Nor do they support his conclusion that "Germanic society from AD 200 to 600 was a small-scale rural society which developed with the family and the farmstead as the centre of the universe" (*ibid.* 136). The references being made are at least as wide as NW Europe, and arguably stretch back in time to at least the early Iron Age. In his chapter below, Howard Williams reminds us that the opportunities for making references to the intellectual repertoire were not confined to the preparation of the burial tableau: the funeral was a drama in several acts, each of which could make the mourners glad or sad or to provoke a resigned recognition of the human dilemma, which, while it might not itself be a religion or a cosmology, comes close to its agenda.

The kind of space-time referential framework more likely to be operating has been sketched for burial in boats. Ship-settings, rock carvings of ships and some boat burials are known around the north sea in the Bronze Age. The idea reappears in the form of boats containing people and buried in pits; in the 1st century AD on Bornholm, in the 5th century in Frisia, in the 6th century in Uppland Sweden, in the 7th century in East Anglia, in the 9th century in Norway, Denmark and Schleswig Holstein and in the 10th century on Orkney (Müller-Wille 1995; Carver 1995; 2005: 301–306). If these were Christian symbols, we would suppose them to plot the locus of a missionary activity. But no-one is even suggesting that boat-burial is a religious sect – let alone that missionaries recruited people to its ethos. It is difficult to draw satisfactory equations with Frey or any other god (Carver 1995), and references to heavenly voyages, and so on, are facile. Instead I have proposed a model of the reification of ideas drawn eclectically from a common northern European cosmology. The ship was a player in the theatre of shared knowledge, its symbolism modified from place to place and time to time like any other hard-worked metaphor. But there came a particular moment when the ship was a symbol necessary to a particular burial, so an actual ship was procured and buried. The distribution of ship burial is thus not religious or ethnic, but the distribution of a shared poetic mood or rather of the moments when that mood was evoked and reified (Carver 2000). It is not excluded that the ship, as a metaphor, has allusions to Egyptian burial ships, as burial mounds may have to pyramids. Sutton Hoo ship 1 contained textiles from Syria, and buried nearby was a bronze bucket, perhaps from North Africa, or at least referring to Nubia. There is no need to cite diffusion: the southern world was already known to the northerners and vice versa. The interest for us lies in what they chose to incorporate in their view of this world (and the next), and why. In this context it can be seen that Christianity can also arrive, not as a package, but as chunks of imported metaphor. Appreciation of the popular stories of King David and Daniel does not require belief in Christ, the Trinity or the Virgin birth. In trying to understand what is intended by the term 'conversion' we need to draw a distinction on the one hand between the selective adoption of Christian notions, and on the other the imposition of a Christian organisational infrastructure. These are two quite different realities and we had better be sure which we mean.

It is also important for the ideology of burial mounds to remember that by the 5th century the landscape had plenty of them. As Richard Bradley (1993), Howard Williams (1997), Andrew Reynolds (2009) and Sarah Semple (this vol.) have shown, people manipulated the face of the land and left mental maps for those that came later. These were maps that later people could read, and perhaps indicated more to them than simply former cultural territories; for the Anglo-Saxons, the prehistoric landscape of east Britain can be seen as a non-literate text as deep as the Bible was to become. Each generation of 'burial experts' had the pre-existing landscape to reckon with; and this, if nothing else, should encourage us to expect a strong local flavour to both burial and belief. In his recent study of *kurgans*, the huge burial mounds of Eastern Eurasia, Bryan Hanks (2001) found that, at a given place, later mounds made reference to earlier ones. The giant 10th century BC mound at Arzhan was 120m across and covered 70 timber rooms as well as the central chamber with its log coffins. 160 horses and 7 servants were sacrificed and laid in the rooms. This mound also signalled the first appearance of Scytho-Siberian animal art. So, the great monument marks one of those historical moments of ideological rebirth, leaving a long trail for others to follow. There was evidence for feasting around this mound, and not just at the time of the funeral: the place attracted festivals of horse racing and feasting up to historic times.

Assembly

If burial can be explained as a kind of poetic utterance, it can be expected to make references to fate, and the hereafter, and the four last things, ideas that beset all humans whether they profess any religious belief or not. It thus remains possible that burial was focussed on celebrating humans rather than gods and its theological content may be in doubt. If so, we are still searching for other sites where the focus was on the supernatural. Did Anglo-Saxons go in for communal worship? And if so, did it need a building or any space we can recognise? The discussion above leaves us with the expectation that there will have been spiritual specialists in early Medieval Britain, as in Viking Scandinavia, and that their activities need not have been confined to private consultations given to eminent persons. We should expect the manifestations of belief to be imprinted in the landscape, in settlements, buildings and on objects – all areas of research that will be explored in the chapters that follow.

　　For many years scholars have resisted the idea that northern religions had or needed temples (*e.g.* Olsen 1966; Hutton 1991: 270; Welinder 2003). For some, worshippers stood in sacred groves or beside dark tarns, occasionally killing something, or someone, to propitiate the unknown and dreaded. Others felt that communal acts of worship were indistinguishable from acts of secular control: the religious space was the hall, where drink was dispensed and decisions made: the ideological was also the social (Herschend 1997). Others again felt that while temples were not endemic to northern belief, the northerners acquired them when they saw the Christians coming: defence by imitation. All this has now been put back into the melting pot by the discoveries at Gudme, Borg and Uppåkra, and the thesis of Leszek Słupecki (discussed below).

　　In Britain, recent studies have identified "shrines" in the form of simple rectangular post settings and deduced from them a quasi-independent development for Anglo-Saxon ritual centres (Wilson 1992, Blair 1995, Meaney 1995). Perhaps the term shrine (Lat *scrinium*, box) is a bit distracting, since it suggests containers for relics rather than places for gathering. It is used in this sense in Ireland, where 'shrines' are generally portable boxes (reliquaries), but may also be large and static as in the rectangular gabled slab-shrines or corner-post slab-shrines (O'Carragain 2003: 143–4), or the square pile of stone slabs (*leacht*) that perhaps functioned as an altar or as the plinth of a cross, or both (Edwards 2000: 116–119). Square settings of posts, with or without ditches are known as burial enclosures in Pictland (Ashmore 1980) and in South Wales (James 1992), as well as at Yeavering (Hope-Taylor 1977: 108–116). Thus the role of the 'Anglo-Saxon shrine' is unclear: given its rather unassertive survival, we may be dealing with burial (as at Yeavering), the enclosure of an idol or with the isolated room of a priest (as in a Roman-Celtic temple). Indeed, the small square enclosure has been cited as a sign of "British" continuity (Blair 1995), which is surprising in view of its ubiquity in Scandinavia and continental Europe (see, for example, Audouze and Büchsenschutz 1989: 63, 128 (granary), 68, 108, 120 (houses)). Obviously houses can also be ritual, but being square is neither a necessary nor a sufficient attribute of religious use.

A better place to hunt might be in the continental *Viereckschanzen*, regular four-sided enclosures with wells and putative temples. At Gournay-sur-Aronde on the same site as, and developed from, an Iron Age timber prototype of the 3rd century BC, is a wide-ditched enclosure 40m square, in which were laid broken weapons and sacrificed animals and people (*ibid.* 150). In Britain, at one of the most comprehensive and best excavated ritual sequences of the Roman and post-Roman periods, Uley in Gloucestershire, the authors track a ritual development through a square post-hole building of the 1st century AD, to a Roman temple (100–400 AD), a polygonal alcove possibly for a statue (Structure III) that served the temple, and a 6th century church (Woodward and Leach 1993). At Whithorn, Peter Hill applies the term 'shrine' to roughly circular places in a cemetery respected by and devoid of burials (1997: 91–6). He remarks that "the three successive 'shrines' do not seem to have close parallels" (*ibid.* 34), but proposes links with circular foci, real or implied, in other cemeteries. Like the rectangular post-settings, this does not get us very far, since circular spaces are also ubiquitous in prehistory and in Europe north, south, east and west. I thus offer the obvious comment that the shape of a structure in plan may not, of itself, be diagnostic of the ritual activity of a particular people, even if one collected examples from the much broader cosmological zone I am advocating. We are looking for more specific indicators, and it is discoveries from the Baltic area that suggest we could soon know how to recognise them.

In his 1996 book, Leszek Słupecki challenged the idea that early Medieval Slavs had no temples; or that, if they did, they were only built in response to Christian interference (*i.e.* 'defiant paganism' as above). He draws a great deal of his evidence from later commentators and especially Saxo Grammaticus, so to some extent we are still in a literary landscape of uncertain date. On this basis he uses archaeological evidence to define two kinds of buildings he would like us to see as sacred. The first are temples, where a hall-like building has particular attributes which appear to set it apart. An example is the timber building at Gross Raden which was surrounded by a paling fence with anthropomorphic posts and which contained six horse skulls, an ox skull and a pottery cup. Another was defined at Parchim, which stood between the fortified settlement and Lake Loddig-See and gave rise to the idea of a cult beach. Słupecki offers, as another attribute of these temples, their orientation towards the four quarters of the world (1996: 101).

His second type of site is unrelated to either burials or halls, although it clearly refers to prehistoric practice. At Perynia, the name of which relates to the god Perun, a circular ditch with a large post hole at the centre was excavated by Syedov in 1951. The ditch was 'scalloped' into petal-shaped areas, all but one of which contained hearths. Słupecki imagined the central post to have supported a wooden effigy of Perun, documented as having been being destroyed in 988. At Khodosoviche, a large post had stood in a similar situation, this time surrounded by a fence and an interrupted ditched enclosure. His star example was the supposed sanctuary sited at a nodal point of the hill-fort on Bogit Mountain. Here a ring of pits has been excavated, at the centre of which was a socket lined with packing stones. It was in this socket, according to Ukrainian archaeologists Timoshuk and Rusanova, that the famous pillar known as the *Sviatovid* originally stood (1996: 182). This remarkable pillar was recovered from the nearby River Zbruch and is now at Cracow. It is carved out of soft limestone, stood originally 2.57m in height and has a figurative scheme on each side. At the top is a head with one hat and four faces, two thought to be male and two female; a horse and other human figures follow lower down. Among the interpretations that academic commentators have seen are a sun god, a spring goddess, a god of the underworld and a giant phallus, which, as Słupecki wryly remarks, is somewhat inconsistent with its square cross-section.

Whether any such equations with mythology are yet possible is less urgent a problem than the obvious echoes that such objects make with the repertoire further west. If the Sutton Hoo sceptre springs to mind, so does the Bewcastle Cross. I am not trying to say that these things influenced each other (the Sviatovid post-dates the other two by some centuries) or refer to each other directly, and certainly not that these echoes have to refer to Christianity or to Rome – all of which have been suggested in each case. For me they say only that North Europe, then as now, is a zone of shared ideas, where imitation and rejection are part of the dialogue of peer polities.

Słupecki's examples are good evidence for some kind of formal religious structure among the Slavs, but his thesis that it developed long before Christian pressure began to build is less secure, because the dating is less secure. His sites are dated 10–11th century from pottery, where it occurs, although this might refer to the date of the site's destruction. However, recent discoveries at Gudme and Uppåkra provide examples every bit as evocative, much better dated and up to a millennium earlier. At Gudme (lit. God's home), on Fyn, attention was drawn to the site by finds of large numbers of *guldgubbar* found in the fields surrounding a filled-in lake. These small gold plaques acquired their nickname, roughly equivalent to 'gold-gaffers', because stamped upon them were small figures resembling old men. But some of the figures depicted are clearly women and couples apparently kissing; whence theories that they represent gods or fertility charms. Although the finds at Gudme focus on a lake or tarn, this is no outdoor nature worship but a managed and prominent ritual centre of some kind, as suggested by the large halls that have now been excavated (Nielsen *et al.* 1997).

The site of Uppåkra, in South East Sweden, has been known since 1930s when the construction of a barn near the round barrow brought to light some *guldgubbar*; but the more recent investigations there were prompted by the revelations at Gudme. Surveys by phosphate and metal detector mapped a distribution of 20,000 finds of gold, silver and bronze with an area of dense occupation at its centre, which was excavated, leading to the discovery of a short hall with bowed walls (Larsson 2007; Walker this vol.). On its south side was found a crystal goblet from the Black Sea area; while at the east end were 115 *guldgubbar*. The *guldgubbar*, which are clearly associated with the building, have been published by Margrethe Watt. She notes figures of men, women and couples, closely paralleled at Gudme and Sorte Muld, and argues that they are "temple money", symbolic votive offerings, with the figures representing Woden and other members of the pantheon. Like Karl Hauck she subscribes to a pagan priesthood enduring at least 500 years up to the 11th century. Among the Uppåkra *guldgubbar* are several featuring a man biting his thumb, attributed to Odin and others carrying a staff, which may indicate the office of shaman (Watt 2004: 210).

These specialist ritual centres have thrown back into conjecture the idea that halls doubled as ritual centres. But it is not always so clear. The giant hall excavated at Borg in Lofoten, NW Norway was also notable for the finding of *guldgubbar*. At its maximum size the hall was 80m long and 7.5–9m in width (*i.e.* slightly bowed). On the basis of the distribution of the objects, or their absence, excavators divided it into 5 rooms, designated "Living room", "Entrance room", "hall", "room" and "byre" (Munch *et al* 2003, 93; Walker this vol.). The objects included farm implements such as sickles and arrowheads, pins, fishhooks, pottery, glass vessels, glass beads and *guldgubbar*. The special objects, the beads and plaques, focussed on the room named as the "hall" (Room C). At this site, the interpretation of the ritual plaques follows the study of Steinsland (1991): although the imagery relates to the sacred marriage, and thus fertility, it depicts a union at divine level (*e.g.* Odin and the giantess Skade), and is actually being used as a metaphor for the union of a leader with his land (Munch 2003: 259). In this case, therefore, the finds do not imply a temple but a "chieftain's farm".

In the future we can expect Scandinavian excavators to bring new questions to these sites: for example, what areas do they serve? Could the hall – especially a hall the size of a farmstead like Borg – have incorporated the ritual space within its rooms, a space which in some settlement contexts (Uppåkra) demands a stand-alone building to fulfil its social function, and in others (Gudme) is a central destination providing ritual and ideological functions for a whole island? From these three great excavations alone we can suppose a variety of ritual provision every bit as sophisticated as the secular, parochial, monastic and episcopal structures of Christianity. The northern regions were well equipped with high investment centres exhibiting strong and varied ideological administration. The minds of such people do not offer a blank slate on which missionaries may write.

Christian variants

Returning from our trip to Scandinavia, it is difficult to believe that Early Anglo-Saxon England, which betrays so many other affinities, did *not* have votive deposits, shrines, ritual gold plaques, standing timber and stone idols, and a range of temple structures, and it seems reasonable to suppose that they will eventually turn up, if displaying differences of emphasis. The trick will be to detach this inquiry – the archaeology of early medieval ideology, its regionalism, its multiple references and its asymmetric change over northern Europe – from the old historical agenda of "the Conversion". In his magisterial review of the conversion of Europe, Richard Fletcher comments: "resistance to Christianity is not a topic about which we should expect much information to have survived" (Fletcher 1997: 285). But only if you mean historical information; the information that has survived is enormous, but it is all archaeological; and what is being resisted, as we have seen, is not Christian ideas, which are welcome to join the party, but Christian political dominance.

This is trying not to be a chapter about early Christianity, and I have presented perverse views on the subject quite enough elsewhere (Carver 1998; 2001; 2003; 2008 ch. 10). In my thesis, paganism and Christianity do not, in this period, describe homogenous intellectual positions or canons of practice. Pagan ideas and material vocabulary were drawn from a wide reservoir of cosmology and were recomposed as local statements with their own geographical and chronological context. I believe that the same kind of evidence, the evidence of monumentality, provokes us to a similar judgment of Christianity. Christianity and paganism were two hands of the same *persona*, and there was considerable interdigitation between the two. Some local practices merely continued under new management. David Stocker and Paul Everson (2003) found votive deposition on the River Witham, from before the 8th century when the Witham pins were thrown in, up till the 14th century when this spiritual resource had been absorbed, without apparent stress, into the stewardship of the monastery. It may be that the use of rivers (as opposed to bogs) is what has inhibited the discovery of Anglo-Saxon period votive offerings (see Lund, this volume).

Other apparently new attributes of early Christianity may have been drawn from local prehistoric sources, rather than being members of the imported package. For example, Ann Woodward (1993) has shown that a cult of relics was active in the Neolithic of southern England, body parts being reserved, presumably for exchange or display. The shrines already mentioned, whether in Britain or Ireland, all have prehistoric roots. Even the stone-lined graves of eastern Scotland, long associated with the Christian conversion, are equivocal in the references they make. Perhaps they do recollect and proclaim the early Christian mortuary sequence of north Italy (*cf.* Carver 1983); but their origins can also be located in the use of stone slabs in Bronze Age and Iron Age graves (*cf.* Close-Brooks 1984).

Carved stone monuments, as collected in the *Corpus of Anglo-Saxon Stone Sculpture* vary from simple slabs with incised names in Latin characters or runes (as at Hartlepool), to tall pillars with complex iconographical schemes involving people and animals in niches (as at Ruthwell and Bewcastle). As already mentioned such schemes may have been commandeered for the pagan pillars of the Baltic (as the *Sviatovid*); or, given the previous exemplars of idols cited by Słupecki, both suites of stone carving may have derived from long periods of experimentation in timber. Two other sequences raise the possibility of more plural origins: the Gotlandic and the Pictish carved stones. Interestingly, both seem to undergo the same kind of evolutionary change, beginning with a basic stone slab that carries a symbol, to a shaped monolith with iconographical pictures, to a more literary finale of the symbol-free cross slabs in Pictland and the runestones in Gotland, both by this time (11th century) overtly declaring a Christian alignment (Nylen and Lamm 1988; Henderson and Henderson 2004). A case has been made for the origins of the Pictish sequence in the imitation of slabs on the Antonine or Hadrian's wall, or as a recognition of Christian grave markers, but an association has also been claimed with barrows, and the square ditched barrows in particular (Ashmore 1980). The competition to assign the affiliation of this sculpture to a pagan or Christian source can have no satisfactory result. Such sources are a figment of our time, not theirs. Picts and Gotlanders could not have known that they were on a trajectory towards ever-increasing ideological control, which would be claimed retrospectively as Christian in character and intent. It therefore behoves us to treat each monumental experiment as a product of its own logic, not as an inept prototype of what we know was to come.

Since ostensibly Christian monumentality varies, it seems to me inherently likely that what we recognise on the ground as Christian would also belong to a varied set of experiments. In some cases, it seemed politically unacceptable to swallow the package whole, since an episcopate would demand the creation of an infrastructure that a local leader could not or would not deliver. Thus the attraction of fiscal solutions such as privately funded churches, or the establishment of monasteries by endowment that did not require taxation, in the way that a full-blown episcopal and parochial system would (Carver 1998). The Christian infrastructure is subservient to the political realities. The variety we encounter in the early centuries means that just as there was no "Anglo-Saxon paganism" there was (pace Blair 2005) no "Anglo-Saxon church" either, at least not before there was a united Anglo-Saxon kingdom. The ideologies of Britain's regions were making their own statements and proclaiming their own alignments as the decades passed.

These things need repeating because some historians and prehistorians seem to be still stuck in a past structured by kings and their religious affiliations. Several years after the Sutton Hoo project had been completed, it was disconcerting to find the same old half-dead horses being flogged at Prittlewell: which king was buried here? Was he a Pagan or a Christian? (MoLAS 2004: 39–42). These are non-questions: burials cannot distinguish kings, even if we knew what a king was in the 7th century (contra Parker Pearson et al. 1993). We can only be sure it was something quite different from a king in the 9th, 13th or 18th century. Similarly it is quite inappropriate and anachronistic to be opposing Christian to pagan in the 7th century. If a contemporary journalist asked whether the Prittlewell prince was Christian or pagan, one hopes he would sit bolt upright, and say "I trust I am neither, and let's pray we never get to the point that we are obliged to declare such a crude choice of allegiance. My burial proclaims the intellectual autonomy of my family, its history, my record as a soldier and estate owner, my broad knowledge of prehistory, my taste, my pride in my people, our inheritance, the current preoccupations of our intellectual arena, our political aspirations and fears." The prince would be disappointed at what was to happen. The dark curtain of Christianity was about to close round Europe, inhibiting original thought about the supernatural there for the next 1000 years.

Conclusion

The administration of dreams is a fundamental human tendency, and the spiritual specialist is likely to have been a player in every human community. In early medieval

Europe, the range of monumentality, and thus the implied variety of ritual behaviour and religious thinking, is prodigious. The references made are to a wide cosmological inheritance from prehistory, from Rome, from continental Europe and from the Mediterranean. Historical terms such as Christianity, paganism and indeed Anglo-Saxon do no justice to the intellect and agency of the people living in eastern Britain at the time. The people of Anglo-Saxon regions drew on a broad repertoire of ideas, particularly from Scandinavia, that we have failed to appreciate because it is only recently that archaeology has had the confidence to claim their discovery.

The 5–8th century was a time of ideological experiment and inventive thinking, for the very good reason that no single power had sufficient might or authority to control it. There was no single orthodox pagan community, and no single orthodox Christian authority. Intellectual positions were adapted to local conditions, in particular the structure of society and the political agendas of the communities. They were worked out – negotiated – between the communities across the seas and across the land, and expressed in monuments, burial practice and other kinds of investment that we have been fortunate enough to inherit. Women were prominent in these investments and thus probably prominent in the administration of the varied belief systems.

But from the time of Charlemagne, authority was achieved over larger and larger territories and with it greater expertise in social and spiritual control. With increasing spiritual control came orthodoxy and the intellectual honeymoon was over. These are trends that I believe we can deduce from the archaeological evidence. Paganism in this period – if it has a useful meaning – refers to the broad repertoire of ideas of enormous time depth on which the inventive thinkers of the day could draw.

The new approaches to Anglo-Saxon paganism, epitomised by the new generation of scholars using this book as a platform, will be multi-disciplinary and will assume no underlying orthodoxies. They search for signs of the spirit in the open air, in the hall, at the grave side and in art, and assemble a synthesis of the Anglo-Saxon soul. In the reflections that follow, the object of our study is the originality of the pre-Christian, non-Christian, mind as a different, not a lesser, way of thinking. Valued for its own sake, it will also be seen to have values that have endured to the present day.

References

Aldhouse-Green, M. (2001) Devotion and Transcendence: Discrepant Function in Sacred Space. *In* A.T. Smith and A. Brookes (eds) *Holy Ground: Theoretical Issues Relating to the Landscape and Material Culture of Ritual Space*, 61–71, BAR International Series, 956, Oxford

Ashmore, P. (1980) Low Cairns, Long Cists and Symbol Stones, *Proc. Soc. Ant. Scot.*, 110: 346–55

Audouze, F. and Büchsenschutz, O. (1989) *Towns, Villages and Countryside of Celtic Europe*, London: Batsford

Bierbrauer, V. (2003) The Cross Goes North: from Late Antiquity to Merovingian Times South and North of the Alps. *In* Carver (ed.), 429–442

Blair, J. (1995) Anglo-Saxon Pagan Shrines and their Prototypes, *Anglo-Saxon Studies in Archaeology and History* 8: 1–28

Blair, J. (2005) *The Church in Anglo-Saxon Society*, Oxford: OUP

Bradley, R. (2001) *Altering the Earth. The Origins of Monuments in Britain and Continental Europe*,

Society of Antiquaries of Scotland Monograph 8, Edinburgh: Society of Antiquitaries, Scotland

Carver, M. (1986) Sutton Hoo in Context, *Settimane Di Studio Del Centro Italiano Di Studii Sull'alto Medioevo* 32: 77–123

Carver, M. (1987) S Maria Foris Portas at Castel Seprio: A Famous Church in a New Context *World Archaeology* 18.3: 312–329

Carver, M. (1993) In Search of Cult. *In* Martin Carver (ed.) *In Search of Cult. Archaeological Investigations in Honour of Philip Rahtz*, V–IX, Woodbridge: Boydell

Carver, M. (1995) Boat Burial in Britain: Ancient Custom or Political Signal? *In* Crumlin-Pedersen and Thye, 111–124

Carver, M. (2000) Burial as Poetry: The Context of Treasure in Anglo-Saxon Graves. *In* E. Tyler (ed.) *Treasure in the Medieval West*, 25–48, Woodbridge: Boydell

Carver, M. (2001) Why that? Why there? Why then? The Politics of Early Medieval Monumentality. *In* H. Hamerow and A. Macgregor (eds) *Image and Power in the Archaeology of Early Medieval Britain. Essays in Honour of Rosemary Cramp*, 1–22, Oxford: Oxbow Books

Carver, M. (2002) Marriages of True Minds: Archaeology with Texts. *In* B. Cunliffe, W. Davies and C. Renfrew (eds) *Archaeology. The Widening Debate*, 465–496, Oxford: British Academy

Carver, M. (ed.) (2003) *The Cross Goes North. Processes of Conversion in Northern Europe, AD 300–1300*, Woodbridge: Boydell

Carver, M. (2003) Introduction: Northern Europeans Negotiate their Future. *In* Carver (ed.), 3–14

Carver, M. (2005) *Sutton Hoo. A Seventh Century Princely Burial Ground and its Context*, Society of Antiquaries Research Report No 69, London: British Museum Press

Carver, M. (2008) *Portmahomack. Monastery of the Picts*, Edinburgh: Edinburgh University Press

Close-Brooks, J. (1984) Pictish and Other Burials. *In* J. G. P. Friell and W. G. Watson (eds) *Pictish Studies: Settlement, Burial and Art in Dark Age Northern Britain*, 87–114, BAR British Series, 125, Oxford

Crumlin-Pedersen, O. and Thye, B.M. (eds) (1995) *The Ship as Symbol in Prehistoric and Medieval Scandinavia*, Copenhagen: National Museum of Denmark

Dickinson, T.M. (1993) An Anglo-Saxon Cunning Woman From Bidford-On-Avon. *In* M. Carver (ed.) *In Search of Cult. Archaeological Investigations in Honour of Philip Rahtz*, 45–54, Woodbridge: Boydell

Drewal, H.J. (1997) Art or Accident: Yoruba Body Artists and their Deity Ogun. *In* S. Barnes (ed.) *Africa's Ogun. Old World and New*, 235–60, Bloomington: Indiana University Press

Edwards, N. (2000) *The Archaeology of Early Medieval Ireland*, London: Routledge

Fletcher, R. (1997) *The Conversion of Europe. From Paganism to Christianity 371–1386 AD*, London: Harper Collins

Geake, H. (1997) *The Use of Grave-Goods in Conversion-Period England c.600–c.850*, BAR British Series, 261, Oxford

Geake, H. (2003) The Control of Burial Practice in Middle Anglo-Saxon England. *In* Carver (ed.), 259–270

Gräslund, A.-S. (2003) The Role of Scandinavian Women in Christianisation: The Neglected Evidence. *In* Carver (ed.), 483–496

Hanks, B.K. (2001) Kurgan Mortuary Practices in the Eurasian Iron Age – Ideological Constructs and the Process of Rituality. *In* A.T. Smith and A. Brookes (eds) *Holy Ground: theoretical Issues Relating to the Landscape and Material Culture of Ritual Space*, 39–48, BAR International Series, 956, Oxford

Henderson, I. and Henderson, G. (2004) *The Art of the Picts*, London: Thames and Hudson

Herschend, F. (1997) *Livet i hallen. Tre fallstudier i den yngre järnålderns aristokrati*, Uppsala

Hill, P. (1997) *Whithorn and St Ninian*, Stroud: Sutton

Hutton, R. (1991) *The Pagan Religions of the Ancient British Isles. Their Nature and Legacy*, Oxford

Hutton, R. (1993) Preface to the Paperback Edition of Hutton 1991

Insoll, T. (2004) *Archaeology, Ritual, Religion*, London: Routledge

James, H. (1992) Early Medieval Cemeteries in Wales. *In* N. Edwards and A. Lane (eds) *The Early Church in Wales and the West*, 90–103, Oxford: Oxbow Books

Lager, L. (2003) Runestones and the Conversion of Sweden. *In* Carver (ed.), 497–508

Larsson, L. (2007) The Iron Age Ritual Building at Uppåkra, Southern Sweden, *Antiquity* 81: 11–25

Lewis-Williams, D. (2002) *The Mind in the Cave*, London: Thames and Hudson

Lutovsky, M. (1996) Between Sutton Hoo and Chernaya Mogila: Barrows in Eastern and Western Early Medieval Europe, *Antiquity* 70: 671–6.

Meaney, A. (1995) Pagan English Sanctuaries, Place-Names and Hundred Meeting Places, *Anglo-Saxon Studies in Archaeology and History* 8: 29–42

MoLAS (2004) *The Prittlewell Prince. The Discovery of a Rich Anglo-Saxon Burial in Essex*, London MoLAS

Müller-Wille, M. (1995) Boat Graves, Old and New Views. *In* Crumlin Pedersen and Thye, 101–110

Munch, G., Stamsø, S., Johansen, O. and Roesdahl, E. (2003) *Borg in Lofoten. A Chieftain's Farm in North Norway*, Trondheim: Tapir Academic Press

Nielsen P.O., Randsborg K. and Thrane H. (eds) *The Archaeology of Gudme and Lundeborg*, Akademisk Forlag: Universitetsforlaget i København

Nylén, E. and Lamm, J.P. (1988) *Stones, Ships and Symbols. The Picture Stones of Gotland from the Viking Age and Before*, Stockholm: Gidlunds

O'Carragáin, T. (2003) A Landscape Converted: Archaeology and Early Church Organisation on Iveragh and Dingle, Ireland. *In* Carver (ed.), 127–152

Olsen, O. (1966) Hørg, hov og kirke. Historiske og arkeologiske vikingetidsstudier. *Aabøger for nordisk oldkyndighed og historie 1965*: 1–307

Parker-Pearson, M., Van De Noort, R. and Woolf, A. (1993) Three Men and a Boat: Sutton Hoo and the East Anglian Kingdom, *Anglo-Saxon England* 22: 27–50

Pemberton J. (1997) The Dreadful God and the Divine King. *In* S. Barnes (ed.) *Africa's Ogun. Old World and New*, 105–46, Bloomington: Indiana University Press

Price, N. (ed.) (2001) *The Archaeology of Shamanism*, London: Routledge

Price, N. (2002) *The Viking Way. Religion and War in Late Iron Age Scandinavia*, AUN 31, Uppsala: University Press

Ramqvist, P.H. (1992) *Högom: The Excavations 1949–1984*, Neumünster: Karl Wachholz Verlag.

Ravn, M. (2003) *Death Ritual and Germanic Social Structure (c. AD 200–600)*, Oxford BAR International Series 1164, Oxford

Renfrew, A.C. (1985a) *Towards an Archaeology of Mind*, Inaugural Lecture, Cambridge: CUP

Renfrew, A.C. (1985b) *The Archaeology of Cult. The Sanctuary at Phylakopi*, British School of Archaeology at Athens. Supp. Vol. 18

Reynolds, A. (2009) *Anglo-Saxon Deviant Burial Customs*, Oxford: OUP

Staecker, J. (2003) The Cross Goes North: Christian Symbols and Scandinavian Women. *In* Carver (ed.), 463–482

Steinsland, G. (1991) *Det hellige bryllup og norrøn kongeideologi*, Oslo

Stocker, D. and Everson, P. (2003) The Straight and Narrow Way. Fenland Causeways and the Conversion of the Landscape in the Witham Valley, Lincolnshire. *In* Carver (ed.), 271–288

Słupecki, L. (1994) *Slavonic Pagan Sanctuaries*, Warsaw: Institute of Archaeology and Ethnology: Polish Academy of Science

Thackeray, J.F. (2005) The Wounded Roan: A Contribution to the Relation of Hunting and Trance in Southern African Rock Art, *Antiquity* 79: 5–18

Van De Noort, R. (1993) The Context of Early Medieval Barrows in Western Europe, *Antiquity* 67: 66–73

Watt, M. (2004) The Gold-Figure Foils ("Guldgubbar") from Uppåkra. *In* L. Larsson (ed.) *Uppåkrastudier 10 Acta archaeologica Lundensia* 48: 167–221

Welinder, S. (2003) Christianity, Politics and Ethnicity in Early Medieval Jämtland. *In* Carver (ed.), 509–530

Williams, H. (1997) Ancient Landscapes and the Dead: The Reuse of Prehistoric and Roman Monuments as Early Anglo-Saxon Burial Sites, *Medieval Archaeology* 41: 1–32

Wilson, D. (1992) *Anglo-Saxon Paganism*, London: Routledge

Woodward, A. and Leach, P. (1993a) *The Uley Shrines. Excavations of a Ritual Complex on West Hill. Uley, Gloucestershire 1977–9*, London: English Heritage

Woodward, A. (1993) The Cult of Relics in Prehistoric Britain. *In* M. Carver (ed.) *In Search of Cult. Archaeological Investigations in Honour of Philip Rahtz*, 1–8, Woodbridge: Boydell

Chapter 2

In the Open Air

Sarah Semple

Introduction

The pre-Christian sacred landscape has long held a special place in Anglo-Saxon and early medieval scholarship. Jacob Grimm envisaged pre-Christian worship taking place within groves: *untouched by human hand, embowered and shut in by self-grown trees* (Grimm 1900: 69). Hill-top sanctuaries and fields devoted to deities, holy stones, trees and wells have all been considered as elements of the pagan spiritual landscape in early medieval England and around the North Sea rim (Stenton 1941: 10–11; Gelling 1978: 158–61; Hines 1997: 385).

Written sources of the Conversion and post-Conversion period are considered to capture and preserve elements of pre-Christian belief and practice (Jolly 1996: 6–34). Texts such as the laws, penitentials and homilies, often condemn or prohibit the veneration of natural places, such as wells, trees and stones (Morris 1989: 57–9) whilst the English herbals confirm a reliance on the natural world as a source of material for charms, amulets, spells and cures (Cockayne 1864–6). Lichen might be scraped from stones, plants and tree bark used in charms, animal and bird movements used for prophesising and auguries (*Ælfric Auguries*, lines 88–91; trans. taken from Meaney 1984: 133). The natural world was fundamental to pre-Christian and post-Conversion popular beliefs. Scholarship over the last century has fully accepted this, but simultaneously adopted a reluctant standpoint that considers this 'nature-led' pre-Christian religion as too vague and diluted by later Christianized written accounts, to be researched with any real clarity. "The unknowable, unknown…" in Stanley's words, has been considered by many to be untraceable in a silence of true prehistory (1975: 122; see Hines 1997 for *contra* argument).

Significant changes in theoretical approaches have begun to expand our limited understanding of pre-Christian sacred topography in England and abroad. The creation of early medieval monuments is now considered in terms of the writing of new ideologies and identities into the landscape (Carver 2001; Carver 2002) and ancient features, natural or human-made, might be drawn upon in these processes of identity creation, to legitimate land ownership, power and lineage (Bradley 1998a; Bradley

2002). The act of raising new monuments and re-using old monuments, drawing on the power of the ancient and the natural, is conceived as an active process of physical myth-making; with the landscape both adopted and used afresh to add emphasis to the legends and narratives used by communities to establish both identity and power (Williams 2006: 145–78). Just as the written stories of the early Christian period such as *Beowulf* may fossilize poetry or legends that had developed over several hundred years of oral tradition (Lapidge 2000) – so the landscape must be seen in similar textual terms, reworked and changed according to alterations in belief, political power, religion and identity.

The landscape has therefore come to the forefront of theoretical approaches that hinge on the belief that changes in religious or political ideology can result in physical changes – as Sam Turner has so appositely concluded: "the things people believe and the way they express their beliefs have influenced not only people's perceptions of the landscape but also its physical form" (Turner 2006: 4). The attention of researchers has moved towards a search for the *signals of belief*: the changes in settlement, land-use and division, burial practices and administrative arrangements that offer evidence for the changing beliefs and ideals of communities (see for example Hoggett 2007). A tension has also arisen in distinguishing the sacred from the secular. Long held ideas that 'sacred' sites were set apart from either settlement or cemetery (Wilson 1992; Meaney 1995) are now in question, with evidence for ritual activity emergent from settlement evidence, buildings and structures and cemeteries (Williams 2006; Hamerow 2006). The later written sources attest to field rituals, healing charms and spells that suggest that even beyond the Conversion, common activities such as collecting herbs or plants or blessing fields included ritualistic and magical elements (Jolly 1995). We should perhaps look, therefore, more carefully at all activities within the landscape. Planting, harvesting, creating or defining boundaries, establishing land ownership, moving through and accessing specific types of natural environment may all have necessitated rituals and activities relating to patterns of belief and superstition. Recent excavation and research on early medieval assembly locations suggests such sites were maintained and defined by the periodic re-cutting of boundary ditches (one might also envisage regular clearance of undergrowth, grass and brambles) (Sanmark and Semple 2008; Semple and Turner *forthcoming*). Although mundane, this suggests that we can capture, in archaeological terms, the regular or repeated physical definition of special places in the landscape; in this instance, locales for assembly and ceremony.

Research thus no-longer centres on establishing evidence that will verify or underpin the written sources, *e.g.* material evidence for temples, idols or shrines. Adopting instead a holistic and landscape-led approach that integrates a full range of multi-disciplinary evidence, we seek to establish medieval perceptions and beliefs about place and how these survive or change over time. Stefan Brink and his colleagues have developed such approaches in Scandinavian scholarship, providing a framework that uses composite evidence spanning millennia to examine sacred topography in terms of long-term ritual activity (Brink 2001).

These new theoretical advances have allowed early medieval research to progress in three ways. Firstly it is interdisciplinary, freeing itself from the narrow parameters of the archaeological evidence of the fifth to seventh centuries AD and drawing upon the full complement of sources for the period. In the 1970s and 1980s, historical sources were shunned in the drive for medieval archaeology to 'come of age', David Austin and Peter Ucko enjoining medieval archaeologists as late as 1990 to reject historical frameworks and sources (Austin 1990). However, the need for an interdisciplinary methodology was continually recognized (Hawkes 1976; Webster 1986), and most researchers dealing with religion pre- or post-Conversion, have continued to adopt an interdisciplinary standpoint: Rosemary Cramp, Audrey Meaney, John Hines and John Blair, to name a few, have all in differing ways fore-fronted the integration of historical, literary and place-names sources with archaeology. The subtle change in the last fifteen years is that more archaeologists have become willing to integrate historical, literary, poetic and linguistic evidence as a means of contextualizing their arguments and interpretations, and have done so without removing the primacy of archaeology in their debates (Carver 1986; 2000; 2005; Reynolds 1997; 2009).

Secondly, it has become far more acceptable to examine the wider panorama of evidence for early medieval communities in North West Europe, and to draw on evidence for Scandinavia, Iceland, the Balkans, Russia and beyond as a means of interpreting and contextualizing English material (*e.g.* Blair 2005; Price 2002). Some scholars always looked towards the Continental and Scandinavian evidence for pagan religion *e.g.* Turville-Petre (1964), Davidson (1943); Ellis Davidson (1964) and Chaney (1970), but there was also a viewpoint in the mid- to late twentieth century that tended to emphasise its dangers. Scandinavian scholarship has itself driven change in English intellectual approaches with the work of Anders Andrén, Lotte Hedeager, Anne-Sofie Gräslund, Stefan Brink, Neil Price among others, demonstrating the effectiveness of interdisciplinarity, the integration of comparative material from England and the Continent, and the use of ethnographic evidence from comparative and connected cultures.

These theoretical developments in Scandinavia have also encouraged researchers of early medieval England to look beyond the Anglo-Saxon period and see how prehistoric and Roman practices and beliefs, landscapes, monuments and rituals may have informed early medieval beliefs and perhaps even moulded the religions, rites and rituals of communities in the pre-Conversion period. Claims have even been made that Christianity itself was varied locally according to its prehistoric forerunner (Carver 2008). Thus the changing theoretical scene in early medieval archaeology has been stimulated too by prehistoric researches, in which scholars have come to view the landscape in terms of the *longue durée*, and human action as informed and altered by knowledge of and/or the remains of past societies and communities.

This chapter takes an approach that is influenced by all three areas of progress. The pre-Christian landscape of England is here re-created by integrating interdisciplinary sources, by looking beyond England and contextualizing English evidence with findings from the Continent and Scandinavia and finally by recognizing the relevance of the prehistoric and Roman past in the beliefs and perceptions of the communities inhabiting the English medieval landscape.

Natural places

The subtlety found in the English topographical place-names affords a valuable insight into the minds of Anglo-Saxon communities and their evaluation of their physical environment (Gelling 1998: 75, 97). Place-names that mention supernatural creatures such as elves, monsters, demons or giants etc. are rare but informative, associating such creatures with fissures and hollows, openings in the ground, pools and wet-places, ancient monuments and ruins (Semple 2002: 286–7; Blair 2005; Semple in preparation). Elves were believed to haunt hills and valleys and 'wild places' (Hall 2006); trees and shrubs could be described as holy or sacred (Hooke 2003: 18); stones, trees and wells might be worshipped or enshrined (Whitelock *et al.* 1981: 320). One rapidly realises that within Anglo-Saxon communities, a wide array of natural features attracted attention: springs and wells, hollows, fissures, openings and caves, hill-tops, knolls and barrow-shaped features; trees, shrubs, thorn bushes, tree stumps, standing stones, stones with holes – indeed one might summarily conclude that the whole landscape was in Stefan Brink's words "sacred and numinous" to greater and lesser extents.

Natural places have an archaeology because they acquired significance in the *minds* of people in the past. This would not necessarily make any impact on their outward appearance, but one way of recognizing the importance of these locations is through the evidence of human activity that is discovered there (Bradley 2000: 35). In some instances this may comprise material culture such as votive deposits or structures built to enhance the site or natural location, however, natural places may also attract activity around in the wider landscape around them – monuments, burial grounds etc. (*ibid.*). Natural places may thus continue to hold significance in the minds of people precisely because they have been revered and physically enhanced over millennia. Such places may be focal – single locations holding special meaning and significance or poly-focal and extended – tracts of landscape within which many aspects are resonant and powerful: the natural, ancient and contemporary. It is perhaps a modern construct, informed by the European classical past, to look for a designated sacred locale: a grove, a temple, a shrine etc. Investigation of 'religious locales' has in recent years taken account of the idea of extended sacred landscapes, with focal points of activity such as monuments and cemeteries created and used to structure how people viewed, experienced and even moved through the landscape (Tilley 1994, 1996; Bradley 2000; Williams 2006: 179–214; Brookes 2007). The significance of natural places may lie not just in terms of their immediate visual impact, but also how they were framed and enhanced by new monumental constructions, by activities in their immediate and wider environment, and by knowledge and understanding or perception of the landscape around them in terms of the past and present. Sacred places might be important too because of how they were reached – their accessibility or indeed inaccessibility, visibility or invisibility, just as significant as their immediate and wider landscape context (Bradley 2000; Scarre 2002a & b, 26; Mulk and Bayliss-Smith 1999; Äikäs 2007). In this sense place-names are crucial to our understanding of 'sacred landscapes', as a resource that offers a means of understanding how elements of the landscape were perceived in terms of their shape, form, colour and even sound. In archaeological terms we can explore places or locations in terms of colour, light, flora, fauna and even their acoustics (Scarre and

Lawson 2006). Early medieval outdoor assembly sites, for example, are often situated in places that enhance the likelihood of hearing speakers and proceedings (*e.g.* Scutchmer Knob, Berkshire and Aspa Löt, Sweden).

Sacred meaning might become attached to places and even extended tracts of landscape because of a combined range of attributes that affect the full realm of human sensory experience, rather than a single aspect such as a spring or stone (Scarre 2002a & b; Skeates 2007). The description by the writer Felix, of the island of Crowland, the retreat of St. Guthlac, is a complex narrative combining descriptions of the real landscape with sensory attributes of the location, evoking a spiritual equivalent of the types of retreat synonymous with the ascetic locations chosen by the desert fathers when attempting to replicate the biblical wilderness of Christ (Meaney 2005). The special topographic attributes of this locality are complex: it is inaccessible, lying within a 'trackless bog within the confines of the dismal marsh' (*Vita Guthlaci* XXV; trans. Colgrave 1956: 89) and *yet also* perhaps a seasonal island; encompassed by marshy and wet ground for only part of the year (Lane 1988; Stocker 1993: 105). Guthlac is the recipient, however, of numerous religious and secular visitors (*VG* XLIV–XLV, trans. Colgrave 1956: 137–42), undeterred by the 'shady grove' surrounded by numerous reedy pools and gloomy thickets (*VG* XXV & XXVII; trans. Colgrave 1956: 89 & 91). Of course the island was marked as well, by a large and ancient *tumulus* which had been dug open to reveal a habitable opening or *cisterna* (*VG* XXVIII; trans. Colgrave 1956: 93–4). It is these combined natural aesthetics relating both to the place and its contrast with the wider setting, that dramatise the location: a watery location, difficult, yet not impossible to traverse, placed in a seasonally changeable environment, covered in shady tree growth and reedy marshland, quiet except for the birdsong, marked by a large and ancient barrow or ruin of some kind, feared as haunted and evil. Sacred places seem to have achieved their significance not just through their natural distinctive environs, their accessibility, visibility and surrounding archaeology but also through contrast with their wider natural setting.

Fields and groves

The existence of fields and groves dedicated to specific deities is attested by a range of place-names, reviewed most recently by John Hines (1997). *Feld* (field) and *Lēah* (grove) occur several times in combination with god's names such as *woden, thunor* and *tiw* (Hines 1997: 386, see also table 12–1). These sites presumably functioned as places of belief or cult locations where sacred activities might have been carried out. The original form and composition of such sites and how they functioned is grossly hampered, however, by their elusiveness in the modern landscape. Sites such as *Thunresfelda* (Wiltshire) and *Tislea* (Hampshire) for example (field dedicated to *Thunor* and a grove or woodland clearing to *Tiw*), are lost places in the modern landscape. Of those listed by John Hines, only a few are readily locatable. The place-name terms do however allow some speculation on human perception, visitation and interaction with such places. *Feld* is a term that was used regularly as early as the sixth and seventh centuries AD and seems to have been applied indifferently to land that might or might not be under the plough, not marsh or woodland or hills, but pasture, particularly unencumbered land with unrestricted access (Gelling and Cole 2000: 269–71). In its earliest application *feld* may have designated open areas of communal rough pasture for groups of settlements. Gelling and Cole point to eight contiguous *feld*-names spanning the Hampshire and Berkshire borders suggestive of a large tract of shared open land (*ibid.* 272). *Feld*-names in the north of England lie close to the 500ft contour implying the term could denote land that separated the upland from the cultivated lowland (*ibid.*).

These communal and yet peripheral or liminal qualities lie in contrast to the sense of place conjured by an examination of *lēah* as a landscape term. This is interpreted variously as 'forest, wood, glade and clearing' (Gelling and Cole 2000: 237) and may have initially been used in reference to especially ancient and long-established woodland, copses and woodland clearings (Rackham 1976: 56; *ibid.* 237). The term may relate as well to OE *leoht* 'light'; in the sense of a clearing in dense woodland flooded with light (Gelling 1984: 23). Margaret Gelling perceived *lēah* as an active term, often indicative of settlements within cleared areas within or at the fringes of the wooded environment (Gelling and Cole 2000: 220), providing some emphasis that *lēah* might be applied to areas of actively managed or maintained woodland clearance. Since the submission of this paper, Della Hooke has argued very convincingly in press, that lēah should be interpreted as a term meaning wood pasture – woodland environments utilised and managed for grazing animals (Hooke 2009). Perhaps we can visualise places such as Thursley, (Thunor's-*leah*) as cut back, coppiced and maintained. Sacred groves or *hijs* in Estonia exist today as recognizable as stands of trees, occupying low-lying rises of land. These relatively undemonstrative topographic features are, in a particularly flat landscape, highly distinctive in visual terms: their appeal dependant on their wider natural context and their contrast with the surroundings (Jonuks 2007).

These English place-names suggest locales similarly distinctive through their contrast with the surroundings: but not only in terms of their visual impact. A *lēah* might be a clearing hidden within the woods or comprise a visually distinct, stand of trees in an open landscape; the *feld* was peripheral but visited, accessible, even commonly used and owned by communities. It is interesting that some of the earliest mentions of *feld* place-names refer to battle sites and meeting-places or councils (Gelling and Cole 2000: 272). Both types of locale (*lēah* and *feld*) are likely to have been subject to sporadic management, by periodic and traditional means such as grazing and coppicing. Whether long established or newly created, the introduction of light within the woodland canopy, or the creation or maintenance of a shaded grove, would develop environments which might stimulate the growth of particular plant species, artificially altering the botanical composition of these natural places. It is possible too that the *feld*, as a distinct environment below the upland pasture and outside the cultivated fields, would similarly have a different ecological make-up and botanical composition which might be enhanced through low-level maintenance such as grazing or clearance. These locations may thus have comprised partially-managed habitats with distinctive flora and fauna (see for example evidence for the management of Tallensi sacred natural groves in Ghana, Insoll 2007).

Hilltops

The dual notion of places hidden or peripheral in visual terms and yet accessible and visited by communities or individuals is found too in the topographic profile of several hill-top sites considered to be of pre-Christian sacred significance. Hill-tops are widely accepted as an indisputable aspect of pre-Christian sacred locales. Tishoe (Surrey) for example is often cited as a distinctive spur dedicated to the god Tiw (Gelling 1978; 1998). Frank Stenton firmly believed the place-name term OE *hearg* 'temple/shrine' referred in many instances to some form of hilltop sanctuary (1941: 10–11), an interpretation upheld by the frequent association of surviving *hearg* place-names with distinctive hill-tops or whale-backs of land *e.g.* Harrow-on-the-Hill, Middlesex. The types of hill-top associated with *hearg* place-names vary however; dominant and distinctive examples such as Harrow-on-the-Hill, Middlesex, contrast with low and rounded rises such as Wood Eaton, Oxfordshire. At least two English 'hill-top temple' sites comprise dramatic rises of land which at a distance, however, are hidden from view. The bulbous spur that lies at the centre of Goodmanham village is invisible from nearly all the approaches to the settlement. The landscape seems flat until one drops down into the deep coombe that bounds the distinctive spur of chalk on which the church still sits (Figure 3.1a). Similarly Harrow Hill, Sussex is set within a wide natural curtain of hills that completely obscures the dramatic whale-back of land from the wider landscape (Semple 2007) (Figure 3.1b). Visibility and invisibility may be significant in terms of accessibility and human movement. These sites, if sacred places, we must presume were visited and used. A hidden location might increase the visual dramatic impact of the approach to a site, just as a steep climb to a spur or hill could serve to enhance the sense of spirituality, in terms of the journey and the place.

Hill-tops associated with *hearg* place-names have a range of other, highly varied associations with natural- and human-altered phenomenon: clusters of spring-lines, for example, are present at Goodmanham (Yorkshire), Harrowden (Wirral) and Wood Eaton (Oxfordshire). At Harrow Hill (Sussex), pits and mineshafts of prehistoric date mark the summit. The significance of particular hill-tops is likely to relate to a combination of distinctive attributes as well as height or prominence, such as spring-lines, ancient monuments, graves, ruins etc. It is worth considering in this context, the frequent positioning of cemeteries in high places with wide view-sheds, particularly some cremation cemeteries and high status barrow burials (Lucy 1998; Williams 1999). Williams has shown that intervisibility and viewshed may have influenced cemetery location. Within communities, families needing to articulate identity, power and authority by means of visual display, often combined prominent and highly visual positioning with the reuse of pre-Saxon earthworks, monuments and ruins and new monuments as well *e.g.* Lowbury (Berkshire) and Cuddesdon (Oxfordshire). Assembly places too can occur in high, hill-top positions with extensive views, although as Aliki Pantos argues, other motivations were clearly in play as well in the choice of these sites (Meaney 1995; Pantos 2002: 147–52): the assembly at Lowbury Hill, Berkshire, took place on a hill which was the site of a Romano-British temple complex and a high-status, late sixth-century barrow burial. Although other factors clearly contributed to the choice of locations for high-status burials and for assemblies, we might consider the association

Figure 2.1a. All Saints' Church, Goodmanham, East Yorkshire, positioned on a bulbous, natural spur on the Wolds.

Figure 2.1b: The long low profile of Harrow Hill, Sussex, visible on the horison. This is the site of extensive prehistoric flint workings and subsequent prehistoric enclosures and a possible Anglo-Saxon site of pre-Christian importance.

of these types of activities with hill-tops as further indication of the special nature of high places as sacred locales – perhaps places especially associated with or related to concepts of an ancestral presence and spiritual ownership of the landscape.

Fissures, hollows and pits

Belief in supernatural inhabitation of the landscape is attested both in the highly evocative and problematic texts such as *Beowulf* and again within Anglo-Saxon place-name record, with elves, water spirits and monsters or goblins mentioned in association with a range of topographic features. Perhaps for obvious reasons, the dark places of the world – clefts, pits, hollows, fissures and caves – were especially evocative. In the tale of St. Cuthman, an old woman who cursed the saint was picked up by the wind and blown across the downs, before being swallowed into the earth at a place later known as Fippa's pit (Blair 1997). Openings in the earth and rock were dangerous places in the minds of late Saxon Christian communities, topographic locations perhaps that fitted their conceptions of hell as a form of living death, trapped in the grave, persecuted by demons and beasts, within the fissures and cracks of the hellish underworld. The sinners drowned in *Andreas* are swallowed by an awesome fissure in the earth (*Vercelli* XIV), a motif that occurs again in the foundation myth for Minster-in-Thanet, in which the wicked councillor Thunor was swallowed into the ground (Hollis 1998: 41). These ideas are also reflected in the artistic renditions of hell created by the innovative artists of the Harley Psalter in the eleventh century (Semple 2003b). Artist F drew from his imagination a landscape filled with a myriad of shafts, fissures and pits: access points to the torments of hell down which a sinner might all too easily fall or indeed be hooked and dragged or swallowed (*ibid.*). Whilst the compilers of the Vercelli or Exeter Books and the illustrators of the Harley Psalter were from firmly Christian communities, their works are influenced by more widely held late Saxon popular beliefs. Place-names attest to superstitions that associated this type of feature with supernatural creatures. A *grendeles pyt* is documented in Crediton, Devon (739; S255) and a *þyrs pytt* in Marlcliffe, Worcestershire (883; S222); with *Grimeshole*, Berkshire (C13th) and Grimes Graves, even if poorly dated, providing further emphasis that holes and pits (in the latter case prehistoric mine-shafts), could be associated with Grim, Woden's alter ego. Thyrspit, Usselby, Lincolnshire (1372) and Poukeput, Harting, Sussex (1350) attest to belief that goblin-like entities might inhabit pits or openings in the ground. In archaeological terms there is little evidence to add. Of note perhaps are the two small ninth-century coin hoards retrieved from Merlewood Cave (Lancashire) and Attemire Cave (Yorkshire) (Rigold and Metcalf 1984: 262), although caves were presumably good hiding places! The ritual or spiritual importance of Harrow Hill, Sussex and its environs could have resulted from the multiple pre-historic mine shafts on the summit of the hill, but no finds of early medieval date have yet been retrieved from flint mines, although the spoil heaps at neighbouring Blackpatch, were occasionally used for burial (Semple 2008).

These sources in combination imply the existence of long-lived and widely-held folk-superstitions or popular beliefs, but little in the way of active ritual or votive practices relating to fissures, pits or caves. In the Anglo-Saxon mind, fearful supernatural creatures existed and lived in, or were to be encountered at, certain places in the landscape, including pits, nooks and hollows. It is possible these beliefs emerged within and after the Conversion period, reflecting new attitudes to landscape influenced and developed by Christian texts and teachings on hell and damnation. The place-name evidence, however, alongside the unusual motifs within some of the *Vitae* point to these folk-superstitions comprising long-running, localized beliefs, able to survive beyond the arrival of a new Christian theology and perhaps even continue to influence the mentality and imagination of Christian writers and artists (Jolly 1996: 6–34; Blair 2005: 471–9). Indeed such elements may have been consciously included, to render the texts and illustrations more real, more terrifying and thus more effective as means of teaching, informing and re-affirming peoples Christian beliefs.

Rivers, pools, springs, wells and wetlands

Watery-places, like fissures and pits, represented special places in the landscape for Anglo-Saxon populations. The OE nicor or 'water spirit/demon', referred to the field-names Nikerpole, Mildenhall, Wiltshire (1272) and aqua de Nikerpoll, Sussex (1263) (see Mawer and Stenton 1939, 499 and Mawer and Stenton 1930, 562), attest the post-conquest survival of folk beliefs closely related to the superstitions captured by the creator of Beowulf, of terrifying monsters, lurking below the surface of reedy pools and fens (Beowulf, lines 702–824). Watery places could be dangerous gateways to other worlds, occupied by less than welcoming inhabitants; 'The monster must dwell in the fen, alone in his realm.' (Maxims II, lines 42–3). Springs, wells, rivers and lakes attracted activity of a ritual or religious nature in the pre-Christian and Conversion period, as attested by finds of metalwork retrieved from rivers and the establishment of churches, standing crosses and the application of Christian dedications to river crossings, springs and wells.

The ritualized hoarding or deposition of metalwork in water is a phenomenon generally associated with late prehistoric communities (Levy 1982; Bradley 1998b; Yeates 2006: 39–56). Evidence for similar activity in the Roman, early medieval and later historic periods at rivers implies such practices may have continued or re-emerged in later periods. Excavations in 1981 at Fiskerton, Lincolnshire produced evidence for late prehistoric and Roman deposition of metalwork and organic material around a timber causeway crossing a wetland and tributary leading to the River Witham (Parker Pearson and Field 2003). Stocker and Everson have tracked these ritual practices along the Witham Valley, into the late medieval period, pointing to metalwork finds of the fourteenth and fifteenth centuries, including several items of weaponry, from six more of the Witham causeways (2003, Table 17.1). The votive deposition of objects in rivers, springs and pools seems to have continued from late prehistory into the Romano-British period and beyond with strong evidence of medieval depositional practices from the Thames and the Witham as well as several fenland tributaries (see Blair 1994: 99; Hines 1997: 381; Halsall 2000: 267–8). Such finds are traditionally explained as casual losses (Wilson 1965), although researchers have increasingly questioned this assumption, pointing to the possibility of intentional rites perhaps related to crossing boundaries (Blair 1994: 99; Halsall 2000: 267–8). Evidence for ritual 'killing', by bending, of swords (Blair 1994: 99), resonates with earlier practices from the Bronze and Iron Ages, emphasizing further the need to consider these practices within the *longue durée* of structured deposition at wet locations. Wider survey is needed, alongside a critical assessment of patterns of deposition in relation to tidal regimes and river activity: not only could some material have eroded from *in situ* dry land deposits, but the types of activities associated with major rivers such as the Thames were significantly varied, for example fairs, fishing, rogation-tide rituals, trading, domestic disposal, river-side churches and burials (Cohen 2003). The recovery of a variety of items other than swords, and objects of varying date (skulls, whole pots, metallic dress accessories etc.), if intentionally deposited, imply a much wider and complex set of traditions; perhaps even differences in practice between region as well as variability over time.

Stocker and Everson emphasize the pre-Christian 'sacred' nature of the Witham river valley suggesting deposition rituals may have been used to facilitate the periodic appropriation of the causeways as access points to the river, or pools and marshy areas adjacent to the river or indeed to boats for crossing or travelling the river. These deposits could, however, relate to decision-making, boundary disputes or oath-taking rituals (Blair 1994: 104). In the late Saxon period the ownership of an island and indeed the march of the shire boundary at the confluence of the Thames and Cherwell, was disputed between Abingdon and the men of Oxfordshire, and resolved by watching the course of a round shield launched on the river carrying a sheaf and taper (*Chron. Ab.* I 88–90; Blair 1994, 104). It is equally possible that such acts were associated with safe passage across liminal or supernaturally charged locations, made at the onset of long journeys or on a safe return (Lund 2005). Blades often appear in modern folklore as 'control devices' regulating contact between the ordinary world and the supernatural: for example a knife struck into a burial mound was thought to open or close access to the supernatural (Grinsell 1976a: 174; Swire 1966: 77; Hole 1995: 210). Spears cast into Viking burial chambers at Birka, Sweden, have similarly been interpreted as closing ceremonial acts, dedicating the chamber, tomb and its inhabitants to deities and closing them off from the real and present world (Price 2002, 139). One might also consider that the pagan priest Coifi who profaned the pagan temple at Goodmanham perhaps closed down its power by casting a spear into the sacred enclosures (HE II, 13). Pools, lakes, springs and rivers all seem to have been considered as potential conduits or interfaces with other places and supernatural entities and powers (see Lund this vol.). It is possible that weapon and artefact deposits were placatory acts as well as closing devices, ensuring safe passage across the bogs, lakes, fens and rivers.

Watery locations with indeterminate topographic status or identity, such as seasonal islands, tidal islands, inter-tidal zones, marshes and fens subject to seasonal inundations, seem to have held a special place in the minds of past communities in the prehistoric and historic periods (see for example the discussion of the ritual or spiritual importance in prehistory of inter-tidal zones and islands in Scarre 2002a & b). The seasonal quality of the fenland isle inhabited by Guthlac, amid marshes subject to winter and spring inundations, describes precisely the type of liminal qualities communities seem to have been recognized and valued (see discussion above). In the early medieval period, watercourses were used as places of assembly. Islands, bridges, rivers and streams often functioned as territorial divisions and boundaries (Cohen 2003). In addition they were of course natural barriers, crossing-places and routes of communication. These

Sarah Semple

Figure 2.2: The River Dee below the walls of Roman Chester: the scene of royal rituals performed in 973 to confirm and symbolise the overlordship of Edgar over the Welsh and British kings.

'liminal' and contrastingly 'accessible' qualities may have been particularly valued for assembly locations (see Pantos 2002, 2003 & 2004). Royal assemblies such as the inauguration rituals for King Edgar in 973, were held on the River Dee (Barrow 2001: 81–93), a free-flowing river without ownership or claim (Pantos 2002), and of course at the intertidal section of the river: again a location perhaps particularly favoured for public rituals (Barrow 2001) (Figure 2.2). The cemetery at Sutton Hoo is well known for its location on the River Deben, considered by Martin Carver the main entrance or access route to the East Anglian kingdom (Carver 2005, 494–499). This positioning is echoed by cemeteries in West Sussex, situated overlooking estuaries to the Arun, Adur, Ouse and Cuckmere river valleys and in some instances enhanced by additional structures or shrines (Semple 2008). These too imply that tidal inlets and river mouths were important locations for signaling identity and ownership and creating visible relationships with the past through the use of ancient remains (Semple 2008).

Rivers, wet places, islands or tidal confluences will have held different meanings for differing communities and people: local, regional and visiting populations. A deep-running element is a common concern with the liminal quality of these sites. Perhaps these places were dangerous because if crossed or travelled upon, there was a risk of moving from the real and present world into another supernatural world, perhaps even from the living to the dead. Julie Lund has argued that water courses were perceived as boundaries between the living and the supernatural in

Old Norse sources and has linked the deposited artefacts found at bridges and fords in Viking Age Scandinavia to the liminal concept of the bridge in the cognitive landscape (2005; see Lund this vol.). Stocker and Everson (2003) also argue for the long-term deposition around causeways in the Witham Valley as evidence for rituals related to traversing or engaging with the river (*cf.* Parker Pearson and Field 2003). The subsequent establishment of medieval monasteries along the valley in relation to these same causeways, is suggested as symbolising the monastic custodianship of these ancient crossing-places and a conversion and appropriation of the rituals surrounding them: *"the prehistoric ritual had been given a meaning that sat acceptably within the ideology of a new religion: a 'conversion' had taken place"* (Stocker and Everson 2003: 280–5). It has also been argued that this process of Christianisation can be applied to the natural wells and springs that emerge in the post-Conversion period as sacred sites with Christian dedications or those enhances by the establishment of Christian shrines or churches.

The western British evidence summarised by Sam Turner (2006: 132–3) points to a two-fold process: the Christianisation of wells and springs with pre-Christian significance and an emerging, newly acquired sanctity around some natural phenomenon, resulting from the establishment of an early medieval or medieval Christian foundation. The former type of association is relevant here, and John Blair has outlined how such natural water sources might have existed as pre-Christian cult foci, surviving as cult sites into the Christian period, representing an aspect of continuing or surviving popular belief (Blair 2005: 226–7, 472–3; Turner 2006: 132–3). Blair notes that this appropriation could certainly happen at minster level (Rattue 1995: 55–61) but also postulates a "much humbler level" of adoption, taking account of less formally developed landmarks (Blair 2005: 226, see too 477–8). The most compelling example of a minster level adoption is Barton-on-Humber, where the tenth-century church is aligned on a group of wells; the alignment pointing to the pre-minster importance of the springs (Rodwell and Rodwell 1982: fig. 6).

Sanctified ruins

So far this chapter has examined a range of natural locations significant to the beliefs of communities: fields and groves, hilltops and watery places. Human-altered places, ancient remains, monuments and ruins, were also important and used in a variety of ways. Ancient sites, monuments and ruins were commonly reused for burial (Williams 1997), but *re-use* was considerably more diverse. Settlements, such as Yeavering, Northumberland and Drayton, Oxfordshire, were situated in the sixth and seventh centuries to take advantage of ancient palimpsests of prehistoric remains (Hope Taylor 1977; Benson and Miles 1974: fig. 1). By the mid to late Saxon period churches were constructed inside or next to hillforts, henges and stone circles (see for example Hanbury, Worcestershire or St. Mary the Virgin, Stanton Drew, Somerset) and more frequently on or next to ancient barrows (*e.g.* Bampton, Oxfordshire or Berwick, Sussex). Pagan or pre-Christian timber shrines were established at prehistoric sites (Slonk Hill, Sussex and see Blair 1995 and 'Shrines' below) and later, standing stones were Christianised (*e.g.* Rudston, Yorkshire), and by the late Anglo-Saxon period, all types of site were

Figure 2.3: Scutchmer Knob, Berkshire, documented as a shire assembly site in the late Anglo-Saxon Period: recorded in AD 990–992 (S 1454) and in 1006 (ASC (E): Swanton 1996, pp. 136–137).

reused as locations for public assembly (Figure 2.3). The 'reuse' of Roman sites is no less diverse and complex, with building material quarried from forts and villas and re-used in new Christian religious structures (*e.g.* Escomb, Co. Durham), churches established in the ruined remains of buildings (exemplified at Vindolanda, Northumberland and St. Paul-in-the-Bail, Lincolnshire) and stone sarcophagi excavated for the burials of dignitaries and saints.

Some of these many exemplars may be no more than co-incidental juxtapositions or functional appropriations; the use of a convenient hill or enclosing earthwork or indeed ruined structure, for the creation of a new focus, or the opportune recycling of a useful resource such as cut stone or architectural fragments for a new structure or burial. It is the sheer diversity of secondary usage or recycling across the period, however, which is compelling, attesting to the interest and curiosity of the population, as well as their intimate knowledge and understanding of their environs and a repeated emphasis by communities on ancient, human-made structures in the processes of identity creation, myth-making and ideological signalling across the period (Semple 2009). Whilst the evidence is ephemeral and direct associations often difficult to pin down, a strong argument can still be made for the potency of monuments of the ancient past in the minds of pre-Christian, Anglo-Saxon populations. In some instances these sites may have held qualities now lost to us; importance as ancestral places, associations with healing or magic, connections to myths and legends about origins, landownership and identity, or very simply, they were recognised, remembered, or perceived as locations with a long-term ritual and spiritual significance.

Cemeteries and mortuary practices are reviewed in this volume by Howard Williams and are not covered in detail here. They must be acknowledged however, as a further element of a wider numinous landscape. Cemeteries were visited, experienced, marked with monuments and placed to draw on the power of the past. Within the landscape of Anglo-Saxon England, it is clear that cemeteries, whether cremation or inhumation, were places of special importance that were created as political and spiritual markers (Carver 2002, 2005), as signals of identity and as complex reflections of social relations within and between communities (Lucy 2002; Devlin 2007). They were also places frequented by the living and used as arenas for ceremonies and assemblies (Williams 2006; Carver 2005). Cemeteries and individual burials were associated frequently with prehistoric and Roman relict monuments (Williams 1997). The diversity and variability in how communities used these remains is extensive *and* the ways in which these monuments were used for funerary purposes changed across the Conversion Period (Williams 1998; 1999; Semple 1998; 2009). Ancient monuments were recycled as funerary sites across the fifth to seventh centuries (Williams 1997). Round barrows were preferred, particularly those close to routes and rivers and visually prominent in the landscape (Williams 1999); however there is a diversity apparent in the choice of monuments and the ways they were used that suggests individual communities and regional groups employed the visible past in processes and actions designed to fix themselves in the landscape (Williams 1998; Lucy 2002; 2003a; 2008; 2009). For example a single ancient barrow at Dover Buckland (Kent) acted as a focus for a cemetery over several generations (Evison 1989); while at Harford Farm (Norfolk) a palimpsest of ancient remains provided a backdrop for several cemeteries in contemporary usage (Penn 2000). In Cossington, Leicestershire, the use of a Bronze Age barrow as a focus for a small Anglo-Saxon cemetery represented the culmination of a series of successive events beginning in the Bronze Age (Thomas 2008). Re-use in this instance represented a long series of negotiations with the past by successive Iron Age, Roman and early medieval communities. This is a pattern echoed on a much larger and more complex scale at other sites such as Dorchester-on-Thames (Oxfordshire), (see Blair 2005 for short discussion of the latter) and Wasperton (Warwickshire) (see Carver, Hills and Scheschkewitz 2009). By the seventh century, the use of ancient remains was largely the preserve of aristocratic groups, seeking to legitimate new hereditary systems of control over enlarged kingdoms, particularly within frontiers and contested areas of the landscape (Semple 2003a). And by the late seventh century, burials utilising ancient earthworks were mainly rich female graves, centred in Bronze Age barrows: a stage perhaps in signalling the consolidation of dynastic identities (Carver 2001).

Ruins, ancient sepulchres and tombs, ancient enclosures and forts were significant places that evoked the ancestral past and could be activated or actively used to underwrite claims to landscape and local identity by the addition of new burial grounds and markers. A single burial might be intentionally placed to make an ancestral connection with the landscape, to express ownership or territorial limits; a community cemetery, across several decades or even several hundred years, could make use of one or more ancient monuments, each burial emphasising the connection between community, land and ancestors (Williams 2006). Although such sites can never be claimed as 'temples' or 'shrines' devoted to pre-Christian worship, the ancient remains in the landscape held a significant place in the Anglo-Saxon mind as part of a wider, numinous, spiritual and resonant landscape. Ancient ruins were special as physical locations in the landscape where an ancestral presence might be sought, evoked or imagined (see Sanmark this vol.).

This connection may have been significant for the builders of churches. Richard Morris drew attention in 1989 to the incidence of medieval churches situated in relation to hengiform monuments, Roman buildings, prehistoric standing stones and barrows. Citing the letters of Pope Gregory, which ask that pagan temples in Britain should not be destroyed, but re-dedicated and turned to the use of Christianity (HE I, 30), Morris argued that the juxtaposition of church and monument seen for example at Avebury, Wiltshire or Knowlton, Dorset, reflected the significance of these monuments in pre-Christian worship and belief (Morris 1989: 46–92, pp. 71–4). In the Conversion Period, the newly established monuments of the Christian church were sometimes juxtaposed with the ancient remains of the past (*ibid.* & Blair 1988; 1992). The recycling of Roman structures and the situating of churches within Roman ruins was relatively commonplace, and the use of Roman stone, ceramic and brick can be found in Northumbria, Kent, the South East, and elsewhere (See Tyler Bell 2005 for a detailed discussion). Such reuse has been explored in ideological terms, argued as evidence that Christian church was itself re-building Roman power and influence, in particular the power and influence of the Roman church. It is interesting, however, that alongside the use of the Roman past within the fabric of the Christian resurgence, prehistoric monuments were appropriated too and in these instances functional motivations are often less plausible. Although as Morris argues, in some examples, we may be seeing evidence of the re-dedication of pre-Christian religious sites (1989), it is extremely difficult to ascribe any single interpretive framework to the wide variety of instances where we find churches juxtaposed with prehistoric remains.

Medieval churches positioned in close and immediate proximity to standing stones and stone circles are rare in the English landscape *e.g.* Awliscombe (Devon), Stanton Drew (Somerset), and Rudston (Yorkshire) (Figure 2.4). Although we might suspect that these monuments were Christianised, having been venerated in a pre-Christian era (Morris 1989, 81–4), particularly given the later laws which mention the worship of springs, stones or trees (see discussion above and below), nevertheless it is difficult to establish with any certainty that these associations represent a Conversion period appropriation of active religious pre-Christian sites. Such evidence is frustratingly elusive. Similarly, although possible associations between medieval churches and prehistoric barrows can be found throughout the country (*e.g.* Fimber, East Yorkshire and Winwick, Northamptonshire), few if any provide incontrovertible evidence of the 'Christianization' of a pagan cult site or shrine. One of the most convincing cases to have emerged through excavated evidence is the close association between an early Christian foundation and Bronze Age barrows at Bampton (Oxfordshire), where a late Saxon/ Norman church and Norman chapel overlay a pair of Bronze-age ring-ditches, one of which had been used for burial as early as *c.* AD 700 (Blair 1998; 1999).

Figure 2.4: The prehistoric monolith in the churchyard of All Saints', Rudston, Yorkshire.

At Taplow (Berkshire), Ogbourne St. Andrew (Wiltshire) and High Wycombe (Berkshire) medieval churches can be found adjacent to prominent barrows and although there are many other potential examples, these offer a useful insight into at least one possible motivation for the appropriation of barrows (prehistoric or indeed pre-Christian Anglo-Saxon) by the Christian church. At Ogbourne, a prehistoric round barrow, lying immediately east of the medieval church, had been reused for burial in the late Anglo-Saxon period. At Taplow and High Wycombe, barrow burials of the sixth to seventh centuries drew a Christian focus by the eighth century or later. The establishment of a church next to a burial mound, whether prehistoric, prehistoric and reused or pre-Christian Anglo-Saxon, strongly attests to a perceived need to appropriate the pre-Christian dead, ensuring the inclusion of ancestors within the new Christian religious enterprise. Prehistoric barrows could, it seems, be viewed alongside reused prehistoric and early-medieval burial mounds, as locations where the pagan dead lay and perhaps where their spirits still resided: a persistent folk tradition or superstition captured in written texts even beyond the Conversion (Semple 1998).

A final category of ancient remains adopted by the Christian church were prehistoric enclosures. Mid-Saxon minsters set within Iron Age hill forts are known at Hanbury (Worcestershire), Tetbury (Gloucestershire), Breedon-on-the-Hill (Leicestershire), and Aylesbury (Buckinghamshire). Whilst a hillfort or henge may have offered a useful boundary for a new minster, such appropriations have been interpreted as actions representing a need to add a political or ritual emphasis to a new religious foundation. (Blair 1988; 1992 and 2005) At some sites, however, neither interpretation is sufficient. Since 1989, field researches at Avebury have confirmed that the famous association between medieval church and henge represent the surviving visible signs of a long-term, ritual dialogue between community and landscape. Settlement at Avebury is attested in the Roman period, adjacent to the major Roman thoroughfare running from Mildenhall to Bath (Corney 1997: 29; Robinson 2001). The centrality and importance of the ancient prehistoric remains at Avebury and West Kennet as a focus for the inhabitants of this late Roman road-side settlement, is suggested by a series of wells containing votive material of late Roman date around Silbury Hill, as well as votive coins and metalwork of the same period inside the Neolithic henge and south of the settlement at West Kennet Long Barrow too (Pollard and Reynolds 2002: 178–80). This pattern of late Roman settlement and ritual activity gave way to a fifth-/sixth-century settlement with post-built structures and sunken-featured buildings around the southern entrance to the henge. The focus of settlement then shifted over-time, skirting the edge of the henge and moving around to the western-side of the monument by the eighth and ninth centuries. Sculptural fragments attest to a ninth-/tenth-century Christian focus outside the western entrance of the monument (Pollard and Reynolds 2002: 235–7), whilst the standing church contains the fossilized remains of a tenth-century structure (*ibid.*; Semple in preparation). Lying at the heart of this late-Roman to late-Saxon activity, is Waden Hill, a natural whale-back of land overlooking the henge, avenues and Silbury Hill and the late-Roman settlement, the name of which derives from OE weōh, or pagan idol/ shrine (Gelling 1978). The relationship between church and henge at Avebury, becomes therefore, instead of an individualised de-paganising act in the Gregorian mould, a physical symbol of a much longer ritual discourse enacted between people and the landscape. This does not imply continuous and unchanging patterns of belief – rather that repeated renegotiation, involving monument construction and monument re-use, at intermittent but significant junctures, connecting community to landscape and the living to the ancestral past across millennia.

Temples and shrines

Although place-name evidence has been used in the opening to this chapter, to underpin the idea that pagan religious activity took place in clearings and open fields, the OE terms *hearg* 'temple', and *woe* 'holy place, idol, altar' (see Meaney 1995: 29) which occur in written sources and place-names, have long been accepted as references to places conceived as 'temples' or 'altars'. The OE term *hearg* occurs in an eighth-century charter (**S**106) and in ninth-century texts (Meaney 1995: 31), whilst the word *weoh* can be found in an authentic late seventh-century charter (S235, Whitelock 1955: 484, no. 58). Bede's description of the heathen temple at *Godmundingham* (Goodmanham, East Yorkshire) refers to sacred enclosures (HE I 30 (completed in AD 731), *templa et altaria* 'temples and altars', *aras et fana idolorum cum septis quibus erant circumdata*, 'altars and temples of idols with the fences/ hedges with which they were surrounded', *fanum cum omnibus septis suis*, 'the temple with all its fences/hedges', translation from Blair 1995, 2). 'Crude pillars' are referred to in a letter written by Aldhelm in the 680's: 'let us raise a hymn…that where once the crude pillars (*ermula cruda*) of the same foul snake and the stag were worshipped with coarse stupidity in profane shrines (*fana profana*), in their place dwellings for students, not to mention holy houses of prayer, are constructed skillfully by the talents of the architect' (Letter V to Heafrith, translation from Lapidge and Herren 1979: 143–6, 160–4, 201 n. 25; Blair 1995, 2–3, 25 nt. 16). Late laws occasionally mention the worship of springs, stones or trees II Cnut V (1020–1: Wormald 1999: 345), and in one rare instance the setting up of sanctuaries at such places: '…if there is on anyone's land a sanctuary [*friþgeard*] round a stone or a tree or a well [=spring] or any such nonsense', (Northumbrian Priests Law see Whitelock *et al.* 1981: 463). This implies that although religious activity might well take place in open-spaces and in relation to natural phenomena, equally these may have been enhanced by the addition of man-made structures. There has been a tendency to envisage the temples or sacred places of the Anglo-Saxons as spatially removed from settlements and cemeteries (Wilson 1985; Meaney 1995: 37), although Audrey Meaney has pointed to potential associations with 'hundred' meeting-places and at the end of the pagan period, with royal estates (1995: 37). While specially dedicated pre-Christian ritual buildings may have existed, in England as in Scandinavia, a well-known candidate being Building D2 at Yeavering (see Walker this vol. and below), we have no concurrence between any place-name containing the OE elements *hearg* 'temple', and *woe* 'holy place, idol, altar' and any physical evidence for either a timber structure or stone-built structure, or indeed settlement evidence of any kind.

Elsewhere I have suggested that places with names incorporating the term *hearg*, were instead naturally distinctive locations with material evidence for long-lived activity from prehistory through to the Romano-British and early medieval periods. In particular, when identifiable, such places have strong evidence for Roman or Romano-British religious activity (*e.g.* Wood Eaton, Oxfordshire and Harrow Fields, Cheshire). Whether driven by the attraction of monumentality or natural features or through memory of past activities, at a few of these sites archaeological evidence attests to repeated activity from late prehistory to the post-Roman era (Semple 2007). We cannot say with any certainty that each of these sites *continued in use*; they may have been renegotiated and reused at different points in time and had different meanings to each successive audience. In each era the activities and physical remains of the previous usage must have added to, and enhanced, the special nature of the site. Such place-names may therefore have been given, not to sites with actively used, pre-Christian Anglo-Saxon religious structures, but to sites remembered, visually recognized or perceived, as places associated with non-Christian religion or ritual in a more distant past.

Ritual or religious built structures are, however, claimed at the well-known site of Yeavering, Northumberland. Building D2 has long been considered a type of temple or cult structure (Hope Taylor 1977, 277–8; Blair 1995, 18–19; Walker this vol.), although this has recently been questioned, with doubt raised regarding the 'ritual' nature of the ox skull deposits, and thus the religious function of the structure per se (Hamerow 2006, 1–30). More significant than the individual status of Building D2, is the extraordinary array and arrangement of buildings that developed over time, and the changing orientation of the site across the sixth and seventh centuries AD (Hope Taylor 1977, Fig. 63; Gittos 1999). Not only is the evidence at Yeavering an insight into how settlements themselves may be ritually orientated and combine and integrate functional and spiritual elements (much as special settlements in Southern Scandinavia have also been shown to do); the settlement sits within, and makes reference to, an array of prehistoric remains (Hope Taylor 1977; Bradley 1987). We might consider Yeavering then in light of the discussion above, as further corroboration that locations used or re-used over time, could become important to communities and populations as places of ancestral and spiritual significance.

Shrines, beams, poles and totems

The existence of more ephemeral cultic structures or foci is suggested by evidence from settlement and cemetery excavations for the existence of square enclosures, standing posts and shrine-type buildings. The square enclosure imposed on the Western Ring Ditch at Yeavering, which has long been identified as a type of cultic structure or shrine (Hope Taylor 1977, 108–16, fig. 52), was positioned around a central post, which attracted a series of radial burials (Hope Taylor 1977, 112–116, Figs. 50–52; Blair 1995: 16; Lucy 2005, 127–44). The enclosure continued to attract burials before a shift in focus occurred and D2, again with a square enclosure/ annexe around a central post, took over as a ritual foci for burial. Square enclosures seem to have a long duration. There are Iron Age and Roman examples, but there are also many undated instances, such as the grouping at Harford Farm which subsequently attracted a small series of early medieval cemeteries (Penn 2000), and the example at Windmill Hill in Wiltshire (Smith

1965). Some can be dated to the sixth to seventh centuries AD, like Yeavering (Blair 1995), and the square structure at Slonk Hill, Sussex (Hartridge 1978). These are occasionally superimposed on, or adjacent to, prehistoric round-barrows or ring-ditches or situated in relation to extensive complexes of prehistoric remains. At least two are associated with Anglo-Saxon settlements (*ibid.* fig. 11). Whilst caution is needed in assuming any of the ubiquitous undated examples are early medieval, the evidence implies a type of ritual monument or structure with a lifespan bridging the Iron Age and Roman periods, still actively in use in pre-Christian England (see Carver this vol.).

At Yeavering, both the square enclosure and its later replacement encompass single standing posts or pillars. John Blair has pointed a range of evidence for standing orthostats or pillars functioning as cultic foci (*cf.* Carver, this vol.). The place-names which include the OE elements *stapol* and *bēam* may evidence sacred trees, tree-trunks, wooden posts or stone pillars (see Gelling 1978; Blair 1995 and Meaney 1995). Once again a handful of documented assembly sites seem to have made use of places associated with standing posts or monuments *e.g. Thurstaple*, Kent, is a lost example of a hundred meeting-place apparently associated with the *stapol* or post of Thor (Meaney 1995). Once again this is a monument with an extensive repertoire of uses: as markers for graves, barrows, cemeteries and ancient barrows, as foci on settlements, and as elements structuring the orientation of both burials and buildings. It is difficult to speculate on the meaning of these monuments, particularly as the wide variety of contexts within which they were deployed implies that standing posts had many differing ritual uses. Some no doubt were grave markers that commemorated the dead and their kin group, some may have signalled kin-based or group identities, marking territory, places of assembly and sacred sites. Others may have been established purely to structure movement and interaction with sites.

A final connection worth emphasizing, however, is with the sacred importance of living trees (Blair 1995: 2005). The world-tree is considered a key and common element of pan-northern European, pre-Christian belief, indeed it is an almost universal element in world religion (Russell 1979). Continental accounts attest to the felling of pagan sacred trees by Charlemagne and Boniface (Mayr-Harting 1996; Talbot 1954: 45–6), whilst a small group of English written sources list prohibitions that include the worship of trees (see above for example). Assemblies of varying kinds were certainly held at specific or chosen trees: Augustine met the British at a place known in the time of Bede as Augustine's Oak (HE II, 2), a synod took place at an unidentified *Aclea*, Northumbria, in 782 and in 789 (ASC (F)) and the West Saxons and Mercian's fought in 851 at an Aclea 'Oak Field' in Surrey (ASC (A)) (See Swanton 1996, 52, 54, 64). More traditional assemblies held at trees are attested widely, by sites such as 'Hundred tree', Buckinghamshire, mentioned in charter of AD 1006 (Pantos 2002: 65–7, 123). Some of the standing posts that once stood at Yeavering or Bampton, must have been elaborately carved, and although monuments of a Christian era, the highly decorated stone crosses of the eighth century, such as Ruthwell, may well reflect an absorption of the world-tree myths into the motifs, symbols and patterns of veneration of Anglo-Saxon Christianity (North 1997: 273–90).

Discussion

Entwined with the idea that places may have been remembered and used over long time periods, is the broader idea that people's communal identity, both in local and regional terms, may have been bound up with the ways in which they used and perceived the landscape. The repeated use of ancient remains for burial, for the positioning of palace sites and for assembly, are all potentially about the need to forge an identity rooted in past and present linking people to landscape, as they are active statements about legitimacy or authority and ownership. However, it is also clear that new sites and untouched places, hidden locations, were also important. This chapter opened with the use of fields, groves and woods as sacred places and identified them as locations that had spiritual meaning to pre-Christian and Conversion period communities. It is possible that such places were chosen for their natural and untamed beauty, for their isolation and secret position. The rare but significant mentions of the need to meet outdoors away from bounded or roofed spaces underpin the idea that open and natural spaces may have been important for their untouched, unaltered state. As Insoll (2007) has shown however, the 'natural' may become the human-altered or -created. Even when we cannot discern in highly visible archaeological terms, a *longue durée* of physical activity, we should not underestimate the vast array of repeated processes – collection or gardening of natural materials, fencing, grazing, enclosing or delimiting of sites which may be very difficult to discern in archaeological terms but which we should now perhaps look at with greater scrutiny.

The combined concepts of the sacred natural place and the numinous landscape, have endured in modern scholarship despite changing perspectives, and have been particularly emphasized within prehistoric research on phenomenological and aesthetic approaches to material remains within their landscape (Bradley 2000; 2002; Tilley 1994). This chapter has identified just some of the types of locale that seem to have been significant within early medieval mentalities, beliefs and superstitions. Even from such a cursory overview, however, it is clear that such places did not exist in isolation – their wider relationship with the landscape, the communities inhabiting it and the people moving through it, seem to have added to or enhanced their special and attractive qualities.

It is clear we can see elements of pre-Christian or non-Christian belief in the way the landscape is labelled: there is an appreciation of natural places and of previous prehistoric practice. The labelling may be verbal, surviving in place-names, and in some documents. Or it may be material and seen in the positioning of burials and other monuments. Both the verbal and material make references to belief systems that are more clearly drawn in Scandinavia (Lund, Sanmark, and Walker, this vol.); it seems likely, however, that Anglo-Saxon paganism made reference to local British and prehistoric practice too. Whether or not these beliefs have their roots in prehistoric practice in Britain or northern Europe more generally (and it is by no means easy to distinguish between the two), the rituals involved the full pre-Christian repertoire: votive deposits, furnished burial, monumental mounds, sacred natural phenomena and eventually constructed pillars, shrines and temples. All these monumental investments however, were, and needed to be, situated in a wider ritual landscape, so that the every day life of the people took place in a theatre which was also occupied by spirits, benign, malevolent and ancestral. Whether local, imported or universal, this numinous landscape provides the substance of Anglo-Saxon non-Christian religion as we so far know it.

Acknowledgements

I would like to thank Martin Carver, Howard Williams and Alex Sanmark for their valuable comments and suggestions during the completion of this paper.

References

Äikiäs, M. (2007) *Quiet Places – GIS Study of Sami Ritual Sites in Northern Finland*. Paper delivered at 'Cognition and Materiality', Nordic Graduate Seminar, Athens 2007

Austin, D. and Thomas, J. (1990) The 'Proper Study' of Medieval Archaeology: A Case Study. *In* D. Austin and J. Thomas (eds), *From the Baltic to the Black Sea*, 29–35, London: Routledge

Barrow, J. (2001) Chester's Earliest Regatta? Edgar's Dee-Rowing Revisted, *Early Medieval Europe* 10(1): 81–93

Benson, D. and Miles, D. (1974a) Cropmarks near the Sutton Courtenay Saxon Site, *Antiquity* 48: 223–6

Bell, T. (2005) *The Religious Reuse of Roman Structures in Early Medieval England*, BAR British Series, 390, Oxford

Blair, W.J. (1988) Minster Churches in the Landscape. *In* D. Hooke (ed.), *Anglo-Saxon Settlements*, 41–47, Oxford: Blackwell Books

Blair, W.J. (1992) Anglo-Saxon Minsters: A Topographical Review. *In* W.J. Blair and R. Sharpe (eds), *Pastoral Care before the Parish*, 226–66, Leicester: Leicester University Press

Blair, W.J. (1994) *Anglo-Saxon Oxfordshire*, Stroud: Sutton

Blair, W.J. (1995) Anglo-Saxon Pagan Shrines and their Prototypes, *Anglo-Saxon Studies in Archaeology and History*, 8: 1–28

Blair, W.J. (1997) Saint Cuthman, Steyning and Bosham, *Sussex Archaeological Collections*, 135: 173–92

Blair, W.J. (1998) Bampton: An Anglo-Saxon Minster, *Current Archaeology*, 160: 124–130

Blair, W.J. (1999) *The Bronze Age Barrows and Churchyard*, Bampton Research Paper 5

Blair, W.J. (2005) *The Church in Anglo-Saxon Society*, Oxford: OUP

Bradley, R.J. (1987) Time Regained: The Creation of Continuity, *Journal of the British Archaeological Association*, 140: 1–17

Bradley, R.J. (1998a) *The Significance of Monuments*, London: Routledge

Bradley, R.J. (1998b) *The Passage of Arms*, (2nd edit.), Oxford: Oxbow Books

Bradley, R.J. (2000) *An Archaeology of Natural Places*, London: Routledge

Bradley, R.J. (2002) *The Past in Prehistoric Societies*, London: Routledge

Brink, S. (2001) Mythologizing Landscape, Place and Space of Cult and Myth. *In* M. Stausberg (ed.) *Kontinuitäten und Brüche in der Religionsgeschichte. Festschrift für Anders Hultgard zu seinem 65. Geburtstag am 23.12. 2002*, Ergänzungsband zum Reallexikon der Germanischen Altertumskunde, 31, 76-107, New York: W. de Gruyter

Brookes, S. (2007) *Economics and Social Change in Anglo-Saxon Kent: AD 400–900, Landscapes, Communities and Exchange*, BAR British Series 431, Oxford

Carver, M.O.H. (1986) Contemporary Artefacts Illustrated in Late Anglo-Saxon Manuscripts, *Archaeologia*, 108: 117–146

Carver, M.O.H. (2000) Burial as Poetry: The Context of Treasure in Anglo-Saxon Graves. *In* E. Tyler (ed.), *Treasure in the Medieval West*, 25–48, York: Medieval Press

Carver, M.O.H. (2001) Why That, Why There, Why Then? The Politics of Early Medieval Monumentality. *In* A. Macgregor and H. Hamerow (eds) *Image and Power in Early Medieval British Archaeology Essays in Honour of Rosemary Cramp*, 1–22, Oxford: Oxbow Books

Carver, M.O.H. (2002) Reflections on the Meaning of Anglo-Saxon Barrows. S. Lucy and A.Reynolds (eds), *Burial in Early Medieval England and Wales*, 132–143, Society for Medieval Archaeological Monograph 17, London: SMA

Carver, M.O.H. (2005) *Sutton Hoo: A Seventh-Century Princely Burial Ground and its Context*, London: Britsh Museum Press

Carver, M.O.H. (2008) *The Pictish Monastery at Portmahomack* (Jarrow lecture 2008), Newcastle

Carver, M.O.H., Hills, C. and Scheschkewitz, J. (2009) *Wasperton. A Roman, British and Anglo-Saxon Community in Central England*, Woodbridge: Boydell

Chaney, W.A. (1970) *The Cult of Kingship in Anglo-Saxon England*, Manchester: University Press

Cockayne, O. (1864–5) *Leechdoms, Wortcunning and Starcraft of Early England*, 3 Vols, London: Longman, Roberts and Green

Cohen, N. (2003) Boundaries and Settlement: The Role of the River Thames, *Anglo-Saxon Studies in Archaeology and History* 12: 9–20

Colgrave, B. (ed.) (1956) *Felix's Life of St. Guthlac*, Cambridge: CUP

Colgrave, B. and Myners, R.A.B. (ed. and trans.) (1969) *Historia Ecclesiastica Gentis Anglorum*, Oxford: OUP

Corney, M., (1997) New Evidence for the Romano-British Settlement by Silbury Hill,*Wiltshire Archaeological and Natural History Magazine*, 90: 139–40

Devlin, Z. (2007) *Remembering the Dead in Anglo-Saxon England: Memory Theory in Archaeology and History*, BAR British Series 446. Oxford

Ellis, H.R., (1943) *The Road to Hel, A Study of the Conception of the Dead in Old Norse Literature*, Cambridge: CUP

Ellis Davidson, H.R., (1964) *Gods and Myths of Northern Europe*, London: Penguin

Evison, V.I. (1987) *Dover: The Buckland Anglo-Saxon Cemetery*. London: HMBC

Gelling, M. (1978) *Signposts to the Past*, Chichester: Phillimore

Gelling, M. (1984) *Place-Names in the Landscape*, London: J.M. Dent and Sons

Gelling, M. (1998) Place-Names and Landscape. *In* S. Taylor (ed.), *The Uses of Place-Names*, 75–100, St. John's House Papers No. 7, Edinburgh: Scottish Cultural Press

Gelling, M. and Cole, A. (2000) *The Landscape of Place-Names*, Stamford: Shaun Tyas

Gittos, H. (1999) Yeavering. *In* M. Lapidge (*et al.*) *The Blackwell Encyclopedia of Anglo-Saxon England*, Oxford: Blackwell

Grimm, J. (1900) *Teutonic Mythology*, 4 vols, trans. J.S. Stallybrass, vol. 1, London

Grinsell, L.V. (1976) *The Folklore of Prehistoric Sites in Britain*, London: Newton Abbot, David Charles

Hall, A. (2006) Are There Any Elves in Anglo-Saxon Place-names? *Nomina*, 29: 61–80

Halsall, G., (2000) The Viking Presence in England? The Burial Evidence. *In* D. Hadley and J. Richards (eds), *Cultures in Contact: Scandinavian Settlement in England in the Ninth and Tenth Centuries*, 267–8, Turnhout, Belgium: Brepols Publishers

Hamerow, H. (2006) 'Special Deposits' in Anglo-Saxon Settlements, *Medieval Archaeology*, 46: 481–30

Hartridge, R. (1978) Excavations at the Prehistoric and Romano-British Site on Slonk Hill, Shoreham, Sussex, *Sussex Archaeological Collections*, 116: 69–141

Hawkes, S.C. (1976) The Early Anglo-Saxon Period. *In* G. Briggs, J. Cook and T. Rowley (eds), *The Archaeology of the Oxford Region*, 64–108, Oxford: OUP

Hines, J. (1997) Religion: The Limits of Knowledge. *In* J. Hines (ed.), *The Anglo-Saxons from the Migration Period to the Eighth Century*, 375–401, Woodbridge: Boydell

Hoggett, R. (2007) Charting Conversion: Burial as a Barometer of Belief?, *Anglo-Saxon Studies in Archaeology and History*, 14: 28-37

Hole, C. (1995) *Encyclopedia of Superstitions*, London: Helicon

Hollis, S. (1998) The Minster-in-Thanet Foundation Story, *Anglo-Saxon England*, 27: 41–64

Hooke, D. (2003) Trees in the Anglo-Saxon Landscape. *In* C.P. Biggam (ed.), *From Earth to Art: The Many Aspects of the Plant World in Anglo-Saxon England*, 17–40, Costerus New Ser. 148, Glasgow University Press

Hope Taylor, B. (1977) *Yeavering: An Anglo-British Centre of Early Northumbria*, Department of the Environment Archaeological Reports No. 7, London: HMSO

Insoll, T. (2007) 'Natural' or 'Human' Spaces? Tallensi Sacred Groves and Shrines and their Potential Implications for Aspects of Northern European Prehistory and Phenomenological Interpretation, *Norwegian Archaeological Review*, 40: 2, 138–58

Jolly, K. (1996) *Popular Religion in Late Saxon England*, Chapel Hill: University of North Carolina Press

Jonuks, T. (2007) Holy Groves in Estonian Religion, *Estonian Journal of Archaeology* 11,1: 3–35

Lane, T. (1988) Some Cropmarks in Crowland, *Archaeology in Lincolnshire 1987–1988*, Fourth Annual Report of the Trust for Lincolnshire Archaeology

Lapidge, M. (2000) The Archetype of *Beowulf*, *Anglo-Saxon England*, 29: 5–42

Lapidge, M. and Herren, M. (1979) *Aldhelm: the Prose Works*, Cambridge: D.S. Brewer

Levy, J. (1982) *Social and Religious Organisation in Bronze Age Denmark: An Analysis of Ritual Hoard Finds*, BAR British Series, 272, Oxford

Lucy, S. (1998) *The Early Anglo-Saxon Cemeteries of East Yorkshire*, BAR British Series, 272. Oxford

Lucy, S. (2002) Burial Practice in Early Medieval Eastern England: Constructing Local Identities, Deconstructing Ethnicity. *In* S. Lucy and A. Reynolds (eds), *Burial in Early Medieval England and Wales*, 72–87, Society for Medieval Archaeological Monograph 17, London: SMA

Lucy, S. (2005) Early Medieval Burial at Yeavering: A Retrospective. *In* P. Frodsham and C. O'Brien (eds), *Yeavering, People, Power and Place*, Stroud: Tempus

Lund, J. (2005) Thresholds and Passages: The Meanings of Bridges and Crossings in the Viking Age and Early Middle Ages, *Viking and Medieval Scandinavia* 1: 109–37

Mawer, A. and Stenton, F.M. (1930) *The Place-Names of Sussex, Part II*, English Place-Name Society Vol. VII, Cambridge

Mawer, A. and Stenton, F.M. (1939) *The Place-Names of Wiltshire*, English Place-Name Society Vol. XVI, Cambridge

Mayr-Harting, H. (1996) Charlemagne, the Saxons, and the Imperial Coronation of 800, *English Historical Review*, 111, no. 444: 1113–33

Meaney, A.L. (1984) Ælfric and Idolatry, *Journal of Religious History*, 13: 119–35

Meaney, A.L. (1995) Pagan English Sanctuaries, Place-Names and Hundred Meeting-Places, *Anglo-Saxon Studies in Archaeology and History*, 8: 29–42

Meaney, A.L. (2005) Felix's Life of Guthlac: Hagiography and/or Truth, *Proceedings of the Cambridgeshire Antiquarian Society*, 90: 29–48

Morris, R. (1989) *Churches in the Landscape*, London: J. Dent and Sons

Mulk , I and Bayliss-Smith, T. (1999) The Representation of Sámi Cultural Identity in the Cultural Landscapes of Northern Sweden: The Use and Misuse of Archaeological Knowledge. *In* P. Ucko and R. Layton, *The Archaeology and Anthropology of Landscape. Shaping Your Landscape. One World Archaeology 30*, London: Routledge

North, R. (1997) *Heathen Gods in Old English Literature*, Cambridge: CUP

Pantos, A. (2002) *Assembly-Places in the Anglo-Saxon Period: Aspects of Form and Location*, Unpublished DPhil thesis, Oxford University

Pantos, A. (2003) 'On the Edge of Things': The Boundary Location of Anglo-Saxon Assembly Sites. *In* D. Griffiths, A. Reynolds & S. Semple (eds), *Boundaries in Early Medieval Britain: Anglo-Saxon Studies in Archaeology and History, 12,* 38–49, Oxford: Oxford University School of Archaeology

Pantos, A. (2004) The Location and Form of Anglo-Saxon Assembly Places. *In* A. Pantos & S. Semple (eds) *Assembly Places and Practices in Medieval Europe,* 155–80, Dublin: Four Courts Press

Parker-Pearson, M. and Field, N. (2003) *Fiskerton. An Iron Age Timber Causeway with Iron Age and Roman Offerings,* Oxford: Oxbow Books

Penn, K. (2000) *Excavations on the Norwich Southern Bypass, 1989–91 Part II: The Anglo-Saxon Cemetery at Harford Farm, Caistor St. Edmund, Norfolk,* East Anglian Archaeology, 92, Dereham: Archaeology and Environment Division, Norfolk Museum Service

Pollard, J. and Reynolds, A. (2002) *Avebury: The Biography of a Landscape,* Stroud: Tempus

Price, N. (2002) *The Viking Way: Religion and War in Late Iron Age Scandinavia,* Uppsala: University Press

Rackham, O. (1976) *Trees and Woodland in the British Landscape,* London: Dent

Rattue, J. (1995) *The Living Stream: Holy Wells in Historical Context,* Woodbridge: Boydell

Reynolds, A. (1997a) The Definition and Ideology of Anglo-Saxon Execution Sites and Cemeteries. *In* G. de Boe and F. Verhaeghe (eds), *Death and Burial in Medieval Europe,* II, 33–41, Zelik: Instituut voor het Archeologisch Patrimonium

Reynolds, A. (1997) Sutton Hoo and the Archaeology of Execution, *Saxon,* 27: 1–3

Reynolds, A. (1999) *Later Anglo-Saxon England: Life and Landscape,* Stroud: Tempus

Reynolds, A. (2009) *Anglo-Saxon Deviant Burial Customs,* Oxford: OUP

Rigold, S.E. and Metcalf, D.M., (1984) A Revised Check-list of English Finds of Sceattas. *In* D. Hill and D.M. Metcalf (eds), *Sceattas in England and on the Continent,* 245–68, BAR British Series 128, Oxford

Robinson, P. (2001) Religion in Roman Wiltshire. *In* P. Ellis (ed.) *Roman Wiltshire and After: Papers in Honour of Ken Annable,* 147–64, Devizes: Wiltshire Archaeological and Natural History Society

Rodwell, W. and Rodwell, K. (1982) St. Peter's Church, Barton-upon-Humber, *Antiquaries Journal* 62: 283–315

Russell, C. (1979) The Tree as a Kingship Symbol, *Folklore* 90: 2: 217–33

Sanmark A. and Semple S.J. (2008) Places of Assembly: Topographic Definitions from Sweden and England, *Fornvännen* 103: 245–59

Sawyer, P.H., (1968) *Anglo-Saxon Charters: An Annotated List and Bibliography,* London Royal Historical Society Guides and Handbooks No. 8

Scarre, C. (2002a) Coast and Cosmos: The Neolithic Monuments of Northern Brittany. *In* C. Scarre (ed.) *Monuments and Landscape in Atlantic Europe,* 84–102, London: Routledge

Scarre, C. (2002b) A Place of Special Meaning: Interpreting Prehistoric Monuments Through Landscape. *In* B. David and M. Wilson (eds) *Inscribed Landscapes: Marking and Making Place,* 154–75, Honolulu: University of Hawaii Press

Scarre, C. & Lawson, G. (2006) *Archaeoacoustics,* McDonald Institute Monographs. Cambridge: McDonald Institute for Archaeological Research

Semple, S.J. (1998) A Fear of the Past: The Place of the Prehistoric Burial Mound in the Ideology of Middle and Later Anglo-Saxon England, *World Archaeology* 30(1): 109–26

Semple, S.J. (2002) *Anglo-Saxon Attitudes to the Past: A Landscape Perspective,* Unpublished DPhil Thesis, Oxford University

Semple, S.J. (2003) Illustrations of Damnation in Late Anglo-Saxon Manuscripts, *Anglo-Saxon England* 32: 31–45

Semple, S.J. (2003) Burials and Political Boundaries in the Avebury Region, North Wiltshire, *Anglo-Saxon Studies in Archaeology and History* 12: 72–91

Semple, S.J. (2004) Locations of Assembly in Early Anglo-Saxon England. *In* A. Pantos & S.J. Semple, *Assembly Places and Practices in Medieval Europe*, 135–54, Dublin: Four Courts Press

Semple, S.J. (2007) Defining the OE Hearg: A Preliminary Archaeological and Topographic Examination of Hearg Place Names and their Hinterlands, *Early Medieval Europe* 15(4): 364–385

Semple, S.J. (2008) Polities and Princes AD 400–800: New Perspectives on the Funerary Landscape of the South Saxon Kingdom, *Oxford Journal of Archaeology* 27(4): 407–429

Semple, S.J. (2009) Recycling the Past: Ancient Monuments and Changing Meanings in Early Medieval Britain. *In* M. Aldrich and R. Wallis (eds), *Antiquaries and Archaists: The Past in the Past and the Past in the Present*, 29–45, Reading: Spire Books

Semple, S.J. (in preparation). *Anglo-Saxon Conceptions of Landscape*

Semple, S.J. and Turner, A. (forthcoming), Excavations at Scutchmer Knob, Berkshire, *SMAJ*

Skeates, R. (2007) Religious Experience in the Prehistoric Maltese Underworld. *In* D. Barrowclough and C. Malone (eds) *Cult in Context: Reconsidering Ritual in Archaeology*, 90–96, Oxford: Oxbow Books

Smith, I.F. (1965) *Windmill Hill and Avebury, Excavations by Alexander Keiller 1925–1939*, Oxford: Clarendon Press

Speake, G. (1989) *A Saxon Bed Burial on Swallowcliffe Down*, London: HMBC

Stanley, E.G. (1975) *The Search for Anglo-Saxon Paganism*, Cambridge: D.S. Brewer

Stenton, F.M. (1941) The Historical Bearing of Place-Name Studies: Anglo-Saxon Heathenism *The Transactions of the Royal Historical* Society, 4th Series, XXIII (1941): 10–11

Stocker, D. (1993) The Early Church in Lincolnshire: A Study of the Sites and their Significance. *In* A. Vince (ed.), *Pre-Viking Lindsey*, 101–22, Lincoln Archaeological Studies 1, Lincoln: City of Lincoln Archaeology Unit

Stocker, D. and Everson, P. (2003) The Straight and Narrow Way: Fenland Causeways and the Conversion of the Landscape in the Witham Valley, Lincolnshire, *In* M.O.H. Carver (ed.), *The Cross Goes North: processes of Conversion in Northern Europe, AD 300–1300*, 271–288, Woodbridge: York Medieval Press

Swire, O.F. (1966) *The Outer Hebrides and their Legends*, Edinburgh: Oliver and Boyd

Talbot C.H. (1954) *The Anglo-Saxon Missionaries in Germany*, London: Sheed and Ward

Tilley, C. (1994) *A Phenomenology of Landscape: Places, Paths and Monuments*, Oxford: Berg

Tilley, C. (1996) The Power of Rocks: Topography and Monument Construction on Bodmin Moor, *World Archaeology*, 28(2): 161–176

Thomas, J. (2008) *Monument, Memory and Myth, Use and Re-use of Three Bronze Age Barrows at Cossington, Leicestershire*, Leicester Archaeology Monograph No. 14

Turner, S. (2006) *Making a Christian Landscape: The Countryside in Early Medieval Cornwall, Devon and Wessex*, Exeter: University Press

Turville-Petre, E.O.G. (1964) *Myth and Religion of the North*, London: Weidenfeld and Nicholson

Webster, L. (1986) Anglo-Saxon England AD 400–1100. *In* I. Longworth and J. Cherry (eds), *Archaeology in Britain Since 1945 New Directions*, London: British Museum Publications

Whitelock, D. (1955) *English Historical Documents I c.500–1042*, London: Eyre and Methuen

Whitelock, D., Brett, M. and Brooke, C.N.L. (1981) *Councils and Synods with Other Documents Relating to the English Church, I. AD 871–1204*, Oxford: Clarendon Press

Williams, H. (1997) Ancient Landscapes and the Dead: The Reuse of Prehistoric and Roman Monuments as Early Anglo-Saxon Burial Sites, *Medieval Archaeology*, 41: 1–32

Williams, H. (1998) Monuments and the Past in Early Anglo-Saxon England, *World Archaeology*, 30(1): 90–108

Williams, H. (1999) Placing the Dead: Investigating the Location of Wealthy Barrow Burials in Seventh-Century England. *In* M. Rundkvist (ed.), *Grave Matters Eight Studies of First Millenium AD Burials in Crimea, England and Southern Scandinavia,* 57–86, BAR International Series 781, Oxford

Williams, H.M.W. (2006) *Death and Burial in Early Medieval Britain,* Cambridge: University Press

Wilson, D.M. (1965) Some Neglected Late Anglo-Saxon Swords, *Medieval Archaeology,* 9: 32–54

Wilson, D. (1992) *Anglo-Saxon Paganism,* London: Routledge

Wilson, D. (1985) A Note on OE *hearg* and *weoh* as Place-Name Elements Representing Different Types of Pagan Worship Sites, *Anglo-Saxon Studies in Archaeology and History,* 4: 179–83

Wormald, P. (1999) *The Making of English Law: King Alfred to the Twelfth Century, Volume 1, Legislation and its Limits,* Oxford: Blackwell Publishers

Yeates, S. (2006) *Religion, Community and Territory: Defining Religion in the Severn Valley and Adjacent Hills from the Iron Age to the Early medieval period,* BAR British Series, Oxford.

Chapter 3

At the Water's Edge

Julie Lund

Introduction

One important area of correspondence between early English and Scandinavian mentalities lies in the central role of rivers and lakes. While the role of waterways was probably not identical for each area, similarities in source material suggest that one way of grasping the ritual role of water in the Anglo-Saxon landscape is to study the better documented Scandinavian perspective. The source material comprises descriptions and references to waterways and wetlands in texts, and archaeological evidence in the form of the deposits of tools, weapons, jewellery and ritual objects that are found in them. Accordingly, in this chapter I will first examine the wetland deposits and the role of lakes and rivers in Scandinavian cosmology with a focus on the Viking Age – then use these as analogies for practices and beliefs in Anglo-Saxon England. I shall touch on the connection between the legendary smith and the water's edge, and finally discuss the role of the wetlands in a Christian context.

The interpretation of the practice of depositing artefacts in wetlands has long been debated in archaeology. In general, wetland finds have been interpreted as votive offerings, whereas most finds from dry land are considered to be hoards of treasure or scrap metal. This division between sacred and profane deposits was established by Sophus Müller in 1886 and maintained over the following 100 years (Müller 1886; Karsten 1994: 24; Bårdseth 1998: 12; Melheim 1999; Needham 2001: 278). Starting from the 1980s, however, a gradual transition be can be identified: from seeing the hoards – including many of the finds from dry land – as *offerings* towards interpreting them as traces of *ritual actions* (Levy 1982; Bradley 1990: 23–24). This has meant a shift from discussing which *gods* were intended as recipients towards focusing on *the social purposes* of ritual acts of deposition (Berggren 2006). In the last ten years, even hoards of treasure have been categorised as exhibiting traces of ritual action (Zachrisson 1998; Hedeager 1999; Andrén 2002; Lund 2004; Ryste 2005; Spangen 2005). Moreover, acts of deposition in the Viking Age and Late Anglo-Saxon Period were not to be seen as isolated in history, but represented the repetition of a very long tradition. It should be noted here that 'rituals' are not always religious, but can be political or judicial acts (Detienne 1989; Rappaport 1999: 24–25, 31; Habbe 2005). This is seen clearly in the

Old Norse sources where oath-taking and the opening of the assembly meetings are accompanied by ritual actions (Habbe 2005). Even acts of deposition have been seen in this light, being interpreted as actions relating to boundary disputes or oath taking (Blair 1994: 104, see Semple this vol.).

These alterations of emphasis in the studies of deposits form part of the general change in landscape studies from the 1990s onwards, which focus on the landscape as a mediator rather than as merely the scene for human actions. Humans formed the landscape, but were also being formed by it (see for instance Barrett *et al.* 1991; Welinder 1992; Bender 1993; Bradley 1993; 2000; Tilley 1994; Thomas 1996). Structuring the landscape can be a means to create and maintain the identity of individuals and groups. Acts of deposition attach meaning to specific places (Brück 2001: 297; Osborne 2004: 7), and the locations of ritual deposits connect to mental structures and perceptions of world-view (Zachrisson 1998: 93–122; Hedeager 1999: 241–243; Ryste 2005: 59–67; Spangen 2005: 33). The landscape is thus a social artefact, in that it bears witness to social relations between humans, artefacts and places; and it is also cognitive, having roots in the mentality, word-view and cosmology of the people who used it. Since acts of deposition stress particular features in the landscape, they should enable us to get a glimpse of how the cognitive landscape was structured.

Personality of objects

The choice of artefacts for deposition was hardly accidental. Janet Hoskins states that "things tell the story of [a person's] life" (Hoskins 1998: 2–11); but based on Anglo-Saxon and Old Norse texts it could equally be stated that in England and Scandinavia "people were telling the stories of things' lives". Most of these texts were written down after the conversion, but some of them arguably contain traces of Anglo-Saxon and Old Norse attitudes towards artefacts and landscape that could inform the interpretation of hoards. In these texts we hear of swords and pieces of jewellery being acquired, passed on as gift or heritage, being buried in a mound with the latest owner, and regained by new owners by breaking into the mound and fighting the spirit dwelling there. Weapons could bear names, such as Arthur's sword *Caliburnus*, and his spear *Ron* (Historia Regum Britanniae, book VII, 189–190), or the stout sword *Mimming* in the Old English poem *Waldhere* stanza 2–4. The sword *Skovnung* in Kormaks Saga complains loudly when it is not treated properly (Drachmann 1967: 28–30). A sword with the same name in Thord Hredes Saga is described as a cool-headed sword (Drachmann 1967; Idsøe 2004: 62). Even where swords were broken and forged into new weapons, they are described in a way that indicates that they were believed to have their own personality which survived through this transformation (Davidson 1962: 171–173). If we look at the archaeological material, some specific artefacts were either hoarded or buried in mounds that were reopened soon after the burial and so it does indeed seem possible that similar ideas could have existed for the contemporary real-life weapons outside of Anglo-Saxon and Viking-Age literature.

Possessing an object implies the creation of a social relation between the person and the artefact – and in this process the artefact surpasses its own materiality (Weiner 1985: 212; Gosden 1999: 120). It can consequently come to exercise the quality of a social agent (Gosden 1999: 120), and if repossessed, the sword would bring along with it the stories of its previous owners even as it circulated between men (Mauss 1954 [1924]; Weiner 1985: 210; Fowler 2004: 57). A central aspect of such inalienable artefacts is that they cannot be destroyed (Weiner 1985: 210). The act of deposition could in this sense be a way of handling an object with a complex social biography – by taking them out of circulation, but keeping them at specific places that bore a special meaning. In that perspective the act of deposition can be seen as the final stage of the social life of the artefact.

If we compare the stories of the artefacts in these sources with the way material culture was handled in England and Scandinavia it is likely that *some*, but certainly not *all* artefacts were considered agents with their own name and identity. It should be noted that the concept of personified objects was still appreciated in the 10th century, as the Christian poem *The Dream of the Rood* demonstrates. Here, the story of Christ is told to the poet by the wood of Christ's crucifix itself. The animation of objects in the early medieval world indicates a deep mind-set towards the character of specific objects – artefacts with complex social biographies, inalienable artefacts such as heirlooms, bride-silver or religious artefacts. In what follows, we should view the objects as having personality and biography, thus broadening the significance of their deposition in wet places.

Objects in Scandinavian waters

Prior to the Anglo-Saxon period, acts of deposition consistently took place in wetlands in both Britain and Scandinavia. The Scandinavian depositions from the first centuries AD consist of huge amounts of destroyed weapons laid down on different occasions. The large weapon sacrifices are part of the extensive water cult that can be found throughout most of Northern European prehistory – in Neolithic sacrifices of animals and humans, the impressive Bronze Age hoards with weapons, jewellery and cult objects, and in the Pre-Roman Iron Age depositions of cauldrons, wagons and humans (Fabech 1991; Kaul 2003; Koch 1998). The Iron Age sacrifices of weapons – mainly spears and swords – shields, tools, and other equipment for an army represent some of the most spectacular wetland finds and are interpreted as sacrifices of the weapons of a defeated enemy (Ilkjær & Carnap-Bornheim 1990; Ilkjær 2003; Kaul 2003; Dobat 2008). They are dated to the period from the 4th century BC to the 5th century AD, with the majority of the deposits placed in the 3rd and 4th century AD. The material consisted of thousands of weapons and the ritual acts included deliberate damage of the artefact and in many cases even the sacrifice of animals (Ilkjær & Carnap-Bornheim 1990; Ilkjær 2003).

Compared to this material the finds from wetlands from the later period are clearly limited in numbers, though not in quality. In Scandinavia, fibulae and bracteates were placed in wetlands or at the edge of wetlands during the 5th to first half of the 6th century (Hedeager 2003). Deposition ceased in the 6th century, but reappeared in the late 8th century (Fabech 1991; Hedeager 1999; Lund 2004). From the late 8th century until the beginning of the 11th century, weapons, jewellery, coins and tools were again deposited in bogs, lakes, rivers and in the sea (Geißlinger 1967; Hines 1989; Zachrisson

1998; Hedeager 1999; Andrén 2002; Lund 2004; 2005; 2006). The wetland deposits of the 8th–11th century are of a quite different character to those of the earlier periods: successive large scale depositions in the same place are relatively rare, and most of the material consists of artefacts laid down either singly or as small hoards. These artefacts only very rarely show signs of being damaged prior to deposition. They tend to cluster in rivers and lakes. A significant number of river finds come from places with sacred names, such as Gudenå in Jutland, Denmark, a name meaning 'stream of the gods' (Lund 2004; 2005; 2007).

One way of approaching an interpretation of the Scandinavian river finds is to examine the role of the watercourses in the Older Edda, Snorri's Edda and the skaldic Poetry. Some of the poems in the Elder Edda – including Völuspá, Hávamál, Grímnismál and *Völundarkviða* – and the skaldic poetry are considered to have a core of pagan myths and beliefs. In the early Middle Ages, rivers and streams were often used as administrative borders for ownership of land (Øeby-Nielsen 2005: 130). Similarly in Old Norse texts, watercourses act as borders, where groups of beings – men, gods and giants – lived on different sides of a river (Østmo 2005: 64). In this sense the rivers organised the different types of beings spatially in the cosmology. Mythical watercourses are listed in *Grímnismál* and Snorri's Þulur with names referring to the very special character of the waterways in question (Vigfusson 1991; Simek 1993). Several of these have names related to warfare and battle, for instance *Gunnþró* (meaning *the groove of battle*), *Gunnþorin* (meaning *eager for battle*), and *Örmt* (meaning *the one that divides armies*) (*Grímnismál*, stanza 27–29; Simek 1993). Another theme in the same poem is the description of watercourses, which contain or 'flow with' weapons, such as *Geirvimul* (meaning *the one bobbing with spears*), *Nöt* (meaning *the stinging*) and *Sliðr* (meaning *the dangerously sharp*). The latter appears in both *Grímnismál* and *Völuspá* stanza 36, where it says that "from the East comes a river through *Eitrdalar* (meaning *the valley of poison*), it falls (that is *flows*) with swords and saxes, *Sliðr* is its name" (*Völuspá* stanza 36, my translation).

It has been stated that the concept of rivers with weapons in this Old Norse poem is simply an adaptation from Christian visionary literature (Simek 1993 [1983]: 294); but as the philologist Jonas Wellendorf points out, the concept of weapon-loaded rivers in Christian visionary literature appears later than in the Old Norse poetry and is more likely an adaptation of a pagan concept (Wellendorf 2006: 23–24). This interpretation is indeed supported by the existence of the material counterparts, that is real physical rivers containing real weapons. According to Grímnismál the weapon-loaded rivers, *Geirvimul* and *Nọt* run around the sanctuaries or homes of the gods, whereas *Sliðr* runs through the area of the humans, but falls from here to *Hel*, the land of the dead. Thus, the weapon-loaded watercourses are also described as borders.

It is clear that oral or written metaphors in Old Norse literature have equivalence in Late Iron Age and Early Medieval material culture – in the sense that the landscape, the material culture and the poems contain intertwined metaphors (Tilley 1999: 4; Domeij Lundborg 2006: 40). The presence of names and description of watercourses 'running with weapons' indicate that people who produced and heard the poems represented in the Old Norse sources knew of real watercourses containing weapons. The ritual acts of deposition and the names and descriptions of watercourses in the skaldic and eddaic poems are in this sense expressions of the same material metaphor: the concept of the sharp, dangerous weapon-loaded watercourses running through the world.

Rivers in the Anglo-Saxon cognitive landscape

Ritual deposits in the wetlands of England show continuity from the 4th to 11th century. Roman lead baptismal tanks, pewter vessels, and tableware mainly from the 4th century were deposited in wells, fens and rivers. It has been debated whether these depositions represent contemporary Christian acts or pagan rituals. It has even been suggested that they are expression of religious belief common to pagans and Christians (Petts 2005 [2003]: 110–111). Not only liturgical objects, but even spearheads were deposited in rivers in this period (Swanton 1974). The material shows that the concept of wetlands as sacred places was present in the mentality of people living in Britain on the eve of the Anglo-Saxon era.

The number of early medieval artefacts found in English rivers is far too high to represent accidental losses. As in Scandinavia, the dominant part of the material consists of weapons, yet jewellery and tools are also represented. The number of hoards in England decreases in the 6th–8th century, but is far from lacking. For instance, in the River Thames more than one hundred spearheads of Anglo-Saxon types have been found, in 25 different places (Swanton 1974: 31–89). Spearheads from the 5th and 6th century dominate (Cohen 2003: 11), but spearheads from the previous and following centuries are represented (Swanton 1974). The deposition of Anglo-Saxon spearheads also took place in the Rivers Cherwell, Kennet and Way (Swanton 1974: 59,75, 88–89), though in far lesser numbers than in the Thames. Swords, spearheads and axes, dating to the 9–10th century and of both Anglo-Saxon and Scandinavian type have been recovered from the English rivers, mainly in the Thames, Lea and Witham (O'Neil 1944; Davidson 1962: xvii–xxi, 56, 64; Wilson 1965: 32–44, 50; 1981: 15). Examples include the sword of Petersen's type X with silver inlays found in the River Thames at Battersea (Wilson 1964: 107), the sword of type O/M found in the Thames at Kew (Peirce 2002: 90–91), a spearhead from the River Thames (BM M&ME 1893, 7–15,2), a scramasax, sword and tools found in a hoard in the bank of a small stream flowing past Greencroft in Lancaster (Wilson 1964: 135–136), and a sword with an inlay of Latin letters, found in the River Witham opposite Monk's Abbey (Wilson 1964: 143).

Not only weapons, but horse equipment, tools and jewellery have appeared in these contexts in significant numbers. A number of bronze stirrups with inlays in copper and silver have been discovered in the Rivers Thames, Witham, and Avon (Shetelig & Bjørn 1940: 58, 88, 99; Hinton 1974: 48–50; Backhouse *et al.* 1984: 105–106). Ornaments in Anglo-Saxon as well as Scandinavian style are also represented in the wetland finds. A gold finger ring with engravings was found in the River Nene, an ornamented bone pin in Ringerike style and the 11th-century Hammersmith plaque were recovered from the River Thames, and the so-called Witham pins – a set of three silver-gilt, linked pins with circular heads from the 8th century – were found in the River Witham (Shetelig & Bjørn 1940: 92; Wilson 1964: 132–134, 158–159; Backhouse *et al.* 1984: 109). The ornaments, riding gear, and tools underline the interpretation of the finds as being ritual depositions and not traces of battle. The majority of finds derive from parts of England where Scandinavians had a strong impact in the Viking Age. Wetland depositions were definitely not introduced by the Scandinavians to Anglo-Saxon England (as the finds of 5th- and 6th-century spearheads and the Witham pins testify), but the practice seems to have had a revival in the Viking Age.

Like the weapon depositions from South Scandinavia, the English river-finds include a high proportion of unique artefacts. One example is the iron scramasax of Anglo-Saxon type from the River Thames found at Battersea, London from the 9th–10th century, which is inlaid in copper, bronze and silver. Runes forming the *futharc* alphabet and the masculine name *Beagnoth* are inscribed on the blade (Wilson 1964: 144–146; Owen-Crocker 1981: 72). This could indeed be the sort of artefact that was believed to have identity and agency in the Anglo-Saxon world. The name on the blade has so far been interpreted as either the name of the producer or the owner of the sword, but could just as well have been the name of the sword itself. The first syllable of the name means either ring or crown and the second either boldness or booty (Michael Benskin, pers. comm.). This may indicate that it was a gift from the crown, and suggests that crucial social relations were materialised in this scramasax. Other examples include a silver-gild binding strip with an animal head and a runic inscription dating it to the late 8th century found in the bank of the River Thames near Westminster Bridge (BM M&ME 1869,6–10,1) and a pair of stirrups decorated with inlaid brass wire found at the bank of River Cherwell, near Magdalen Bridge (Hinton 1974: 48–50). The objects found in the rivers represent some of the highest level craft of the time. The concept of weapon-loaded watercourses is not found in the Anglo-Saxon texts, but the material from the English rivers does demonstrate that their material counterparts existed – rivers 'running with unique objects'.

Bridges, fords and crossings point – thresholds and passages

In southern Scandinavia, hoards of weapons, jewellery, keys and whetstones are often found clustering around fords and bridges, a phenomenon that can relate to both the practical and the symbolic role of the bridge in the landscape, being a threshold and a passage between the living and the dead (Lund 2005). Between the 5th and 10th century, settlement and cemetery in Scandinavia are often divided by a watercourse and connected by a bridge or a ford (Hedeager 2002: 14; Adamsen 2004: 22ff.). This has its counterpart in the Old Norse texts, where the land of the living and the land of the dead is divided by a river and connected by a bridge (Hedeager 2002: 14; Lund 2005). The same line of thought seems to have been expressed in the structure of many of the Viking Age runestones, where the word 'bridge' is often placed at the top point of the arch of the inscription, dividing the name of the bereaved on the one side from the name of the deceased on the other (Lund 2005: 126–127). The same structure can even be identified on stones that do not actually include the word 'bridge' in the inscription. Thus, the placing of the inscriptions seem to be expressing a general metaphorical thinking of living and dead being placed on each side of a border, such as a watercourse. After the establishment of Christianity in Scandinavia the bridge maintained its role as a threshold for the dead – with a shift from having the dead *body* crossing the bridge to a concept of the *soul* of the dead individual crossing the bridge on its journey. In continental Christian sources the bridge was also described as a place for judgement or trial of the soul (Lund 2005). The ritual of depositing artefacts at the bridges and fords in Scandinavia presumably refers to these layered meanings of crossing points.

River crossings also feature in the creation of assembly places, in that the journey to the assembly place often involves crossing a bridge (Sanmark & Semple 2008). This finds a striking parallel in the Old Norse *Grímnismál*, which states that every day the god Thor crosses the rivers *Kǫrmt, Ǫrmt* and *Kerlauger two* on his way to the assembly place at the tree of life Yggdrasil (*Grímnismál*, stanza 29). According to Snorri, the Asir gods ride across the bridge to the assembly place at *Urðar brunni* every day (*Edda*, Snorri Sturlason, 'Gylfaginning', 14). The bridge is also the scene of a number of battles described in early medieval written sources, such as the Norwegian Sagas of the Kings. This could be due to the fact that watercourses often formed administrative borders for ownership, parishes and counties – borders that could have older roots and formed subjects of contention (Øeby-Nielsen 2005: 130). Yet the artefacts found in the vicinity of the bridges and fords can hardly only be objects lost during battles, since they include jewellery, keys, mounts, tools and decorated stirrups.

The aspect of the bridge as an entry gate to the settlement is clearly expressed in the spatial structure of the significant Viking Age residential, trade and cult centre of Tissø, Sjaelland. The only access to this spectacular site is across the stream Halleby Lake, via a 50 m long wooden bridge dated to the Viking Age. Close to the bridge an unusual double grave has been excavated, containing the skeletons of two men, both of whom were decapitated. Their heads have been placed between their legs facing upwards. These skeletons have been carbon-dated to *c.* 1030–1040 AD (Jørgensen 2002: 221), and are the latest finds from the Tissø complex. The liminal place of the bridge apparently formed a suitable place for burying the executed men.

In Anglo-Saxon England, there are indications from archaeological material and place names that bridges and fords were also central to the cognitive landscape. Many of the finds from the English rivers are found in close vicinity to bridges and crossing points. This was the case for the deposition of spears from the early Saxon centuries, as in the River Thames, or the River Wey at Weybridge, Surrey (Swanton 1974: 88). Similarly, in the River Witham, swords, long knives, axe heads and spearheads are found clustering around crossings and causeways (Stocker and Everson 2003: 280). Place-names also indicate that crossings were important in the early Anglo-Saxon cognitive landscape. In the names Weeford in Staffordshire and Wyfordby in Leicestershire the first part of the name comes from *wēoh*, meaning idol, shrine or sacred place (Wilson 1985: 179–181).

These sacral names and practices show that the role of the bridge in the world-view, and possibly also in the cosmology, was not simply passively adapted from the Scandinavians in the Later Anglo-Saxon period, but must have already been part of the Anglo-Saxon mentality. From the 10th century, in areas with strong Scandinavian influence, the location of the bridge was certainly ritually significant. At an excavation at Skerne, East Yorkshire, the oak logs of a wooden bridge were discovered along with four knifes, a spoon bit, an adze, a sword, and the bones of several animals (Dent 1984: 253). The sword was of JP type V / X, dating from the 10th – early 11th century

(Petersen 1919). The bones represent more than 20 animals – horses, cows, sheep, and dogs. They showed no traces of butchery or consumption except for one horse, struck down by an axe in the forehead (Richards 2000: 33). The occurrence of a weapon and tools with the animal bones, and the fate of the horse, indicate that a religious ritual – a sacrifice – was intended.

Thus, on many levels the bridge or ford formed a central point in the cognitive landscape; moving from one bank to the other could signify entering the area of another owner, an assembly place or the land of the dead.

Lakes in the Scandinavian cognitive landscape

When we turn from rivers to lakes we find quite a different pattern in the comparison of Scandinavian and English material. In South Scandinavia in the 7th–11th centuries, weapons and jewellery are found in lakes, clustering around the bank of the lake, for instance in Lake Tissø (meaning *the lake of the god Tyr*) on Sjaelland, Denmark, in Gudingsåkrarna (meaning *the holy fields of the gods*) on Gotland, Sweden and in Råbelöv Sjö in Skåne, Sweden (Müller-Wille 1984: 188f; Jørgensen and Sørensen 1995; Jørgensen 2002; Lund 2007: 106–108; Lund 2008). The latter does not have a theophoric place-name, but its name presumably derives from *Ball* from Old Norse *ballr* (meaning *dangerous, damaging*, or *the one, which gives fear*) (Kousgård Sørensen 1968: 114). An analysis of the distribution of deposited artefacts in Lake Tissø shows that the weapons and jewellery were thrown in the water from the bank (Jørgensen 2002). The tendency, that weapons and tools are found *at the bank* or have been thrown *from the bank of the lake*, also appears in several other places in south Scandinavia (Lund 2007, 2008).

In Old Norse texts numerous lakes and bogs are related to female gods, and are mainly described as their residence (Näsström 1997: 96–97). One term denoting a body of water, *brunnr*, appears in several different contexts in the sources. *Brunnr* has mostly been translated as 'a well' and only rarely 'a spring'. However, *brunnr* can also be translated as a spring, stream or watering place, and actually the term *brunns-munni* means the bank of a pond (Vigfusson 1874). According to *Völuspá* (st 19–20) the *brunnr* Urð is termed both *brunnr* and *sæ*, meaning lake. Another occurence of *brunnr* in the Old Norse sources is *Mimisbrunnr*, appearing in *Völuspá* (st 28) and Snorri's Edda (*Gylfaginning*). The place-name *Mimirs Lake* occurs in several places in Scandinavia (Simek 1993: 216f). This supports the idea that the *brunnr* of the Old Norse sources could signify a lake. A third *brunnr*, *Hvergelmir*, is in *Grímnismál* 26 described as the source of all rivers. According to the eddaic poems the third world has its roots in *Urð* and *Mimisbrunnr* and according to Snorri's *Gylfaginning* the third root is in *Hvergelmir*. Thus, it seems possible to translate the concept *brunnr* as a lake, a wetland, a pond – and not just to a humanly constructed well. This forms a much more useful connection to understanding which type of landscape the poems are actually describing (Lund 2008).

Armed with this re-reading, I would suggest that deposition in lakes can be equated with pagan practice recorded in literature as taking place at a sacred *brunnr*, or at its bank or *Urð*. According to *Hávamál* (st 111), the *Þulr* (the cult speaker) or the god Odin himself has his speaker's chair placed at *Urðar brunni*. The *norns*, who are in charge of fate live at or in *Urð*, as stated in *Völuspá* (st 19–20) and the skaldic poem *Sigurðardrápa* (Jónsson 1967: 69), and the gods place for judgement is at *Urð*, according to Snorri (*Gylfaginning*). Further indications come from Adam of Bremen's description of the pagan sacrifices in Uppsala, where it says *Ibi etiam est fons, ubi sacrificia paganorum solent exerceri*: "there is also a *fons* in which pagan sacrifices are made" (*Adam, skolie* 138). The word *fons* in this context is often translated as 'a well', presumably to relate it to *Urðr* and *Mimisbrunnr*. *Fons* is, however, more correctly translated as 'a spring' (Lund 2004: 208). In this sense the *skolie* states that in Old Norse paganism, sacrifices were performed at springs. The hoards from lakes could be traces of this type of activity.

Even in a Christian context, the bank of the water stands out. In *Heliand*, a Saxon Gospel from around 830 we find elements from the Palestinian landscape being replaced with more familiar northern European features. Christ consistently addresses his disciples at the water's edge (Murphy 1992: 40, n. 63). In the skaldic poem *Kristið Kvæði* by Eilífr Goðrúnarson from the 10th–11th century, Christ is placed at *Urðr* (Simek 1993 [1983]: 243): "In this way the strong king of Rome has strengthened his power over the Pagan countries; it is said that he has his seat in the south at *Urðar brunni*" (Jónsson 1967: 144; my trans.). This has a remarkable resemblance to the location of the seat of the *Þulr* or *Odin*. The poem indicates that as a pragmatic adaptation to local customs in the course of Christianisation, Christ was placed in an already established cognitive landscape. This implies that the bank of water was considered to be a liminal place, where god(s) and humans communicated. The bank of the lake thus formed a central point in the cosmology and consequently in the use of the landscape.

The lake in Anglo-Saxon mentality

That the lake was central to the Anglo-Saxon cognitive landscape is strongly suggested by the epic poem *Beowulf*. The action of the poem takes place in the 5th or 6th century, but the text was written down between the 8th and 10th century and represents a fusion between Old Norse and Anglo-Saxon mentalities. Considering that the narrative was placed in Scandinavia, but written down in England, it is striking that the natural landscape described could as easily be in England as South Scandinavia. Two episodes in the poem are worth noticing in this context: Firstly, Beowulf demonstrates his status as a hero by participating in a swimming competition holding his sword all the way and even killing nine beasts with it (*Beowulf* 538–541; 574–575). Secondly, to take the fight to Grendel's mother he goes to the moors and enters the lake she lives in (*Beowulf* 1492–1496). In her underwater hall he uses a huge ring sword from the hall to kill her (*Beowulf* 1557–1569). The strange sword then melts and is burned up from the hot blood of the beast (*Beowulf* 1605–1617). This sword could indeed be defined as a potentially dangerous artefact which could or should not leave the lake. Considering the long debate on the dating of the poem, it is interesting to note that the idea of a dangerous lake that contains a remarkable and tabooed sword, matches the type of hoards known from South Scandinavia in the 8th–11th century rather than the 6th–7th century.

In England there is at least one lake that has a theophoric place-name, Tyesmere in Worcestershire, a name meaning the mere of the God Tiw (Wilson 1992: 13). In essence this place-name is identical to Tissø, the lake of the God *Tyr*, one of the most significant places for weapon deposition in Scandinavia. But in contrast to Tissø, no weapons have so far been discovered in Tyesmere. This follows a general picture: whereas the English rivers contain a large number of weapons, as of today no weapons from the Anglo-Saxon period have been found in English lakes. Whether this represents a different pattern of ritual behaviour in Scandinavia and England, or whether it is due to insufficient examination of the lakes is unknown.

The smith on the bank

In the late 10th and early 11th century there were a number of depositions of smith's tool chests in South Scandinavia. These too tend to be found at the banks of waters – mainly lakes – but in a few instances they are placed at the banks of rivers (Lund 2006: 323–326). In legend, myth and saga, smiths with supernatural powers are situated at a water obstacle separated from the settlement (Lund 2006: 331–334). The social role of the smith has been a major focus of recent research, emphasizing the links between metal technologies and processes of transformation – the smith, so to say, giving life to the objects (Burström 1990; Hedeager 2002; Rønne 2002; Jakobsson 2003; Gansum and Hansen 2004; Barndon 2005). If certain special artefacts were considered in the Late Iron Age as having a social identity – the smith's kit was pivotal in the process of transformation. Depositing the tool chests could indeed be a way of handling potentially dangerous tools (Lund 2006: 331–334).

Tool chests were also deliberately hoarded in England. The number of finds indicates that these hoards cannot have been lost accidentally or intended to be recovered. The Anglo-Saxon tool hoards are found at Hurbuck, near Lanchester, Durham (Hodges 1905: 215), at Flixborough, Scunthorp (Leahy 1995), at Westley Waterless, Cambridgeshire (Wilson 1976: 268), at Nazeing, Essex (Morris 1983), and in Stidriggs, Dumfries (Leahy 2003: 170). The English hoards are dated from the 8th–11th century, in other words the analogous period to the Scandinavian immediately following the introduction of institutional Christianity. Some are found on dry land, but a few are placed in wetland contexts. The Hurbuck hoard was found in the stream Shallhope Burn, the Nazeing hoard at the bank of the River Lea. A tool chest found in a bog at Birsay (Orkney) was decorated in Anglo-Saxon style (Arwidsson and Berg 1983: 26). It is even possible that the Westley Waterless hoard was a wetland find, as it was found while digging drainage (Morris 1983: 37). The Flixborough hoard was found on dry land, but shows strong resemblance to the Scandinavian finds in terms of content. It consisted not only of tools, but even included large metal containers and an iron bell, just as the Scandinavian tool hoards from Mästermyr, Veksø and possibly Nosaby (Leahy 1995; Lund 2006). Legendary smiths had a central role in the early medieval world view. Regin and Weland appear in the iconography with pagan as well as Christian motifs (Hauck 1977; Müller-Wille 1977: 131; Staecker 2004: 57). As the smiths' use of the landscape in the legends matches the location of the deposits of tool chests, these could be actions relating to the special role of the smith in the early medieval period.

Did Christianity dry out wetland thinking?

Early Christian laws from Norway forbade sacrifices to rocks, trees and shrines, whereas these texts do not mention sacrifices in wetlands. However, the prohibition of pagan ritual practices described in the English Laws of Knut included the veneration of rivers and wells (Sanmark 2004: 151). In Latin versions, the rivers and wells are termed *aquam* and *fontes*; in the Old-English versions they are termed *flod* and *wæterwyllas* (II Cnut 5 – 5,1). Whereas both *aquam* and *flod* are clearly rivers, the term *fons* normally refers to a spring. The term *wæterwyllas* can also be translated as a spring of water (Bosworth and Toller 1898). Thus the sacrifices forbidden in the Law of Knut took place in the very type of wetlands where acts of deposition took place at this time.

Objects of the 5th–10th century have been found in lakes and bogs in Ireland, nominally already a Christian country at the time. For instance, a sword dated to the 6th–7th century has been discovered in the River Lung, and a sword of a type known from the 7th–8th century has appeared in the River Boyle at Tivannagh – both of them found at places where artefacts had been deposited in earlier periods (O'Sullivan *et al.* 2000: 174; Fredengren 2002: 259). In Ireland, a number of liturgical objects – books, book shrines, bells and a crucifix – from the Irish Early Middle Ages have also been recovered from the wetlands (Fredengren 2002: 259; Fredengren *et al.* in press: kap. 7). For instance at Clonmacnoise, a monastery in the midlands of Ireland, finds from the vicinity of a wooden bridge included a liturgical bronze vessel of the 7th–8th century (O'Sullivan *et al.* 2000: 174). As these finds pre-date the period of Viking influence, they could possibly be expressions of a pagan practice incorporated in early Irish Christianity. Based on a combined analysis of the contemporary written sources and the archaeological material, it has been suggested that the Irish wetlands in this period were perceived as inhabited by supernatural creatures, to which sacrifices should be made (Aitchison 1996; Fredengren 2002). The Christian religious objects found in Irish wetlands have been interpreted to represent blessings of the wetlands performed by clergymen, as described in contemporary hagiographies (Fredengren 2002: 259). This would mean that the act of deposition continued, but its meaning changed.

A similar mentality towards wetlands may be present in early Christian England. According to the *Vita sancti Guthlaci* and the later poems *Guthlac A & B*, the Anglo-Saxon saint Guthlac chose to stay in a barrow on an island in a fen – a place conceived as the home of evil spirits (Semple 1998: 112–113). This indicates that the concept of supernatural creatures situated in wetlands was part of Anglo-Saxon mentality even within a Christian source. Many saints were also connected to specific wells and springs, and baptism could in some cases take place in rivers (Meaney 1995: 35; Hines 1997: 381; Stocker and Everson 2003: 282). This use of the wetlands may have been a way of altering places already pervaded with layers of meaning and making them acceptable in a Christian context. In a sense Guthlac's placement in a dangerous, liminal landscape approached by crossing a fen inhabited by evil beings aligns to the use of water as a boundary, dividing living and dead, marking ownership or bordering the assembly places.

Early monastic sites in England, Ireland and Scotland were often located on liminal places accessed by crossing water. In Ireland a large number of the silver hoards are found at the bridge or ford entering the monastic area (Krogsrud 2009). Thus, the use of waters as a division between 'them' and 'us' seems to have been fundamental in a Scandinavian and Anglo-Saxon and also Celtic mentality, but was used in varying ways in the different contexts.

The conversion to Christianity was a long and irregular process, and institutionalised Christianity was probably not incorporated and established in Britain until the 8th century (see Carver this vol.). The archaeological material of the previous periods shows a mosaic of different people, social groupings and varying rituals. As identity is created from the dispositions of the *habitus* of people, and the habitus is formed by and forms social practice (Jones 1997: 90; 2007b: 48–49); performing a ritual – like acts of deposition – can be a means to create and maintain identity. Knowing where, how and why an object should be deposited in wetlands was the product of the group's habitus. By performing a ritual, a group reproduces its identity and constructs a collective memory (Assmann 1995: 128–131).

It has been suggested that the presence of the Scandinavians in England in the late Viking Age could have caused a resurgence of the Anglo-Saxon cult (Sanmark 2004: 151). If we acknowledge that this paganism included concepts of mentality and world view on a general level and not just belief in its narrowest sense, it is clear that the depositions of weapons, jewellery and tools from mainly the 9th and 10th century could be expressions of a new blossoming of cultural paganism. This tradition of mobilising specific landscape features through ritual acts had its roots in pre-Christian Anglo-Saxon England, revitalised in the fusion of Anglo-Saxon and Scandinavian traditions. The objects deposited in this period were of distinct Anglo-Saxon as well as Scandinavian types. Specific types of artefacts, such as stirrups, are found in the English rivers and this phenomenon seems to be singular to Britain (there is no evidence of their being deposited in Scandinavia); several of these objects have Anglo-Saxon runic inscriptions. Thus, the acts of deposition were most likely shared ritual practices, which could also contribute to merging the different ways of perceiving the landscape and the different types of objects.

Conclusion

The practice of depositing material in wetlands took place in Northern and Central Europe through prehistoric and early historic times. However, the material is so diverse that it must be considered as relating to associations and meanings specific to the different contexts of time and place. The types of objects being deposited vary from massive hoards of destroyed artefacts to deposits of single whole artefacts, from objects, humans and animals with very different and complex social lives, to artefacts with very short biographies. Diversity can also be found in place-names, pointing in one context towards a fertility cult, in another to a war cult. Clearly, the meanings of the wetland varied regionally and inter-regionally, as is expressed in the many deposits from the rivers Thames, Lea and Witham, and the apparent lack of deposits in English lakes from the 6th century onwards.

Acts of hoarding reflected a mentality and world view where specific artefacts, especially weapons, but even jewellery and liturgical objects, were treated as social agents, which were deposited as a way of handling tabooed items or dealing with the place itself. The wetland finds can, in this sense, be seen as expressions of the heterogeneity of religious practice in Anglo-Saxon England. The English deposits from the Middle Anglo-Saxon period can hardly have been actions prompted by early Christians. The finds from the Late Anglo-Saxon period include Anglo-Saxon as well as Scandinavian types of objects. Thus, while they shared a northern European tradition of ritual deposition in water, these were hybrid acts from a period in which a mosaic of people with different identities met and fused in England.

Acknowledgments

Thanks to Neil Price, University of Aberdeen for drawing my attention to the *Heliand* as a source or water-related rituals, to Michael Benskin, University of Oslo for discussing the name Beagnoth, and especially Sarah Semple and Martin Carver for the editing.

References

Primary Sources

Adam of Bremen Gesta Hammaburgensis ecclesiae pontficum ed. C.A. Christensen, 1948. København: Rosenkilde og Bagger

Beowulf. Text and Translation 2000. Translated by John Porter. Anglo-Saxon Books

II Cnut. In: Die Gesetze der Angelsachsen. Herausgegeben im Auftrage der Savigny-Stiftung von F. Liebermann, 1960. Scientia Aalen

Edda Snorra Sturlusonar. Udgivet efter håndskrifterne af kommissionen for det Arnamagnæanske legat; ved Finnur Jónsson, 1931. Gyldendal, København

Grímnismál. In: Eddadigte II. Udgivet af Jón Helgason, 1971. Ejnar Munksgaard, København

Kristið kvæði, by Eilífr Guðrunarson. Den norsk-islandske Skjaldedigtning, ved Finnur Jónsson

Sigurðardrápa, by Kormákr Øgmundarson. Den Norsk-islandske skjaldedigtning, ved Finnur Jónsson

The Dream of the Rood. In: Anglo-Saxon Poetry. Selected and translated by R.K. Gordon. Dutton, New York

The Historia Regum Britanniae of Geoffrey of Monmouth. V: Gesta Regum Britannie. Edited and translated by Neil Wright, 1991. D.S. Brewer, Cambridge

Vǫlundarkviða. In: Eddadigte III. Udgivet af Jón Helgason, 1971. Ejnar Munksgaard, København

Vǫluspá, Hávamál. In: Eddadigte I. Udgivet af Jón Helgason, 1971. Ejnar Munksgaard, København

Waldhere/Waldere. In: Anglo-Saxon Poetry. Translated and edited by S.A.J. Bradley

Secondary Sources

Adamsen, C. (2004) På den anden side, *Skalk* 5: 20–28

Aitchison, R.B. (1996) Votive Deposition in Iron Age Ireland: An Early Medieval Account, *Emania* 15: 67–75

Andrén, A. (2002) Platsernas betydelse. Norrön ritual och kultplatskontinuitet. *In* K. Jennbert, A. Andrén and C. Raudvere (eds) *Plats och praxis. Studier av nordisk förkristen ritual*, 299–342, Vägar till Midgård, vol. 2. Lund: Nordic Academic Press

Arwidsson, G. and Berg, G. (1983) *The Mästermyr Find: A Viking Age Tool Chest from Gotland*, Stockholm: Almqvist & Wiksell

Assmann, J. (1995) Collective Memory and Cultural Identity, *New German Critique* 65: 125–133

Backhouse, J., Turner, D.H. & Webster, L. (1984) *The Golden Age of Anglo-Saxon Art 966–1066*, London: British Museum Publications

Barndon, R. (2005) Metall og myter – magi og transformasjon. Refleksjoner omkring den norrøne smedens kunnskap og identitet i et komparativt perspektiv, *Primitive Tider* 8: 61–74

Barrett, J.C., Bradley, R. and Green, M. (1991) *Landscape, Monuments and Society: The Prehistory of Cranborne Chase*, Cambridge: Cambridge University Press

Bender, B. (1993) *Landscape: Politics and Perspectives*, Berg. Providence, R.I.

Berggren, Å. (2006) Archaeology and Sacrifice. A Discussion of Interpretations. In A. Andrén, K. Jennbert and C. Raudvere (eds) *Old Norse Religion in Long-Term Perspectives. Origins, Changes, and Interactions*, 303–308, Vägar till Midgård, vol. 8. Lund: Nordic Academic Press

Blair, W.J. (1994) *Anglo-Saxon Oxfordshire*, Stroud: Alan Sutton Publishing

Bosworth, J. and Toller, T.N. (1898) *An Anglo-Saxon Dictionary: Based on the Manuscript Collections of the Late Joseph Bosworth*, Oxford: Oxford University Press

Bradley, R. (1990) *The Passage of Arms: An Archaeological Analysis of Prehistoric Hoards and Votive Deposits*, Cambridge: Cambridge University Press

Bradley, R. (1993) *Altering the Earth. The Origins of Monuments in Britain and Continental Europe: the Rhind Lectures 1991–92*, Monograph series, vol. 8. Edinburgh: Society of Antiquaries of Scotland

Bradley, R. (2000) *An Archaeology of Natural Places*, London and New York: Routledge

Brück, J. (2001) Body Metaphors and Technologies of Transformation in the English Middle and Late Bronze Age. In J. Brück (ed.) *Bronze Age Landscapes: Tradition and Transformation*, 65–82, Oxford: Oxbow Books

Burström, M. (1990) Järnframställning och gravritual. En strukturalistisk tolkning av järnslagg i gravar i Gästrikland, *Fornvännen* 85: 261–272

Bårdseth, G.A. (1998) *Depot som arkeologisk kjeldekategori: en analyse av depot og depotskikk frå mesolitikum til førromersk jernalder i Sande og Volda Kommunar, Møre og Romsdalfylke*, Hovedfagsoppgave i arkeologi. Oslo: Universitetet i Oslo

Cohen, N. (2003) Boundaries and Settlement: The Role of the River Thames, *Anglo-Saxon Studies in Archaeology and History* 12: 9–20

Davidson, H.R.E. (1962) *The Sword in Anglo-Saxon England: Its Archaeology and Literature*, Oxford: Clarendon Press

Dent, J. (1984) Skerne. *Current Archaeology*, 91: 251–253

Detienne, M. (1989) Culinary Practices and the Spirit of Sacrifice. In J.-P. Vernant and M. Detienne (eds) *The Cuisine of Sacrifice among the Greeks*, 1–20, Chicago, IL: Chicago University Press

Dobat, A.S. (2008) *Werkzeuge aus kaiserzeitlichen Heeresausrüstungsopfern. Mit besonderer Berücksichtigung der Fundplätze Illerup Ådal und Vimose*. Højbjerg: Jernalderen i Nordeuropa, Jysk arkæologisk selskab

Domeij Lundborg, M. (2006) Bound Animal Bodies. In A. Andrén, K. Jennbert and C. Raudvere (eds) *Old Norse Religion in Long-Term Perspectives: Origins, Changes and Interactions: An International Conference in Lund, Sweden, June 3–7, 2004*, 39–44, Vägar till Midgård, vol. 8. Lund: Nordic Academic Press

Drachmann, A.G. (1967) *De navngivne sværd i saga, sagn og folkevise*. Studier fra sprog- og oldtidsforskning, vol. 264. Det filologisk-historiske samfund. København

Fabech, C. (1991) Samfundsorganisation, religiøse ceremonier og regional variation. *In* C. Fabech and J. Ringtved (eds) *Samfundsorganisation og regional variation. Norden i romersk jernalder og folkevandringstid. Beretning fra 1. nordiske jernaldersymposium på Sandbjerg slot 11.–15. april 1989*, 283–352. Jysk arkæologisk selskabs skrifter, vol. 27. Højbjerg: Jysk arkæologisk selskab

Fowler, C. (2004) *The Archaeology of Personhood: An Anthropological Approach*, Themes in Archaeology, London: Routledge

Fredengren, C. (2002) *Crannogs: A Study of People's Interaction with Lakes, with Particular Reference to Lough Gara in the North-West of Ireland*, Wicklow: Wordwell

Gansum, T. and Hansen, H.J. (2004) Fra jern til stål. *In* L. Melheim, L. Kedeager, K. Oma (eds) 344–376, *Oslo Arkeologiske Serie*, vol. 2. Mellom himmel og jord. Foredrag fra et seminar om religionsarkeologi, Isegran 31. januar – 2. februar 2002. Oslo: Institutt for arkeologi, kunsthistorie og konservering

Geisslinger, H. (1967) *Horte als Geschichtquelle, dargestellt an den völkerwanderungs- und merowingerzeitlichen Funden des südwestlichen Ostseeraumes*, Neumünster: Wachholtz

Gosden, C. and Marshall, Y. (1999) The cultural biography of things, *World Archaeology* 31: 2: 169–178

Habbe, P. (2005) *Att se och tänka med ritual: kontrakterande ritualer i de isländska släktsagorna*, Vägar till Midgård, vol. 7. Lund: Nordic Academic Press

Hauck, K. (1977) Wielands Hort. Die sozialgeschichtliche Stellung de Schmiedes in frühen Bildprogrammen nach und vor dem Religionswechsel, *Antikvarisk arkiv* 64

Hedeager, L. (1999) Sacred Topography. Depositions of Wealth in the Cultural Landscape. *In* A. Gustafsson and H. Karlsson (eds) *Glyfer och arkeologiska rum – en vänbok till Jarl Nordbladh*, 229–52. Gotarc Series A, Vol. 3. Göteborg: Göteborg University, Department of Archaeology

Hedeager, L. (2002) Scandinavian 'Central Places' in a Cosmological Setting. *In* L. Larsson and B. Hårdh (eds) *Central Places in the Migration and Merovingian Periods; papers from the 52nd Sachsensymposium, Lund, August 2001*, 3–18, s. 362 s. Uppåkrastudier, Nr. 6, Acta archaeologica Lundensia. Stockholm

Hedeager, L. (2003) Kognitiv topografi: Ædelmetalldepoter i landskapet. *In* P. Rolfsei and F.-A. Stylegar (eds) *Snartemo-Fumene i nytt lys. Skrifter*, Vol. 2. Oslo

Hines, J. (1989) Ritual Hoarding in Migration-Period Scandinavia: A Review of Recent Interpretations, *Proceedings of the Prehistoric Society* 55: 193–205

Hines, J. (1997) Religion: The Limits of Knowledge. *In* J. Hines (ed.) *The Anglo-Saxons. From the Migration Period to the Eighth Century. An Ethnographic Perspective*, Studies in Historical Archaeo-Ethnology, Vol. 2, 375–410, Woodbridge: Boydell Press

Hinton, D.A. (1974) *A Catalogue of the Anglo-Saxon Ornamental Metalwork 700–1100 in the Department of Antiquities, Ashmolean Museum*, Oxford: Clarendon Press

Hodges, C.C. (1905) Anglo-Saxon Remains. *In* I.W. Page (ed.) *The Victoria History of the Counties of England, Durham. A history of the County of Durham*, vol. 1, London

Hoskins, J. (1998) *Biographical Objects: How Things Tell the Stories of People's Lives*, New York: Routledge

Idsøe, R. (2004) *Fortellinger om sverdet: våpenverdighet, ære og krigerideologi i yngre jernalder*, Hovedfagsoppgave i arkeologi med vekt på Norden. Bergen: Arkeologisk institutt. Universitetet i Bergen

Ilkjær, J. and Carnap-Bornheim, C.V. (1990) *Illerup Ådal*, Århus: Jutland Archaeological Society Publications, Distributed by Aarhus University Press

Ilkjær, J. (2003) Danske krigsbytteofringer. *In* L. Jørgensen, B. Storgaard and L. Gebauer Thomsen (eds) *Sejrens triumf. Norden i skyggen af det romerske imperium*, vol. 44–65. København: Nationalmuseet

Jakobsson, A.H. (2003) *Smältdeglars härskare och Jerusalems tillskyndare. Berättelser om vikingatid och tidig medeltid*. Stockholm Studies in Archaeology, Vol. 25. Stockholm: Stockholms Universitet

Jones, S. (1997) *The Archaeology of Ethnicity: Constructing Identities in the Past and Present*, London: Routledge

Jones, S. (2007) Discourses of Identity in the Interpretation of the Past. *In* T. Insoll (ed.) *The Archaeology of Identities: A Reader*, 44–58, London: Routledge

Jónsson, F. (1967) *Den norsk-islandske skjaldedigtning*. vol. B1. København: Rosenkilde og Bagger

Jørgensen, L. (2002) Kongsgård – kultsted – marked. Overvejelser omkring Tissøkompleksets struktur og funktion. *In* C. Raudvere, A. Andrén and K. Jennbert (eds) *Plats och praxis: Studier av nordisk förkristen ritual*, 215–286, Vägar till Midgård, Vol. 2. Lund: Nordic Academic Press

Jørgensen, L. and Sørensen, P.Ø. (1995) Den gådefulde Sø, *Skalk* 6

Karsten, P. (1994) *Att kasta yxan i sjön: en studie över rituell tradition och förändring utifrån skånska meolitiska offerfynd*. Acta Archaeologica Lundensia. Series in 8°, vol. 23. Stockholm: Almqvist & Wiksell International

Kaul, F. (2003) Mosen – Porten til den anden verden. *In* L. Jørgensen, B. Storgaard and L. Gebauer Thomsen (eds) *Sejrens triumf. Norden i skyggen af det romerske imperium*, 18–43, København: Nationalmuseet

Koch, E. (1998) *Neolithic Bog Pots: From Zealand, Mön, Lolland and Falster*, Nordiske Fortidsminder. Serie B, Det Kgl. København: Nordiske Oldskriftselskab

Kousgård Sørensen, J. (1968) *Danske sø- og ånavne, 1, A–D*. Navnestudier, Vol. 61. Akademisk forlag. København

Krogsrud, L.M. (2009) *Viking Age Silver Hoards in Ireland: Regional Trade and Cultural Identity*, Department of Archaeology, Conservation and History, Oslo, University of Oslo

Leahy, K. (1995) The Flixborough Hoard, *Current Archaeology* 141: 352

Leahy, K. (2003) *Anglo-Saxon Crafts*, Gloucestershire: Tempus

Levy, J.E. (1982) *Social and Religious Organization in Bronze Age Denmark, An Analysis of Ritual Hoard Finds*, Oxford BAR International Series, 124, Oxford

Lund, J. (2004) Våben i vand. Om deponeringer i vikingetiden, *Kuml. Årbog for jysk arkæologisk selskab*: 197–220

Lund, J. (2005) Thresholds and Passages: The Meanings of Bridges and Crossings in the Viking Age and Early Middle Ages, *Viking and Medieval Scandinavia* 1: 109–137

Lund, J. (2006) Vikingetidens værktøjkister i landskab og mytologi, *Fornvännen*, 5: 323–341

Lund, J. (2007) Vikingetidens våbenofringer: Ting finder sted. *In* H. Lyngstrøm, P. Foss and B. Storgaard (eds) *Specialer i forhistorisk arkæologi 2004–2005*. København: SAXO-instituttet, Afdeling for Forhistorisk Arkæologi.

Lund, J. (2008) Banks, Borders and Bodies of Water in a Viking Age Mentality, *Journal of Wetland Archaeology*, Volume 8: 51–70

Mauss, M. (1954 [1924]) *The Gift: Forms and Functions of Exchange in Archaic Societies*, London: Cohen & West

Meaney, A.L. (1995) Pagan English Santuaries, Place-Names and Hundred Meeting-Places, *Anglo-Saxon Studies in Archaeology and History* 8: 29–43

Melheim, L. (1999) Om arkeologi og religion, med utgangspunkt i Worsaae anno 1866, *Nicolay. Arkeologisk tidsskrift* 79: 4–16

Morris, C.A. (1983) A Late Saxon Hoard of Iron and Copper-Alloy Artefacts from Nazeing, Essex, *Mediaeval Archaeology* XXVII: 27–40

Murphy, S.J.G.R. (1992) *Heliand. The Saxon Gospel. A Translation and Commentary by S.J.G. Ronald Murphy*, Oxford: Oxford University Press

Müller-Wille, M. (1977) Der frühmittelalterliche Schmied im spiegel Skandinavischer Grabfunde.

Frühmittelalterliche Stüdien. Jahrbuch des Instituts für Frühmittelalterforschung der Universität Münster 11: 127–201

Müller-Wille, M. (1984) Opferplätze der Wikingerzeit, *Frühmittelalterliche Studien* 18

Müller, S. 1886 Votivfund fra sten- og bronzealderen. *Aarbøger for nordisk oldkyndighed og historie*: 216–251

Needham, S. (2001) When Expediency Broaches Ritual Intention: The Flow of Metal between Systemic and Buried Domains, *The Journal of the Royal Anthropological Institute* 7: 2: 275–298

Näsström, B.-M. (1997) Stucken, hängd och dränkt. Rituella mönster i norrön litteratur och i Adam av Bremens notiser om Uppsalakulten. *In* A. Hultgård (ed.) *Uppsala och Adam av Bremen*, 222 s. Religionshistoriska forskningsrapporter från Uppsala, Vol. 11. Falun: Nya Doxa

O'Neil, B.H.S.J. (1944) The Silchester Region in the 5th and 6th Century AD, *Antiquity* 18: 113–122

Osborne, R. (2004) Hoards, Votives, Offerings: The Archaeology of the Dedicated Objects, *World Archaeology* 36: 1: 1–10

O'Sullivan, A., Brady, N. and Boland, D. (2000) Clonmacnoise. *In* I. Bennett (ed.) *Excavations 1998*, Brookfield. Bray: Wordwell

Owen-Crocker, G.R. (1981) *Rites and Religions of the Anglo-Saxons*, David & Charles. Newton Abbot

Peirce, I. (2002) *Swords of the Viking Age*, Woodbridge: The Boydell Press

Petersen, J. (1919) *De norske vikingesverd: En typologisk-kronologisk studie over vikingetidens vaaben.* Videnskabsselskapet i Kristiania skrifter, historisk-filosofisk klasse, vol. 2. I kommission hos Jacob Dybwad. Kristiania

Petts, D. (2005 [2003]) Votive Deposits and Christian Practice in Late Roman Britain. *In* M. Carver *The Cross goes North. Processes of Conversion in Northern Europe AD 300–1300*, Woodbridge: The Boydell Press

Rappaport, R.A. (1999) *Ritual and Religion in the Making of Humanity*, Cambridge: Cambridge University Press

Richards, J.D. (2000) *Viking Age England*, Stroud: Tempus

Ryste, B. (2005) *Edelmetalldepotene fra folkevandringstid og vikingtid i Norge: gull og sølv i kontekst*, Hovedfagsoppgave i Arkeologi. Oslo: Universitetet i Oslo

Rønne, O. (2002) Smeden i jernalder – ildens hersker, *Primitive tider. Arkeologisk tidskrift* 5: 55–63

Sanmark, A. (2004) *Power and Conversion: A Comparative Study of Christianisation in Scandinavia*, OPIA, vol. 34. Uppsala: The Department of Archaeology and Ancient History, Uppsala University

Sanmark, A. and Semple, S. (2008) Places of Assembly: Topographic Characteristics in Sweden and England, *Fornvännen*, 103: 245–259

Sanmark, A. and Semple S (2010) The topography of outdoor assembly sites in Europe. *In* H. Lewis and S. Semple (eds) *Perspectives in Landscape Archaeology*, 107–115, BAR British Series, 2103, Oxford

Semple, S. (1998) A Fear of the Past: The Place of the Prehistoric Burial Mound in the Ideology of Middle and Later Anglo-Saxon England, *World Archaeology* 30: 1: 109–126

Shetelig, H. and Bjørn A. (1940) *Viking Antiquities in England with a Supplement of Viking Antiquities on the Continent of Western Europe. Viking Antiquities in Great Britain and Ireland.* Part IV, Oslo: H. Aschehoug & Co.

Simek, R. (1993 [1983]) *Dictonary of Northern Mythology*, Cambridge: D.S. Brewer

Spangen, M. (2005) *Edelmetalldepotene i nord-Norge: Komplekse identiteter i vikingtid og tidlig middelalder*, Hovedfagsoppgave i arkeologi. Tromsø: Universitetet i Tromsø

Staecker, J. (2004) Hjältar, kungar och gudar. *In* Å. Berggren, S. Arvidsson and A.-M. Hållans (eds) *Minne och myt. Konsten att skapa det förflutna*, Vägar till Midgård, Vol. 5. Lund: Nordic Academic Press

Stocker, D. and Everson, P. (2003) The Straight and Narrow Way: Fenland Causeways and the Conversion of the Landscape in the Witham Valley, Lincolnshire. *In* M.O.H. Carver (ed.) *The Cross Goes North: Processes of Conversion in Northern Europe, AD 300–1300*, Woodbridge: York Medieval Press

Swanton, M. (1974) *A Corpus of Pagan Anglo-Saxon Spear-Types*, BAR British Series, 7, Oxford

Thomas, J. (1996) *Time, Culture and Identity: An Interpretive Archaeology*, London: Routledge

Tilley, C. (1994) *A Phenomenology of Landscape: Places, Paths and Monuments*, Oxford: Berg

Tilley, C. (1999) *Metaphor and Material Culture*, Oxford: Blackwell

Vigfusson, G. (1847) *An Icelandic-English Dictonary*, Oxford: Clarendon Press

Weiner, A.B. (1985) Inalienable Wealth, *American Ethnologist* 12: 2: 210–227

Welinder, S. (1992) *Människor och landskap*, AUN: Archaeological Studies, Uppsala: Societas Archaeologica Upsaliensis

Wellendorf, J. (2006) Over mytologiske floder, *Maal og minne* 1

Wilson, D. (1964) *Anglo-Saxon Ornamental Metalwork AD 700–1100 in the British Museum*. Catalogue of Antiquity of the Later Saxon Period, Vol. 1, London: The Trustees of the British Museum

Wilson, D. (1965) Some Neglected Late Anglo-Saxon Swords, *Medieval Archaeology* 9: 32–54

Wilson, D. (1981) *The Archaeology of Anglo-Saxon England*, Cambridge: Cambridge University Press

Wilson, D. (1985) A Note on OE *hearg* and *weoh* as Place-Name Elements Representing Pagan Saxon Worship Sites, *Anglo-Saxon Studies in Archaeology and History* 4: 179–83

Wilson, D. (1992) *Anglo-Saxon Paganism*, London & New York: Routledge

Wilson, D.M. (1976) *The Archaeology of Anglo-Saxon England*, London: Methuen

Zachrisson, T. (1998) *Gård, gräns, gravfält. Sammanhang kring ädelmetalldepåer från vikingatid och tidigmedeltid i Uppland och Gästrikland*, Stockholm Studies in Archaeology, Vol. 15. Stockholm: Stockholm University

Øeby-Nielsen, G. (2005) De danske runestens oprindelige plads. *Kuml. Årbog for jysk arkæologisk selskab*

Østmo, M.A. (2005) *Tilhørighet i tid og rom: om konstruksjon av kollektiv identitet og bygdefellesskap i jernalderen*, Hovedfagsoppgave i arkeologi. Oslo: University of Oslo

Chapter 4

At the Funeral

Howard Williams

Introduction

Religious interpretations of early medieval graves have a long tradition in England. The 'pagan grave' can be seen as part of a nineteenth-century romantic-nationalist desire to portray the Germanic successors of Rome as primitive yet noble ancestors (Content and Williams this vol.). Such rites as cremation, the deposition of grave goods, animal sacrifice, boat-burial and mound-burial, have all been seen as 'customs' inspired by pagan perceptions of the afterlife. Following critiques of culture-historic approaches in the 1970s, archaeologists tended to leave religious interpretations to one side and focus on social and economic explanations for burial rite. Merovingian archaeologists in particular have been profoundly critical of attempts to identify pagan religious belief in the burial record (*e.g.* Effros 2003). Mortuary symbolism was seen as constituting and displaying the socio-political identity of the deceased, rather than eschatologies, cosmologies or mythologies. Thus, furnished graves of the later fifth and sixth centuries have been increasingly viewed as multi-dimensional and idealised expressions of age, gender, kinship, status and ethnicity (*e.g.* Härke 1992; Stoodley 1999).

The emergence of furnished cremation and inhumation graves is thus no longer regarded as reflecting a single and coherent 'Anglo-Saxon paganism'; nor need the decline in accompanied burial relate directly or exclusively to Christian conversion (*e.g.* Geake 1997). Indeed, the very term 'pagan Anglo-Saxon burial' compounds the conceptually naïve assumption that there existed a one-to-one correlation between ethnic affiliation, religious beliefs and ritual practice that archaeologists have been so keen to move beyond (*e.g.* Carver this vol.). Therefore, on both theoretical and methodological grounds, pagan mortuary ritual is an area of study bedevilled with problems and recent considerations of religion that have sometimes avoided the burial evidence all together (*e.g.* Hines 1997).

Archaeologists who remained in the hunt for evidence of belief in burial have tended to fasten on those aspects of mortuary ritual that seemed unusual or 'irrational' – for example distinctive, specialist artefacts, including objects regarded as 'amulets' because of their decoration, non-functional form or diminutive size (Dickinson 1993; Meaney 1981). Another approach has been to attempt to identify the burials of individual pagan ritual specialists, such as the 'cunning woman' from Bidford-on-Avon (Dickinson

1993). High status or princely burials, such as those at Sutton Hoo, have also been regarded as suitable theatres for the study of ritual performance, even if the emphasis has been on the ideological or political context of the burials rather than their religious meaning (see Carver 2005, ch. 14). Another unusual type of burial at the other end of the scale, is the so-called 'deviant' early Anglo-Saxon inhumation studied by Andrew Reynolds (2009).

Most recently there have been reconsiderations of the ritual significance of the act of mortuary deposition itself as a form of cultic practice. This includes viewing furnishing graves itself as a dedicatory or votive rite (Crawford 2004) and the fragmentation and deposition of artefacts in the closing and filling of graves as 'prestations' to appease and/or commemorate the dead (King 2004). The role of food and drink in funerary rites (Lee 2007) and the importance of animal sacrifice (particularly in the cremation rite) have both received detailed attention in terms of pre-Christian practice and worldviews including the possibility of shamanistic themes linked to soul-journeying influencing the early Anglo-Saxon cremation rite (Fern 2007; Williams 2001).

Current research on two key aspects of burial that might conceal religious thinking is addressed in other chapters of this book: the sacral geography implied by the location of cemeteries in the landscape (Semple, Sanmark and Lund this vol.) and the use of animals in the art of objects used as grave goods (Dickinson 2002; 2005; Pluskowski and Fern this vol.). In this chapter the focus will be on the performance of the funeral, addressing both the cremation and inhumation practices found throughout southern and eastern England. I intend to look for religion in *practice*, focusing on the treatment and transformation of the human body in death.

Mortuary performance

Mortuary practices are performed by the living, who make choices about how the dead are disposed of, drawing on the social relationships between the living and the dead. Yet simultaneously funerals involve engagement with mortality, the afterlife, ancestors and the supernatural. Funerals focus upon the transformation of the body, soul and mourners through a liminal, polluting phase in which the dead are often regarded as dangerous to the living and in need of rituals to reconstitute them into an afterlife or an ancestral identity (see Metcalf & Huntingdon 1991). From this perspective, death rituals are rites of passage concerned with transforming the living and the dead through a sequence of ritual performances. The dead are being turned into new states of being; an ontological engagement with death and mortality (Vitebsky 1993). Equally, the mortuary process involves *cosmology*, that is, the creation and re-creation of ways of seeing the world in which both the living and the dead have a place. This may involve beliefs about soul-journeying to join the ancestors or deities in other-worlds, hence mortuary practices can frequently concern *eschatology*. These eschatologies are often linked to myths of world-creation – *cosmogonies* – and may be based on the archetypes provided by the deeds and even the funerals of gods and heroes, and so can be described as *mythological*.

It is certainly possible that extensive pagan mythological traditions relating to death and the afterlife were perpetuated over long periods of time by oral traditions throughout early medieval Europe. Yet not all pre-literate and semi-literate early medieval societies can be presumed to have had well-formularised and singular afterlife destinations, nor clear ideas about how funerals are intended to get the dead to them. Even so, early Anglo-Saxon funerals may have served to perform and affect the way the world is perceived, and are particularly geared to the creation and citation of concepts of the person in life and death – *personhood* (Fowler 2004). These concepts of personhood, cosmos and myth rarely exist in a power-vacuum; they are geared to particular ways of seeing the world used in strategies of domination and resistance and in asserting claims to resources and identities. In this sense, mortuary practices are simultaneously concerned with promoting *ideologies*. These need not be static, but are situational constructs, drawing upon and manipulating existing values and concepts of the world to make specific statements about the living and the dead (see Carver this vol.).

It may remain questionable whether medieval Icelandic written sources seemingly recording aspects of pagan mythology are applicable to the societies and beliefs of many centuries earlier in other parts of north-west Europe. Yet certainly in recent years, a number of Scandinavian archaeologists have led the way in re-engaging with the eschatological and cosmological interpretations of first millennium AD mortuary practices drawing analogies for both Norse literature and ethnographic sources (for a review, see Andrén 2007). In part this has involved the search for ritual specialists in the presence of distinctive grave-assemblages (Price 2002), the investigation of explicitly religious artefacts such as Thor's hammer pendants (Staecker 1999) or the presence of mythological themes such as the possible materialisation of the world-tree Yggdrasil as tricorn stone-settings (Andrén 2007: 125–26). Notably, Anders Andrén (1993) has considered how the depictions of boats and carts on Gotlandic picture stones can be considered to be an evolving materialised ideology, situating them as one version of a broader ideology for commemorating the dead that had different material manifestations over time and space in later first millennium AD Scandinavia.

Yet while pursuing rigorous social approaches to later first millennium AD mortuary variability at individual sites (*e.g.* Rundkvist 2007) and regions (*e.g.* Svanberg 2003), Scandinavian archaeologists have also explored mythological and cosmological themes within mortuary performances themselves. These include the study of the provision of food and drink (*e.g.* Back Danielsson 2007; Ekengren 2004), animal sacrifice and the portrayal of heroic and martial lifestyles in death (Herschend 2001; Jennbert 2006; Rundkvist and Williams 2008) as well as the overall varied and theatrical nature of death-rituals (Price 2008).

Of particular relevance for this study have been recent investigations of the ritual transformations by fire that appear central to late Iron Age mortuary practices in many regions of Scandinavia. Terje Østigård (1999) has developed a theoretical approach to cremation practices inspired by ethno-archaeological research in order to consider the importance of the post-cremation transportation and containment of cremated remains, the metaphors of cooking and consumption that may have connected funerary feasts and the cremation process in later Iron Age Norway. This allows Østigård to perceive cinerary urns as dedicatory vessels by which the dead are offered to ancestors or deities (Østigård 2000). Terje Gansum has drawn upon analogies from later written sources and ethnographic analogy to explore metaphors and mythologies connecting cremation and iron-working in late Iron Age Scandinavia (2004a; 2004b). The relationship between ritual performance, metal-working, monumentality and myth-making has been explored in Gansum and Østigård's investigation of the fire-rituals connected with ninth-century mound-building at Haugar in Tønsberg, Norway (Gansum and Østigård 2004). Most recently, Goldhahn and Østigård (2007; 2008) have developed an explicit argument that furnaces were used for cremation and smiths were the ritual specialists controlling both metalworking and cremation ceremonies.

A theme running through these studies is the powerful connection between the ambiguity and transformation of the human body depicted on metalwork and the cremation process itself (see also Williams forthcoming). Therefore, these studies create a connection between mortuary performance and the cosmological themes of animal-person transformation and otherworld journeys thought to be depicted upon selected late Iron Age artefacts bearing animal art as well as gold bracteates and gold-foil figurines (*e.g.* Back-Danielsson 2007; Hedeager 2001). The importance of fire-transformations for forging relationships between the dead, the supernatural and the landscape have been considered in relation to both cemeteries and sacred groves (Andersson 2005; Larsson 2005; Nielsen 1997; Semple and Sanmark this vol., Wickholm and Raninen 2006).

Other writers have developed specific cosmological interpretations of the transformed products of late Iron Age and Viking cremation rituals in Scandinavia. Even the occurrence of natural stones in graves has been regarded as potentially laden with symbolism linked to pre-Christian cosmology (Artelius and Lindqvist 2005). Meanwhile, items chosen for interment with the ashes may have been specifically selected due to their symbolic connection with fertility and regeneration, seemingly appropriate for the closing of mortuary procedures and the creation of ancestors. Such an argument is made for the significance of Thor hammer-rings found in some cinerary urns from Viking-period central Sweden (Anderson 2005). Other artefacts linked to rituals of transformation and dedication found in both cremation and inhumation graves include instances of the 'killing' of the dead. These might include spears being thrown into cremation deposits (Artelius 2005) or across chamber graves (Price 2002).

Early Anglo-Saxon archaeologists have long been reluctant to search for evidence of an Anglo-Saxon Valhalla in their data and they should remain cautious in adopting the sometimes uncritical application of literary and ethnographic analogies seen in recent Scandinavian studies (see discussions by Price 2006; Rundkvist 2007). Yet equally, recent approaches in Scandinavian archaeology have recognised the shifting and situational nature of northern religions and their manifestations in ritual practices (see Andrén 2007). Moreover, there are already existing examples of the careful exploration of religious themes that may connect together late first millennium AD Scandinavia and early Anglo-Saxon England in terms of mortuary practice, material culture and art (*e.g.* Dickinson 2005; Pluskowski 2006 and this vol; Williams 2001 and forthcoming). Certainly, the long-term historical connections that bound together the North Sea world from the Roman period onwards cannot be ignored (Hines 1984). Moreover, these approaches encourage an interdisciplinary engagement between mortuary practice, ideology and cosmology, in particular when focusing on the treatment and transformation of the body in death in the construction and commemoration of personhood (see also Back-Danielsson 2007; Wickholm and Raninen 2006). At the very least, these perspectives provide a powerful antidote to those studies that are content to explore the material manifestations of Christian beliefs in mortuary practice through both archaeological and written sources whilst doggedly denying any connection between pre-Christian worldviews and the mortuary arena.

Yet if our aim is to reconnect religion and society in our study of pre-Christian early medieval mortuary practices, a common problem remains a focus on 'meaning'. Archaeologists seem obsessed with the de-coding of symbolism to find out what mortuary practices such as the killing of horses, the placing of weapons with the dead or the raising of burial mounds approach 'meant' to past people. Not only does this set us with very high expectations when considering the material evidence of non-literate or semi-literate societies with little in the way of contemporary documentation, it also puts a questionable primacy on thought over embodied practice, the discursive over *habitus*, and of intention and design over performance. This point relates to broader debates in mortuary archaeology over the extent that we should be focusing on elite expressions of power and authority or seeing funerals as contexts where different forms of agency and emotion were expressed and negotiated. For our discussion, it is unrealistic to put an emphasis upon *belief* over what people actually did, and what experiential impact their actions may have had.

One way of by-passing some of the limitations of a primarily meaning-focused approach to early Anglo-Saxon mortuary ritual might be to regard funerals as contexts for the production and reproduction of social memories and cosmologies through mnemonic practices: sequences of performances that aim to transform the identities of the living and the dead. In this regard, a useful concept is one developed by Andy Jones in relation to Neolithic and early Bronze Age mortuary practices; namely regarding funerals as 'technologies of remembrance' (Jones 2007). In Jones' formulation, this serves to emphasise how mortuary practices are sequences of acts and practices ('techniques') that together create chains of actions that connect to transform the social person and reconstitute them in a new form in death. The intended outcome may not always be reached, might be the subject of negotiation between different groups, and a range of practical, economic, socio-political and religious factors might influence how the technology of the funeral proceeded. Yet it helps us to understand that funerals in the past were not repeated and formulaic procedures reflecting the identity of the dead directly, but ritualised performances that were essentially of their time and place. Conversely, mortuary practices in this light were not unstructured and impromptu, but the result of informed decisions and choices by mourners who actively remembered past funerals and sought to reproduce and reformulate remembered templates in appropriate but also innovative ways.

This approach is particularly appealing when applied to the diverse and variable mortuary practices of early Anglo-Saxon England. This is because in the fragmentary and shifting socio-political context of the early medieval kingdoms of this period, there is no expectation of a uniform and static world-view and cosmology, but a diverse and rapidly altering set of practices drawing upon diverse traditions concerning the treatment of the dead and afterlife beliefs. In this light, the focus on mortuary ritual as 'technologies of remembrance' allows us to emphasise the importance of the mortuary process as a performance that *made* ancestors and connected the living with the dead and the supernatural. Simultaneously it focuses our appreciation on the diversity and contrasting mnemonic technologies employed within and between early Anglo-Saxon communities through their funerals.

Two main modes of disposing of the dead have been identified in eastern England for the fifth and sixth centuries AD: furnished cremation and furnished inhumation. Both the inhumation and cremation rites are found across southern and eastern England and these rites often occur upon the same cemeteries. They are internally complex and variable, both in terms of the treatment of the body, the quality and quantity of artefacts associated with the dead, grave structures and their deployment in terms of cemetery organization and location.

Let us consider the two disposal methods in turn, contrasting their technologies of remembrance. Each involves the transformation of the social person and the construction of their social memory. The repeated addition of new graves, and hence the accretion of burials at a cemetery site, can be regarded as the accumulative citation of memories onto place – a means of performing, affirming and reproducing social and religious identities through the successive and evolving relationships created between the living and the dead during mortuary practices.

Performing cremation

Studies of Anglo-Saxon cremation rituals can now draw on important cemetery excavations and syntheses from Spong Hill (Hills 1980; 1999), Sancton (Timby 1993) and Newark (Kinsley 1989), together with osteological analyses of cremated bone by Jackie McKinley (1994) and Julie Bond (1996). Analyses of the variability in the decoration and form of the cinerary urns and the artefacts and bones they contain were conducted by Julian D. Richards (1987) and augmented by more recent studies by Mads Ravn (2003) and the present author (Williams 2003; 2007).

These studies have demonstrated that early Anglo-Saxon cremation rites involved a complex sequence of interactions and transformations. The process would have begun with the washing and clothing of the corpse, perhaps with objects that had been possessions, but also gifts from kin and others attending the funeral. The costume of the deceased may have denoted an idealised or aspired social identity and perhaps also a political or religious affiliation. This was followed by the construction of the pyre. The pyre would have provided a mnemonic focus for the cremation and may have been decked with artefacts, textiles and furs. The transportation and placing of the cadaver on the pyre may have been important elements of the ceremony during which social relationships among the living were affirmed through mourning for the dead. These elements of the funeral are lost to us. Equally important however might have been the killing of animals and the cooking of food prior to the cremation, perhaps to honour the dead. Offerings of food evidenced by cremated animal remains (usually pig or sheep/goat) and charred plant remains found within cinerary urns may indicate the sharing of the feast with the dead. Drink may have also been added to the pyres given the presence of burnt pot-sherds and heavily burnt glass drinking vessels found from cremation burials. Furthermore, it appears that domestic animals; particularly horses but less commonly cattle, dogs, foxes could be slaughtered and placed whole upon the pyre, possibly as sacrifices to spirits or gods, as otherworld transportation and guides, or as statements of social status and wealth of the deceased's kin.

This would have been followed by the visible destruction of the body and its transformation into heat, flame, smoke, steam, ash and burnt bone. Unlike in the modern crematorium, this process would have been a public experience witnessed by mourners, participants and onlookers; the sensory interaction with the body as the skin was destroyed and flesh and bone were broken apart may have been an integral element to the symbolism and commemorative functions of the ritual process.

The corporeal interaction of the living and the dead did not end there; it would continue once the pyre had cooled and the ashes were searched. The selection of artefacts and bone from the ashes and their placement in an urn would have involved an intimate engagement between the bodies of the dead and the living. The actual sites of cremation pyres are rarely preserved (although see Carnegie & Filmer-Sankey 1993). Yet from the artefacts that are absent from cremations but common in inhumation graves of similar date, it is possible to suggest that many items were placed on the pyre but selected out from among the ashes for re-circulation among the living, including knives and weapons (Williams 2005). It is also clear from the archaeological evidence for cremation from sites like Spong Hill that not all of the ashes seem to have ended up in the cinerary urn. While it is possible that 'inefficiency' of retrieval may explain this variability and consequently the remaining ashes were simply left on the pyre site, it is equally possible that cremated bone was circulated among the mourners (McKinley 1994).

Finally, after a procession to the burial site, the interment of the ashes in the cinerary urn would be the final connection between the living and the dead. It is also possible that cinerary urns were stored above ground for long periods of time before the decision was taken to inter them in the cemetery either singly or as a group of cinerary urns. During this post-cremation period, there could have been numerous commemorative rituals that would not leave any archaeological trace.

In this light, we can challenge a view of cremation as a rapid and singular event of destruction concerned solely with theatrical display, and instead regard it as a process in which the living and the dead were connected through a staged and sequential corporeal interaction (Williams 2006). The impact of the animated fire upon the body would be a multi-sensuous experience: a memorable event in which all senses would have been affected. The variable evidence in the form, content and scale of the cremation rituals may be connected to the deceased's social identity (Ravn 2003; Richards 1987; Williams 2003), the shared themes linking the rites are as important and may have been connected to broader ideologies in contemporary society. In particular, the transformation of animals and people together may allude to shape-shifting themes (see Fern, Pluskowski this vol.)

However, this was not the end of the cremation's *châine opératoire*, and we open a new window on the process by considering those artefacts that were excluded from the pyre but added to cinerary urns during a post-cremation ritual. The most frequent unburned items found in cremation graves are the cinerary containers themselves.

It remains unclear whether these richly and (sometimes) bizarrely decorated vessels were made especially for the funeral, or selected for their qualities from among pots used in the domestic setting, but it does appear that they differ from the normal range of domestic assemblages found in early Anglo-Saxon settlements (Richards 1992). Moreover, as Richards (1987) has argued, the identity of the deceased seems to have had a bearing on the form and decoration of the pot selected to contain the remains of the dead (see also Williams 2005). Leaving aside the details of this variation, we need to ask what these objects were doing in the post-cremation rite after the spectacle of the burning pyre was long passed? The early Anglo-Saxon cremation rite placed great emphasis upon the urn as container for a sizeable proportion of the human and animal bone from the pyre. In this sense, urns provided a new corporeal and material 'body' for the deceased, and the decorated surface of the urn articulated a new surface or 'skin' for the ancestor.

The most common items that escaped the pyre and were placed in the urn unburnt had associations with hair, including 'toilet implements' consisting of bronze and iron tweezers, razors and blades, shears and earscoops, some of them full-sized functional objects, others miniatures possibly serving as amulets among the living or specially made for the funerary ritual. There is clearly a social dimension to the provision of these items in cinerary urns. For instance, only a minority of urns contained combs suggesting that this was a practice restricted to a particular group or groups. Indeed, combs appear to be associated with cremation burials that also had more pyre goods, suggesting a possible status association (Williams 2003: 111). Yet equally, the practice was widespread enough to be employed in a significant minority of graves. Other aspects of comb symbolism are more elusive. Both genders could receive these items although there is a slight female bias (Williams 2003: 108). All age groups could be provided with combs but there appear to be different age-associations at different sites. For Spong Hill, miniature and double-sided combs are most common with infants and young children (four years and younger) while triangular and barred and zoomorphic combs are most common with older children and adolescents (Williams 2003: 110). One suggestion is that combs need not reflect the social identity of the dead person directly, but aspects of an idealised, even aspired identity, not fully achieved during the lifetime and so created by the survivors during the funeral. If so, then the combs may have ascribed and commemorated a new identity in death that cross-cut age, gender and status roles in life. Therefore these items were not primarily about the display of social identities as much as emotive acts to affirm and commemorate the relationships between the living and the dead.

Many combs were added to the tops or bottoms of urns and were clearly only associated with the ashes during the filling of the urn (Williams 2003: 107). Many appear to represent fragments, a portion of a whole item broken off for burial with the ashes, usually an end-piece (Williams 2003: 107–08). This implies that a portion of the object was offered up for the dead while the remainder was kept by the mourners as mementos of the deceased. The act of fragmentation mirrored the dissolution of the pyre while the sharing of the item between the living and the dead evoked an ongoing connection. The placing of comb fragments therefore simultaneously articulated remembering and forgetting in material form. In at least one instance at

Spong Hill, two pieces of the same comb were distributed in adjacent urns containing an adult male and adult female respectively. Each urn was afforded a set of miniature toilet implements. These were buried together with a third pot containing a juvenile accompanied by iron tweezers. The fragmentation of the comb in this instance, together with the provision of toilet implements, created connections *between* interments buried contemporaneously and interpreted by Catherine Hills as a possible family group (Hills 1994: 44–46). This underlines how these objects were not exclusively about personal adornment or personal identity, but how they created selective mnemonic connections between the dead and the survivors through their placing in urns.

This interpretation can also be applied to 'toilet implements', including tweezers, blades, shears and razors, whether iron or bronze, full-sized or miniature. Again both males and females could receive these items although in this case there is a clear male bias to their provision (Williams 2007: 84). The age correlations are also interesting, with tweezers most common with adults, while shears and razors are more common among infants, children and adolescents (Williams 2007: 81–82). The length of tweezers can be shown to relate in crude terms to the age at death, with the smaller items tending to be found in the urns of infants and younger children (Williams 2007: 82–83). As with combs it appears that some miniatures may have been made simply for the funeral. Furthermore, only a small number of these items show signs of heat-damage that, for the copper-alloy objects at least, strongly suggests that they had not been placed with the corpse on the pyre. These items may have had many functions and uses, but a simple association with the identity of the living person is difficult to affirm.

Since the vast majority of urns did not produce these artefacts, it is tempting to speculate about what circumstances singled out a minority of individuals for this distinctive treatment. It is possible that those who received the miniature objects were the graves of ritual specialists or a particular status-group. Considering the presence of combs and toilet implements in cinerary urns from Lackford, Suffolk, Lethbridge (1951) interpreted their role in managing human hair as a form of magical protection for the dead against sorcery. A few commentators have developed the idea further (*e.g.* Wilson 1992: 139–40; King 2004: 226–7). Certainly the practice can be seen of one variant of a broader theme of 'amuletic' and regenerative objects, many of them 'miniatures', added in cremation practices throughout northern Europe in the middle and later first millennium AD (*e.g.* Anderson 2005; Callmer 1995; Price 2002: 203–4). The emphasis upon hair and bodily transformation also finds a resonance in the broadly-contemporary portrayal of the human body — and the human head in particular — in Style I animal art found on selected sixth-century dress accessories and weaponry (Dickinson 2002; see Williams forthcoming).

Yet why were hair and the objects connected with its management, particularly poignant in commemorating the cremated dead? Combs were likely to have been used for cleaning and presenting hair and in some instances for fixing hair in place. Combs sometimes bear signs of being pierced for suspension and hence may have been prominent elements of dress. As an element of apparel as well as bodily management, it is possible (but impossible to prove) that combs and toilet implements may have as much of an amuletic role in protecting the body as any non-functional item of dress such as beads and pendants (Meaney 1981).

Yet for all this, in the end the objects all serve the most affectionate of human symbolic actions, that of grooming. Toilet implements and combs were deployed to reconstitute social memories and create ancestors from ashes, perhaps bonding, marking out and sharing those who were, and wished to remain, closest to the deceased.

Performing inhumation

The idea of the early medieval furnished inhumation burial as a *tableau* created for the display of the deceased's identity as envisaged by the mourners has become a common theme in recent research. This approach emphasises the *context* of the grave as the appropriate scale at which to examine the interaction of bodies and material culture.

Discussing this approach in relation to Mounds 1 and 17 at Sutton Hoo, Martin Carver (2000) suggested that the rich assemblages of artefacts operated in a manner analogous to the theatrical performance of early medieval poetry, where the cadaver, grave goods and structures could be regarded as props making bold and complex statements about the dead person and the mourners:

> "A grave is not simply a text, but a text with attitude, a text inflated with emotion …
> like poetry it is a palimpsest of allusions, constructed in a certain time and place."
> (Carver 2000: 37).

While concurring with Carver's approach, we can take his poetry analogy further by suggesting that both poetry and graves can act not only as statements in the present, but serve to connect and conflate past, present and future in a ritual spectacle, evoking different types of memory including origin myths, heroes, ancestors and genealogies. Like Carver, Halsall (2003) regards furnished burials as the strategic construction of mourners. Burial rituals, including the choice of clothing for the body, grave goods, structure, orientation and position, are always a dynamic and innovative social display rather than a rigid conservative tradition of ritual behaviour (Halsall 2003: 62–3). Early medieval funerals are seen as involving many different texts, words, and acts culminating in the creation of memorable 'scenes' within the grave that 'compose' an idealised portrayal of the dead as perceived and negotiated by the mourners (Halsall 2003: 68). Crucially, Halsall emphasises that the brevity of these displays was central to their nature and efficacy.

This approach as developed by Halsall and Carver among others has the advantage of focusing attention of the role of funerals as an ideologically-laden performance by the living. This is particularly appropriate when applied to the richest 'princely' burials from the Rhineland and eastern England. However, for an appreciation of the role of funeral ceremony for furnished burials as a whole, this approach is less satisfactory and requires qualification. The archaeological evidence often shows that the aim of furnished burial rites was *not* the creation of a single scene, but often involve a sequence of different 'scenes' in a logical progression of change, from death-bed, funerary procession to burial and monument raising.

The implications of this argument are twofold. First, the final composition of the grave, as seen by archaeologists, may not have been as important as the process of making it. As with cremation rituals, inhumations involved a connected sequence of displays in which the dead are transformed and translated by mourners. The sequence of performances leading from scene to scene created social memories and identities rather than the creation of a static *tableau* at the end. Second, the mnemonic connections between the sequence of memorable scenes is not simply about display, but the tension between display and staged concealment leading to the final burial of the dead at the end of the process. The materials, substances and artefacts placed with the dead can be as much concerned with the management of sensory experience – protecting, containing, wrapping and shrouding the dead – as with display *per se*. From this perspective, early Anglo-Saxon inhumation rites create memories of the dead through a process of both display and concealment, just as early Anglo-Saxon cremation rites involved commemoration by display, transformation and fragmentation (see Küchler 2002). In this light, inhumation and cremation are related but alternate pathways to commemoration through transformation.

The narrative that was deduced from the excavation of the horse and rider grave at Sutton Hoo is a prime example of a funeral as performance. The pit was dug and lined with cloth, two spears and a shield were placed in the grave and the coffin containing a young man and his sword was laid on top of them. A horse's bridle and saddle were stacked at the head end of the coffin, and then a bucket, a pot and a haversack of foodstuffs were placed beside it. At the last minute a comb was thrown in, hitting the side of the coffin and sliding down it. Then the back filling began, eventually raising a mound over both pits (Carver 1998, 110–113). The excavator explored an even more detailed biography for the Mound 1 burial, taking the story beyond the composition of the grave tableau to its temporary display to visitors, its roofing with rafters and its eventual backfilling perhaps many months later (Carver 2005, 177–199).

However, the vast majority of furnished burials do not approach the wealth of these princely burials, and the grave goods are less easily interpreted as evidence of overt display and conspicuous consumption. These graves of lesser wealth should reflect the close relationships between the living and the dead body hence may relate to concepts of personhood and emotional ties, less overtly linked to political propaganda. At the mixed-rite early Anglo-Saxon cemetery of Snape, in Suffolk William Filmer-Sankey and Tim Pestell revealed a number of plough-damaged cremation and inhumations graves with poor bone preservation (Filmer-Sankey & Pestell 2001). As at neighbouring Sutton Hoo (Carver 2005, Ch. 4–6), the excavators looked for the full sequence of ritual practices associated with the sixth-century furnished inhumation rites from the digging of the grave and its preparation, the range of grave linings and structures, and diversity of artefacts placed with the dead, and evidence for ritual practices associated with the back-filling of the graves. Insect pupae mineralised on select artefacts hint that the bodies were displayed for some days before burial, suggesting a lengthy funerary process (*e.g.* Filmer-Sankey & Pestell 2001: 75, 77–9). In most cases, the grave-cuts at Snape were considerably larger than that necessary to contain a body, suggesting the explicit intention to create a sizeable container in the earth to receive and display the body, including ledges, steps and in some cases evidence of a platform or canopy constructed within the grave (Filmer-Sankey & Pestell 2001: 36–8, 238). There was also evidence of ritual activities taking place throughout the burial procedure. The preparation of the grave to receive the body could include evidence of soil pillow-pads and in one case a deposit of ash. 28 out of the 40 graves investigated had some form of organic container or structure. Rather than coffins, it is likely that many were biers or grave-linings. In four cases the organic layer was seen to extend up the sides of the grave cut suggesting that the entire grave was lined to receive the body (sometimes folded to make double layers), perhaps attached to wooden structures to maintain their rigidity (Pestell 2001: 241). For instance, in grave 16 tablet weaves were identified suggesting that large blankets lining the grave and clothing the body may have been adorned with woven horsehair patterns (Crowfoot in Filmer-Sankey & Pestell 2001: 211). Two boat-burials from the site illustrate a further ritual use of grave containers.

The artefacts placed with the dead body itself probably represent earlier stages of the funeral; the washing, dressing, adorning and posturing of the body for the funeral, although further objects were added within the grave context. For this discussion it is important to recognise that many objects were not 'on display' in the grave, but were hidden from view within bags, boxes and swathes of textile and other organic linings. The cadaver itself may not have been on-view since mineralised textiles hint that clothing was augmented by veils that may have covered the heads of many of the cadavers (Crowfoot in Filmer-Sankey & Pestell 2001: 211). Weapons may have been wrapped separately for burial (Crowfoot in Filmer-Sankey & Pestell 2001: 212: and there is evidence that the lyre in grave 32 was buried in a bag (Crowfoot in Filmer-Sankey & Pestell 2001: 212). Textiles had many roles within the mortuary arena of the furnished grave: they were used for expressing wealth, status and the identity of the deceased as well as serving to contain, consign and conceal artefacts within the burial context.

The covering and burial of the body is also evidently a staged and ritual process at Snape. In two graves, 36 and 37, textile layers were found overlying the body (Crowfoot in Filmer-Sankey & Pestell 2001: 208). The excavators also suggest that grasses, bracken or flower stems may have been strewn over the bodies. Stems and leaves were found to overlie the corpse in grave 47 while bracken and vegetation was identified in graves 3, 32 and possibly for grave 8. Other ritual acts involve the deposition of charred wood, from small flecks to large burnt timbers in 33 out of 40 graves (Filmer-Sankey & Pestell 2001; 243). There seems a particular emphasis upon the placing of charred timbers over the head of the cadaver, as in graves 8 and 39. In grave 9, it appears from the section of the grave that the burnt oak timbers formed a pile rising in height towards the head (west) end of the grave. At the foot (east) end of the grave was a shelf upon which no burnt timbers were found. It is possible that a mourner or mourners could have used this step upon which to stand to place the timbers over the corpse during the burial rites (Filmer-Sankey & Pestell 2001: 36–38).

This brief review of the Sutton Hoo and Snape inhumation graves suggests that at each stage of the funeral, different artefacts and layers were present, revealed and then enclosed and hidden from view. Rather than a single tableau, or 'image of death', the graves were formed from a sequential arrangement of both display and concealment.

Conclusion

The details of belief and practice in Anglo-Saxon paganism remain obscure and the mortuary arena will not provide us with all the answers. However, by considering the social and religious dimensions of both the form and variability of early Anglo-Saxon mortuary practices, embodied beliefs can be discerned. We cannot use this evidence to 'read off' cosmologies from mortuary practices any more than we can reconstruct social structures. The mortuary rituals were not primarily about representation, nor were they primarily about symbolising religious or social concepts. Instead, they were mnemonic performances, enabling the living to transform the dead and to reconstitute the relationship between them. The variability we find in early Anglo-Saxon mortuary practices, and the contrasting uses of cremation and inhumation, are testimony to the complex local negotiations of these broader themes in using the ritual process as a technology of remembrance. These were not geared to manifesting a single afterlife belief, but localised variants of pagan practice geared to the construction of cosmologies, ancestors and social memories.

Acknowledgements

I would like to acknowledge the discussions and feedback of numerous audiences to earlier versions of this paper presented at conferences and research seminars between 2005 and 2008. These included the Anglo-Saxon paganism conference at Rewley House, Oxford organized by Sarah Semple and Alex Sanmark in 2005, the Sutton Hoo Society conference in 2006 and research seminars presented at the Universities of Lund, Kalmar, Stockholm and Uppsala in September 2007, the British Museum in March 2008 and the University of Gotland in May 2008. In particular, I am grateful to Martin Carver, Alex Sanmark and Sarah Semple for their comments on earlier drafts of this paper.

References

Anderson, G. (2005) With Thor on Our Side: The Symbolism of the Thor Hammer-Ring in Viking Age Burial Ritual. *In* T. Artelius & F. Svanberg (eds) *Dealing with the Dead: Archaeological Perspectives on Prehistoric Scandinavian Burial Ritual*, 45–62, Stockholm: National Heritage Board

Anderson, G. (2006) Among Trees, Bones, and Stones. *In* A. Andrén, K. Jennbert and C. Raudvere (eds) *Old Norse Religion in Long-Term Perspectives: Origins, Changes and Interactions*, 195–199, Lund: Nordic Academic Press

Andrén, A. (1993) Doors to Other Worlds: Scandinavian Death Rituals in Gotlandic Perspectives, *Journal of European Archaeology* 1: 33–56

Andrén, A. (2007) Behind Heathendom: Archaeological Studies of Old Norse Religion, *Scottish Archaeological Journal* 27(2): 105–138

Artelius, T. (2005) The Revenant by the Lake: Spear Symbolism in Scandinavian Late Viking Age Burial Ritual. *In* T. Artelius & F. Svanberg (eds) *Dealing with the Dead: Archaeological Perspectives on Prehistoric Scandinavian Burial Ritual*, 261–76, Stockholm: National Antiquities Board

Artelius, T. & Lindqvist, M. (2005) Bones of the Earth – Imitation as Meaning in Viking Age Burial Ritual, *Current Swedish Archaeology* 13: 25–39

Back Danielsson, I.-M. (2007) *Masking Moments: The Transitions of Bodies and Beings in Late Iron Age Scandinavia*, Stockholm Studies in Archaeology, University of Stockholm

Bond, J. (1996) Burnt Offerings: Animal Bone in Anglo-Saxon Cremations, *World Archaeology* 28(1): 76–88

Callmer, J. (1994) The Clay Paw Burial Rite of the Åland Islands and Central Russia, *Current Swedish Archaeology* 2: 13–46

Carver, M. (1998) *Sutton Hoo: Burial Ground of Kings?* London: British Museum

Carver, M. (2000) Burial as Poetry: The Context of Treasure in Anglo-Saxon Graves. *In* E. Tyler (ed.) *Treasure in the Medieval West*, 25–48: York Medieval Press. Woodbridge: Boydell

Carver, M. (2005) *Sutton Hoo: A Seventh-Century Princely Burial Ground and its Context*. London: British Museum

Crawford, S. (2004) Votive Deposition, Religion and the Anglo-Saxon Furnished Burial Ritual, *World Archaeology* 36(1): 83–102

Dickinson, T. (1993) An Anglo-Saxon 'Cunning Woman' from Bidford-Upon-Avon. *In* M. Carver (ed.) *In Search of Cult: Archaeological Investigations in Honour of Philip Rahtz*, 45–54, Woodbridge: Boydell

Dickinson, T. (2002) Translating Animal Art. Salin's Style I and Anglo-Saxon Cast Saucer Brooches, *Hikuin* 29: 163–86

Dickinson, T. (2005) Symbols of Protection: The Significance of Animal-Ornamented Shields in Early Anglo-Saxon England, *Medieval Archaeology* 49: 109–63

Effros, B. (2003) *Merovingian Mortuary Archaeology and the Making of the Early Middle Ages*, Berkeley: University of California Press

Ekengren, F. (2004) Drinking and the Creation of Death: New Perspectives on Roman Vessels in Scandinavian Death Rituals, *Lund Archaeological Review* For 2004: 45–61

Fern, C. (2007) Early Anglo-Saxon Horse Burial of the Fifth to Seventh Centuries AD. *In* S. Semple and H. Williams (eds), *Early Medieval Mortuary Practices*, Anglo-Saxon Studies in Archaeology and History, 14, 92–109, Oxford: Oxford University School of Archaeology

Filmer-Sankey, W. & Pestell, T. (2001) *Snape Anglo-Saxon Cemetery: Excavations and Surveys 1824–1992*, East Anglian Archaeology Report 95. Ipswich: Suffolk County Council

Fowler, C. (2004) *The Archaeology of Personhood*, London: Routledge

Gansum, T. (2004a) The Archaeology of Earth, *Current Swedish Archaeology* 12: 7–21

Gansum, T. (2004b) Role the Bones – From Iron to Steel, *Norwegian Archaeological Review* 37(1): 41–57

Gansum, T. & Østigård, T. (2004) The Ritual Stratigraphy of Monuments that Matter, *European Journal of Archaeology* 7(1): 61–79

Geake, H. (1997) *The Use of Grave-Goods in Conversion-Period England*. BAR British Series 261. Oxford

Goldhahn, J. & Østigård, T. (2007) *Transformatøren – ildens mester i jernalderen*, Göteberg: Götebergs Universitet

Goldhahn, J. & Østigård, T. (2008) Smith and Death – Cremations in Furnaces in Bronze and Iron Age Scandinavia. *In* K. Childis, J. Lund & C. Prescott (eds) *Facets of Archaeology: Essays in Honour of Lotte Hedeager on her 60th Birthday*, 215–242, OAS 10. Oslo: Oslo Academic Press

Halsall, G. (2003) Burial Writes: Graves, Texts and Time in Early Merovingian Northern Gaul. *In* J. Jarnut & M. Wemhoff (eds) *Erinnerungskultur im Bestattungsritual*, 61–74, Munich: Wilhelm Fink

Härke, H. (1992) *Angelsächsische Waffengräber des 5. bis 7. Jahrhunderts,* Zeitschrift für Archäologie des Mittelalters. Beiheft 6. Köln, Rheinland Verlag

Hedeager, L. (2001) *Asgard* Reconstructed? Gudme – A 'Central Place' in the North. *In* M. de Jong and F. Theuws (eds) *Topographies of Power in the Early Middle Ages*, 467–508, Leiden, Brill

Herschend, F. (2001) *Journey to Civilization: The Late Iron Age View of the Human World,* Uppsala: Department of Archaeology and Ancient History, University of Uppsala

Hills, C. (1980) Anglo-Saxon Cremation Cemeteries, with Particular Reference to Spong Hill,

Norfolk. *In* P. Rahtz, T. Dickinson & L. Watts (eds) *Anglo-Saxon Cemeteries 1979*, 197–208, BAR British Series 82, Oxford

Hills, C. (1994) The Chronology of the Anglo-Saxon Cemetery at Spong Hill, Norfolk. in B. Stjernquist (ed.) *Prehistoric Graves as a Source of Information*, 41–49, Kungl. Vitterhets-, historie och antikvitets akademien, Konferenser 29. Stockholm: Almqvist and Wiksell

Hills, C. (1999) Spong Hill and the *Adventus Saxonum*. *In* C.E. Karkov, K.M. Wickham-Crowley and B.K. Young (eds), *Spaces of the Living and the Dead: An Archaeological Dialogue*, 15–26, American Early Medieval Studies 3. Oxford: Oxbow

Hines, J. (1984) *The Scandinavian Character of Anglian England in the Pre-Viking Period*, BAR British Series 124, Oxford

Hines, J. (1997) Religion: The Limits of Knowledge. *In* J. Hines (ed.) *The Anglo-Saxons from the Migration Period to the Eighth Century*, 375–400, Woodbridge: Boydell

Hoggett, R. (2007) Charting Conversion: Burial as a Barometer of Belief? *In* S. Semple & H. Williams (eds) *Early Medieval Mortuary Practices: Anglo-Saxon Studies in Archaeology & History 14*, 28–37, Oxford: Oxford University School of Archaeology

Jennbert, K. (2006) The Heroized Dead: People, Animals and Materiality in Scandinavian Death Rituals, AD 200–1000. *In* A. Andrén, K. Jennbert and C. Raudvere (eds) *Old Norse Religion in Long-term Perspectives: Origins, Changes and Interactions*, 135–40, Lund: Nordic Academic Press

Jones, A. (2007) *Memory and Material Culture*, Cambridge: Cambridge University Press

King, J. (2004) Grave-Goods as Gifts in Early Saxon Burials, *Journal of Social Archaeology* 4(2): 214–38

Kinsley, A. (1989) *The Anglo-Saxon Cemetery at Millgate, Newark-on-Trent, Nottinghamshire*, Nottingham: University of Nottingham

Küchler, S. (2002) *Malanggan. Art, Memory and Sacrifice*, Oxford: Berg

Larsson, L.K. (2005) Hills of the Ancestors: Death, Forging and Sacrifice on Two Swedish Burial Sites. *In* T. Artelius & F. Svanberg (eds) *Dealing with the Dead: Archaeological Perspectives on Prehistoric Scandinavian Burial Ritual*, 99–124,. Stockholm: National Heritage Board

Lee, C. (2007) *Feasting the Dead: Food and Drink in Anglo-Saxon Rituals*, Woodbridge: Boydell

Lethbridge, T.C. (1951) *A Cemetery at Lackford, Suffolk,* Cambridge: Cambridge Antiquarian Society

Mckinley, J. (1994) *The Anglo-Saxon Cemetery at Spong Hill, North Elmham. Part VII: The Cremations,* East Anglian Archaeology 69. Dereham: Norfolk Museums and Archaeology Service

Meaney, A. (1981) *Anglo-Saxon Amulets and Curing Stones*, BAR British Series 96, Oxford

Metcalf, D. and Huntingdon, R. (1991). *Celebrations of Death – The Anthropology of Mortuary Ritual*, 2nd Edition, Cambridge: Cambridge University Press

Nielsen, A.-L. (1997) Pagan Cultic and Votive Acts at Borg. The Central Significance of the Farmstead in the Late Iron Age. *In* H. Anderson, P. Carelli and L. Ersgård (eds) *Visions of the Past. Trends and Traditions in Swedish Medieval Archaeology*, 372–92, Lund Studies in Medieval Archaeology 19. Lund: Almqvist and Wiksell

Nilsson Stutz, L. (2003) *Embodied Rituals and Ritualized Bodies*, Acta Archaeologica Lundensia No. 46. Stockholm: Almqvist & Wiksell

Østigård, T. (1999) Cremations as Transformations: When the Dual Cultural Hypothesis was Cremated and Carried Away in Urns, *European Journal of Archaeology* 2(3): 345–64

Østigård, T. (2000) Sacrifices of Raw, Cooked and Burnt Humans, *Norwegian Archaeological Review* 33(1): 41–58

Pluskowski, A. (2006). Harnessing the Hunger: Religious Appropriations of Animal Predation in Early Medieval Scandinavia. *In* A. Andrén, K. Jennbert and C. Raudvere (eds) *Old Norse Religion in Long-term Perspectives: Origins, Changes and Interactions*, 119–23, Lund: Nordic Academic Press

Price, N. (2002) *The Viking Way: Religion and War in Late Iron Age Scandinavia,* Uppsala: University of Uppsala

Price, N. (2006) What's in a Name? An Archaeological Identity Crisis for the Norse Gods (and Some of their Friends). *In* A. Andrén, K. Jennbert and C. Raudvere (eds) *Old Norse Religion in Long-Term Perspectives: Origins, Changes and Interactions,* 179–83, Lund: Nordic Academic Press

Price, N. (2008) Bodylore and the Archaeology of Embedded Religion: Dramatic License in the Funerals of the Vikings. *In* D.M. Whitley and K. Hays-Gilpin (eds) *Faith in the Past: Theorizing Ancient Religion,* 143–65, Walnut Creek: Left Coat

Ravn, M. (2003) *Death Ritual and Germanic Social Structure,* BAR International Series 1164, Oxford

Reynolds, A. (2009) *Anglo-Saxon Deviant Burial Customs,* Oxford: Oxford University Press

Richards, J.D. (1987) *The Significance of Form and Decoration of Anglo-Saxon Cremation Urns,* BAR British Series 166, Oxford

Rundkvist, M. (2007) Early Medieval Burial Studies in Scandinavia 1994–2003. *In* S. Semple & H. Williams (eds) *Early Medieval Mortuary Practices, Anglo-Saxon Studies in Archaeology & History 14,* 47–55, Oxford: Oxford University School of Archaeology

Rundkvist, M. & Williams, H. (2008) A Viking Boat Grave with Gaming Pieces Excavated at Skamby, Östergötland, Sweden, *Medieval Archaeology* 52: 69–102

Staecker, J. (1999) Thor's Hammer. Symbol of Christianization and Political Delusion, *Lund Archaeological Review* for 1999: 89–104

Stoodley, N. (1999) *The Spindle and the Spear,* BAR British Series 288, Oxford

Svanberg, F. (2003) *Death Rituals in South-East Scandinavia AD 800–1000,* Decolonizing the Viking Age 2. Stockholm, Almqvist and Wiksell International

Timby, J. (1993) Sancton I Anglo-Saxon Cemetery. Excavations Carried out between 1976 and 1980. *Archaeological Journal* 150: 243–365

Vitebsky, P. (1993) *Dialogues with the Dead – The Discussion of Mortality among the Sora of Eastern India,* Cambridge: Cambridge University Press

Wickholm, A. and Raninen, S. (2006) The Broken People: Deconstruction of Personhood in Iron Age Finland, *Estonian Journal of Archaeology* 10(2): 150–66

Williams, H. (2001) An Ideology of Transformation: Cremation Rites and Animal Sacrifice in Early Anglo-Saxon England. *In* N. Price (ed.) *The Archaeology of Shamanism,* 193–212, London: Routledge

Williams, H. (2003) Material Culture as Memory: Combs and Cremation in Early Medieval Britain, *Early Medieval Europe* 12(2): 89–128

Williams, H. (2005) Keeping the Dead at Arms Length: Memory, Weaponry and Early Medieval Mortuary Technologies, *Journal of Social Archaeology* 5(2): 253–275

Williams, H. (2006) *Death and Memory in Early Medieval Britain,* Cambridge: Cambridge University Press

Williams, H. (2007) Transforming Body and Soul: Toilet Implements in Early Anglo-Saxon Graves *In* S. Semple & H. Williams (eds) *Early Medieval Mortuary Practices: Anglo-Saxon Studies in Archaeology & History 14,* 66–91, Oxford: Oxford University School of Archaeology

Williams, H. (Forthcoming) Transforming Heads in Early Anglo-Saxon England.

Wilson, D. (1992) *Anglo-Saxon Paganism,* London: Routledge

Chapter 5

In the Hall

Jenny Walker

Introduction

From the early days of Anglo-Saxon archaeology there has been uncertainty about where pre-Christian religion was practised, whether outside or inside a building, and, if inside, whether such a building was dedicated solely to religious use – in other words a temple – or whether religious ritual was one function among many in a high-status building of more general purpose, a building which we might term a hall. Linguistic analyses of sagas, epic poetry, and chronicles suggested that, whilst in some cases religious rites were performed in the hall for socio-political reasons, in other instances the practice of ritual appeared to take place in a building physically separated from the secular hall. For many years the verdict was that the pagan Scandinavians had no temples, and the English inherited this mantle too (Olsen 1966; Carver this vol.)

This chapter reconsiders the proposition that the hall was itself a ritual theatre. Developments in theory have provided the archaeologist with a new toolkit not only for understanding the role of ritual in the hall but also the definition of the hall as itself an ideological construct. Changes in thinking have highlighted the importance of agency in archaeological interpretations, an agency that enabled the expression of a socio-religious ideology best suited to local and contemporary needs. Yeavering is currently the site in Britain that can claim both the best range of excavated halls and a probable ritual function within and beside them. This paper examines the ritual geography of Yeavering, but within the context of the more graphic examples that have been recently brought to light in Scandinavia. This case study shows how the designers of the hall, and the settlement, built ideology into the architectural components of the site. The need to examine the ideological expression contained in buildings is shown to be of crucial importance in the study of the development of early medieval society as a whole.

Literary sources and the early years of hall study

Studies of the hall first arose out of an interest, both in Britain and in Scandinavia, in sagas and epic poetry. To begin with, these sources were largely investigated as a means of demonstrating the longevity and importance of rising and competing nations (Trigger 2000: 48–49). In Norway, for example, the series of saga-histories entitled the *Heimskringla* became a "potent factor in awakening Norway's desire for independence […] by reminding Norwegians of their heroic past" (Magnusson and Pálsson 1966: 13). The hall was naturally seen as a player in these narratives, and sources like *Beowulf*, *Egil's saga*, and *Njal's saga* provided abundant detail of its appearance and layout (Anon. 1975; Bradley 1995; Cook 2001). The sources feature a building of great physical grandeur, richly decorated and lavishly furnished. They also made it clear that the hall was a central feature of early medieval life, and it was within its purview that all the important social, religious, and political events took place (see, for example, King Edwin's decision to convert to Christianity as described by Bede (HE II, 13; McClure and Collins 1999: 95).

Such descriptions led to great expectations amongst the archaeological community in Britain. However, whilst large halls were being discovered in Scandinavia from the beginning of the twentieth century onwards, such as at the Swedish site of Svintuna (Nordén 1933; Lindeblad 1997), no such buildings had then been recovered on British soil. Leeds' (1923; 1927; 1947) excavations at Sutton Courtenay in Berkshire, southern England revealed only pit-buildings, which in no way matched the halls described in the literary sources. The Council for British Archaeology in 1948 (cited in Radford 1957: 27) described the inhabitants of Anglo-Saxon England as, "for the most part, in a culturally primitive condition … a rectangular scraping in the ground with wattle walls and a thatched roof seem to have been the limit of their known architectural competence". All this changed with the discovery of sites like Doon Hill in Midlothian, southern Scotland, and the English sites of Yeavering in Northumbria, Cheddar in Somerset and Cowdery's Down in Hampshire (Hope-Taylor 1966; 1977; 1980; Rahtz 1963; 1979; Millett and James 1983). Finally, sites had been found that contained grand halls, apparently just like those described in the literary sources. They put paid to any suggestions of inferior 'architectural competence', and provided archaeologists with a fresh body of data through which to study early medieval life.

At first, studies of the hall were undertaken with culture-historical and processual approaches. Studies focused on the fifth-century AD invasions described by Bede, and placed heavy emphasis on the supposed relation between architecture and ethnicity (*HE* I, 15; McClure and Collins 1999: 27; see for examples, Hope-Taylor 1977; Dixon 1982; James *et al.* 1984). As Ware (2003: 9) says, the result was that "architectural styles and settlement types, and how these relate[d] to the incursion of Germanic ethnic groups, [took] precedence over the people who created and dwelt within them". These matters of provenance are not irrelevant, and it is clearly important to understand how a building type has come to be, as well as how it is (Boas 1920: 315). Part of such 'coming-into-being' must surely root in geographical and cultural influence. However, early accounts of the hall generally did not attempt to address issues such as the reasons that architectural elements were adopted, ignored, retained, discarded, or adapted. This was largely because while culture-historical approaches tended to chronicle change in terms of influence or migration, processual approaches analysed buildings in terms of social structure. Both these approaches assumed that practice and behaviour could be explained by archaeology, but not the thoughts behind them (Johnson 2001: 86).

Post-processual archaeology and the hall

Post-processual archaeologies introduced the role of the individual and the community as agents in the manipulation of cultural material (Bender and Edmonds 1999: 158; Hodder 2001: 8, 27). As a result, archaeologists studying ancient architecture began to appreciate the motives and agency of the builders. Although speaking of the modern world, Giddens provided an inspiration for the new thinking: "the individual could, at any phase in a given sequence of conduct, have acted differently. Whatever happened would not have happened if that individual had not intervened"(1984: 9). This implies that, whilst the architect of a hall would have been limited by social and structural restrictions, s/he would have been free to choose from all the available architectural elements in order to build his/her hall. In the early medieval period, the degrees of freedom are debatable, but it seems clear that we should assume an agency in a time and place. In this paper I define the force driving such shared agency as the local ideology.

Ideology has three main purposes: to legitimate a current social situation, to make sectional needs and desires appear to be of universal importance, and to hide any conflict-causing inequalities (Abercrombie *et al.* 1980; Shanks and Tilley 1982: 132–133; Thompson 1985). Clearly there are other functions for ideology, such as helping people cope with the common fear of death, but, focusing on these three main functions, it is possible to argue that the hall is an intellectual premise, concerned with what society and individuals were, but also with what they wished it and themselves to be (Zevi 1957: 73; Rapoport 1969: 48: DeMarrais *et al.* 1996: 16: Carver 2001: 1). Post-processual thinking has allowed the hall to be seen as a political act with the implicit intention of emphasising certain meanings at the expense of others (Kirk 1997: 63). In the same way that later architects took care to create the spaces needed to ensure that Christianity endured, early medieval pre-Christian builders used the hall to 'spatially inscribe' (Soja 1996: 46) the ideology that they wished to construct and survive. British halls could now be seen not simply as emulations of the "new, politically ascendant élite" (James *et al.* 1984: 206) but, instead, as deliberately designed to create and maintain the desirable social order. This means that the questions that can now be asked of the hall are not about the surrounding external influences but those that address the meaning of the local ideological expression.

The *hov*: hall or temple?

The ideological character of the hall itself is closely connected with its possible function as the theatre for religious ceremonies. The interpretation of texts that describe religious usage in pre-Christian Scandinavia has remained ambiguous. Early twentieth-century interpretations of the word *hof* translated it as denoting a building separate to the hall and used for ritual activities, *i.e.* what we might call a temple (Olsen 1915; 1926; Gunnell 2003: 1). One reason that such buildings remained archaeologically invisible for so long was assumed to be a function of the re-use of sacred ground by early Christian churches, as demonstrated, for example, by the presence of a structure underneath the eleventh-century stave church at Mære in Trøndelag, Norway (Lidén 1969). However, after Olsen

(1966) had spent much time analysing texts like the *Landnámabók*, he concluded that there was no evidence to suggest that the early medieval pagan peoples used separate temple buildings. The phrase in the *Landnámabók* that stated that *hoftollr* had to be paid to the pagan religious hierarchy, for example, was probably introduced into the text in a deliberate attempt to (re)construct pagan laws in order to justify the Christian Church's demand for tithes (Olsen 1966: 277). Such detail could not be taken as evidence for the existence of temples. Instead, it was proposed that the *hof* was a farm "where cult meetings were held for more people than those living there" (Olsen 1966: 280), *i.e.* the word *hof*, in fact, just denoted a hall. Its translation as a 'temple' might simply have been caused by its compatibility with Christian understanding of the physical organisation of religion, in other words by Christian *habitus* (see Bourdieu 1977; 2004). Attempts to identify cult sites from place-names have concluded that the words that might have been used to denote a temple could just as easily have been used to describe a banqueting hall (see, for example Brink, 1996: 13; Słupecki 1994: 12). This led to the description of the hall as an "élite multi-functional building where cultic activities [...] took place, [...] or [...] a building [...] intended for social interaction involving cultic activities" (Söderberg 2003: 294). However, the decision to perform religious activities in the hall must have been one with ideo-political objectives, as by moving cult into the hall a "personal institution [could be made of] religious practice"(Fabech 1994: 174). This has the advantage of assisting in the legitimation of secular élite powers by fusing all the power 'arenas' into one building (Fabech 1999: 459; Söderberg 2003: 307). Political power is based on "hidden structures anchored in authority [which is] embedded in the cosmological order" (Hedeager 1999: 151), and, as such, esoteric control becomes crucial to the security of secular power and a powerful weapon in the political armoury of the élite (Gräslund 1991: 45). The hall could act as both a domestic farm building and, at the same time, be symbolic of the pagan cosmos (Gunnell 2003: 14). The morning after a ceremony, the chief/priest would revert to being a farmer, and the temple of the night before would revert to being his domestic hall. However, the role of this person in the ceremonies would have made an indelible impression on the local community, and would have bolstered his socio-political standing (Gunnell 2003: 19). This equation between the religious and secular facets of life in the early medieval period might have meant that high status buildings had multiple uses and multiple meanings throughout the days and seasons (see Gurevich 1985: 26–27; Rapoport 1993: 15; Kleinschmidt 2000: 34). And even if there were separate buildings, dedicated to divine or to secular performance, these are likely to have been closely linked.

To examine how these matters might be expressed on the ground I will focus on Yeavering, an English site with strong secular and religious signals, examine them briefly and use them to draw some general observations on the special character of those high status early medieval buildings which we gloss as 'the hall'.

The spatial organisation of ritual at Yeavering

Yeavering has been selected because the building plans are exceptionally well defined, meaning that their spatial organisation can be studied in order to assess their ideological expression. This is not to say that the report is without difficulties. For example, the dating scheme used by Hope-Taylor (1977: 337) relies on the attribution of the two archaeological horizons of burning to attacks made on Northumbria by Penda in AD 633 and again in AD 651/655 (HE II, 20; III, 1; McClure and Collins 1999: 105). There is, however, no evidence to suggest that Yeavering was one of the victims of these attacks, and there are no supporting ^{14}C-dates (O'Brien 2005: 148). This has had knock-on effects for all subsequent datings and interpretations of the site, but the episodes of burning might just as easily have been either accidental or a deliberate means of clearing the site for new building works (Welch 1992: 46). Other difficulties concern the stratigraphy of the site. These will not be discussed here as they fall out with the remit of this paper and are covered extensively elsewhere (see Hope-Taylor 1977; Miket 1980; Scull 1991; contributions to Frodsham and O'Brien 2005). The plans of the buildings, however, are good enough to make meaningful statements about how ritual, be it socio-political or religious, might have been organised. The variety of buildings, assemblages (meagre as they are) and burial rites provide a useful arena to test the ideas outlined above. The site contains early medieval burials in mounds and post-structures that Hope-Taylor determined as pagan (WR-DC and ER-DC) and orientated burials that he designated as Christian (Area B). The buildings were designated as secular halls (A1–4), as an assembly place (Building E), as a pagan temple (D2), converted to Christian use, and as a possible church (Building B) (1977: 250, 278). I plan to revisit three of the principal structures and examine them for their possible roles in the ideological sphere.

The site of Yeavering was located by aerial photography in 1949 (Hope-Taylor 1958: 403). It stretched over a 350m long area of a low gravel ridge above the River Glen at the foot of Yeavering Bell, from where it was looked out over by a first-century AD hillfort (Rollason 2003: 82). It is located approximately 35km from the historic royal centre at Bamburgh (Hope-Taylor 1977: 3). The site was identified with the place

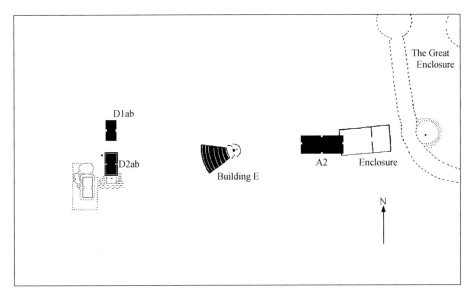

Figure 5.1: Yeavering: structures of Phase IIIa, b (sixth century) (Walker after Hope-Taylor 1977: Fig. 76).

Ad Gefrin cited by Bede as the place where Paulinus baptised the local population into the Christian faith following the conversion of King Edwin (HE II, 14; McClure and Collins 1999: 97). The area had, however, been witness to human activity since Mesolithic times, with the Neolithic represented by numerous ceramic finds and by a number of henge monuments and standing stones (Frodsham 2005: 19, 29, 32). The 'Anglo-British centre' (Hope-Taylor 1977) at Yeavering is argued to have begun in the sixth century AD and to have continued into the seventh (Rahtz 1980: 265; Welch 1984: 77–78; Scull 1991: 57–58).

Building A2

Building A2, the first of the designated halls, was built in Phase IIIAB, the third of the Yeavering phases (Hope-Taylor 1977: 160, Figs 59 & 60; here Figures 5.1 & 5.2). It measured 25m by 11m (82ft by 36ft) and had been built using walls of tongue-and-groove planks set straight into the ground (Fernie 1983: 17). Posts around the outside edge of the walls indicated that the building had been buttressed, and lateral lines of internal postholes were probably a 'system of piles' used to support a wooden floor (Hope-Taylor 1977: 161). Inside, the hall was divided into three chambers, a large central room accessed by doorways in the mid point of the long walls, plus two much smaller rooms at both of the gable ends, accessed from the outside by doorways in the short walls and from the inside by entrances placed in the mid point of each partition wall (Hope-Taylor 1977: 127). The aisles of the building allowed for a large open area in the middle of the central chamber, and this is where Hope-Taylor (1977: 161) believed the hearth would have been. The arrangement of posts indicated in Figure 5.2a was interpreted as a "chair or throne flanked by tall posts" (Hope-Taylor 1977: 161; here Figure 5.2b). A2 was also accompanied by an enclosure attached to its eastern gable end, which could only be accessed by passing through both the large central chamber and the smaller eastern side-room. This enclosure was also divided into two parts, with a smaller section separated from the larger outdoor area by a palisade wall with a doorway placed in the mid point (Hope-Taylor 1977: 160).

     It is easy to see how the nature of space could have been used to its full advantage by the builders of A2. Following Giddens' (1979; 1984) theories of structuration, which can be defined as an approach to the 'interpretation of social systems as both the result of, and the means by which, human relations are organised and reinforced' (Brumfiel 2000: 249), it is possible to argue that the hall would be structured by the performance of its users, and the performance, in turn, would be structured by the hall. The way that the doorways were placed in A2 both created and maintained a hierarchical social order. Different groups of people, perhaps according to rank or tribal affiliation, could enter the hall through three alternative routes. Those that entered from the west, however, had further to progress through the building until they reached the central chamber, perhaps indicating some kind of control over who was allowed to attend the events carried out inside. This entrance can also be envisaged as a ceremonial approach for supplicants to the high-seat, a seat that may have been positioned directly in front of the door to the eastern chamber and, thus, effectively controlled access to the outside area. The leader might also have used the western entrance in order to approach the high-seat in pomp and ceremony after all the other attendees were in place. Whichever the case, the spatial organisation of hall A2 allows for the hierarchical performance of ritual activities in their widest sense. It provided the leader, be it in a social and/or religious context, with the opportunity to display his/her power, a power that was inscribed on to the architecture (see Herschend 1998: 171). In this way, the hall can be viewed as an expressive instrument of thought (Bourdieu 1977: 89) that could not only provide a setting for action but that could also "remind people what those activities [were], signify power, status, or privacy, express and support cosmological beliefs, communicate information, help establish individual or group identity, and encode value systems" (Rapoport 1980: 299).

Building D2b

Figure 5.1 shows the other buildings that are believed to have been contemporary with Hall A2. As can be seen, there is a large wedge-shaped structure in the centre of the site (E), which has been interpreted as an assembly stand (Hope-Taylor 1956: 650; 1977: 129; Alcock 2003: 242). However, to the far west of the area are two further buildings, D1ab to the north, and, more importantly, D2ab in alignment with it to the south (Hope-Taylor 1977: 159). D2a and D2b were rectangular buildings like A2, although they were orientated north to south rather than east to west. D2a was built in Phase II, *i.e.* in the phase preceding the construction of Hall A2, with D2b being contemporary with the latter (Hope-Taylor 1977: 159–160). In both phases there were just two doorways, placed opposed to each other in the long walls. Inside the building, the structure was broken into three aisles by the use of four post pairs. Three posts running across the building at the southern end might indicate a partitioned area.

What is mostly of interest in the context of this paper is the fact that ritual activity can be seen in the remains of D2ab. Immediately north of the eastern doorway, there was a pit containing a large number of ox bones, most of which were skulls (Hope-Taylor 1977: 98, 100, 326). The stratigraphy of these deposits indicated that "special provision [had been] made for [the] formal stacking of [...] bones" (Hope-Taylor 1977: 326). Moreover, the nine episodes of deposition revealed patterning that might indicate seasonal cultic activity (Hope-Taylor 1977: 146–147).

D2ab also appears to have been closely associated with a number of burials. During the period of D2a, burials at Yeavering centred on the Western Ring Ditch to the far west of the site (Hope-Taylor 1977: 70–78, 102; Frodsham 2005: 38; Lucy 2005: 128–130). There were, however, a number of burials to the south of D2a inside a small enclosure attached to the building and in association with a number of freestanding, possibly totemic, posts (Hope-Taylor 1977: 153; Wilson 1992: 44, 46). After D2a was burnt down and the 'totemic' posts removed from this area, D2b was built on exactly the same spot, perhaps indicating a need for some form of continuity and legitimisation (Hope-Taylor 1977: 153; Fernie 1983: 19). It was also at this point that burials began to be made in what has been labelled the Western Cemetery (WR-DC), the northernmost of which respected the building and its enclosed area (Hope-Taylor 1977: 70–78, 102; Frodsham 2005, 38; Lucy 2005: 128–130).

Hope-Taylor (1977: 153) argued that "all the evidence falls consistently in place when [D2ab] is seen as a building with potent religious associations [making] it a focus for

Jenny Walker

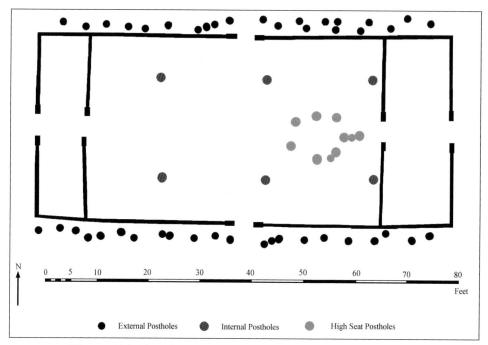

Figure 5.2(a): Plan of Building A2 (Walker after Hope-Taylor 1977: 127).

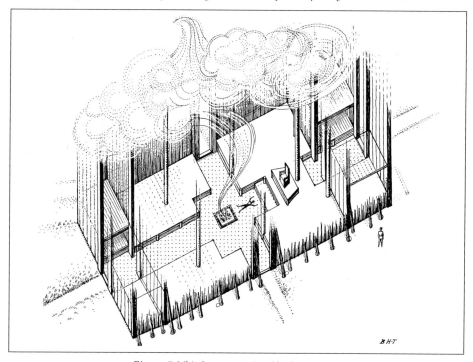

Figure 5.2(b): Interpretation (ibid. Fig. 60).

both burial and for seasonal festivals". Furthermore, Wilson (1992: 46–47) has speculated that the removal of the posts coupled with the destruction and rebuilding of D2 might represent the conversion of a pagan temple to an area for Christian use sometime around Paulinus' visit in AD 627 (see HE I, 30; McClure and Collins 1999: 57). Thus, D2ab might represent supporting evidence for Pope Gregory's demand that the pagan temples be taken over as part of a deliberate ideo-political strategy (Olsen 1966: 279; Wilson 1992: 34).

Building Bab

Building D2b continued in use throughout Phases IIIAB and IIIC (Hope-Taylor 1977: 160, 162). In Phase IV it appears to have been replaced in function by building Ba, to the east of the hall of that period, A3a (Hope-Taylor 1977: 165; see Figures 5.3 & 5.4).

Building B was built on an east to west alignment, and in its first expression, Ba, was a simple rectangle with a doorway placed in each of its four walls (Hope-Taylor 1977: 80). In its second phase, Bb, an annexe was added to the western gable end, which could be accessed via the off-centre doorway in the internal wall (Alcock 2003: 274). In association with the structure, during both phases, was the so-called Eastern Cemetery, which contained more than two hundred and fifty burials placed in closely packed lines (Lucy 2005: 133). Moreover, in the same way that the putatively pagan 'temple' D2a had been built in association with the Western Ring Ditch, building Bab was placed in association with the Eastern Ring Ditch. This could mean that both the Western and Eastern Ring Ditches were regarded as of religious and ceremonial importance (Frodsham 2005: 38). Hope-Taylor (1977: 252, 258) interpreted building Bab at Yeavering as a Christian church, and the density of interments does resemble that found in other Christian cemeteries (Lucy 2005: 133).

A Scandinavian excursion

For comparative purposes, we can refer briefly to two Scandinavian sites that have greatly enlarged the understanding of the way early medieval monumental buildings are brought into the service of religion. The first and most graphic is Uppåkra in Skåne, Sweden (Larsson 2007), where an unmistakeable cult building lies at the centre of an excavated area that has yielded over 20,000 finds (Figure 5.5). The timber building is a stave hall measuring 13.5m by 6m, with a central tower reminiscent of a stave church and it has been reconstructed with this in mind (Figure 5.6). The excavator estimates that the site at Uppåkra was active from the 2nd century to the 10th century AD and that the stave hall remained functional over most of the period. The finds include richly ornamented vessels, a deposit of destroyed weapons and 115 gold-foil plaques featuring images of men and women both alone and in pairs.

These *guldgubbar* have so far been found only found in Scandinavia (Watt 1991; Ratke and Simek 2006). Often, they are interpreted as votive deposits, or, more specifically, as 'temple-money' (Watt 1991: 107; 2004: 210; Thomsen *et al.* 1993: 88). In this religious understanding, the paired figures are thought to represent the god, Frey, and his giantess bride, Gerd, from eddaic lays in *Skírnismál*, which, in the line with the *hieros gamos*

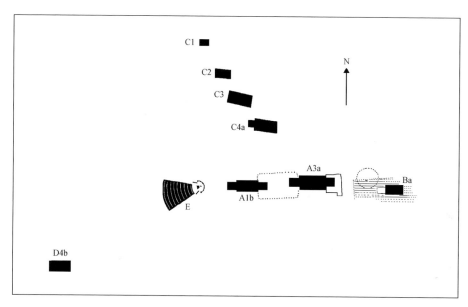

Figure 5.3: Yeavering: structures of Phase IV (seventh century) (Walker after Hope-Taylor 1977: Fig. 78).

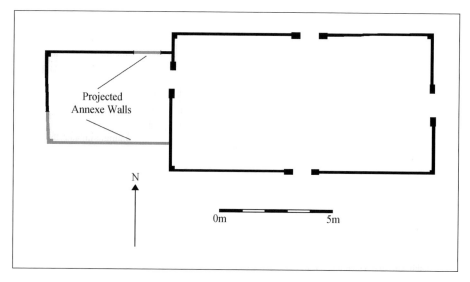

Figure 5.4: Building B (Walker after Alcock 2003: 274).

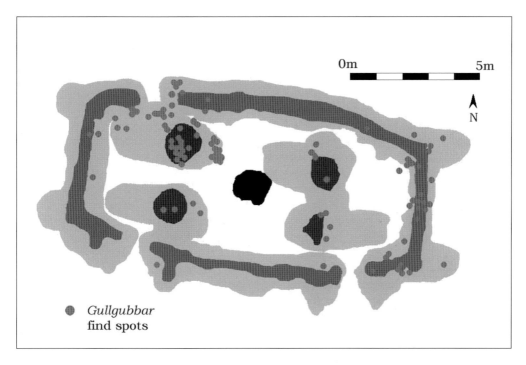

Figure 5.5: The temple/hall at Uppåkra, showing the distribution of gold foil plaquettes (guldgubbar) (Larsson 2007: Fig. 3).

myth (see below), are taken to be indicative of a fertility cult being carried out within the hall (Steinsland 1990a: 316). Lamm (2004: 46) has also proposed that the figures could be real people dressed in masks and costumes "either participating in a religious ceremony or personifying the gods themselves". A more socio-political function might also be plausible, as a number of scholars have suggested that the *guldgubbar* were, instead, or perhaps also, significant of secular interaction between the leading families (see, for example, Larsson 2002: 28). Following this proposal, analysis of more than two hundred and fifty examples of *guldgubbar* has concluded that the paired figures might represent dynastic marriages and rights of inheritance (Ratke and Simek 2006). Single-person examples and those that appeared to show wraith-like figures might have symbolised coming-of-age rituals and movement into the afterlife (Parker-Pearson pers. comm. June 2004). This would give the *guldgubbar* both secular and religious facets, with their function, perhaps, analogous to later Christian church registers that recorded births, marriages, and deaths (Price pers. comm. June 2004). This is not an interpretation that stands in contradiction to the earlier religious ones, as they do, in fact, have much common ground. The myth of the *hieros gamos* describes the enthronement of a Norse king and his wedding to the land, personified in the body of the giantess (Steinsland 1990: 86; 1991: 126–127). However, it is a myth that deals with the "foundation of the principality and legitimates the claim [to] political power of the prince" (Steinsland 1991: 86). Thus, the iconography of the *guldgubbar* found in the hall at Borg, can be

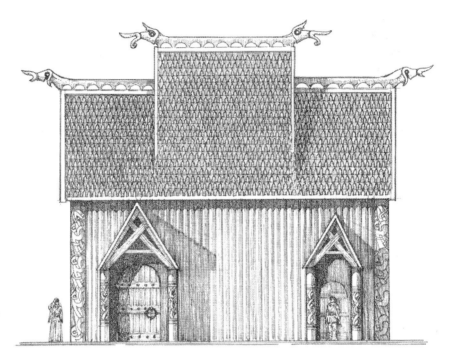

Figure 5.6: Reconstruction of the Uppåkra temple reproduced with permission of the artist Löic Lecareux.

argued to reinforce the link between secular and religious power, as discussed above, and represent the performance of socio-religious rites in the hall.

From this clear definition of a structure dedicated to cult activities we can turn to the site at Borg on Vestvågøy on the Lofoten Islands (Munch *et al.* 1987; Munch *et al.* 2003), where two hall-houses were excavated, the later of which, I: 1a, was very well-preserved (Figure 5.7). Hall I: 1a was built in the first half of the seventh century (Munch *et al.* 1987: 165). It was a three-aisled construction and used a trench to support an inner wooden wall that was then insulated with sod (Johansen and Munch 2003: 13). The entire building measured 80m by 7.5m–9m with slightly curving long walls and rounded corners (Herschend and Mikkelsen 2003: 51). Finally, the house was divided up into five rooms, of which Room C was the hall room (Herschend and Mikkelsen 2003: 65). As can be seen, the space was organised in such a way as to control the users. The main room itself could not be entered directly from the outside allowing access to be restricted and directed. Inside the hall, in the northeast corner of the room, there was a posthole, Posthole 1, which appeared to act not only as a support for the roof, but also as an integral part of the high-seat (Johansen and Munch 2003: 18; Munch 2003a: 261). Thus, as in Hall A2 at Yeavering, the chief could progress past the already attending guests to his/her seat, by entering the hall via Room B and walking up the central aisle. Suppliants could also approach the high-seat in this way once the chief was seated. The chief could also enter the hall after the guests by using the doorway between Rooms C and D, thus, emphasising his/her own importance (Herschend 1998: 28, 170; Herschend and Mikkelsen 2003: 66). The organisation of the space reinforced and reified a society hierarchical in nature, and maintained the élite position at the centre of hall rituals. The way the hall was built in both cases ritualised the secular power of the chief/king and made the hall and social power synonymous with each other. At Borg, moreover, there are specific signs that religious rites were also incorporated into the secular power base. Recovered from Posthole 1 were a number of artefacts that have been interpreted as having had socio-religious function. These included fragments of Tating-ware and three *guldgubbar* that are believed to have been deposited intentionally (Holand 2003: 133; 2003a: 203–204; Munch 2003: 249; Munch 2003a: 254).

On the basis of the artefacts recovered at Borg, which included domestic items such as pottery, glass-wares, tools, loomweights, and spindlewhorls (see contributions to Munch *et al.* 2003), it is obvious that the hall was a multi-functional building, and that part of that function included the performance of both socio-political and socio-religious rituals. Thus, it can be argued that the Borg building was a *hof* under the re-definition presented by Olsen (1966). Rituals of both a secular and religious nature appear to have been carried out under its roof, most probably with the express intention of uniting both types of power in the body of the one leader, and taking full advantage of the spatial recursivity of the hall.

The diversity of religious expression

It seems safe to argue that the hall at Borg was a *hof*, under the definition of such a place as a building used for both secular and religious ceremonies, aimed at the construction and maintenance of a hierarchical society reinforced by the recursive nature of architecture. There are similar examples, such as the Swedish site of Slöinge, where similar ritual activities are likely have been carried out within the confines of the hall itself (Lundqvist 2000; Lundqvist and Callmer 1994). By contrast, a number of sites have come to light that seem to contain a separated cult building within the settlement

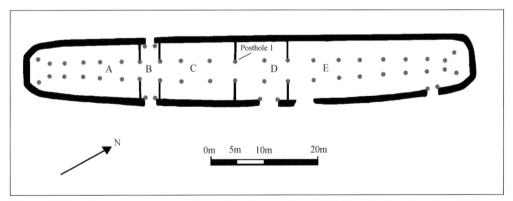

Figure 5.7: Borg House 1: 1a interpretations of the division of space (Walker after Herschend and Mikkelsen 2003: 68).

complex, including Lejre and Tissø in Denmark, Borg in Östergötland and most clearly at Uppåkra in Skåne (see Christensen 1991; 2007; Nielsen 1997; 2006; Jørgensen 2001; 2003; Larsson 2006; 2007). Even at Uppåkra, the 'Iron Age ritual building' is seen to have had a social role. Its excavator sees it as "an especially stable central place.... representative of a solidly established social order" (Larsson 2007: 22).

Discussion

Assignments of such roles are not so easy for Britain in the sense that many of the putative hall-sites discovered are either unexcavated or have fundamental problems with their recorded remains. For example, halls and/or temples might exist at the English sites of Atcham in Shropshire, Long Wittenham in Berkshire, Milfield in Northumberland, and Sprouston in Roxburghshire, southern Scotland, but these settlements are only known by aerial photography, further interpretation cannot yet be made (see Knowles and St. Joseph 1952; Reynolds 1980; Smith 1984; 1991; Booth *et al.* 2007). Flat sites with little stratification, such as Chalton or Cadbury make assessments of ritual inside or outside the hall difficult (see Addyman *et al.* 1972; Addyman and Leigh 1973; Alcock 1995). At Cowdery's Down in Hampshire, Building C12 has been interpreted as the hall, with C13 as a cult building, on the basis of the remains found in nearby Pit 6 (Millett and James 1983: 221, 247). However, aside from the animal remains found in this pit, virtually no other cultural material remained on the site (Millett and James 1983: 197). Thus, the identification of C13 as a cult building must remain tenuous.

At Yeavering, the 'temple' building identified in D2a preceded the construction of the first hall, indicating that the selection of the site had primarily religious rather than secular objectives. Consequently, it is plausible to argue that Hall A2 was supplementary to the religious ceremonies taking place in D2a, rather than the other way round. However, this still means that the halls at Yeavering had a religious context due to the fact that they were an addition to an already religious site, and, consequently, were inextricably linked to religious activities. This is partly what makes Yeavering such an interesting site, inasmuch as the ideology expressed in the hall architecture cannot have been tied to any particular religion. Halls existed in both the pagan and the Christian settlements, and, thus, the architecture must be expressive of a wider early medieval ideology. It is an inter-mixing of initially pagan architecture with Christian buildings that can also be seen in the architecture of what have commonly been interpreted as refectories and dormitories on monastic sites like Jarrow, Monkwearmouth, and Northampton (Cramp 2005; Williams and Shaw 1982; Blair 1992; 1996).

Even at Yeavering the architecture of both the halls and the cult buildings is so similar as to indicate linked function and ideology, in the same way that religion and secular power was fused in just the one building at Borg in Lofoten. The presence of two different types of ritual building (D2 and B) suggests that the way of expressing the link between the two types of power varied according to the needs of those controlling the architecture of hall-sites. The élite might have chosen the architectural medium of religious expression that was most suitable for their own individual circumstances.

At Borg in Lofoten, the appropriation of religion as a political tool was implemented via the introduction of a ritual room into the domestic longhouse. At Yeavering, a separate space was provided. Once the control of religion was in the hands of the élite, the organic nature of pagan cult might have allowed the chief to select which rites should be conducted in the hall and which in the temple. I see this as a function of how well established the leading family was in its political ascendancy, and, thus, on how necessary it might have been to strengthen the bonds between religious and secular power. In other words, different personal emphases and developmental levels may have led to religious and political ideas being expressed as local expressions dependent on the specific geographical and temporal context. This would account for the *guldgubbar* being found in both the hall-room at Borg in Lofoten and in the cult building at Uppåkra (Larsson 2006: 250). The chief at Borg in Lofoten may have felt much more need to associate him/herself with religion in order to create and/or maintain his/her power base than the chief or king at Yeavering did, despite the fact that they existed at broadly the same time. Diversity appears to be the key facet of religious expression, not only in the type of buildings included on hall-sites but also in the types and location of socio-religious rituals. Ultimately, the religious ideology first expressed in the temple at Yeavering, for example, became amalgamated with the ideology of the secular hall. Over time, this socio-religious ideology was incorporated into Christian expressions of power, as seen in the continued use of hall architecture at both Yeavering and at other, monastic sites. Clearly it was powerful ideology, as demonstrated by its longevity and the Christian desire to include it in settlements of their own.

The deduction has to be that the placement of religious rituals was not fixed. There may have been a cultural and "symbolic vocabulary [...] held in common by the people of the North Sea and the Baltic littoral" (Carver 1995: 121), however, the execution of religion during the British, Anglo-Saxon and Scandinavian Iron Age pagan periods appears to have been an eclectic mix dependent on the preferences and/or status of the owner of the local hall.

Conclusion

The nature of religious performance on hall-sites, whilst retaining common elements of North Sea culture, could be tailored to individual needs and was a function of the agency of the hall-builder. Decisions regarding the construction of a separate cult building might have depended on the current power base of the hall-builder and the degree of need for the physical proximity of secular and religious rites. Thus, arguments surrounding the definition of a *hof* might be unproductive. If religious expression in architectural terms was a function of the needs and desires of the hall-builder then no template need be applied to the patterning of ritual on hall-sites. The use of the word *hof* in any one text must surely be a function of the author's understanding of the hall, as produced by his/her own experience of its use, which in turn depended on the way religious and secular rites had been organised. Thus the study of ritual on hall sites must be anchored in the local context and take into account the individual agency and needs of the hall and temple builders. Ritual was not performed in a prescribed way, and to fail to take this agency into account would be to fail in our attempt to understand the ritual nature of hall sites and, thus, of early medieval society as a whole.

References

Abercrombie, N., Hill, S. and Turner, B. (1980) *The Dominant Ideology Thesis*, London: George Allen & Unwin

Addyman, P. and Leigh, D. (1973) The Anglo-Saxon Village at Chalton, Hampshire: Second Interim Report, *Medieval Archaeology*, 17: 1–25

Addyman, P., Leigh, D. and Hughes, M. (1972) Anglo-Saxon Houses at Chalton, Hampshire, *Medieval Archaeology*, 16: 13–31

Alcock, L. (1995) *Cadbury Castle, Somerset. The Early Medieval Archaeology*, Cardiff: University of Wales Press

Alcock, L. (2003) *Kings and Warriors, Craftsmen and Priests in Northern Britain AD 550–850*. Edinburgh: Society of Antiquaries of Scotland

Anon (1975) *Egil's Saga*, trans. Christine Fell. London: J.M. Dent and Sons Ltd

Bender, B. and Edmonds, M. (1999) Postscript. In M. Edmonds (ed.), *Ancestral Geographies of the Neolithic*, 155–162, London: Routledge

Blair, J. (1992) Anglo-Saxon Minsters: A Topographical Review. In J. Blair and R. Sharpe (eds), *Pastoral Care Before the Parish*, 226–266, Leicester: Leicester University Press

Blair, J. (1996) Palaces or Minsters? Northampton and Cheddar Reconsidered, *Anglo-Saxon England*, 25: 97–121

Boas, F. (1920) The Methods of Ethnology, *American Anthropologist*, XXII: 314–315

Booth, P., Dodd, A., Robinson, M. and Smith, A. (2007) *The Thames Through Time. The Archaeology of the Gravel Terraces of the Upper and Middle Thames. The Early Historical Period: AD 1–1000*, Oxford: Oxford University School of Archaeology

Bourdieu, P. (1977) *Outline of a Theory of Practice*, Cambridge: Cambridge University Press

Bourdieu, P. (2004) Habitus. In J. Hillier and E. Rooksby (eds), *Habitus: A Sense of Place*, 27–34. Aldershot: Ashgate

Bradley, S. (1995) *Anglo-Saxon Poetry*, London: Everyman: J.M. Dent

Brink, S. (1996) Political and Social Structures in Early Scandinavia. A Settlement-Historical Pre-Study of the Central Place, *Tor*, 28: 235-81

Brumfiel, E. (2000) On the Archaeology of Choice. Agency Studies as a Research Stratagem. In M.-A. Dobres and J. Robb (eds), *Agency in Archaeology*, 249–255, London: Routledge

Carver, M. (1995) Boat-Burial in Britain: Ancient Custom or Political Signal? In O. Crumlin-Pedersen and B. Munch Thye (eds), *The Ship as Symbol in Prehistoric and Medieval Scandinavia*, 111–124, Copenhagen: National Museum

Carver, M. (2001) Why That? Why There? Why Then? The Politics of Early Medieval Monumentality. In H. Hamerow and A. Macgregor (eds), *Image and Power in the Archaeology of Early Medieval Britain. Essays in Honour of Rosemary Cramp*, 1–22, Oxford: Oxbow Books

Christensen, T. (1991) Lejre Beyond Legend – The Archaeological Evidence, *Journal of Danish Archaeology*, 10: 163–185

Christensen, T. (2007) A New Round of Excavations at Lejre (to 2005). In J. Niles and M. Osborn (eds), *Beowulf and Lejre*, Trans. F. Ingwersen, 109–126, Tempe: Arizona Centre for Medieval and Renaissance Studies

Cook, R. (2001) *Njal's Saga*, London: Penguin

Cramp, R. (2005) *Wearmouth and Jarrow Monastic Sites*. Swindon: English Heritage

Demarrais, E., Castillo, L.J. and Earle, T. (1996) Ideology, Materialization and Power Strategies, *Current Anthropology*, 17 (1): 15–31

Dixon, P. (1982) How Saxon is the Saxon House? *In* P. Drury (ed.), *Structural Reconstruction. Approaches to the Interpretation of the Excavated Remains of Buildings*, 275–287, BAR British Series 110. Oxford

Fabech, C. (1994) Reading Society from the Cultural Landscape. South Scandinavia between Sacral and Political Power. *In* P. Nielsen, K. Randsborg and H. Thrane (eds), *The Archaeology of Gudme and Lundeborg*, 169–183, Copenhagen: Institute of Prehistoric and Classical Archaeology

Fabech, C. (1999) Centrality in Sites and Landscapes. *In* C. Fabech and J. Ringtved (eds), *Settlement and Landscape: Proceedings of a Conference in Århus, Denmark*, 455–473, Moesgård: Jutland Archaeological Society

Fernie, E. (1983) *The Architecture of the Anglo-Saxons*, London: Batsford

Frodsham, P. (2005) The Stronghold of its Native Past. Some Thoughts on the Past in the Past at Yeavering. *In* P. Frodsham and C. O'Brien (eds), *Yeavering. People, Power, & Place*, 13–64, Oxford: Tempus

Frodsham, P. and O'Brien, C. (eds) (2005) *Yeavering. People, Power, & Place*, Oxford: Tempus

Giddens, A. (1979) *Central Problems in Social Theory: Action, Structure and Contradiction in Social Analysis*, London: Macmillan

Giddens, A. (1984) *The Constitution of Society. Outline of the Theory of Structuration*, Cambridge: Polity Press

Gräslund, A.-S. (1991) Some Aspects of Christianisation in Central Sweden. *In* R. Samson (ed.), *Social Approaches to Viking Studies*, 45–52, Glasgow: Cruithne Press

Gunnell, T. (2003) Hof, Halls, God(ar) and Dwarves. An Examination of the Ritual Space in the Pagan Icelandic Hall. Paper presented at the Cosmology Society Conference. Structure and Belief in Northern Europe, University of Edinburgh

Gurevich, A. (1985) *Categories of Medieval Culture*, Trans. G.L. Campbell. London: Routledge & Kegan Paul

Hedeager, L. (1999) Myth and Art: A Passport to Political Authority in Scandinavia during the Migration Period. *In* T. Dickinson and D. Griffiths (eds), *The Making of Kingdoms: Anglo-Saxon Studies in Archaeology and History*, Vol. 10, 151–156, Oxford: Oxford University Committee For Archaeology

Herschend, F. (1998) *The Idea of the Good in Late Iron Age Society*, Uppsala: Uppsala University.

Herschend, F. and Mikkelsen, D.K. (2003) The Main Building at Borg. *In* G. Munch, O. Johansen and E. Roesdahl (eds), *Borg in Lofoten. A Chieftain's Farm in North Norway*, 41–76, Trondheim: Tapir Academic Press

Hodder, I. (2001) *Reading the Past*, Cambridge: Cambridge University Press

Holand, I. (2003) Finds Collection and Documentation, Distribution and Function. *In* G. Munch, O. Johansen and E. Roesdahl (eds), *Borg in Lofoten. A Chieftain's Farm in North Norway*, 131–140, Trondheim: Tapir Academic Press

Holand, I. (2003a) Pottery. *In* G. Munch, O. Johansen and E. Roesdahl (eds), *Borg in Lofoten. A Chieftain's Farm in North Norway*, 199–210, Trondheim: Tapir Academic Press

Hope-Taylor, B. (1958) The Anglo-Saxon Royal Palaces at Yeavering, Northumberland, England. Paper Presented at the *Bericht über den V Internationalen Kongress für Vor- und Frühgeschichte*, Hamburg

Hope-Taylor, B. (1966) East Lothian: Dunbar, Doon Hill, *Medieval Archaeology*, 10: 175–176

Hope-Taylor, B. (1977) *Yeavering: An Anglo-British Centre of Early Northumbria*. London: HMSO

Hope-Taylor, B. (1980) Balbridie...and Doon Hill, *Current Archaeology*, 72: 18–19

James, S., Marshall, A. and Millett, M. (1984) An Early Medieval Building Tradition, *Archaeological Journal*, 141: 182–215

Johansen, O. and Munch, G. (2003) Introduction and Summary. *In* Gerd Munch, O. Johansen and E. Roesdahl (eds), *Borg in Lofoten. A Chieftain's Farm in North Norway*, 11–18, Trondheim: Tapir Academic Press

Johnson, M. (2001) *Archaeological Theory*, Oxford: Blackwell

Jørgensen, L. (2001) From Tribute to the Estate System, 3rd to 12th Century. *In* B. Arrhenius (ed.), *Kingdoms and Regionality. Transactions from the 49th Sachsensymposium 1998 in Uppsala*, 73–82, Stockholm: Archaeological Research Laboratory, Stockholm University

Jørgensen, L. (2003) Manor and Market at Lake Tissø in the Sixth to Eleventh Centuries: The Danish 'Productive' Sites. *In* T. Pestell and K. Ulmschneider (eds), *Markets in Early Medieval Europe*, 175–207, Macclesfield: Windgather Press

Kirk, T. (1997) Towards a Phenomenology of Building: The Neolithic Long Mound at La Commune-Sèche, Colombiers-Sur-Seulles, Normandy. *In* G. Nash (ed.), *Semiotics of Landscape: Archaeology of the Mind*, 59–70, BAR International Series 661, Oxford

Kleinschmidt, H. (2000) *Understanding the Middle Ages. The Transformation of Ideas and Attitudes in the Medieval World*, Woodbridge: Boydell Press

Knowles, D. and St Joseph, J.K. (1952) *Monastic Sites from the Air*, Cambridge: Cambridge University Press

Lamm, J. P. (2004) Figural Gold Foils Found in Sweden: A Study Based on the Discoveries from Helgö. *In* H. Clarke and K. Lamm (eds), *Exotic and Sacral Finds from Helgö. Excavations at Helgö XVI*, 41–142, Stockholm: Almqvist & Wiksell International

Larsson, L. (2002) Uppåkra – Research on a Central Place. Recent Excavations and Results. *In* B. Hårdh and L. Larsson (eds), *Central Places in the Migration and Merovingian Periods*, 19–30, Lund: Almqvist & Wiksell International

Larsson, L. (2006) Ritual Building and Ritual Space. Aspects of Investigations at the Iron Age Central Site Uppåkra, Scania, Sweden. *In* A. Andrén, K. Jennbert and C. Raudvere (eds), *Old Norse Religion in Long-Term Perspectives. Origins, Changes, and Interactions*, 248–253, Lund: Nordic Academic Press

Larsson, L. (2007) The Iron Age Ritual Building at Uppåkra, Southern Sweden, *Antiquity*, 81: 11–25

Leeds, E. T. (1923) A Saxon Village near Sutton Courtenay, Berkshire, *Archaeologia*, 73: 147–192

Leeds, E. T. (1927) A Saxon Village at Sutton Courtenay, Berkshire (Second Report), *Archaeologia*, 76: 12–80

Leeds, E. T. (1947) A Saxon Village at Sutton Courtenay, Berks.: A Third Report, *Archaeologia*, 112: 73–94

Lidén, H.-E. (1969) From Pagan Sanctuary to Christian Church. The Excavation of Mære Church in Trøndelag, *Norwegian Archaeological Review*, 2: 3–32

Lindeblad, K. (1997) The Town and the Three Farms. On the Organisation of the Landscape in and around a Medieval Town. *In* H. Andersson, P. Carelli and L. Ersgård (eds), *Visions of the Past. Trends and Traditions in Swedish Medieval Archaeology*, 491–512, Lund: Institute of Archaeology

Lucy, S. (2005) Early Medieval Burial at Yeavering: A Retrospective. *In* P. Frodsham and C. O'Brien (eds), *Yeavering. People, Power, & Place*, 127–144, Oxford: Tempus

Lundqvist, L. (2000) 'http://hem.passagen.se/lalu0144/sloinge/eng/slo_hom.htm'. Page consulted 18th August 2004

Lundqvist, L. and Callmer, J. (1994) Slöingeprojektet 1993. Fortsatt undersökning på en fyndplats med guldgubbar, *Fornvännen*, 89: 257–263

Magnusson, M. and Pálsson, H. (1966) Introduction. *In* M. Magnusson and H. Pálsson (eds), *King Harald's Saga. Harald Hardradi of Norway*, 9–39, London: Penguin

McClure, J. and Collins, R. (1999) *The Ecclesiastical History of the English People*, Oxford: Oxford University Press

Miket, R. (1980) A Restatement of Evidence from Bernician Anglo-Saxon Burials. *In* P. Rahtz, Tania Dickinson and L. Watts (eds), *Anglo-Saxon Cemeteries 1979. The Fourth Anglo-Saxon Symposium at Oxford*, 289–305, BAR British Series 82. Oxford

Millett, M. and James, S. (1983) Excavations at Cowdery's Down, Basingstoke, Hampshire, 1979–81, *Archaeological Journal*, 140: 151–279

Munch, G. (2003) Jet, Amber, Bronze, Silver and Gold Artefacts. *In* G. Munch, O. Johansen and E. Roesdahl (eds), *Borg in Lofoten. A Chieftain's Farm in North Norway*, 241–252, Trondheim: Tapir Academic Press

Munch, G. (2003a) Borg as a Pagan Centre. *In* G. Munch, O. Johansen and E. Roesdahl (eds), *Borg in Lofoten. A Chieftain's Farm in North Norway*, 253–263, Trondheim: Tapir Academic Press.

Munch, G., Johansen, O. and Larssen, I. (1987) Borg in Lofoten. A Chieftain's Farm in Arctic Norway, *Proceedings of the Tenth Viking Congress*, 149–170, Oslo: University of Oslo

Munch, G., Johansen, O. and Roesdahl, E. (eds) (2003) *Borg in Lofoten. A Chieftain's Farm in North Norway*, Trondheim: Tapir Academic Press

Munch, G., Johansen, O. and Roesdahl, E. (2003a) Preface. *In* G. Munch, O. Johansen and E. Roesdahl (eds), *Borg in Lofoten. A Chieftain's Farm in North Norway*, 9–10, Trondheim: Tapir Academic Press

Nielsen, A.-L. (1997) Pagan Cultic and Votive Acts at Borg. *In* H. Andersson, P. Carelli and L. Ersgård (eds), *Visions of the Past. Trends and Traditions in Swedish Medieval Archaeology*, 373–392, Lund: Institute of Archaeology

Nielsen, A.-L. (2006) Rituals and Power. About a Small Building and Animal Bones from the Late Iron Age. *In* A. Andrén, K. Jennbert and C. Raudvere (eds), *Old Norse Religion in Long-Term Perspectives. Origins, Changes, and interactions*, 243–247, Lund: Nordic Academic Press.

Nordén, A. (1933) Svintuna och dess kastal vid Eriksgatan. Ett arkeologiskt bidrag till ortnamnsforskningen, *Fornvännen*, 263–279

O'Brien, C. (2005) The Great Enclosure. *In* P. Frodsham and C. O'Brien (eds), *Yeavering. People, Power, & Place*, 145–152, Oxford: Tempus

Olsen, M. (1915) *Hedenske kultminder i norske stedsnavne. Vitenskapsselskapets skrifter, II. Hist.-filos. klasse, 1914, No. 4*, Kristiania: Dybwad

Olsen, M. (1926) *Ættegård og helligdom: norske stedsnavn socialt og religionshistori belyst*, Oslo: Aschehoug

Olsen, O. (1966) *Hørg, hov og kirke: historiske og arkæologiske vikingetidsstudier*, Copenhagen: Det kongelige nordiske oldskriftselskab

Radford, C.R. (1957) The Saxon House: A Review and Some Parallels, *Medieval Archaeology*, 1: 27–38

Rahtz, P. (1963) The Saxon and Medieval Palaces at Cheddar, Somerset – An interim Report of the Excavations in 1960–62, *Medieval Archaeology*, 6: 53–66

Rahtz, P. (1979) *The Saxon and Medieval Palaces at Cheddar*, BAR British Series 65, Oxford

Rahtz, P. (1980) Yeavering: An Anglo-British Centre of Early Northumbria, *Medieval Archaeology*, 24: 265–270

Rapoport, A. (1969) *House Form and Culture*, Englewood Cliffs, NJ: Prentice-Hall

Rapoport, A. (1980) Vernacular Architecture and the Cultural Determinants of Form. *In* A. King (ed.), *Buildings and Society. Essays on the Social Development of the Built Environment*, 283–305, London: Routledge and Kegan Paul

Rapoport, A. (1993) Systems of Activities and Systems of Settings. *In* S. Kent (ed.), *Domestic Architecture and the Use of Space*, 9–20, Cambridge: Cambridge University Press

Reynolds, N. (1980) Dark Age Timber Halls and the Background to Excavation at Balbridie, *Scottish Archaeological Forum*, 10: 41–60

Rollason, D. (2003) *Northumbria, 500–1100. Creation and Destruction of a Kingdom*, Cambridge: Cambridge University Press

Ratke, S. and Simek, R. (2006) *Guldgubbar*. Relics of Pre-Christian Law Rituals? *In* A. Andrén, K. Jennbert and C. Raudvere (eds), *Old Norse Religion in Long-Term Perspectives. Origins, Changes, and Interactions*, 259–264, Lund: Nordic Academic Press

Scull, C. (1991) Post-Roman Phase I at Yeavering: A Re-consideration, *Medieval Archaeology*, 35: 51–63

Shanks, M. and Tilley, C. (1982) Ideology, Symbolic Power and Ritual Communication: A Reinterpretation of Neolithic Mortuary Practices. *In* I. Hodder (ed.), *Symbolic and Structural Archaeology*, 129–154, Cambridge: Cambridge University Press

Słupecki, L. (1994) *Slavonic Pagan Sanctuaries*, Warsaw: Institute of Archaeology and Ethnology Polish Academy of Sciences

Smith, I. (1984) Patterns of Settlement and Land Use of the Late Anglian Period in the Tweed Basin. *In* M. Faull (ed.) *Studies in Late Anglo-Saxon Settlement*, 177–196, Oxford: Dept for External Studies

Smith, I. (1991) Sprouston, Roxburghshire: An Early Anglian Centre of the Eastern Tweed Basin, *Proceedings of the Society of Antiquaries of Scotland*, 121: 261–294

Söderberg, B. (2003) Integrating Power; Some Aspects of a Magnate's Farm and Presumed Central Place in Järrestad, South-East Scania. *In* L. Larsson and B. Hårdh (eds), *Centrality-Regionality: the Social Structure of Southern Sweden during the Iron Age*, 283–310, Stockholm: Almqvist & Wiksell International

Soja, E. (1996) *Thirdspace: Journeys to Los Angeles and Other Real and Imagined Places*, Oxford: Blackwell

Steinsland, G. (1990) De nordiske gullblekk med parmotiv og norrøn fyrsteideologi. Et tolknings-forslag, *Collegium Medievale*, 3: 73–94

Steinsland, G. (1990a) Pagan Myth in Confrontation with Christianity: Skírnismál and Genesis. *In* Tore Ahlbäck (ed.), *Old Norse and Finnish Religions and Cultic Place-Names*, 316–328, Åbo: the Donner Institute for Research in Religious and Cultural History

Steinsland, G. (1991) *Det hellige bryllup og norrøn kongeideologi*, Oslo

Thompson, John (1985) *Studies in the Theory of Ideology*, Berkeley: University of California Press,

Thomsen, P. O., Blaesild, N., Hardt, N. and Michaelsen, K. (1993) *Lundeborg – en handelsplads fra jernalderen*. Vol. 32. Svendborg: Svendborg/Omegns Museum

Trigger, B. (2000) *A History of Archaeological Thought*, Cambridge: Cambridge University Press.

Watt, M. (1991) Sorte Muld. A Chieftain's Seat and Cult Site from the Late Iron Age in Bornholm. *In* P. Mortensen and B. Rasmussen (eds), *Høvdingesamfund og kongemagt*, 107. Moesgård: Jysk Arkæologisk Selskab

Watt, M. (2004) The Gold-Figure Foils from Uppåkra, *Uppåkrastudier 10, Acta Archaeologica Lundensia*, 48: 167–221

Williams, J. and Shaw, M. (1982) Middle Saxon 'Palaces' at Northampton, *Current Archaeology*, 84 (viii): 38–41

Welch, M. (1984) The Dating and Significance of the Inlaid Buckle Loop from Yeavering, Northumberland. *In* S. Chadwick Hawkes, J. Campbell and D. Brown (eds), *Anglo-Saxon Studies in Archaeology and History 3*, 77–78, Oxford: Oxford University Committee For Archaeology

Welch, M. (1992) *Anglo-Saxon England*, London: Batsford

Wilson, D. (1992) *Anglo-Saxon Paganism*, London: Routledge

Zevi, B. (1957) *Architecture as Space. How to Look at Architecture*, New York: Horizon Press

Chapter 6

Animal Magic

Aleks Pluskowski

Introduction: a world of animals

The symbolic repertoire of early Anglo-Saxon society can broadly be described as 'zoocentric'. Animals were central to the ornamentation applied to every type of object, animal elements in personal names were common and animals were actively incorporated into mortuary rites, both as whole carcasses and portions of meat. But not all species of animal were equally represented in the symbolic repertoire; in fact many did not feature at all. This paper attempts to discover how and why were animals chosen, and how the semiotic system they belonged to was constructed.

In pre-Christian northern Europe, animals appear to have played an organising role in society and cosmology (Hedeager 1998; 1999; 2003). In Anglo-Saxon society, as on the Continent and in Scandinavia, the symbolic repertoire appears in a hierarchical context, expressing above all the ideology and identity of the fighting elite. Given the menagerie of Anglo-Saxon iconology, it is useful to consider the animals represented with their contemporary ecology. In the chapter, my objective is the relationship between physical and conceptual reality. I explore the material culture of the symbolic repertoire, surveying the links between those animals experienced in the landscape, those employed in a range of representations on personal effects and those incorporated into the funerary process.

The ecological background to the symbolic repertoire

Despite the apparent importance of wild species in the symbolic repertoire of early Anglo-Saxon society, analyses of animal bones recovered from settlements indicate that the majority of people were most familiar with their own domesticates, even if the relative exploitation of cattle, sheep, goats, pigs and poultry for meat and secondary products, as well as the use of dogs and horses, varied from region to region (Crabtree 1989). Furthermore, this readily accessible and controllable faunal group represented most of the animal sacrifices and food offerings incorporated into the mortuary theatre (Crabtree 1995). It is important to stress that the rhythms of the predominantly rural Anglo-Saxon society would have been inevitably linked to the passing of seasons and their impact on crops and livestock. The patterns of hunting as well as associated ritual systems would have also followed a predictable, annual cycle. Numerous wild species could be encountered at the fringes of human activity; at the periphery of settlements, in meadows used for pasture and beyond in the wilderness. Anglo-Saxon migrants arriving in England would have been familiar with the howling of wolves, but the bear – the other top terrestrial predator in northern Europe – appears to have become extinct in England by the Roman period (Yalden 1999: 113–6). Medium-sized carnivores included red foxes, wild cats and various mustelids (otters, badgers and weasels) which, alongside a range of other raptors, preyed on a diversity of small mammals, birds and fish. Eagles and ravens would have been highly visible in their respective habitats (Hooke 1998: 30–1). The largest non-predatory fauna included aurochs, wild boar, red deer, roe deer, beaver and hare; all were hunted but their representation in the symbolic repertoire varied dramatically. A few species of snake were also indigenous to England, but later Anglo-Saxon literature conceptualised these as a sub-category of *wyrmas* along with dragons and maggots. Although there are no detailed 'zoological' descriptions of these animals, they were considered to be poisonous, subterranean and closely associated with the transformation of the dead (Semple 1998: 109–11; Thompson 2004: 132).

Pollen data variously indicate a continuity as well as a reduction in the intensity of landuse in the post-Roman period, which would have enabled certain habitats, particularly woodland in the north, to regenerate (Dark 2000: 156). Indeed, the Roman legacy of landuse left fundamental distinctions between the sparsely wooded central regions of England and the more densely wooded peripheries (Rackham 1994: 11). Nonetheless, it is clear that the exploitation of wild fauna was very limited. The relative proportion of wild mammals in Anglo-Saxon faunal assemblages is minute, increasing in varying frequencies and diversity from the early to the late Saxon period, a pattern which may be particularly linked to the growth in demand for wild products in towns (Sykes 2001: 149). The products of hunting and hawking were tied to expressions of rank, and the later urban demand for game may well have reflected a desire to emulate what was becoming a socially distinct pattern of consumption (*ibid.* 261–2). There is also evidence for the use of luxury furs in late Anglo-Saxon visual display (Owen-Crocker 1998: 36–7), which were also obtainable from towns (in England or from Scandinavian/Continental trading hubs) where evidence for fur-working is concentrated. The increased exploitation of game alongside the extension of agriculture and pasture would have increased the likelihood of contact with wolves, and despite the extreme paucity of lupine remains in early medieval archaeological contexts, place-name evidence suggests their general absence from southern England by the 11th century may have been partly the result of human pressure (Aybes and Yalden 1995).

At the fringes of the terrestrial environment, people came into contact with a range of wetland and marine species. The marine environment represented a blue wilderness (in many respects it continues to do so) and careful analysis of fish remains indicates that both marine and freshwater fishing in early Anglo-Saxon England were relatively limited and localised, developing and becoming more intensive in the course of the 10th century (Sykes 2001: 123–7; Barrett *et al.* 2004). Nonetheless even before the 'commercial revolution' in English fishing, people came into contact with some of the most impressive marine animals in their local waters, particularly a range of whale species (Dobney, Jaques, Barrett and Cluny 2007), which were consumed, their bones processed into artefacts, and whose role as a formidable oceanic predator would be evoked with fear and admiration in later Anglo-Saxon poetry. Bodies of water found inland, such as rivers and lakes, were home to a diversity of fish and mammals, a number of which were exploited for food, including the carnivorous pike. During the first millennium across northern Europe, some of these bodies of water became important sites for votive deposits, and in later literature were envisaged as the haunts and havens of monstrous beings, the most famous example from Old English poetry being Grendel's mere in *Beowulf* (Lund this vol.). By the time its description was written down – as a hellish parody of the great hall Hereot – the representation of wilderness as a physically and spiritually challenging environment was well established (Pluskowski 2006a: 56–60; Lund this vol; Semple this vol.).

Despite this increasing contact with the wilderness, the exploitation of animals for economic and ritual usage was generally limited to domesticates. Horses, dogs and livestock were readily incorporated into the 'mortuary theatre' of pagan Anglo-Saxon society, and wild species are only infrequently represented; a pattern comparable to funerary assemblages in southern Scandinavia. Here, the prevalence of domesticates, particularly horses and dogs, has been tentatively interpreted as reflecting both a lack of access to wild fauna and, perhaps as a result, a more limited and arguably exclusive relationship between humans and wild animals, in contrast to more northern regions, where, for example, the inclusion of bears in burials continued into the second millennium.

The presence of bears in Scandinavian iconography and their virtual absence in early Anglo-Saxon England suggests that the development of the symbolic repertoire was related in some way to ecological reality. On the other hand, the use of bear pelts in funerary contexts suggests the memory of the symbolic roles played by Continental bears may have been transferred or re-activated during the Anglo-Saxon settlement of England. This split between 'wild' and 'domestic' animals is convenient for the purpose of analysis, but the evidence suggests that a select group of animals from both categories met in the ritual feast. Ken Dowden (2000: 159) in his synthesis of common and diverging features of cultic practice across pre-Christian Europe, observed that 'paganism is about eating', and the consistent emphasis on dietary prohibitions and attacks on sacrificial meat in early medieval pastoral literature, underlies the significance attached to sacral food in both pre-Christian societies and in Christian constructions of the pagan 'other' (Filotas 2005: 341–2). Thus a concept of sacrality was determined which transcended biogeographic categories, excluding many domesticates as well as many wild species.

The ecology of early Anglo-Saxon England represents an important backdrop for situating the use of animals in the symbolic repertoire, first and foremost in the popularity of zoomorphic (animal-shaped) art, which challenges us to consider the overwhelming popularity of animal forms in early Anglo-Saxon aesthetics and the meanings behind the choice of certain species.

Zoomorphism: the visual language of the symbolic repertoire

Animal ornament in the north of Europe has been analysed and defined as a sequence of styles. Salin's Styles I and II, the two animal-art styles most relevant to the subject of this book, were both developed in southern Scandinavia, but spread to other parts of Scandinavia, the Continent and Anglo-Saxon England (Figure 6.1). Style I emerged during the second half of the fifth century, although its origin lay in Late Roman artistic traditions and their localised fifth-century manifestations outside the Empire; in England Style I persisted into the later sixth century. Style II appeared towards the middle of the sixth century and developed through the next century; it was current in England from the later sixth century into the seventh, eventually being selectively incorporated into the artistic outputs of Christian religious houses (Salin 1904; Haseloff 1981; Kristoffersen 2000; Speake 1980; Hawkes 1997; Høilund Nielsen 1998; 1999; 2001).

Style I animals are conceptually the most challenging (Figure 6.1(a)). Their biological identity is limited to traits such as heads or hands with outstretched thumbs that might be called 'human', coiled beaks that suggest raptors, and heads or limbs (with claws) that belong to quadrupeds; often these are combined to form an 'animal-man' or even an 'animal-bird-man' – mythical or transformational rather than mundane species. Body-parts are emphasized, often at the expense of completely coherent, articulated creatures, and elements, which might thus have iconic independence, could be subtracted, added or transposed to create ambiguity and unnaturalness. Style II animals are more balanced and integrated, markedly fluid or 'serpentine' in profile and with a strong tendency to interlace; species traits, such as those of raptors, wolves, boars, snakes and perhaps horses, appear more evident (Figure 6.1(b)). Both styles seem arcane, however, designed to absorb, puzzle or deceive a viewer (*cf.* Lindström and Kristoffersen 2001). Despite this obscurity, it is possible to begin to see patterns in the use of certain animal motifs, most visibly in the fittings attached to shields.

Stylised animal art is a hallmark of the material record for post-Roman northern Europe, beguiling scholars for over a century and a half. That it was valued not simply as decoration but for its symbolic roles in social practice, ritual and ideology does not now seem in doubt, though whether its specific meanings can be recovered, and how, remains problematic and controversial (Høilund Nielsen and Kristoffersen 2002; *cf.* Hines 1997 and Hawkes 1997).

Two routes can be taken to recovering their symbolic value. One, obviously, is to search for iconographic meaning. Of particular salience to deciphering Style I are Scandinavian gold bracteates (Figure 6.2), small metal-foil pendants which overlap in time and share some motifs with Style I, but being inspired by Late Roman medallions are much more pictorial (quasi-narrative) in character. Some bear runic inscriptions, albeit of highly disputed meaning. They have been studied most intensively by Professor Karl Hauck using a hermeneutic methodology (Axboe *et al.* 1985–1989). His conclusions, that the bracteates embodied an evolving Scandinavian cosmology centred on a pre-Viking Odin, a shaman-like god of healing, magic and warfare, have been widely cited, but are still contentious. Perforce this route involves drawing analogies from one visual context to another, and ultimately to written testimony which tends to be found either in mainly south European and Late Antique sources or in very much

Figure 6.1 (a) (top): Style I and (b) (above): Style II animal ornament [reproduced with permission from the British Museum Photo Archive].

later, Old Saxon and Old Norse texts that relay Nordic mythologies. The problem is that motifs do not have to maintain their meaning: they can be malleable, changing form and meaning according to context.

The other route to explanation is through social context. Style II was first and foremost used supra-regionally on men's prestige weaponry and equipment, including horse-gear, being transferred only later and more locally to female jewellery. In England, although relatively few in numbers, the style is especially associated with items in precious materials and coincides with changes in social structuring represented in burial practice (Speake

Figure 6.2: A bracteate with zoomorphic design from Faversham, Kent. Reproduced from Speake, G. (1980) Anglo-Saxon Animal Art and its Germanic Background. Oxford: OUP. By permission of the author.

1980; Stoodley 1999, esp. 138–42). There is then an argument that it is related (through the gifting and display of iconic objects) to newly emergent political leaders and their aristocratic warrior retinues, who defined and legitimated their status by manifesting a Norse ancestry (Høilund Nielsen 1997; 1998; 1999). Professor Lotte Hedeager would extend this reading to all post-Roman animal art, seeing it as a material-culture analogue of the beliefs enshrined in Germanic royal genealogies and origin legends. Drawing on arguments similar to those of Hauck, she stresses that it is the shamanistic, socio-cosmological referents of the animal art, particularly the cult of Odin, that powered its role in sustaining barbarian social hierarchies (Hedeager 2000; 2005).

Whether the usage and meaning of animal art varied between Style I and Style II also ought to be considered, however, although this is not easy to do because of differences between South Scandinavia and the other regions where the two styles were cultivated in terms of their access to precious metals and their practice of burial with grave-goods or deposition of votive hoards. In its South Scandinavian homeland, despite common assumptions, Style I is more associated with precious metals than is Style II and may have been as much a feature of the male as of the female realm, if not more so (Karen Høilund Nielsen, pers. comm.). Elsewhere, however, notably in Norway and in England, Style I was indeed overwhelmingly used on women's dress accoutrements, especially brooches, which mostly seem to be locally produced (Kristoffersen 2000; Dickinson forthcoming a). These facts suggest diversity in the role of animal art, but they also highlight the particular importance potentially of Style I on male-associated items. Rather than signifiers of spiritual status, these items express social control. At this point I propose to focus the argument on Anglo-Saxon shields.

Woden's armour: beasts on shields

In 2000 an Anglo-Saxon cemetery of considerable significance was excavated at Sutton Hoo, some 500 m north of (but mainly pre-dating) the famous mound-burials (the Tranmer House cemetery, Bromeswell 018: Anon 2002 Carver 2005: esp. 483–6). The mixed-rite burials, some of evident high status, included one, grave 868, with a remarkably decorated shield. Crowning the apex of its iron boss was a copper-alloy disc decorated between its silver-plated borders with a gilded relief field depicting two chasing 'quadrupeds' in Salin's Style I. Smaller bichromatic discs, carrying only a simple relief field of radial-bars, capped the rivets which fastened the boss-flange to the shield, and another eight were mounted on the shield-board in two opposing rows either side of the boss. Bisecting one half of the board between these rows were two bichromatic, animal-shaped mounts: an elongated fish-like creature facing out from the boss towards a raptor (eagle) which, apart from the fact that it grasped a snake, was like the much larger bird in Salin's Style II that, with a so-called 'dragon' mount, dominates the front of the great south Scandinavian shield from Sutton Hoo mound 1 (Bruce-Mitford 1978: pls. 1–3). According to previous studies, the new shield belongs to a distinctive group buried in the sixth and early seventh century with men of some significance, mainly in eastern England (Dickinson 2005; also Dickinson forthcoming a and b). These studies reached no agreement, however, on an interpretation of the zoomorphic decoration itself. The new Sutton Hoo shield, with its different animal-styles and animal-types combined in a single suite and its provenance in a well recorded, fully equipped weapon-inhumation, presents the sort of rich contextual data that could help unlock the meanings of such ornament.

Nineteen insular shields with animal-ornamented fittings have been identified at the time of writing, as well as twenty fittings of comparable type which have been found separately either in a secondary function in a woman's grave or as casual losses. The Style II Scandinavian shield from Sutton Hoo Mound 1 and possibly another in Mound 2 need also to be brought into consideration, though their fittings are mostly exceptional in nature (Figure 6.3). Apart from these two, almost all the fittings consist of either boss-apex discs decorated in relief-cast Style I or shield-board mounts with

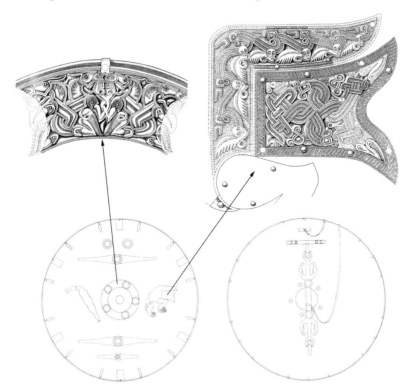

Figure 6.3: Shield ornament from Sutton Hoo Mound 1. Reproduced from Bruce Mitford, R. (1975–83) The Sutton Hoo Ship Burial. Volume 2. Arms and Armour and Regalia. *London: British Museum Press. By permission of the British Museum.*

similar decoration and/or in the shape of an animal. Style I and animal-shaped mounts for the boss-cone or boss-flange are represented only once each. Analysis of this repertoire suggests that the Style I and figural mounts are twin manifestations of a single iconography, which finds its best analogies among the gold bracteates.

The Style I motifs are surprisingly intelligible. Most, typically, are either animal-(bird)-men or quadrupeds, occurring in friezes of two, in which case they are generally forward-facing and the same, or of three or multiples thereof, in which case creatures are sometimes individualised as to 'species' and stance. Occasionally such motifs occur singly. Especially pertinent are the 'flying' anthropomorphic figure on the apex disc from Empingham II, grave 112, Rutland, and the backward-turning long-beaked creature on mounts from the back of the shield in Westgarth Gardens grave 41, Suffolk, for these find their most striking analogies on some B-bracteates. Compare the former with the central 'man' on IK 61 Galsted, Jutland and IK 176 Söderby, Uppland, and the latter with the left-hand beast on IK 74 Heide, Schleswig-Holstein, one of a series in which a central 'man' contends with two backward- and/or forward-facing open-jawed or beaked creatures, just as the Galsted/Söderby 'man' opposes an open-jawed beast (Axboe *et al.* 1985–9). In turn, these may explicate the animals on the Barton Seagrave apex disc, where an animal-(bird-)man is confronted by two creatures, one again with a long curved beak (as well as several others, apparently dismembered), and perhaps also those on the Sheffield's Hill 115 disc, where an animal-man faces open-jawed creatures, one facing forward, the other backward.

Now in Hauck's interpretations, these bracteate scenes relate to the struggle of gods, and specifically Odin, with demons of the underworld, whose artistic ancestry and iconic identity lie in Late Antique sea monsters. The Galsted/Söderby series might even depict an epiphany of Odin after his defeat of a final monster and as a new age was dawning (Lamm *et al.* 2001). It is not difficult to transfer this explanation to the Style I shield fittings, especially if the various hybridised animal motifs are taken, as they often have been, as icons of shape-shifting, shamanic or supernatural beings (*e.g.* Leigh 1980; 1984; Magnus 2003). On their own, animal-men or monstrous creatures might stand as mnemonics for the larger cosmological cycle, whilst the friezes of the Barton Seagrave and Sheffield's Hill discs perhaps evoke specific details of encounters between transcendental gods and monstrous beings.

This interpretation is reinforced by consideration of the figural mounts. They are dominated by aquatic creatures (now up to seventeen examples). Rarely are these true fish, though the pike from Spong Hill grave 31, Norfolk, is reasonably identifiable (Figure 6.4), and pike-like traits seem to underlie nearly all the others; the symmetrical arrangement of their fins or flippers is more consistent, however, with land animals. They should be regarded as mythical underwater creatures, conceived on the basis of the pike, one of the most ferocious freshwater fish known to north Europeans. More mythical are the hippogriffs (eagle-headed horses) from Bergh Apton grave 26, Norfolk, and the wolf-headed 'dragons' from Sutton Hoo mounds 1 and 2, though the latter might also have an aquatic aspect, given the parallelism between the paired mounts on the shields from Sutton Hoo mound 1 and the new grave 868: elongated 'dragon' and aquatic respectively plus eagle (Bruce-Mitford 1978: fig. 29). Pertinently, the eagle, with seven examples, is the second most frequent figural mount

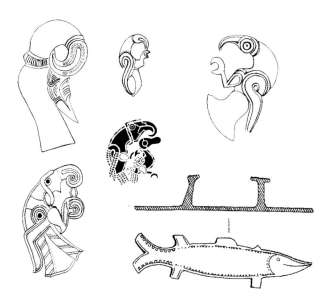

Figure 6.4: Aggressive aquatics and aerials from shields. Reproduced from Speake, G. (1980) Anglo-Saxon Animal Art and its Germanic Background. *Oxford: OUP. By permission of the author.*

(Figure 6.4a–d) although its distribution is confined to Kent and Suffolk, whereas other types of fitting predominate more widely north of the Thames. The best analogies for the aquatic and eagle figural forms come again from bracteates, such as some of the 'Three-gods' series of B-bracteates where an aquatic being attacks a central (divine) figure and the C-bracteate, IK 33 (in the British Museum) where one confronts – just as on the Sutton Hoo 868 shield – an eagle, whose form, replicated on other C-bracteates, is the closest parallel for the shape taken by the majority of the Anglo-Saxon bird mounts (that is not with Style II traits). Readings of an eagle as an emblem specifically of Oðinn or of some other supernatural being or merely as an imperial icon are all possible. However, the consistency of the images chosen for figural mounts, taken with the evidence from the mounts in Style I with which in some cases they co-occur, encourages an explanation of the shields' iconography as one focused on a Nordic cosmology of supernatural and shamanistic engagements crossing the boundaries of life and death. Perhaps these were believed to determine the circumstances of the living (and dying) during battle (*cf*. Price 2002: 393–4), and hence their iconic presence on a shield – normally the only defensive piece of armament buried in an Anglo-Saxon grave – provided extraordinary protection against a 'bad' outcome.

Shields in context

The shield had a special place in early Anglo-Saxon burial ritual: with, or often instead of, the sword, it was the principal token by which adult masculinity was symbolised, a masculinity that was plainly tied to martial conduct, raised social status and, arguably, an ethnicised identity (Dickinson and Härke 1992; Härke 1997b; Stoodley 1999). Animal-ornamented shields were a special and elevated class of this symbol. Although not all were buried with assemblages that outdid the average shield-burial, some certainly were (up to the stupendous level of the Sutton Hoo mound-burials). They stand out particularly, however, by the very high level of their armament – 94 per cent also had a spear and 39 per cent a sword. These were graves, and so arguably men, that stood out within their local communities and in some cases much further afield. Their shields – a highly visible element in the burial tableau, though in terms of the modest size of the mounts rather less so in a battlefield – signalled a special relationship with the supernatural, perhaps even with Woden. They manifested a man's special capability and responsibility to protect, and so perhaps affirmed his affiliation to a warrior retinue and/or claims to power over others, from kindred to even kingdom.

When the heyday of animal-ornamented shields in England should be placed is not easy to specify, and current suggestions may prove too conservative once the results of the English Heritage project integrating high-precision carbon-14 dating with new typological seriations is published. At present, it seems to lie in the two middle quarters of the sixth century, but it might have started earlier and lasted later, with the Sutton Hoo mound-burials of the early seventh century clearly the latest depositions (Dickinson 2005, 139–44). Distribution patterns show that it was practised primarily in the Anglian material-culture regions of England, but extending to and across the lower Thames into Kent. Although some fittings were re-used as jewellery in women's graves in the Upper and Middle Thames and further south, it was not apparently a custom of Saxon districts. However, before too much is read into the fact that Anglian and Kentish but not initially Saxon dynasties took Woden as their divine ancestor, it should be noted that Style I occurs on scabbard-mouths (protecting the sword) primarily in Saxon areas, and while their motifs, mainly an (animal-) man between two quadrupeds, are less varied than those on shields, they might well refer to the same iconography as the shields.

The layout of richly ornamented fittings on shields and their associated contexts may have together engendered specific stories about these objects and the events surrounding them. Style I, both generally and particularly in its majority use on female dress accoutrements, has been interpreted in terms of Norse cosmology (*e.g.* Leigh 1980; 1984; Magnus 2001; Hedeager 2005: 504–14). It does raise the question, however, of how an ideology embedded in a model of the battlefield, real and supernatural, operated in the female realm of jewellery. Exemplars from shields may have provided or inspired designs for brooches, or both may have drawn on a common stock of iconography. Second-hand shield fittings (as also horse-fittings: Fern this vol.) were selectively transferred from men to women. That women's zoomorphic brooches and pendants were protective amulets (apotropaic) has long been argued, and some round brooches and bracteates seem almost literally 'little shields', so it is not difficult to understand how the overall ideology could embrace women, and even that, vicariously, they should be the more numerous bearers of it.

The versatile boar

The way animals helped to constitute mythology and embodied its presence in prestige artefacts used for gift exchange and social display is a behaviour of wide occurrence, and one which possibly finds particularly apt resonances in the social and ideological rituals embedded in later Old English and Old Norse poetry (Bazelmans 1999; North 1997b). The dissemination of aggressive animal symbolism beyond the margins of battlefield ideology can be further demonstrated by the image of the wild boar, one of the more distinctive animals of the early Anglo-Saxon symbolic repertoire (see also Sanmark this vol.). The boar featuring as a crest fitting on helmets is attested in both England and Scandinavia in the 7th century; in the former region by excavated examples from Benty Grange, Northampton and Guilden Morden, whilst the ends of the brow fitting on the Sutton Hoo helmet terminate in boar heads. Several centuries later, the memory of the function of boar-helmets was preserved in *Beowulf*:

> "... the weapon-smith wrought it thus, worked it with magic
> set it with swine shapes so that thereafter no
> blade nor battle sword might bite through. . ."

The consistent use of the boar on helmets is complemented by its representation on women's bracelets, brooches and pendants, the use of boar tusks in female graves and the representation of the boar on men's jewellery such as buckles and shoulder clasps, harness mounts and swords (Hawkes 1997: 316). A seventh-century sword blade stamped with three figures of boars was recovered from the River Lark (Davidson 1962: 49–50). A similar diversity in use is also evident in Scandinavia, but what *is* interesting is the consistent use of the boar on personal effects, often in very similar ways, in the two regions. It is likely that the multiple uses of the boar, as suggested by varied contexts, probably revolved around its flexible association with protection, aggression, fertility and identity (Glosecki 2000: 14).

The multiplicity of meanings associated with the same animal would inevitably vary depending on the context and perhaps even the level of knowledge possessed by the viewer of the image. When considering the reception of the symbolic repertoire, we cannot assume the omnipresence of an immobile, captive audience and must take into account the shape, size and visual access to every example (Belting 1990; Mathews 2000: 7). Whilst some of the most 'accessible' uses of symbolic animals were to be found on shields, even the popular raptor fittings do not appear to have been made to take advantage of the full widths of shields, which would have presented the best opportunities for visual display on the battlefield. Shield decoration appears at five levels of ostentation, from the most luxurious metal fittings found in Mound 1 at Sutton Hoo to a complete absence of any fittings (Dickinson and Härke 1992). The addition of relatively small decorative fittings would have allowed the shields of high ranking warriors to be personalised, without impinging on the use of their backgrounds as markers of a group or unit identity (Stephenson 2002: 114). Visibility and clear identification of these fittings would have been limited, their militaristic use secondary, suggesting the symbolic repertoire functioned on personal as well as communal levels. This may have also been the case for the role of animals in the mortuary theatre, simultaneously serving living audiences and dead individuals.

Animals in the mortuary theatre

A limited number of animal species were actively incorporated into funerary rites across the Germanic world where they were used in the construction of mortuary identities or 'personhood', as well as performing metaphysical functions (Williams 2006: 11). In early Anglo-Saxon England, the inhumation of whole animals (such as the horse in Mound 17 at Sutton Hoo) is comparatively limited both in number and diversity. By contrast, whole animals in large numbers were placed on pyres for cremation, where they were more clearly active players in the mortuary theatre, most probably killed for this particular purpose (see Bond 1996; Bond and Worley 2006). The cremated remains of as many as seven animals were placed together in urns at Spong Hill (Lucy 2000: 90–94, 112–3). These fragments hint at sacrificial slaughter at the graveside; a violent, disturbing and dramatic ritual, most likely conducted with axe hammers – the weapons and symbols of cult leaders (Dobat 2006: 887–8). Decapitation within such contexts is certainly attested by finds of ox and horse skulls (Richards 1992: 141).

The limited economic exploitation of wild animals is paralleled in their representation in the mortuary theatre; they feature in a few cremations in the largest cemeteries and are represented by a small group of artefacts interred with a diverse range of people. At least one fox was recorded in a cremation at both Sancton and Spong Hill, with a further probable four at the latter represented by mandibles, three of which were associated with females. These were almost certainly the remains of fox pelts with the crania left intact, whereas the Sancton animal appears to have been a whole carcass. Bear claws have been found in cremation burials from Elsham, Sancton (two) and Spong Hill (six) – presumably bear-skins included on the pyre. A bear metacarpus was also recovered from West Stow. They are evidence of personal possessions, almost certainly imported and point to a comparable use of wild animal products to that found on the Continent from the Iron Age and in parts to Scandinavia, where they have been linked with specific cultic activity. In early Anglo-Saxon England, pelts – alongside joints of meat and whole animals – would have played a key role in the construction of mortuary identity. It is not excluded that the ritualistic use of animal disguise was practiced. Other representations of wild fauna in the mortuary theatre included teeth, found in early Anglo-Saxon graves across the country from both the 6th and 7th centuries. Salin (1959 (4): 28) speculated that such teeth may have been remnants of skulls fixed on posts over the graves, but more recently, and more plausibly, they have been interpreted as amulets (Meaney 1981). Unfortunately, so few have been found that it is impossible to identify a particular chronological or regional pattern. Moreover, there is difficulty assigning them to particular species, particularly canid teeth which could be dog, fox or wolf. They are outnumbered by perforated boars' tusks, typically associated with female burials, as are beaver teeth, set in copper alloy or in two cases in gold. Two boar tusks have been found outside cemetery contexts – in West Stow and Waterbeach, both perforated, and an unusual example of a buckle constructed from a large boar tusk (or possibly hippopotamus ivory) from a 7th century grave at Castledyke.

The animals collaborating in the elite hunt were horses and dogs, and their quarry, deer. All of these animals feature in cremations at Spong Hill, Sancton and Sutton Hoo. Dog inhumations are relatively infrequent and quite mixed in character, representing a range of breeds associated with males and females of varying ages. This has made it difficult to interpret them, although the dog, like the wolf, may have been perceived as an appropriate mediator between the world of the living and the dead, alongside its other potential roles in the mortuary theatre (Gräslund 2004). Whilst the most common combination of animal offerings on funeral pyres at Spong Hill were horses and sheep/goats, the latter were represented by joints of meat – food; dogs on the other hand, most likely placed on the pyre whole and joined horses in eight instances (Williams 2005: fig. 10). Mound 4 at Sutton Hoo contained the cremated remains of an adult male, an adult female, a horse and possibly a dog – accompanied by gaming pieces and textiles. Mound 7 contained cremated animal bones from horse, cattle, sheep/goat, pig and red deer (a piece of un-worked antler), in addition to fragments of a drinking horn, a copper alloy cauldron, textile, gaming pieces and a glass bead, possibly part of a sword suspension system (Bond 2005). Dogs and horses are not found together in any other early Anglo-Saxon cemeteries.

The earliest example of a raptor used in falconry in early medieval England is the complete skeleton of a peregrine falcon from the Middle Saxon settlement of Brandon (Crabree pers. comm.). But this was simply discarded after the animal expired. Unlike at Scandinavian sites such as Rickeby (Vallentuna, Uppland), in Anglo-Saxon England raptors do not appear to have been incorporated into funerary rites. So although it is clear that dogs and horses were interred as whole carcasses, sometimes together in 6th and 7th century Anglo-Saxon burials, there is little evidence for the display of hunting and fighting assemblages that one finds on the Continent and in Scandinavia. However, in terms of scale and chronology, the role of the horse in cremation rites is unparalleled in contemporary Europe. There is evidence for innovation in Anglo-Saxon England amongst early generations of migrants in what would become a widespread north European phenomenon (Fern 2007: 102). Does this reflect the relative importance of aristocratic hunting in these regions? Does it reflect regional differences in the relationships between people and animals, in different funerary performances?

The uses of animals in early Anglo-Saxon funerary rites point to multiple roles that, in turn, can arguably be linked back to a consistent semiotic system. A bear pelt and a horse may have been incorporated into the same funerary performance for very different reasons, but both would have contributed to the construction of an individual's mortuary identity, worldly and otherworldly. With the widespread acceptance of Christianity, animals – as active players – vanish from the mortuary theatre although they continued to be buried in ritualistic contexts such as foundation deposits. To date, a total of four late Anglo-Saxon examples of animals interred with people in three execution cemeteries can all be interpreted as the outcome of a judicial process, most probably convictions for bestiality; at Stockbridge both man and dog buried together in grave 19 had been decapitated, suggesting that both had been perceived as malefactors (Reynolds 1998: 164–5).

Animals as windows into early Anglo-Saxon cosmology

The use of animals as active, rather than simply metaphorical, mediators between the natural and supernatural worlds is a characteristic of shamanic religious systems

(Eliade 1989). Stephan Glosecki (1989) has argued for a shamanic view of early Anglo-Saxon society on the basis of traces of totemism and ecstatic techniques found in later Anglo-Saxon literature, whilst Howard Williams (2005) has suggested that early Anglo-Saxon society shared an 'ideology of transformation' with other groups in the North Sea, expressed through animal use and representation in 5th and 6th century funerary rites. More specifically, Glosecki and Williams have argued for an animistic pagan Anglo-Saxon society, where the spiritual was accessible through the natural. The earliest written sources providing information on the mechanics of pagan beliefs in England are fragmentary and unreliable. There is very little direct evidence for the actual veneration of animals as deities in England, although the practice is attested in other regions of northern Europe. A letter written by Aldhelm of Sherborne (d. 709) mentions shrines which had been converted to Christian uses, where previously *ermuli cervulique* had been worshipped, perhaps referring to an image of a stag or hybrid stag-deity (Filotas 2005: 144). Such examples are exceptional. On the other hand, early Anglo-Saxon material culture shares both form and context with the symbolic repertoire deployed by pagan societies in other parts of northern Europe, particularly Scandinavia. In all of these regions, the centrality of zoomorphic ornament, the incorporation of animals into funerary rites, personal display and hints in later literature of their original totemic functions such as their use in personal names, all point to a paradigm where animals played a key role in social and cosmological organization. Here, the conceptual boundary between human and animal was mutable, certain species were used to facilitate ecstatic connections with the otherworld, and desirable qualities expressed particularly in wild animals, could be tapped, perhaps even controlled.

Deities were consistently linked with a select group of animals, and were also attributed with the ability to shape-shift and travel between worlds. In later Anglo-Saxon sources, Woden (like the Scandinavian Odin) is consistently, if fragmentarily, described as a highly animalistic deity. Brian Branston (1974: 104) had argued on the basis of the limited literary evidence that the English Woden never evolved into his Scandinavian equivalent: a fickle, predatory battle god (Grundy 1995; Price 2002). However, Christian authors writing about pagan cosmologies in England, Scandinavia and elsewhere were unlikely to have had any first-hand understanding of these semiotic systems, and rigidly defined gods in relation to the familiar forms of Roman and Mediterranean culture outlined in early Christian literature (Fell 1995: 19). Recent studies of Odin have blurred earlier characterisations, breaching the boundaries of function, gender and appearance (Grundy 1995, Price 2002). For example, the earliest link between the god and wolves is found on an 8th century runic inscription from Ribe, an association that may have been represented on Migration period bracteates, but one which is not elaborated upon until the 12th and 13th centuries. Taking just this one example, it is clear that Odin's complex relationship with wolves exemplified his role in contemporary understandings of death, particularly death in battle.

Hints of cultic similarities between the English Woden and Scandinavian/Continental equivalents may be deduced from a buckle design recovered from Finglesham and on the Sutton Hoo helmet, on which 'dancing warriors' wear helmets that bear horns terminating in zoomorphic beaked heads, perhaps representing birds circling overhead (Price 2002: 388). Both English examples parallel images of horned figures in southern

Scandinavia and on the Continent, which in the case of a helmet plate-die from Torslunda and pressed mounts from Gutenstein and Obrigheim, are accompanied by wolf-coated or lupine hybrid warriors. These and related motifs can be convincingly linked to the cult of Odin (*ibid.* 372–3), which appears to have derived from a cult of Mercury as it developed in Roman Gaul. Given contemporary entomological links between Anglo-Saxon Woden and Scandinavian Odin, their cults appear to have been expressed in the symbolic repertoires of both regions in comparable ways, although the regal traits of the deity appear to have been adopted in Scandinavia from the West Saxons (North 1997a: 78). In this instance the use of dancing warriors and birds in both England and southern Scandinavia may have alluded to a personal affinity with the deity or his cult, where the stylised birds can be identified as his accompanying ravens. The use of wolves on the Sutton Hoo purse lid, echoing another contemporary composition from Torslunda, may reflect an Anglian variant reflecting the local totemic importance of the wolf on one level (Newton 1993), and the lupine Woden on another.

The absence of direct evidence for battle gods in pagan Anglo-Saxon society is almost certainly related to the increasing reliance on Christ for success and protection in battle during the 7th century (see below). During this time, and into the 8th century, the raptor and serpent continued to be used but in different settings, whilst representations of boars and stags declined in early Anglo-Saxon Christian art, perhaps because they were more distinctive and therefore less flexible symbols (Hawkes 1997: 321–326). This break with the past was not always comprehensive, since memories of the early world view appear to have been preserved in later literature and surviving pagan practices were widely and persistently condemned (Filotas 2005).

If animals were employed in socio-cosmological organisation, it is unsurprising to find that predatory species and the concept of predation featured prominently in the expression of rank. Through the fundamental relationship between predator and prey, consumer and consumed, people situated themselves both ecologically and cosmologically in relation to other organisms (including each other), on a physical and metaphysical level (Pluskowski 2006a; 2006b). In the symbolic repertoire, predatory animals were employed most of all in the defining activities of the élites: fighting (on shields), and feasting (drinking horns, musical instruments). In a society where individuals could be closely identified with certain animals through names, visual allusions, disguises or actions, the élites legitimised themselves both socially and cosmologically as predators – instigators of violence and the top consumers in their group. The animals they identified with were wild, uncontrollable, some of them with the potential to display impressive aggression and ferocity; the sights and sounds of large carnivores hunting, killing and fighting. These animals were the least experienced by early Anglo-Saxon society, and they would have been vividly contrasted with those animals under human management, particularly livestock, experienced on a daily basis (see below). This may have lent a disconcerting sense of otherness to those who regularly employed the symbols of the wolf, boar and eagle. Hunting these animals was both difficult and dangerous, characteristics which may have extended to the deployment of their symbolic forms. The otherness of those individuals at the conceptual 'cutting-edge' of mutability is perhaps echoed in an aspect of the representation of heroic dragon slayers in later Germanic literature, where both slayer and dragon shared more affinities with each other than with the rest of humanity, and where the slayer adopted 'dragonish' behaviour and characteristics (Lionarons 1998: 110). On the other hand, it is equally possible that animals depicted on arms and armour were references to gods, who were defined adjectively by those species. Rather than drawing on the character of the animal, the bearer of the zoomorphic shield, helmet and sword derived support from the represented deities. This form of empowerment could even extend to animals; the horse in Mound 17 at Sutton Hoo wore human ornament on its bridle (Carver 1998: 112); strap ends decorated with moustached masks flanked by stylised birds reminiscent of Scandinavian motifs interpreted as representing Odin (Price 2002: 386–388). Here, there is good evidence to suggest that individuals most closely linked to the cultic activities of Odin were also perceived as dangerous 'others' (Breen 1999; Grundy 1995). So whilst pagan North Sea societies may have shared a comparable 'ideology of transformation', this encompassed a spectrum of participation which, in early Anglo-Saxon England, is perhaps visible in the deployment of the symbolic repertoire. Moreover, whilst it is clear that animal symbolism permeated multiple aspects of early Anglo-Saxon society, the battlefield represented one of its most striking and popular theatres.

Animals in conflict

Neil Price (2002) has convincingly argued for the presence of a strong ritualistic element in Scandinavian warfare, characterised by systems of magic and divine support. Battles were fought on two planes; the physical and the metaphysical, both inter-linked through the use of objects and gestures. This organisation of warfare was guided by élite groups, but it was not exclusively under their control. Early Anglo-Saxon warfare may have functioned in a similar way, although the only evidence hinting at its supporting ritualistic structure is the prevalence of comparable symbolic elements in surviving material culture. If we accept this, the differences may partly be due to the comparative chronologies of religion and warfare in both regions. The period of 'pagan' warfare in Scandinavia spanned almost half a millennium, perhaps even longer if we tentatively push its origins to the organisation of military combat and ritual deposition of arms in the pre-Roman Iron Age (Randsborg 1995; Engström 1997).

In Anglo-Saxon England, a visible sense of hierarchy developed in the second half of the 6th century, with increasing evidence for social stratification, and became more clearly marked in the 7th century, especially in individual barrow burials. John Moreland (2000) links the appearance of this social differentiation with the construction of distinctive regional material cultures – expressions of affiliation and allegiance to regional aristocratic elites. In Eastern England, this included the reaffirmation of cultural links with Scandinavia – here Anglo-Saxon elites were most visibly part of that supra-regional elite culture expressed in the lavish material culture of the Vendel period, particularly associated with the Swedish province of Uppland and the island of Gotland. This also involved a change in the perception of military status, from a wide inclusion of the male population in the 5th and 6th century to a more selective involvement of smaller numbers in the 7th and early 8th century, reflecting increasing *selectivity* of military service with a growing importance of ordered styles of combat, the role of nobility as leaders and organisers of this type of warfare (Härke 1997a). The burials at Sutton Hoo exemplify the expression of this new ideology through the language of an animalistic symbolic repertoire, oriented towards prowess in battle and exultation in death. However, by the 8th century, many of the Anglo-Saxon élite class had converted to Christianity.

The acceptance of Christianity by north European political élites realigned the metaphysics of battle: the military successes of the early Carolingians were closely linked to divine aid and spiritually bolstered by victory sermons, the presence of military chaplains who heard confession, provided absolution and assurance of salvation to soldiers, as well as the use of relics and religious banners on the battlefield (Bachrach 2001: 147–158). In England, King Edwin's victory against the pagan West Saxons in 626 was the first recorded demonstration of the power of the Christian god in battle, exemplifying divine aid in the protection and advancement of Edwin's regime (Higham 1997: 168). Politics, religion and warfare were just as closely linked during and after the conversion period as they had been before; in the theatre of battle, the use of decorative martial equipment continued, but its cultural significance and its metaphysical role changed. The use of 'life stones' in sword hilts functioning as charms was replaced with relics (Davidson 1962: 182–3). Even so, the battle of gods was not one-sided, as demonstrated by Penda of Mercia's continuing military successes against a string of Christian armies. The ultimate triumph of Christ in battle came with Penda's death in 655, which signalled the beginning of the end for English paganism as a political ideology and public religion (*ibid.* 241). This was paralleled by victory in the realm of symbols. The cross on the Benty Grange helmet and the inscription on the Coppergate helmet reflect the gradual adoption of a new symbolic repertoire by the fighting élite, representing the continuing use of apotropaic devices, albeit drawing their power from Christ (Stephenson 2002: 110–111).

So what is the evidence for the active use of symbols on a pagan Anglo-Saxon battlefield? It is highly likely that the spiritual qualities of raptors on shields, boars on helmets, and 'serpentine' pattern-welded swords would have been activated in battle, as a form of shamanic empowerment (Glosecki 1989). Later Anglo-Saxon poets described the battle-fallen as food for the wolf, raven and eagle. But whereas poets in Scandinavia, as well as in Wales, employed the beasts of battle to glorify the actions of individual warriors, in later Anglo-Saxon literature they were employed to signify the horror and tragedy of battle (Jesch 2002). These differences may well reflect contrasts in the metaphysical development of warfare in England and Scandinavia, however they probably originated under similar circumstances, reflecting comparable symbolic interpretations of social phenomena (*ibid.* 267). The Anglo-Saxon battlefield resonated with bestial energy; wild, uncontrollable animals were invoked for protection, to inspire aggression and fighting prowess, and the killing of foes was conceptualised in the terms of bestial violence and consumption. The metaphorical consumption of the battle-dead became ritualistic consumption as participants called upon the symbolic power of predatory animals, on a predatory god through his animalistic allusions, with some going as far as to engage in bestial mimicry, and by doing so deliberately breach the behavioural boundary between human and animal. It is uncertain whether pagan Anglo-Saxon armies went as far as ritual disguise, but perhaps early medieval clerical attacks on masquerades targeted such practices on a more general level (Breen 1999; Filotas 2005). As a self-proclaimed predatory class, élite warriors would have dominated both the physical and metaphysical organisation of battle. The potentially complex role of Woden on the battlefield is lost to us, although Bede associated the clash of pagan and Christian armies in the 7th century with the struggle of deities. The process of conversion in England was closely linked to the actions of the political élite, and by the 8th century the more overt links with a pagan warrior ideology would have been broken and recast within a Christian mould. So even though boar helmets are mentioned as protective devices in *Beowulf*, there is no evidence this reflected anything more than a memory of the potentially earlier totemic semiotic language (Fell 1995: 24).

The symbolic repertoire in context: comparisons with the Continent and Scandinavia

Early Anglo-Saxon society initially derived its symbolic repertoire from its homeland cultures, and it subsequently emulated, blended and invented, within the framework of a broadly shared north European pagan semiotic system. Later Anglo-Saxon sources shed some light on the function of symbols in pre-Christian society but they do not provide us with the level of mythological detail found in 12th- and 13th-century Old Norse literature, which, written by Christians, represents only a fragmentary and indirect source for the role of symbols in pagan Scandinavia, let alone Anglo-Saxon England (Hawkes 1997: 315). As a result we are left with little first hand information on the potential complexity of the symbolic repertoire.

On the other hand, the consistent use of a limited group of symbols revolving around animal ornament in England, Scandinavia and the Continent in the 6th and 7th centuries points not only to a shared aesthetic milieu, but most likely comparable expressions of political and religious allegiance. The context and chronology of this symbolic repertoire corresponds to the development of new political structures in the North Sea region revolving around the control of military resources, and the use of visual display in social communication and organisation. The multiple roles of the new élites were expressed, in part, through the visual language of predation. The conceptualisation of the élite class as ecologically dominant would continue following the acceptance of Christianity, but in England, and indeed other parts of Europe, would manifest most explicitly through the development of aristocratic hunting culture. In high medieval fables, this ecological play on the cosmic order was exemplified by representing the aristocracy as wild carnivores – the truly independent and native citizens of the realm – compared to the lower servile orders and their animal equivalents (Salisbury 1994: 130–131).

The adoption of Christianity resulted in the abandonment of animal burial, but not animal ornamentation, some of which was incorporated into Christian religious art, accompanied by a shift from a zoocentric to an anthropocentric iconography, and, I would argue, world-view. The range of animal iconography on Anglo-Saxon coinage from the so-called 'secondary phase' (*c.* 710–50), breaching political and geographical boundaries included birds on or with crosses, peacocks, hens, lions, wolves, largely inherited from Roman rather than Germanic culture, and snakes, omnipresent in pre-Christian northern Europe, sometimes in conflict with birds (Gannon 2003). The elaborate birds and beasts of Insular manuscripts – a highly original yet synthetic art form – may have reclaimed the apotropaic properties from the gods of the previous generation. By the 11th century, the new symbolic menagerie rooted in Biblical tradition was firmly in place, and the visual language of Germanic animal forms was reaching its final 'native' phase in both Britain and Scandinavia in the Urnes style. Nonetheless, pagan animism influenced the development of Anglo-Saxon Christianity, where "spiritual understanding and change could be accomplished and manifested in and through the physical realm" (Jolly 1993: 236). Similar meetings between pagan and Christian semiotics in material culture during the course of the 7th century are evident in other parts of the Germanic world, such as Burgundy (Schutz 2001: 237).

During the 9th and 10th centuries, Scandinavians colonised the northern parts of British Isles, and briefly re-introduced pagan burial rites involving the interment of animals. Some also took advantage of native stone sculptural traditions to express elements of their world-view, perhaps within the context of adopting or absorbing elements of Christianity. The only known Scandinavian cremation cemetery in England is at Heath Wood in Ingleby, where excavations in the 1940s and 50s revealed the remains of cremated animals; in mound 1, the bones of an adult, sheep, ox and possible dog, mound 2 included an ox and a horse, and mound 11 potentially a small dog and sheep (Richards 2004: 196). This is comparable to the barrow burial at Chapel Hill in Balladoole on the Isle of Man, where a layer of cremated bone covered the burial of a man and a (potentially sacrificed) woman, and included ox, horse, sheep and dog (Bersu and Wilson 1966: 10). A comparable funerary assemblage was also discovered in nearby Ballateare (*ibid.* 51). Animal bones were also discovered in a Viking cremation burial at Hesket-in-the-Forest in Cumbria, and feature in Viking burials in Scotland (Barrett 2003: 219).

These visible trappings of paganism were adopted by some Anglo-Saxon communities, especially in northern England and the Isle of Man where regionally specific and short-lived expressions of the lupine apocalypse appear in monumental art. At Skipwith, Sockburn, Gosforth, Ovingham and Kirk Andreas, they form a visible cosmological interface between Anglo-Saxon Christian and Scandinavian pagan paradigms (Pluskowski 2004). The impact of these Anglo-Scandinavian uses of predation was limited, for although their symbolic role was active rather than mnemonic (as with contemporary poetry evoking the wolf and eagle in battle), their use was short-lived. Risden's (1994) observations on *Beowulf* suggest that a late Anglo-Saxon audience would have understood the broad messages of this fresh injection of actively used pagan symbols in England; the basic meanings of the wolf, boar, eagle and raven – their association with the life and death of warriors – would have been recognised. But there is no indication the composer of *Beowulf* had anything more than a vague awareness of Germanic pagan practices (Fell 1995: 28), even though communication between 'pagan' Scandinavia and 'Christian' England would have facilitated some level of knowledge (Johnson 1995: 48). Indeed, a familiarity with the significance of cosmic predation in Scandinavian semiotics is evident in the pictorial development of the bestial hellmouth; a tool of conversion originating in southern England in the 10th century (Schmidt 1995).

Epilogue: the impact of Christianity

When comparing Anglo-Saxon paganism with other pre-Christian cultic practices in northern Europe, particularly ones which continued to function into the second millennium, there is a sense that the acceptance of Christianity in England briefly stimulated the use of the pagan symbolic repertoire in new and imaginative ways, and at the same time terminated its further development. Comparisons with other religious paradigms in northern Europe are both inevitable and problematic, but the deployment of symbols in early Anglo-Saxon England expressed an ideology shared with groups across the North Sea region. Our understanding of the symbolic repertoire of pagan Anglo-Saxon society must be based on iconography and the ritualistic treatment of animal remains from the 5th–7th centuries, with much of the surviving evidence represented by the trappings and mortuary compositions of the élite class. It is important to acknowledge the complex and dynamic contexts of this corpus of material culture, and the use of applied zoomorphic ornament into the 11th century cannot be accounted for under a single explanation (Schutz 2001: 219; Thompson 2004: 132–3). Originally, the symbolic repertoire as it developed in the 6th and 7th centuries would have presented an opportunity for political organisation, as was most probably the case in contemporary Scandinavia (Hedeager 1999), in turn associated with a supra-regional ideology that emphasised the grave and battlefield as its fundamental inter-related theatres, and which negotiated the mutable relationship between the categories of human and animal.

But although we should expect diversity in practice and belief within early Anglo-Saxon England, as across southern Scandinavia, the corpus of material culture points to the existence of a relatively cohesive semiotic system, with a consistently skewed relationship between ecological experience and imagination. The concepts expressed through these symbols were at first firmly rooted in a pagan world-view, but from the late 7th century onwards they became increasingly repositioned within a Christian framework. Veneration of Woden was dying out in England in the 8th century, and by the 10th century, his role in superstition had waned (North 1997a: 80–3). Zoomorphic ornamentation on the other hand continued to be used into the 11th century, now more widely applied to religious artefacts than martial equipment, whilst poets employed the battlefield animals to mourn rather than glorify the deeds of warriors. If animal art had been used to signify the old gods, Christianity's rich symbolic bestiary would have enabled the meanings attached to zoomorphic images to be readily re-deployed. Those species which had little place in the new iconology – such as the wolf – faded into comparative obscurity (Pluskowski 2004; 2006b). Scandinavian colonisation in England in the 9th and 10th centuries did not revive a pagan symbolic repertoire, for although Scandinavian animal ornament was adopted, the cremation and interment of animals at cemeteries, as well as the use of predatory imagery on monumental sculpture in the northern counties and the Isle of Man, was localised and short-lived. The incomers eventually adopted Christianity, and when

England fell under the political hegemony of Denmark in 1017, both were Christian kingdoms. The use of animals in both regions in ritual, magic and art continued, perhaps with little change in form, but there is no evidence for a devotional link to pagan deities, and the symbolic repertoire used to organise and explain this world, and the next, had been completely transformed.

References

Anon. (2002) Sutton Hoo before Raedwald, *Current Archaeology* 180: 498–505

Axboe, M., Düwel, K., Hauck, K. and Von Padberg, L. (1985–89) *Die Goldbrakteaten der Völkerwanderungszeit. Ikonographische Katalog 1–3*. Münstersche Mittelalterschriften 24/1,1–3,2. Munich: Wilhem Fink

Aybes, C. and Yalden, D.W. (1995) Place-Name Evidence for the Former Distribution and Status of Wolves and Beavers in Britain, *Mammal Review* 25/4: 201–227

Bachrach, B.S. (2001) *Early Carolingian Warfare: Prelude to Empire*, Philadelphia: University of Pennsylvania Press

Barrett, J.H. (2003) Christian and Pagan Practices during the Conversion of Viking Age Orkney and Shetland. *In* M. Carver (ed) *The Cross Goes North*, 207–226. Woodbridge: Boydell

Barrett, J.H. Locker, A.M. and Roberts, C.M. (2004) Dark Age Economics Revisted: The English Fish Bone Evidence AD 600–1600, *Antiquity* 78(301): 618–636

Bazelmans, J. (1999) *By Weapons Made Worthy. Lords, Retainers and their Relationship in Beowulf*, Amsterdam: Amsterdam University Press

Belting, H. (1990) *The Image and its Public in the Middle Ages*, New Rochelle: Ad Caratzas

Bersu, G. and Wilson, D.M. (1966) *Three Viking Graves in the Isle of Man*, London: Society for Medieval Archaeology

Bond, J.M. (1996) Burnt Offerings: Animal Bone in Anglo-Saxon Cremations, *World Archaeology* 28(1): 76–88

Bond, J.M. (2005) The Cremated Animal Bone from Mounds 5, 6 and 7. *In* A.E. Evans, Seventh Century assemblages. *In* M. Carver (ed.) *Sutton Hoo: A Seventh-Century Princely Burial Ground and its Context*, 275–280, London: British Museum Press

Bond, J.M. and Worley, F.L. (2006) Companions in Death: the Roles of Animals in Anglo-Saxon and Viking Cremation Rituals in Britain. *In* R. Gowland and C. Knüsel (eds). *The Social Archaeology of Funerary Remains*, 89–90, Oxford: Oxbow Books

Branston, B. (1974) *The Lost Gods of England*, London: Thames & Hudson

Breen, G. (1999) *The Berserker in Old Norse and Icelandic Literature*, Unpublished Ph.D. thesis, University of Cambridge

Bruce-Mitford, R.L.S. (1978) *The Sutton Hoo Ship-Burial Vol. 2. Arms, Armour and Regalia*, London: British Museum Publications Ltd

Carver, M.O.H. (1998) *Sutton Hoo: Burial Ground of Kings?* Philadelphia: University of Pennsylvania Press

Carver, M.O.H. (2005) *A Seventh-Century Princely Burial Ground and its Context*, Society of Antiquaries Research Report 69. London: the British Museum Press

Crabtree, P. (1989) Sheep, Horses, Swine and Kine: A Zooarchaeological Perspective on the Anglo-Saxon Settlement of England, *Journal of Field Archaeology* 16: 205–13

Crabtree, P. (1995) The Symbolic Role of Animals in Anglo-Saxon England: Evidence from Burials and Cremations. *In* K. Ryan and P. Crabtree (eds), *The Symbolic Role of Animals in Archaeology*, 21–26, Philadelphia: University of Pennsylvania; Masca

Dark, P. (2000) *The Environment of Britain in the First Millennium AD*, London: Duckworth

Davidson, H.R.E. (1962) *The Sword in Anglo-Saxon England*, Woodbridge: Boydell

Dickinson, T. (2002) Translating Animal Art. Salin's Style I and Anglo-Saxon Cast Saucer Brooches, *Hikuin* 29: 163–86

Dickinson, T.M. (2005) Symbols of Protection: The Significance of Animal-Ornamented Shields in Early Anglo-Saxon England, *Medieval Archaeology* 49: 109–163

Dickinson, T.M. (Forthcoming A) Medium and Message: Some Observations on the Contexts of Salin's Style I in England. *In* L. Webster, H. Hamerow and S. Crawford (eds) *Shaping Understanding: Form and Order in the Anglo-Saxon World, 400–1100. Anglo-Saxon Studies in Archaeology and History 15*. Oxford: Oxford University School of Archaeology

Dickinson, T.M. (Forthcoming B) Iconography, Social Context and Ideology: the Meaning of Animal-Ornamented Shields in Early Anglo-Saxon England. *In* L.W. Heizmann (ed) *Die Goldbrakteaten der Völkerwanderungszeit 4,2: interdisziplinäre Auswertung*. Reallexikon der germanischen Altertumskunde, Ergänzungsband. Berlin/New York: De Gruyter.

Dickinson, T.M. and Härke, H. (1992) *Early Anglo-Saxon Shields*, Archaeologia 110. London: Society of Antiquaries of London

Dobat, A. (2006) The King and his Cult, *Antiquity* 80: 880–893

Dobney, K. Jaques, D. Barrett, J. and Cluny J. (2007) *Farmers, Monks and Aristocrats: The Environmental Archaeology of Anglo-Saxon Flixborough*, Oxford: Oxbow Books

Dowden, K. (2000) *European Paganism: The Realities of Cult from Antiquity to the Middle Ages*. London: Routledge

Eliade, M. (1989) *Shamanism: Archaic Techniques of Ecstasy*, London: Arkana

Engström, J. (1997) The Vendel Chieftains: A Study of Military Tactics. *In* A.N. Jorgensen and B.L. Clausen (eds) *Military aspects of Scandinavian Society in a European Perspective, AD 1–1300*, 248–255, Copenhagen: National Museum

Fell, C.E. (1995) Paganism in *Beowulf*: A Semantic Fairy-Tale. *In* T. Hofstra, L.A.J.R Houwen, and A.A. Macdonald (eds) *Pagans and Christians: The Interplay Between Christian Latin and Traditional Germanic Cultures in Early Medieval Europe*, 9–34, Groningen: Egbert Forsten

Filotas, B. (2005) *Pagan Survivals, Superstitions and Popular Culture in Early Medieval Pastoral Literature*, Toronto: Pontifical institute of Mediaeval Studies

Gannon, A. (2003) *The Iconography of Early Anglo-Saxon Coinage: Sixth to Eighth Centuries*, Oxford: Oxford University Press

Glosecki, S.O. (1989) *Shamanism and Old English Poetry*, Garland: New York

Glosecki, S.O. (2000) Movable Beasts: The Manifold Implications of Early Germanic Animal Imagery. *In* N.C. Flores (ed) *Animals in the Middle Ages*, 3–23, New York: Routledge

Gräslund, A-S. (2004) Dogs in Graves – A Question of Symbolism? *In* Frizell, B.S. (ed) *Man and Animal in Antiquity*, 167–76, Rome: The Swedish Institute

Grundy, S.S. (1995) The Cult of Odin: God of Death? Unpublished Ph.D. Thesis, University of Cambridge

Härke, H. (1997a) Early Anglo-Saxon Military Organisation: An Archaeological Perspective. *In* A.N. Jørgensen and B.L. Clausen (eds) *Military Aspects of Scandinavian Society in a European Perspective, AD 1–1300*, 93–101, Copenhagen: National Museum

Härke, H. (1997b) Material Culture as Myth: Weapons in Anglo-Saxon Graves. *In* C. Kjeld Jensen and K. Høilund Nielsen (eds), *Burial & Society. The Chronological and Social Analysis of Archaeological Burial Data*, 119–127, Århus: Århus University Press

Haseloff, G. (1981) *Die germanische Tierornamentik der Völkerwanderungszeit*. Vorgeschichtliche Forschungen 17,1–3. Berlin/New York: De Gruyter

Hawkes, J. (1997) Symbolic Lives: The Visual Evidence. *In* Hines, J. (ed.), *The Anglo-Saxons from the Migration Period To the Eighth Century. An Ethnographic Perspective*. Studies in Historical Archaeoethnology 2, 311–338, San Marino/Woodbridge: The Boydell Press

Hedeager, L. (1998) Cosmological Endurance: Pagan Identities in Early Christian Europe, *European Journal of Archaeology* 1(3): 382–396

Hedeager, L. (1999) Myth and Art: A Passport to Political Authority in Scandinavia during the Migration Period. *In* Dickinson, T. and Griffiths, D. (eds) *The Making of Kingdoms: Anglo-Saxon Studies in Archaeology and History, 10,* 154–156, Oxford: Oxford University School of Archaeology:

Hedeager, L. (2000) Migration Period Europe: The Formation of a Political Mentality. *In* F. Theuws and J.L. Nelson (eds), *Rituals of Power from Late Antiquity to the Early Middle Ages,* (15–57,) Leiden: Brill

Hedeager, L. (2003) Beyond Mortality – Scandinavian Animal Style AD 400–1200. *In* J. Downes, and A. Ritchie (eds) *Sea Change: Orkney and Northern Europe in the Later Iron Age AD 300–800,* 127–136, Balgavies: Pinkfoot Press

Hedeager, L. (2005) Scandinavia. *In* P. Fouracre (ed), *The New Cambridge Medieval History Vol. I c.500–c.700,* 496–523, Cambridge: Cambridge University Press

Hicks, C. (1993) *Animals in Early Medieval Art,* Edinburgh: Edinburgh University Press

Higham, N.J. (1997) *The Convert Kings: Power and Religious Affiliation in Early Anglo-Saxon England,* Manchester: Manchester University Press

Hines, J. (1997) Religion: The Limits of Knowledge. *In* Hines, J. (ed.), *The Anglo-Saxons from the Migration Period to the Eighth Century. An Ethnographic Perspective.* Studies in Historical Archaeoethnology 2, (375–410,) San Marino/Woodbridge: The Boydell Press

Hinton, D.A. (2005) *Gold and Gilt, Pots and Pins: Possessions and People in Medieval Britain,* Oxford: Oxford University Press

Høilund Nielsen, K. (1997) Animal Art and the Weapon-Burial Rite. *In* Jensen, C.K. and Høilund Nielsen, K. (eds), *Burial & Society. The Chronological and Social Analysis of Archaeological Burial Data,* 129–48, Århus: Århus University Press

Høilund Nielsen, K. (1998) Animal Style – A Symbol of Might and Myth: Salin's Style II in a European Context, *Acta Archaeologica* 69: 1–52

Høilund Nielsen, K. (1999) Style II and the Anglo-Saxon Elite. *In* Dickinson, T. and Griffiths, D. (eds), *The Making of Kingdoms. Anglo-Saxon Studies in Archaeology and History 10,* 85–202, Oxford: Oxford University School of Archaeology

Høilund Nielsen, K. (2001) The Wolf-Warrior – Animal Symbolism and Weaponry of the 6th and 7th Centuries. *In* E. Pohl, U. Becker and C. Theune (eds), *Archäologisches Zellwerk. Beiträge zur Kulturgeschichte in Europa und Asien: festschrift für Helmut Roth zum 60. Geburtstag,* 471–81, Rahden: Verlag Marie Leidorf Gmbh

Høilund Nielsen, K. and Kristoffersen, S. (2002) Germansk dyrestil (Salins stil I-III): et historisk perspektiv, *Hikuin* 29: 15–74 (English Summary at 301–2)

Hooke, D. (1998) *The Landscape of Anglo-Saxon England,* Leicester: Leicester University Press.

Hutton, R. (1993) *The Pagan Religions of the Ancient British Isles: Their Nature and Legacy,* Oxford: Blackwell

Jesch, J. (2002) Eagles, Ravens and Wolves: Beasts of Battle, Symbols of Victory and Death. *In* J. Jesch (ed) *The Scandinavians from the Vendel Period to the Tenth Century: An Ethnographic Perspective,* 251–280, Woodbridge: Boydell

Johnson, D.F. (1995) Euhemerisation Versus Demonisation: The Pagan Gods and Ælfric's *De Falsis Diis.* *In* T. Hofstra, L.A.J.R. Houwen. and A.A. Macdonald (eds) *Pagans and Christians: The Interplay Between Christian Latin and Traditional Germanic Cultures in Early Medieval Europe,* 35–70. Groningen: Egbert Forsten

Jolly, K. (1993) Father God and Mother Earth: Nature-Mysticism in the Anglo-Saxon World. *In* J.E. Salisbury (ed) *The Medieval World of Nature,* 221–252, New York: Garland

Kristoffersen, S. (2000) *Sverd og spenne: dyreornamentik og sosial kontekst,* Studia humanitatis Bergensia 13. Kristiansand: Høyskoleforlaget

Lamm, J.-P., Hydman, H., Axboe, M., Hauck, K., Beck, H., Behr, C. and Pesch, A. (2000) "Der Brakteat des Jahrhunderts". Über den Einzigartigen zehnten Brakteaten aus Söderby in der

Gemeinde Danmark, Uppland. Ikonologie LVIII, *Frühmittelalterliche Studien* 34: 1–93

Leigh, D. (1980) The Square-Headed Brooches of Sixth-Century Kent. Unpublished PhD Thesis, Department of Archaeology, University College: Cardiff

Leigh, D. (1984) Ambiguity in Anglo-Saxon Style I, *Antiquaries Journal* 64: 34–42

Lindström, T.C. and Kristoffersen, S. (2001) "Figure It Out!" Psychological Perspectives on Perception of Migration Period Animal Art, *Norwegian Archaeological Review* 34: 65–84

Lionarons, J.T. (1998) *The Medieval Dragon: The Nature of the Beast in Germanic Literature*, Enfield Lock, Middx

Lucy, S. (2000) *The Anglo-Saxon Way of Death: Burial Rites in Early England*, Sutton: Stroud

Magnus, B. (2001) The Enigmatic Brooches. *In* B. Magnus (ed), *Roman Gold and the Development of the Early Germanic Kingdoms.* Konferenser 51. Stockholm, 279–96 Kungl., Vitterhets historie och antikvitetsakademien

Magnus, B. (2003) Krigerens insignier: en parafrase over gravene II og V fra Snartemo i Vest-agder. *In* P. Rolfsen and F.-A. Stylegar (eds), *Snartemofunnene i nytt lys,* 33-52 Oslo, Universitetets kulturhistoriske museer

Matthews, K.R. (2000) Reading Romanesque Sculpture: The Iconography and Reception of the South Portal Sculpture at Santiago De Compostela, *Gesta* 39/1: 3–12

Meaney, A. (1981) *Anglo-Saxon Amulets and Curing Stones*, BAR British Series 96, Oxford

Moreland, J. (2000) Ethnicity, Power and the English. *In* W.O. Frazer and A. Tyrrell (eds) *Social Identity in Early Medieval Britain*, 23–51, London: Leicester University Press

Newton, S. (1993) *The Origins of Beowulf and the Pre-Viking Kingdom of East Anglia*, Cambridge: D.S. Brewer

North, R. (1997a) *Heathen Gods in Old English Literature*, Cambridge: Cambridge University Press

North, R. (1997b) *The Haustlöng of Þjóðólfr of Hvinir*, Enfield Lock, Middx., Hisarlik Press

O'Connor, S. (1998) The Boar Tusk Buckle. *In* G. Drinkall and M. Foreman (eds) *The Anglo-Saxon Cemetery at Castledyke South, Barton-on-Humber*, 272–3, Sheffield: Sheffield Academic Press

Owen-Crocker, G.R. (1998) The Search For Anglo-Saxon Skin Garments and the Documentary Evidence. *In* E. Cameron (ed) *Leather and Fur: Aspects of Early Medieval Trade and Technology,* 27–43, London: Archetype for the Archaeological Leather Group

Pluskowski, A.G. (2004) Lupine Apocalypse: The Wolf in Pagan and Christian Cosmology in Medieval Britain and Scandinavia, *Cosmos* 17: 113–131

Pluskowski, A.G. (2006a) *Wolves and Wilderness in the Middle Ages*, Woodbridge: Boydell

Pluskowski, A.G. (2006b) Harnessing the Hunger: Religious Appropriations of Animal Predation in Early Medieval Scandinavia. *In* A. Andrén *et al.* (eds) *Old Norse Religion in Long-Term Perspectives,* 119–123, Lund: Nordic Academic Press

Price, N.S. (2002) *The Viking Way: Religion and War in Late Iron Age Scandinavia*, Uppsala University, Dept. of Archaeology and Ancient History: Uppsala

Rackham, O. (1994) Trees and Woodland in Anglo-Saxon England: The Documentary Evidence. *In* J. Rackham (ed.) *Environment and Economy in Anglo-Saxon England*, 7–11, York, CBA

Randsborg, K. (1995) *Hjortspring. Warfare and Sacrifice in Early Europe*, Aarhus: Aarhus University Press

Reynolds, A. (1998) Anglo-Saxon Law in the Landscape. Unpublished PhD Thesis, Institute of Archaeology, University College London

Richards, J.D. (1992) Anglo-Saxon Symbolism. *In* M. Carver (ed.) *The Age of Sutton Hoo: The Seventh Century in North-Western Europe*, 131–47, Woodbridge: Boydell

Richards, J.D. (2004) *Viking Age England*, Stroud: Tempus

Rollason, D. (2003) *Northumbria, 500–1100, Creation and Destruction of A Kingdom*, Cambridge: University Press

Salin, B. (1904) *Die altergermanische Tierornamentik*, Stockholm: Asher

Salin, E. (1959) *La civilisation mérovingienne d'après les sépultures, les textes et la laboratoire*, 4 Volumes, Paris

Salisbury, J.E. (1994) *The Beast Within: Animals in the Middle Ages*, New York: Routledge

Schmidt, G.D. (1995) *The Iconography of the Mouth of Hell: Eighth-Century Britain to the Fifteenth Century*, London: Associated University Presses

Schutz, H. (2001) *Tools, Weapons and Ornaments: Germanic Material Culture in Pre-Carolingian Central Europe, 400–750*, Leiden: Brill

Semple, S. (1998) A Fear of the Past: The Place of the Prehistoric Burial Mount in the Ideology of Middle and Later Anglo-Saxon England, *World Archaeology* 30(1): 109–126

Speake, G. (1980) *Anglo-Saxon Animal Art and its Germanic Background*, Oxford: Clarendon Press

Stephenson, I.P. (2002) *The Anglo-Saxon Shield*, Tempus: Stroud

Stoodley, N. (1999) *The Spindle and the Spear: A Critical Enquiry into the Construction and Meaning of Gender in the Early Anglo-Saxon Burial Rite*, BAR British Series 288, Oxford

Sykes, N.J. (2001) The Norman Conquest: A Zooarchaeological Perspective, Unpublished PhD Thesis, Department of Archaeology, University of Southampton, Southampton

Thompson, V. (2004) *Dying and Death in Later Anglo-Saxon England*, Woodbridge: Boydell

Wicker, N.L. (2003) The Scandinavian Animal Styles in Response To Mediterranean and Christian Narrative Art. *In* M. Carver (ed) *The Cross Goes North*, 531–550, Woodbridge: Boydell

Williams, H. (2005) Animals, Ashes and Ancestors. *In* A.G. Pluskowski (ed.) *Just Skin and Bones? New Perspectives on Human-Animal Relations in the Historical Past*, 19–40, BAR International Series 1410, Oxford

Yalden, D. (1999) *The History of British Mammals*, London: Poyser

Chapter 7

Horses in Mind

Chris Fern

Introduction

The use of animal symbolism and ritual to convey ideology, and notions of cosmology, is well attested in cultures, past and present (Pluskowski 2007; this vol.). In the Germanic Migration Period (AD 400–550), animal art and related mythologies are believed to have played a leading role in the ordering of society, by encapsulating knowledge of gods, ancestors and the supernatural world (Høilund Nielsen 1997; 1998; Gaimster 1998; Hedeager 2000; Dickinson 2005). In the early Anglo-Saxon mind the horse stands out as a motif with socio-political, heroic and spiritual significance. There is evidence for sacrifice in burial grounds, representation on artefacts, and the citation of human-horse ancestors in the foundation myths of kingdoms and the genealogies of kings. It is argued here that horse symbolism and ritual was a major ingredient of pre-Christian Anglo-Saxon belief and cult.

Both the written and archaeological sources make manifest the value of horses in secular society. For the period following the 7th-century conversion, Christian texts show a strong association between equestrianism and warleaders, with a *topos* of kings as givers of horses (and weaponry) to loyal 'hero' figures. They also allude to the specifically high value of stallions, whose worth was emphasised by the decoration of their harness, using precious materials. The horse-burial evidence of the preceding period (AD 450–600) reinforces this association between 'warriors', elaborate harness and male steeds (Fern 2005; 2007).

These themes are married in the foremost Anglo-Saxon legend of Hengist (stallion) and Horsa (horse/gelding). Their embodiments, it is suggested, can be understood as characterisations of the concept of a warhorse-mounted warleader, with half-human and half-horse connotations. As the most famous brothers and warriors of the age, their story represents an origin myth for the Anglo-Saxons that probably had its source in oral traditions of the Migration Period (Moisl 1981: 232ff.; Brooks 1989: 58ff.; Yorke 1993). Within this early 5th- to 6th-century context, this animal-named doublet may be paralleled by the 'animal-men' and double-horse motifs found in the animal art of the period.

Whilst literary evidence provides only limited verification for the existence of a 'Hengist and Horsa cult', archaeological and art historical sources demonstrate a considerable zeal for horse beliefs: the animal stands out as a motif in burial rites, and equine iconography is demonstrably widespread on brooches and pottery. The inspiration for much of this imagery and mythology is traceable to the Germanic north Continent and south Scandinavia. Within this wider European context, horse ideologies have been linked to shamanistic beliefs, with the animal viewed as a guardian spirit and mode of transport to the afterlife (Williams 2001: 204). Hence, Anglo-Saxon horse beliefs, whilst demonstrating notable insular traits, need also to be viewed as part of a wider pan-Germanic cosmological belief-system.

Ultimately, the disappearance of horse rituals from Anglo-Saxon England and beyond is argued to reflect their incompatibility with Late Antique Christian philosophy, and the prohibition of animal sacrifice by Imperial Edict in the late 4th century (Gilhus 2006: 160). Fundamental mythological and ideological vestiges of pre-Christian beliefs, as attested by the Hengist and Horsa legend, survived to be recorded in 8th-century Anglo-Saxon England, but as the result of church influence, they emerged sober and reticent.

Horse ideology – the prehistoric and Roman periods

Horse ideologies were not unique to Germanic cultures, but are attested in the archaeological and historical record amongst Indo-European peoples from the Neolithic (Bökönyi 1974: 230ff.; Kuzmina 2006; Olsen *et al.* 2006). A famous literary episode from the ensuing Bronze Age is that in *The Iliad* (23: 170), usually dated to the 8th century BC, of the four-horse sacrifice at the Mycenaean funeral of Patrocolus. But perhaps the best known of such offerings are those of the 10th- to 4th-century BC Scythian-Siberian peoples, the grandest of whose tombs contain many dozens of horses (Talbot Rice 1957: 69ff.).

Horse culture and ritual remained prevalent across the Asian Steppe into the medieval period, in the form of tribal horse-borne nomads. Chief amongst these were the Sarmatians, Huns, Avars and Hungarians, who made successive incursions into the Carpathian Basin throughout the first-millennium AD (Bálint 1982; Kiss 2001; Bóna 2002). The essential importance of equestrianism to the Huns was noted by a number of Roman commentators, with Ammianus Marcellinus observing that they were "almost glued to their horses", as if half-man and half-horse (Thompson 1996: 57). It is very likely that European Celtic and Germanic horse ritual and art was influenced by the traditions of these eastern peoples, for whom horse culture was integral to their famous military and political successes. A number of horse-riding technologies certainly came to the west via contact with such groups, including in the early medieval period the Steppe saddle, stirrup and *caftan* riding coat (László 1943; Seaby and Woodfield 1980, 88ff.; Walton Rogers 2007: 210ff.).

According to Tacitus, funerary horse sacrifice and divination was practised by 1st-century AD Germanic Rhineland tribes (*Germania* 10, 27; Benario 1999: 22–5, 38–9). But for the Romans too there is evidence for horse beliefs, in the form of the Gallo-Roman goddess Epona, especially popular with cavalry units of the Western Empire

(Oaks 1986). In addition, horse offerings were also an aspect of Scandinavian tribal culture, with evidence for a continuous tradition, dating from the Bronze Age to the Viking era (Müller-Wille 1970/71: Abb. 43).

In England, occasional horse burials in both cemetery and settlement contexts are a feature of the Iron Age and pre-Christian Roman periods (Collins 1952/3: 39; Barber and Bowsher 2000: 20, fig. 16). Moreover, the recent scientific dating of the famous chalk horse carved into the hillside at Uffington, Wiltshire, has shown that equine representation was already important in the late Bronze Age/early Iron Age (Miles *et al.* 2004: 75ff.).

It is the horse's special status, gained through its enduring social and functional interaction with humans, which lies at the root of such beliefs (Olsen 2006; Kuzmina 2006). It is not the only such animal with a long history of human domestication, however, unlike the dog, the economic demands of stabling, coupled with the animal's intimate association with warfare, hunting and journeying, served from an early period in Europe to equate horsemanship with high status and political ascendancy. In Roman society this was given expression in the social institution of the *eques Romanus* (cavalryman), a title of nobility (Birley 1988: 20, 57ff.; Dixon and Southern 1992: 20, 24). Indeed, Classical commentators believed the horse to be an intelligent, faithful and noble beast, reserved for war. And it was on this basis that Roman culture reviled horse meat (Arbogast *et al.* 2002: 59ff.).

Buried horses in inhumations, cremations and settlements

Horses were killed to accompany some of the most politically-charged funerals of early medieval Europe. In *c.* AD 482 at Tournai, Belgium, King Childeric was buried with the head of a horse, and his grave surrounded by some twenty sacrificed horses (Müller-Wille 1970/71: 132; 1998). In Sweden too, 'royal' power is suggested by the enormous Västhögen (West Mound) at Gamla Uppsala, with its horse and other animal offerings (Duczko 1996: 82).

From the 5th to 7th centuries, the practice of horse burial was widespread east of the Rhine, including amongst the Alamanni, Bavarians, Lombards, Rhineland Franks, Saxons and Thuringians (Müller-Wille 1970/71: Abb.1–2). A single source of inspiration for the rite in the era seems unlikely, since horse sacrifice had been practiced in both south Scandinavia and *Germania* since at least the Roman period (*Germania* 10, 27; Benario 1999: 22–5, 38–9; Hagberg 1967: 55–60). Nevertheless, a renewed impetus at the start of the period may have been given by the horse funerary customs of the Huns, whose influence had reached Frankia and Scandinavia by the era of Attila's political dominance (Bóna 2002: 100–29; Hedeager 2007).

Oexle's (1984) study of the Continental horse-inhumation rite argued that the animal with its harness represented an economic possession, placed in the grave to reflect the status of the deceased and their family, rather than representing a 'sacrifice' to accompany the dead individual to the spiritual afterlife or sate pagan gods. Support for this secularist viewpoint comes from the early medieval law codes of the Alamanni and Bavarians. These contain clauses that both protect and define an elite equestrian class; they include penalties for injuring or killing quality steeds, and others which assert that rulers be able to fight and command from horseback (Rivers 1977: 77, 90–1, 126–7, 132).

Examples of Anglo-Saxon horse burial includes both the practice of inhuming an animal with the deceased (or in a separate adjacent pit), as well as cremating horse and human together, with the remains usually placed in one or more ceramic urns (Vierck 1970/71; Bond 1996; McKinley 1994: 92ff.; Fern 2007: 97ff.). Several-hundred horse cremations are known, the great majority of which come from just one cemetery, of over 2000 burials, at Spong Hill, Norfolk (Hills 1977; McKinley 1994; Fern 2007: tab. 1). Horse inhumations are rarer, with only thirty-two known examples (Fern 2007: 92). They are also regionally differentiated, with horse cremations largely restricted to a territory reaching from north Norfolk to the Humber Estuary, and inhumations most common in the East Midlands and East Anglia (*ibid.*). Overall, the horse represents the most frequent funerary animal sacrifice.

Typically, as on the Continent (where over 700 examples are known), the Anglo-Saxon horse inhumations accompany adult male burials with weaponry and often prestige artefacts, such as swords and bronze vessels (Figure 7.1; Müller-Wille 1970/71: 124, 140ff.; Fern 2007: 95). The wealthiest examples, like those at Sutton Hoo, mound 17, and Eriswell (104), grave 4116, both in Suffolk, contain gilded horse-harness decorated with animal art (Figure 7.2; Fern 2005: figs 5.1, 5.9). In addition, items of harness have also been found in more ordinary graves, adapted for use as dress-fasteners, or else occur as casual losses, recovered by metal-detectorists (Fern 2005: 46; Dickinson *et al.* 2006). Whilst still relatively rare, these finds attest a widespread elite culture of equestrianism in early Anglo-Saxon England (Fern 2005).

In the inhumation rite, the animals were normally either buried in their harness, or with the horse-equipment placed with the deceased, indicating that they were trained riding animals (Fern 2007: 100). *Contra* Oexle (1984), the burial of a bridled animal would appear to support the theory that the animal had been prepared for a journey to the afterlife.

On the Continent, impressive male animals were typically selected for sacrifice (Müller 1980: 150, Tab. 1). Where analysis has been possible, the majority of the Anglo-Saxon horses too were young adult males, with the Sutton Hoo and Eriswell steeds large in stature by early medieval standards, at around 14 hands (1.44–45m) at the withers (Crabtree 1989: 56ff.; Fern 2005: fig. 5.21). This suggests deliberate selection, yet some horse remains have demonstrated evidence for minor pathological traumas. For example, the Eriswell animal probably had a slight limp, indicating that in this case a physically imperfect (though still visually striking) animal was used (O'Connor unpublished). In addition, a minority were either immature or old, raising the question of their suitability as mounts. Such was the 20–30 year old horse found at Snape, Suffolk, of which only the bridled head was buried, associated with weapon-and-boat grave 47 (Davis 2001; Filmer-Sankey and Pestell 2001: 102–11). Although such animals may have been lame in life, perhaps they were still considered viable as sacrifices, their vital animism remaining intact?

The rite of horse decapitation is again one that is well paralleled east of the Rhine, particularly in Alamannic-Bavarian and Thuringian regions (Kerth 2000: 128; Fern 2007: 101). This act, whilst rendering impossible a physically intact 'mount for the afterlife', evokes a strong sense of the accompanying graveside ritual. Five Anglo-Saxon examples are known, including that at Springfield Lyons, Essex, which had

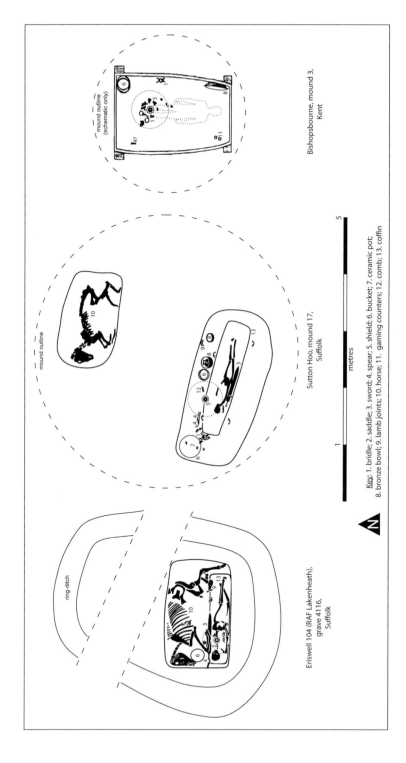

Figure 7.1: Anglo-Saxon horse and bridle burials of the 5th to 7th centuries (redrawn after Wright 1844; Carver 1993; Fern 2005; 2007). Scale 1:67).

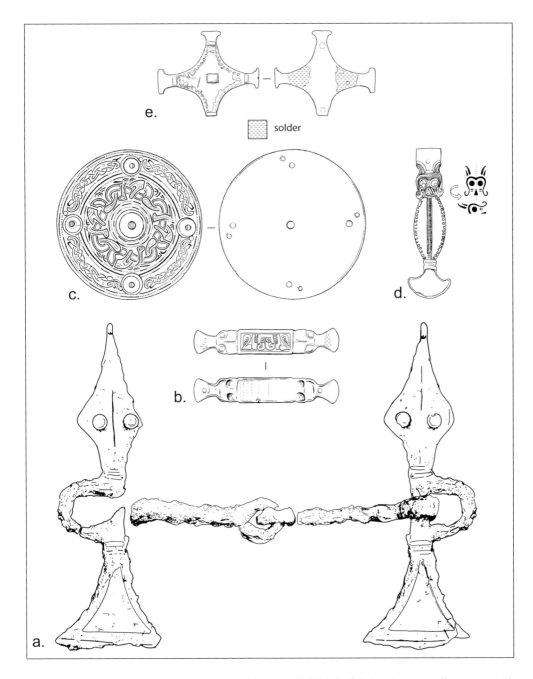

solder

Figure 7.2: Anglo-Saxon horse-harness: a. iron bit, Eriswell 4116, Suffolk; b. gilt copper-alloy mount with Style I ornament, Loxton, Somerset; c. gilt copper-alloy mount with Style II ornament, Allington Hill, Cambridgeshire.; d. gilt copper-alloy mount with Style I ornament, Eriswell 4116; e. gilt copper-alloy mount, Cheesecake Hill, East Yorkshire (after Fern 2005. Scale 1:2).

been buried without any obviously associated human burial (Tyler and Major 2005: 31, fig. 22; Fern 2007: 96, 100).

In comparison to the inhumation rite, Anglo-Saxon horse cremations occur with both adult males and females in broadly equal numbers, and occasionally with children (McKinley 1994: tab. 2; Fern 2007: 99). High-status artefacts, including bronze and glass vessels, and gaming counters, occur with around a third of this demographic, confirming an above-average social standing for a proportion of those cremated with horses (Fern 2007: 100). In addition, a small but significant sub-group of 5th- to 6th-century cremations, found to contain sword and scabbard fittings, may represent a martial elite of the status of Eriswell 4116, hinting at a broadly equivalent equestrian class in both inhuming and cremating societies (Hills 1998: 152–3). However, no definite evidence for harness has been forthcoming from the cremation corpus so far, and hence it is unclear if the majority of the sacrifices were of trained riding animals or perhaps less valuable draft horses (Crabtree 1989: 95; Bond 1994: 124; Fern 2007: 100). Nevertheless, the horse is marked out by its treatment in the rite, for unlike the meat offerings represented by sheep and pig remains, horses (and dogs) were included as whole adult individuals, and hence must instead signify 'companion' animals (Bond 1994).

The large number of horse cremations from England is so far unparalleled in the 'ancestral homelands' of the Anglo-Saxons, with only small numbers recorded for Migration Period cemeteries in Jutland, Lower Saxony and Schleswig-Holstein (Fern 2007: 101, tab. 1). Evidence that the horse burials are not those of north Germanic incomers, but of a settled (perhaps second or third generation) local population is inferred at Spong Hill; horse cremations predominate in areas of the burial ground associated with locally inspired, stamp-decorated, ceramics and away from the central area of first-generation 'immigrant' burial (*ibid.* 99). This suggests that in the horse-cremating region, by the 6th century, a distinctly insular horse ideology had developed, with up to around ten per cent of the population being treated in this funerary tradition (*ibid.*).

By the late 6th to 7th century in England, the act of inhuming or cremating horses with the dead had become a rare and exclusively elite mode of burial (Hills 1998: 151; Carver and Fern 2005: 289; Fern 2007: tab. 2). We see this most clearly at the 'royal' cemetery of Sutton Hoo, with its multiple horse sacrifices (Figure 7.3; Carver and Fern 2005). The cemetery is of course most famous for its ship burials, but this custom too may have alluded to horse culture; in Anglo-Saxon poetry, ships could be described as *sund-hengesta* (sea-stallion) and *yð-mēares* (wave-steed) (Collins 1959: 1).

The combination of a warhorse and harness, weaponry and prestige goods, in horse burials may be argued to reproduce the Continental creed; the model image of a mounted 'Hengist' warleader, with connotations for a secular-equivalent spiritual status in the afterlife. However, the killing of healthy and valuable animals for inclusion in human burial grounds – the setting for highly emotive rites of passage, ultimately concerned with the translation of the dead to the afterlife of the ancestors – also asserts a link with religious belief and cosmology (Härke 2001: 13). Further support for this argument is the evidence for food offerings, which the pre-Christian Anglo-Saxons placed with both their buried and cremated dead, that were very probably intended as rations for the deceased's 'spiritual' journey (for example, lamb

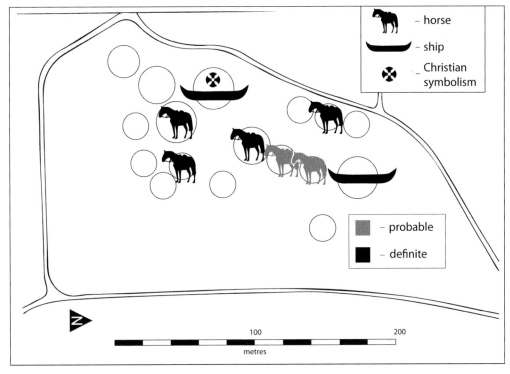

Figure 7.3: Funerary symbolism at Sutton Hoo, Suffolk (redrawn after Carver 2005).

cuts were included in both the Sutton Hoo and Eriswell burials (Figure 7.1; Carver 2005: 245–6, no. 17).

There are also a small number of buried horses, both whole and decapitated, from settlements; including Mucking, Essex, West Heslerton, North Yorkshire, and Sutton Courtenay, Berkshire (Hamerow 2006; tab. 1; Powlesland pers. comm.). Archaeological studies of such remains have emphasised the intrinsically ritual character of these non-economic sacrifices, which represent deliberately structured events, located in purposeful spaces and intended to achieve specific ends (Hill 1996; Hamerow 2006). It has been suggested that such 'special deposits', which also include burials of human infants and dogs in or near buildings, were intended to either protect the settlement or dwelling, or were offered as part of a 'termination' ceremony linked to its abandonment (Hamerow 2006: 26ff.).

Horses in art

The Germanic animal arts of the period have been studied for their chronological development, faunal detail and cosmological significance (Speake 1980; Hawkes 1997; Høilund Nielsen 1998; 1999; Gaimster 1998; Hedeager 2000). Boars, dragons, eagles, fish, ravens, wolves and serpents have all been suggested for the Anglo-Saxon corpus, but horses less so, yet they are a demonstrable component of Scandinavian art of the period (Olsén 1945; Bruce-Mitford 1978: 88, 524; Speake 1980: 77ff.; Hawkes 1997; Høilund Nielsen 2002; Dickinson 2005). In Anglo-Saxon England, animal art is divided into Style I (*c.* 475–575) and Style II (*c.* 550–650), both of which originated in south Scandinavia (Haseloff 1974; 1984; Høilund Nielsen 1998). By the 7th century, animal-decorated weaponry, horse-harness and jewellery had become the preserve of elites, the monopolisation of its imagery arguing for its function as a legitimising force for political, socio-economic and ideological dominance (Earle 1990; DeMarrais, Castillo and Earle 1996).

Interpreting the meaning of animal art is crucial to understanding the role it played, in terms of belief and social display, and when used on elite objects how it influenced socio-political relations (Høilund Nielsen 1997). Detailed readings have been made of the Germanic religious content of figural Scandinavian bracteate art (Hauck 1972; Gaimster 1998), but the abstract aesthetic of most animal art has proved an obstacle to 'translating' its narrative. Yet, far from representing a loss of meaning, abstraction and schematisation should be recognised as the cultural encoding of motifs, well understood to their intended contemporary audience (Morphy 1989: 2). Hence, the stylisation of Germanic animal art may have been a deliberate strategy, designed to restrict access to its narrative, the interpretation of which brought psychological enlightenment to its 'learned' viewer (Leigh 1984: 40; Hawkes 1997: 333; Lindstrøm and Kristoffersen 2001). Very probably the art's intended references were to the gods and mythologies of pan-Germanic Europe (Hedeager 2000). In this sense, its departure from the naturalistic aims of Christian Mediterranean art, from which many of its models were ultimately drawn, may also have been a conscious act, creating an aesthetic that was distinctly non-Christian (Wicker 2003).

Recurrent in Style I are motifs of *Tiermenschen* (animal-men), depictions of four-legged animals with human helmeted-heads and limbs, which can be 'read' following rotation

Figure 7.4: Horses and 'animal-men' a. brooch motif, Bifrons, Kent; b. horse profile stamps used on pottery urns (redrawn after: a. Leigh 1984; b. Hills 1983. Not to scale).

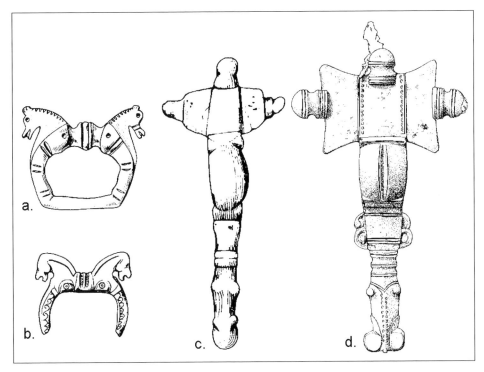

Figure 7.5: Horse iconography on buckles and cruciform brooches: a. Alwalton, Huntingdonshire; b. Clipsham, Rutland; c. Wakerley, Northamptonshire. d. Spong Hill, Norfolk (a. & b. after Hawkes and Dunning 1961. © Reproduced with the permission of the Society for Medieval Archaeology, www. maney.co.uk/journals/ma; c. after Adams and Jackson 1988/89 © Reproduced with the permission of the Northamptonshire Archaeology Society; d. after Hills et al. 1984. © Copyright Norfolk Museums and Archaeology Service, EAA 21. fig. 79. Scale 1:1, a.-c.; 2:3, d).

and mirroring (Figure 7.4a; Haseloff 1974: 9, 13; Leigh 1984: 39). The transformation of the image by the observer serves to animate the static pattern and gives the object an animism of its own. It is possible that this was the intended aim, bringing the viewer into an interactive relationship with the art's mythological narrative and its metamorphic performance (Lindstrøm and Kristoffersen 2001). As such, objects bearing such motifs may have played a sacred role in the religious beliefs and ceremonies of the communities that made and used them. Significantly, in this early context, such Anglo-Saxon animal-men may be argued to offer a parallel for the Hengist and Horsa identities (see below). Coupled with which, is the considerable evidence for the use of a double-horse motif.

Our earliest evidence for this comprises moulded ornament on bronze buckles and brooches, datable to the late and post-Roman periods (Figure 7.5). The buckles, manufactured in Britain between the late 4th and mid-5th centuries, are characterised by pairs of horse-heads, executed to varying degrees of naturalism, and occasionally with harness detail (Type 1b: Hawkes and Dunning 1961: fig. 15). These buckles are insular products, but their motif inspiration probably draws on double-horse imagery employed on Germanic metalwork from the Roman Rhine frontier, south Scandinavia and Frankia. One such is that which decorates the 'vandyke' mounts of a small 4th- or 5th-century bucket from Giberville, France (Figure 7.6g). There are problems with uncritically identifying the buckles from Britain as the badges of mercenary Germanic *foederati* however, as their distribution may instead suggest the accoutrements of indigenous militias (Leahy 2007). Nevertheless, they are a clear manifestation of horse symbolism in a military context at this period of interface between Roman and 'barbarian' identities.

A strong degree of cultural melding is also apparent in the form of the cruciform brooch, a Germanic (Anglian) hybridisation of the Roman cross-bow brooch, to which crucially was added a horse-head foot-plate (Åberg 1926: 33–56; Richards 1992: 139; Bode 1998). In England, the brooch type was introduced from north Germany or south Scandinavia in the early 5th century, and was subsequently produced in large numbers, with a distribution from Kent to Yorkshire (Figure 7.5c–d). The elongated horse-head is heavily stylised, with prominent eyes and exaggerated flared or 'scrolled' nostrils. This last detail, in particular, supports an equine identification, in the context of the comments of a 4th-century Roman veterinarian, who cited 'open nostrils' as one of the ideal characteristics of a horse (Hyland 1990: 6). This motif is also interesting in view of the Anglo-Saxon practice of slitting horses' nostrils (see below), which may have been thought to assist breathing and improve performance. Unlike in the Continental homelands, where a single brooch was worn, in Anglo-Saxon England the brooches were typically worn in pairs at the shoulders. In part this was due to their use for fastening a peplos-type costume, although this doubling of cruciform brooches may have served also as an evocation of a 'Hengist and Horsa' type motif.

Figure 7.6 shows how the motif of a pair of horses can be identified repeatedly in the animal art corpus of England and Europe. It illustrates how it was ultimately derived from an observation of stallion combat, progressing through stages of increasing stylisation, to a finality of cultural encoding (it is not in chronological order). Such is the extent of the abstraction of the Figure 7.6e motif, that it would be as unrecognisable as the majority of Style I species, were it not for our understanding of that expressed on the brooch from Apple Down, West Sussex (Figure 7.6d).

In a naturalistic form this confronted-horses icon occurs on Scandinavian picture stones, such as that from Häggeby (Uppland), Sweden, the likely model for which was stallion duelling (Figure 7.6a–b; Hagberg 1967: 81; Nylén 1980/2: fig. 10). In the wild, stallions will fight for the control of herds of mares and foals. Also, it has been suggested, in this and earlier periods the deliberate baiting of horses for sport may have taken place, perhaps in the context of religious rituals (Hagberg 1967: 81).

In Anglo-Saxon England, the motif figures prominently on an early series of Style I square-headed brooches found in Kent, or in 'Kentish' cultural areas. One of the clearest examples is that from the Apple Down cemetery, which shows two animals rearing at each other on the head-plate of an early 6th-century brooch, the hind-leg of each creature shown dislocated and bent back against its neck (Figure 7.6d; Down and Welch 1990: 95, fig. 2.21). Another occurs on a typologically related brooch from Bifrons, Kent, this time showing a horse galloping down each of the brooch's opposite sides (Figure 7.4a: Hawkes 2000: fig. 27). The motifs display varying degrees of equine morphology, including pointed ears, flared nostrils, tails, extended necks, manes and

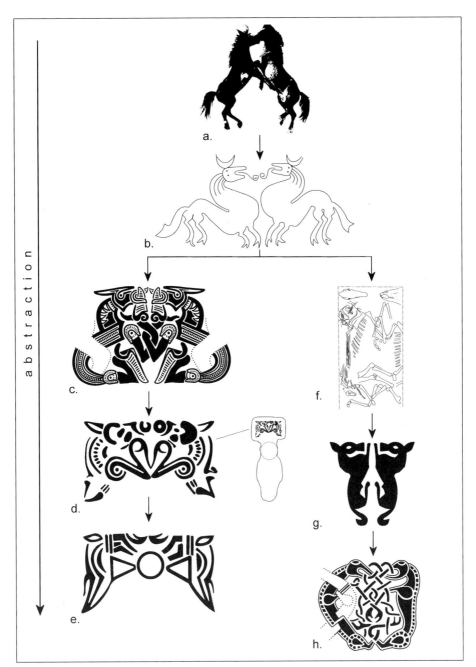

Figure 7.6: The double-horse motif: a. stallions fighting; b. picture stone, Häggeby, Sweden; c. shield-boss motif, Sutton Hoo, Suffolk; d. brooch motif, Apple Down, West Sussex; e. brooch motif, Dover, Kent; f. horse burial, Quedlinburg, Germany; g. bucket motif, Giberville, France; h. purse-lid motif, Sutton Hoo (redrawn after: b. Nylén 1980/2; c. & h. Bruce-Mitford 1978; d. Down and Welch 1990; e. Leigh 1984; f. Müller-Wille 1970/71; g. by the author. Not to scale. Not in chronological sequence).

perhaps feathered fetlocks. Both these gilt-silver brooches, undoubtedly elite items, have affinities to Continental Jutlandic forms and may be imports.

Such motifs were, however, rapidly copied on brooches of definite Kentish manufacture (Leigh 1984: fig. 1). Examples are those from Dover (Figure 7.6e) and Howletts, Kent, as well as new metal-detected finds from Highborough Hill (Eastry), Kent, and West Wight, Isle of White (TAR 2004: figs 88.1–2; Richardson pers. comm.). All demonstrate the further abstraction of the initial image, but like their Jutlandic models remain examples of *Tiermenschen*. Many other quadrupeds in the Style I and successive Style II menageries defy identification, yet others too may be 'lost' equine mythological motifs.

We encounter the Apple Down motif once more on the famous Sutton Hoo mound 1 shield, which again may be a 6th-century south Scandinavian import (Figure 7.6c. Høilund Nielsen 1999: 186). Confronted horses, their manes clearly apparent, are repeated in gilt-silver repoussé patterning around the iron shield-boss (Bruce-Mitford 1978: 88, fig. 36). A further representation is to be found on the garnet-inlaid purse-lid from the same burial (Figure 7.6h); the intertwined limbs of the animals reminded Bruce-Mitford of double-horse burials from Continental cemeteries (Figure 7.6f; *ibid.* 522, fig. 384).

Also from Sutton Hoo, is the helmet with its iconographic programme, comprising two repeated figural panels: the first shows a horse and rider, supported by a second smaller figure, trampling a defeated foe; and on the second, two *Gemini*, dancing with spears and wearing *caftan* riding coats (Figure 7.7; Bruce-Mitford 1978: 190ff., fig. 143). The horse-and-rider design is one known from both the Continent and Scandinavia in the period, but is traceable in its origin to Roman triumphal iconography (MacKintosh 1986). It is also similar to that adapted from imperial imagery for use on Scandinavian gold bracteates (Gaimster 1998: 22, figs. 19, 52). On this series of pendants, which undoubtedly influenced the formation of south Scandinavian animal art, the mounted human figure was increasingly morphed with the steed beneath it, to create the impression of a half-horse, half-warrior deity, in this context variously interpreted as Odin or Thor (Hauck 1972; Gaimster 1998: 25ff.; Hedeager 2007: 53–4, fig. 11). Hence,

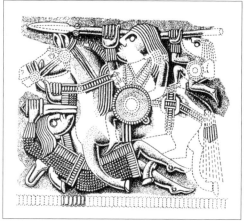

Figure 7.7: Horse-and-rider motif from the Sutton Hoo helmet (after Bruce-Mitford 1978. Scale 1:1. © Reproduced with the permission of the Trustees of the British Museum).

we are dealing with the manipulation of a Roman motif of victory, nobility and equestrianism, to convey Germanic mythology and political ambition. None of the equestrian figures on the Sutton Hoo helmet has been securely identified, though it is likely that they are images of gods or heroic ancestors. It is not impossible, therefore, that in their Anglo-Saxon context both panels were intended to reference the Hengist and Horsa legend.

At a less exclusive level, horse iconography was also employed to stamp-decorate pottery. On a small number of funerary urns from cremation cemeteries a horse-profile stamp was used, including at Sancton, East Yorkshire, and Spong Hill (Figure 7.7b; Hills 1983). In addition, the foot-plates of cruciform brooches were occasionally used to impress horse-nostril patterns on pots, imparting perhaps some of the animism of a sacred object (Briscoe 1985). Less obviously equine is the commonly occurring U-shaped stamp, which is actually a representation of a horse's foot (Figure 7.8; Type G: Briscoe 1983). The detail of the physiology of the foot is lacking in most cases, but in the best examples features can be made out, including the horny outer wall, inner sole and fleshy wedge-shaped 'frog', with its characteristic V-form. This popular symbol is also notable for its association with the swastika, a widespread and acknowledged religious icon of the Roman and Germanic worlds (Wilson 1992: 115). Furthermore, it is possible that some of the linear and moulded designs found on pots, specifically the 'standing-arch' and 'hanging-arch' motifs, are abstract representations of the same horse-foot motif (Hills 1977: no. 1341 & 1431).

After even greater miniaturisation, this symbol was also widely employed to punch-decorate brooches, buckles and other artefacts (Figure 7.8). Again, in most cases the punch motif is reduced to a simple U-shape, but in a minority of cases the detail of the V-form frog was also added. Examples can be found on objects from burials at Bifrons (grave 10), Great Chesterford, Essex (graves 69, 73), Morning Thorpe, Norfolk (graves 35, 80, 90, 96, 114, 131, 396), and Spong Hill (grave 18) (Green *et al.* 1987: figs. 307, 321, 323, 327, 335, 340, 447; Hills *et al.* 1984: fig. 77; Evison 1994: fig. 36; Hawkes 2000: fig. 6). Interestingly, the use of this motif shows a correlation with cruciform brooches that, as noted above, are distinguished by their horse symbolism.

A link between pot and metalwork decoration has been previously recognised, but the symbolic significance of the full range of largely geometric stamps and linear designs is still poorly understood (Richards 1992: fig. 27). The identification of the meaning of the horse-foot motif on both Anglo-Saxon funerary urns and jewellery is a clear indication of the potential of such miniature iconography, as well as demonstrating the degree to which horse symbolism could be abstracted. The rationale for the choice of this icon may have a basis in equestrian best practice, since the condition and care of the hoof and foot is critical to the health of a horse, and by extension its value.

It is also possible that many of the other geometric symbols used as pottery stamps, including circles, grid-squares and crosses, reference horse culture. Representations of branded horses on Roman pottery show a strong correlation with these stamp forms (Klumbach 1952; Type A4a: Briscoe 1983, 58). It is not known whether the early Anglo-Saxons branded their animals, though if they did perhaps the stamps used on pots served to identify horse-owning families, by employing a miniature version of the brand-symbol of their stables.

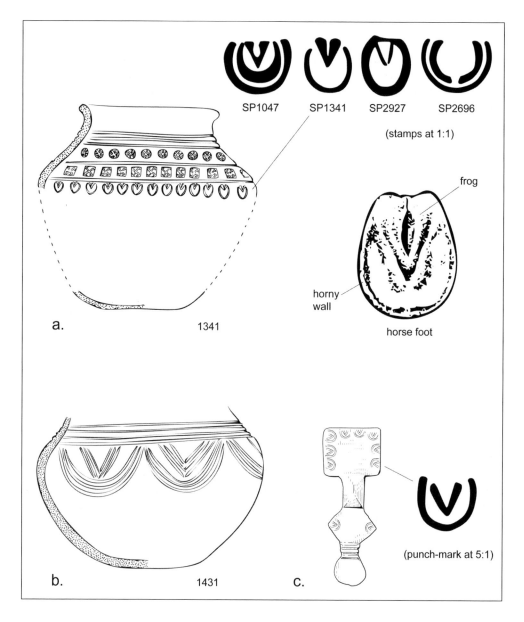

Figure 7.8: Horse symbolism on pottery and metalwork: a. horse-foot stamps on urns at Spong Hill, Norfolk; b. incised decoration on an urn from Spong Hill; c. horse-foot punch decoration on a brooch from Great Chesterford, Essex (a. & b. after Hills 1977. © Copyright Norfolk Museums and Archaeology Service, EAA 6. figs. 33 & 69; c. redrawn after Evison 1994. Scale 5:1, metalwork punch; 1:1, pot stamps & brooch; 1:4, pottery).

There is evidence too for the use of horse-derived materials in the manufacture of artefacts and clothing, which may have had amuletic significance. Horse bone is ideal for the production of a range of objects, including pins, while teeth were used as pendants and gaming counters (Boyle *et al.* 1995: 222–223; Geake 1997: 98–9; Arbogast *et al.* 2002: 108ff.). In addition, horse hair was used to decorate clothing, its coarseness and effulgence making it ideal for hand-plaited details, including, based on the Scandinavian evidence, figural and zoomorphic motifs (Walton Rogers 2007: 94, fig. 3.28b).

Horses in documents

The early Anglo-Saxon written sources reinforce the notion of the high status attached to horsemanship, and of the value of male steeds and harness. Moreover, they provide good evidence for the primacy of horse imagery in pre-Christian religious mythology. The sources date from the 8th to 9th centuries, but it has been shown that they incorporate legends and themes that originated in the early Anglo-Saxon period (Yorke 1993: Mitchell and Robinson 1998: 8–13).

Central to the issue of horse symbolism are the most celebrated brothers of Anglo-Saxon mythology, the aforementioned Hengist and Horsa, who are recorded as descendants of the pre-eminent pagan god Woden, and in the case of Hengist as the patriarch of the Kentish royal dynasty (Turville-Petre 1957; Brooks 1989: 55–74). In Old English, *Hengest* is a masculine noun, with the semantic range 'stallion', 'gelding', 'steed' or 'horse' (Clark Hall 1960: 177). However, in modern German and Dutch *Hengst* (in Swedish *hingst*) is unambiguously 'stallion', making this the most likely intended meaning. *Hors* in Old English is the neuter noun of the genus 'horse' (*equus*), though possibly its usage in this context referenced a castrated steed, establishing the male pairing of stallion and gelding (*ibid.* 190).

Their legend is first documented in Bede's *Historia Ecclesiastica* (HE I.15; II.5; Plummer 1896: 31, 90), though as with other myths recorded by early churchmen, its origin in pre-Christian oral traditions of the 5th to 6th centuries seems likely (Moisl 1981: 219–23, 235–6; Brooks 1989: 58–64; Yorke 1993). Resembling other kingdom founders, such as Hampshire's Port and his sons, their characters are undoubtedly fictional constructs. However, we should not doubt that they mattered in early Anglo-Saxon society, being important and credible enough to be incorporated both into early regnal lists and Bede's Christian history (Yorke 1993). In short, early medieval rulers sought political and dynastic legitimacy by claiming descent from such pseudo-historical hero characters.

The veneration of twin heroes has a long history in Indo-European and Classical tradition. Duos such as Pollux and Castor, and Romulus and Remus, are examples of such *Gemini* deities. And before these, the legend of part-divine and part-mortal, twin horse-cum-hero figures was expressed in the *Dioscuri* and the *Aśvinau*, examples respectively from 2nd-century BC Sparta and 13th-century BC Vedic India (Turville-Petre 1957: 274; Burket 1985: 212). The motif of long-haired brothers and their horses was one that had reached Scandinavia by the 5th century, figuring prominently as a motif on brooches and weaponry, with Odin's sons Vidar and Vále one possible interpretation

(Magnus 2003). In addition, the renown of martial equestrianism is evoked for the preceding Roman period by the institution of the *eques Romanus* (cavalryman), a secular class identified by wealth and propertied status, from which the officer ranks of the Roman army were recruited (Birley 1979: 57–71; Dixon and Southern 1992: 20, 24). It is the conviction of the author that the personalities of Hengist and Horsa were intended to signify a similar status and divinity, with their Woden ancestry taking their relevance well beyond the secular, and extending to a sacred representation of part-warhorse and part-warrior demi-gods.

As long ago as 1957, Turville-Petre argued that the legend of Hengist and Horsa was evidence for a pre-Christian 'cult of the horse'. Direct evidence for this in the historic record is limited to Bede's recollection of a *monumentum* bearing Horsa's name, still to be seen in east Kent at his time of writing (*HE* I.15). Their wider importance is, however, indicated by the account of them as the *duces primi* (first leaders) of the Anglo-Saxons, not only of the peoples of Kent, but of the Saxons, Angles and Jutes inclusively. And they are described ultimately as the progeny of a divine genealogy, "from which stock the families of many kingdoms claimed their descent" (*HE* I.15; trans. McClure and Collins 1994: 26–8). Hence, their legend is likely to have had considerable significance beyond Kent from an early period. Additionally, there are further elaborations on the adventures of Hengist and Horsa in *Beowulf*, the *Anglo-Saxon Chronicle* and the *Historia Brittonum* (Turville-Petre 1957).

The Hengist in *Beowulf*, and the related *Finnsburg Fragment*, is a Jutish warrior hero, hinting that in its Anglo-Saxon context the legend of Hengist and Horsa may represent a myth of Jutlandic origin (Behr 2000). A more recent 19th-century tradition from Schleswig-Holstein may ultimately echo this cultural link; here carved horse-head finials on buildings, considered protective, were termed 'Hengist' and 'Hors' (Yorke 1993: 47). Origin myths linked with south Scandinavia are a common theme amongst Germanic groups of the period, including, for example, the Lombards and Goths (Høilund Nielsen 1998: 37ff.; Hedeager 2000: 18ff.). This is because in the post-Roman period south Scandinavia was politically and ideologically ascendant, and hence such myths, together with the animal art of the region, may have been adopted in an attempt to foster cultural associations, as a means of reinforcing local power relations (Hedeager 1992). Indeed, it has been argued that animal art, as noted above, was a primary means of objectifying such aspirational mythologies (Høilund Nielsen 1998). Hence, to reiterate, we are left once more to ponder whether the Scandinavian-style brooches from Apple Down and elsewhere (Figure 7.6d–e) might very well be such iconographic vehicles for, in this instance, Scandinavian-style legends concerning Hengist and Horsa.

Bede also provides insight into the perceived value of different horses in early Anglo-Saxon society. In a paradigm used to illustrate Aidan's humility, the bishop is gifted by King Oswine of Northumbria (AD 642–670) an *equus optimus* (excellent horse), *stratus regaliter* (regally saddled); but confronted by a needy beggar he gives away the king's animal. Hearing of this, the king admonishes the bishop: "My Lord bishop, why did you want to give a beggar the royal horse intended for you? Have we not many less valuable horses or other things which would have been good enough to give to the poor, without letting the beggar have the horse which I had specially chosen for your own use?" To which Aidan replies: "O King, what are you saying?

Surely this son of a mare is not dearer to you than the son of God?" (*HE* III.14. Plummer 1896: 156; trans. McClure and Collins 1994: 131–134). A number of important details appear within this passage: the royal animal is marked out by its *regalia*, indicating a tradition of decorated harness and saddlery; it is clear evidence for the gift-giving of quality steeds from royal stables (Campbell 1986: 96); and importantly the horse is described as a *filius equae* (son of a mare), denoting a male animal. However, as well as these empirical details, it is also possible that Aidan's final caution against the king's reverence of the stallion had a more fundamental and instructive message from the author of the history – to warn his intended 'princely' audience that horse veneration was spiritually transgressive.

The famous account of the pagan priest Coifi's conversion at Goodmanham, East Yorkshire, in which he profanes the shrine of his old faith, confirms that such details are not merely incidental. It reads: "And at once, casting aside his vain superstitions, he asked the king to provide him with arms and a stallion; and mounting it set out to destroy the idols. Now a high priest of their religion was not allowed to carry arms or to ride except on a mare. So, girded with a sword, he took a spear in his hand and mounting the king's stallion, he set off to where the idols were…But as soon as he approached the shrine, without hesitation he profaned it by casting the spear which he held into it…" (*HE* II.13; Plummer 1896: 113; trans. McClure and Collins 1994: 94–96). Again, it is an incidence of the royal gifting of horses and weaponry, with the priest specifically requesting an *equum emissarium* (stallion of the royal stables), which is contrasted with the *equa* (mare) he is permitted. This episode is often interpreted as a descriptive memory of English paganism (Wilson 1992: 30–31), but conversely may be argued to represent a literary inversion of the contemporary masculine norm, as we see it expressed in both the archaeological and written sources: the combination of a stallion and arms. Bede's account may be, therefore, instead read as an emasculation of the pagan faith. Incidentally, the Coifi episode also illustrates the preferred mode of fighting from horseback used in the period, which is also shown on the Sutton Hoo rider motif, with the spear used over-arm as a throwing or thrusting weapon (Figure 7.7; Bruce-Mitford 1978: fig. 36; Cessford 1993).

The gift-giving of horses between a ruler and his retinue is a motif also found in the *Beowulf* poem (Lines 1035–1045; Trans. Bradley 1997: 438–439; Mitchell and Robinson 1998: 82–83; Webster 1998). The poet provides only the briefest physical description of the *eahta mearas* (eight horses) given by Hrothgar to Beowulf, choosing instead, as elsewhere in the poem, to emphasize the treasure. The horse-equipment includes *fætedhleore* (gold-plated bridles) and a *sadol searwum fah since gewurþad* (saddle skilfully and richly wrought), that is specifically the *hildesetl heahcyninges* (the high king's war saddle). Their bestowal immediately follows the gift of weaponry to the hero, mirroring Coifi's request for arms and a steed, while their harness echoes the *regalia* of Oswine's *equum regium*.

All three episodes suggest a *topos*, probably well known to a contemporary audience, that extolled the value of male warhorses with decorated harness, gifted from royal stables to loyal followers. In each case this motif is likely to have been selected by the author to have maximum appeal to his audience, in portraying Oswine and Hrothgar as the model of generous warleaders, and Aidan, Beowulf and Coifi as the most deserving of their supporters. Although the Christian writers of these works give little embellishment to the nuanced rituals that must have accompanied such significant acts of gift-giving, representing in effect a pre-Christian elite institution, the sacred essence of such actions can again be argued to find expression in the ancestral divinities of Hengist and Horsa.

Horse religion and horse eating

The Hengist and Horsa myth, and much of the identified horse iconography, therefore, has its likely origin in the historically claimed homelands of the Anglo-Saxons, the modern-day regions of Schleswig-Holstein and Jutland. Whilst ultimately inspired by the cosmological beliefs of northern Europe, however, the numerous horse cremations in Anglo-Saxon cemeteries suggest the vigorous energy of an insular horse culture, so far unmatched in Migration Period Continental cremation grounds. By the 7th century, this burial ideology had become predominantly the preserve of an elite class, as is evidenced at the Sutton Hoo cemetery (Figure 7.3). This can be said to mirror the inclusion of horse deities in royal genealogies, developments which point ultimately to the appropriation of horse ideology by the upper echelons of Anglo-Saxon society. Combined, these different threads of evidence may be said to illuminate one crucial truth of pre-Christian Anglo-Saxon religion – that horses mattered.

We find further confirmation of this fact on the famous Franks Casket, a whale

Figure 7.9: Horses on the Franks Casket: a. Ark of the Covenant, back panel; b. 'Hos' scene, right-hand end panel; c. profiled horse and bird, central scene, right-hand end panel; d. horse icon, upper border, right-hand end panel (drawn by author. Scale approx. 3:4).

bone box, made in an early 8th-century Northumbrian monastery (Webster 1999). This artefact is decorated with a complex world-vision of Germanic and Christian episodes, intended as a moral 'mirror for princes', and was doubtless a gift to an elite patron (*ibid*. 244). Horse iconography figures in two episodes, as well as serving as marginalia (Figure 7.9; and see Chapter 9, Figure 9.4).

The back-panel shows the Fall of Jerusalem in AD 70, with the Temple of Solomon its central motif, besieged by Titus' army; within the Temple resides the Ark of the Covenant (Figure 7.9a; *ibid*. 236).Via an Anglo-Saxon re-imagining, however, the cherubim that typically guard this Christian Holy of Holies were replaced by a Germanic quartet of eagles, while crucially the Ark itself sits above a pair of back-to-back rearing horses, their manes clearly shown (*contra* Webster 1999: 236, "winged bovine creatures"). Although the product of a Christian workshop, it is tempting to see this zoomorphic programme, with its very modest interlace ornament, as echoing the same formula of birds and quadrupeds (*i.e.* horses) that decorated many a brooch and buckle of the 6th century. Hence, in the early 8th century, an Anglo-Saxon monastic atelier could produce a gift for a ruler, or possibly another ecclesiastic, that logically united at the centre of one of its compositions the Christian Holy of Holies with the Germanic double-horse icon.

A profiled male horse is also the central motif on the enigmatic right-hand end-panel, which in three scenes illustrates a now 'lost' Germanic legend (*ibid*. 241). The accompanying text to this panel tells of 'Hos' (i.e. OE Hors?), a character exiled and forced to reside upon a 'sorrow mound' (barrow), a 'wretched den of sorrows and torment', by Ertae her oppressor (Figure 7.9b). The left-hand scene shows Hos, a half-human creature sat upon her barrow; she appears to have an equine head, the jaw of a boar, and a serpent-like appendage. She confronts a warrior, possibly Ertae, at whom she wields leafed branches. In the following scene is the profiled male horse, surrounded by a wilderness of rushes, woodland and 'biting' thorns (Figure 7.9c). In the foreground stands another (or possibly the same) barrow containing a shrouded body, beside which stands a cloaked figure holding a 'rod and goblet' (*ibid*. 243). In the final scene, two further cloaked figures appear to have captured a third.

Webster (*ibid*.) viewed the panel as dealing with the themes of wilderness and exile, in the wider context of oblivion in the absence of Christian mercy. The Germanic essence of the piece, however, warrants further exploration. The male horse, together with a small bird that flies across the bottom of the scene, *vis-à-vis* the vision of bereavement they confront, evokes again the importance of animals in pre-Christian belief. Yet, this scene carries none of the political thump of the 'princely' horse burials of archaeology, but is purely concerned with the emotional context of death and the afterlife. Significantly, Hos is another Anglo-Saxon half-human, half-animal character of mythology. Her juxtaposition with the burial mound and her leafy wands may indicate that she is a shamanic-type personality; a religious specialist with abilities to heal the living and speak to dead ancestors, via animal souls and shape-shifting (Williams 2001: 205; see too Sanmark this vol.). In this interpretation, the horse and bird motifs may be illustrative of communicating spirits.

The potential for such beliefs as an aspect of pre-Christian Anglo-Saxon religion has been explored by a number of scholars (see Williams 2001 for a concise summary). The 'ideology of transformation' implied by the cremation rite and art of the 5th to

6th centuries, with their 'mixing' and 'recombination' of human and animal elements, supports the view that a form of shamanism existed in northern Europe in the Migration Period (Leigh 1984; Williams 2001: 206; this vol.).

Significantly, in shamanic practice, horses and birds represent ideal totems on account of their ability to travel large distances, necessary for journeying to the afterlife; whilst the 'noble' character of steeds and hawks also makes them attractive spirit guardians (Lepp 2004). In Scandinavian mythology, it has been suggested that Odin's eight-legged horse, Sleipnir, perhaps represents a shamanic mount (Ellis Davidson 1964: 142). In an early English context, Hengist and Horsa may signify another surviving vestige. In line with the arguments proposed, not only do they combine animal and human elements, but importantly they occupy in the early Anglo-Saxon consciousness a cosmological position between the ancestral world of mortal kings and the Woden-ruled universe.

Proving evidence for shamanism in the archaeological record is difficult. However, as noted above, the horse-burial evidence does offer some tantalising details. The sacrifice of a bridled mount and provisioning of the dead suggests preparations for a journey into the next world. In addition, the act of horse decapitation may have had some link to shamanistic practice, the removal of the head perhaps being intended to release the animal's spirit.

No documentary evidence survives to indicate that the Anglo-Saxon church ever attempted to ban animal burial. The author is also unaware of any such documents from the Continent, that relate to the disappearance of the rite in Alamannic, Saxon, Thuringian or Scandinavian regions. Nevertheless, it is clear that horse burial in all of these territories ultimately ceased following conversion, though this process was gradual rather than immediate.

Christian philosophy of the period, with its emphasis on an anthropocentric universe, was unambiguously hostile to animal sacrifice and veneration (Gilhus 2006). Augustine's (d. 430) teachings instructed that *bestia* were irrational, soulless and created only for Man's utility, consumption and dominion (Clark 1998). It was acceptable for Christians to care for animals, but not to direct to them the affection due to people. The Late Antique church viewed the killing of animals for ritual purposes as implying sacrifice to non-Christian gods. This was because in Christian thinking the sacrifice of Christ for the salvation of Man was the only efficacious and legitimate offering (Gilhus 2006: 154ff.). In practical terms, the Imperial Cult of animal sacrifice ended under Constantine, with acts of public or private ritual killing banned by law in AD 391, in the reign of Theodosius (*ibid.*). The burial or cremation of animals with humans thus afforded certain species a spiritual and corporeal equivalence incompatible with Late Antique thought, with their ritual sacrifice viewed as an act of religious abomination.

A notable change in the horse-burial rite, occurring in the course of the 6th century, both in Anglo-Saxon England and on the Continent, may relate to a growing unease about the polluting effect of animal rituals upon the grave and 'soul'. This is represented by a shift away from the burial of animal and human in the same grave to their separate interment (Oexle 1984: 123, 139). Figure 7.1 illustrates this by the comparison of the early 6th-century burial at Eriswell 4116 (date provided by Hines pers. comm.), with that almost a century later at Sutton Hoo, under mound 17; whilst increasingly in the 7th century, 'horse' burials were marked with bridle-gear only, such as that at Bishopsbourne, Kent (Wright 1844). No burials containing animal sacrifices can be dated after the mid-7th century in England, the era of Christian consolidation. However, the custom did make a brief reappearance in the 9th to 10th centuries as a result of Viking influence, for example at the cremation cemetery of Ingelby, Derbyshire (Richards *et al.* 2004: 79, 92).

In early 6th-century Frankish Neustria, the influence of Christianity may be inferred from a sudden shift in royal funerary tradition. This was marked by the transition from Childeric's burial with its horse sacrifice, to that of his convert son, Clovis (baptised *c.* AD 508), in St Denis Basilica, Paris (James 1988: 123; Müller-Wille 1998). Indeed, the almost total absence of horse burials from the Frankish heartlands, where Gaulish Christianity remained robust into the 5th century and beyond (Hen 1995: 13, 251ff.), stands in contrast to the frequency of the rite east of the Rhine, where Christianity was long resisted. It can be no coincidence too that horse burial continued longest in the territories where conversion was effected only step-by-step between the 8th to 11th centuries, in Frisia, Lower Saxony, Thuringia and Scandinavia (Müller-Wille 1970/71: Abb. 21, 26; Fletcher 1997: 193–228, 403–16). However, conversion rarely achieved the immediate eradication of pre-Christian practice. In Alamannia, officially converted in the late 6th century, horse burial continued into the second half of the 7th century, being for a time syncretistic with the use in cemeteries of Christian gold-foil crosses (Bierbrauer 2003: 436–42).

There is, however, evidence for church prohibitions against other horse-related activities. Theodore's Penitentials, dated *c.* AD 690, one of the Anglo-Saxon church's earliest circulated texts, includes the clause: "they do not forbid horse [flesh]', but 'nevertheless it is not the custom to eat it" (trans. McNeil and Gamer 1990: 208). This ban was reiterated in the canons drawn up by papal legates visiting England in AD 786, suggesting that their consumption was still in evidence, together with a clause against the pagan practice of slitting horse nostrils (Haddan and Stubbs 1896: 458–459). In addition, horse racing was banned by the Synod of Clovesho in *c.* AD 746 (*ibid.* 368).

That horse eating was a wider Germanic activity, rather than one limited to Anglo-Saxon England, is indicated by the letters of the Anglo-Saxon missionary, Boniface. In *c.* AD 732, he reported the consumption of wild and tame horses amongst the Thuringians. Rome's response, that it was: a "filthy and abominable practice", and was to be suppressed "in every possible way" (Emerton 1976: XX, 57–59). The typical interpretation of these prohibitions is one of Christian hostility to a long-lived pagan ritual involving horse sacrifice (Turville-Petre 1957: 279). More recently, historians have situated them within the wider context of early medieval Christian debate concerning the danger of cosmological transgression, by the consumption of animals considered unclean or taboo (Meens 1995). Ultimately, however, Rome's opposition had its likely roots in the long-established Classical aversion to eating horse meat (Arbogast *et al.* 2002: 59).

Archaeology does not support the position that eating horse meat was 'common' in the pre-Christian period in Anglo-Saxon England. Typical faunal assemblages from settlements show that horses were rarely consumed, their remains usually accounting for less than five per cent of total 'domestic' waste (Crabtree 1989: 95, 106; 1996: 71). This pattern does not differ greatly from rural sites of the Christian Roman period in

Britain (Mackreth 1996: 218, 225). It is likely that in this everyday context, horse meat was only eaten when the opportunity was afforded, perhaps by an old animal that had reached the end of its working life, or in periods of privation.

However, finds of 'special deposits', both inside and outside settlements, offer a strong case for a ritual dimension and suggest that horse eating was rare precisely because, rather than being mundane, it could be a sacred activity. Such a ceremony may be inferred from horse remains recently excavated at the site of Melton, East Yorkshire (Fenton-Thomas: forthcoming). Here, two pits contained pottery and the remains of several horses, represented by head-and-foot elements, one of which has been radiocarbon dated between the late 6th and mid-7th century. The evidence suggests that, following a feast of horse, the remains were displayed as skins with head and feet attached, before their burial at the margins of a marshy lake; part of a wider ritual landscape that also included a square 'temple' feature (Blair 1995) and an Anglo-Saxon burial ground. Another similar find is that from Cresswell Field (Yarnton), Oxfordshire, of two skulls and five horse mandibles, found in a sunken-featured building (SFB 7325) (Hey 2005: 75). In addition, the examples of horse-head burials in cemeteries, cited above, may also suggest a scene of horse feasting, and possibly display, at the graveside.

Head-and-hoof rituals are a recognised aspect of horse cult dating back to the Bronze Age (Piggott 1962; Hagberg 1967: 59), though the practice is historically recorded only for the Roman and Viking eras, including at a 9th-century ship burial on the Volga (Frye 2005). Such rituals are most apparent in south and east Scandinavia in the Roman Iron Age, continuing into the Migration Period. Most famous, is the site of Skedemosse, Öland, in Sweden, where over one-hundred horses have been found, and where it is argued, horse racing, stallion combat and religious feasting took place (Hagberg 1967: 59ff., 79ff.).

Conclusion

Hence, it can be established that horse culture loomed large in the consciousness of the early Anglo-Saxons. There is evidence for elite equestrianism, horse deities and iconography, as well as widespread horse funerary rites. Combined, it is argued, these elements illuminate a crucial component of Anglo-Saxon pre-Christian religion. Ultimately, kings and rulers controlled stables of stallions with ceremonial harness, with which they rewarded loyal supporters. And beyond this institution of equestrianism, it is argued, is the fundamental fact that Anglo-Saxon kings claimed equine blood in their veins.

The origin of these horse beliefs, including the Hengist legend and double-horse motif, is traceable to south Scandinavia and north Germany, the supposed ancestral homelands of the Anglo-Saxons. Beyond this, twin horse-cum-hero divinities and horse funerary rituals have their roots in much earlier Indo-European, Asian and Classical cultures. Nevertheless, these themes were culturally renewed by the Anglo-Saxons to play a fundamental role in the formation of new identities, social orders and kingdoms. Anglo-Saxon horse ideologies do not, however, appear in isolation, but were clearly formed out of a broader pan-Germanic cosmology. Shamanism is very likely to have been an element of this belief-system, to which the identified motifs of animal-men, transformation and animal sacrifice conform. Such rituals may also have included horse feasting, as well as perhaps racing and stallion combat.

That Anglo-Saxon horse beliefs could themselves be dynamic and distinctive is, moreover, indicated by the hundreds of 5th- to 6th-century horse cremations which occur, a phenomenon that is so far without parallel in Migration Period northern Europe. Significantly, the popularity of the rite is matched at this period by the widespread use of miniature horse symbolism on cruciform brooches and pottery, objects thus imbued with a sacred animism. It seems more than a coincidence too, that the prominence of the Hengist (stallion) and Horsa (horse/gelding) legend in the history of the kingship and kingdom of Kent, is matched in that region by the adoption of the double-horse motif on high-status jewellery. Combined, this evidence suggests that horse mythologies prevailed at multiple levels of pre-Christian society, in households, communities and, in due course, royal courts.

By the 7th century, such ideological expression had become the preserve of an elite – the emblem of a regally-harnessed stallion and weaponry standing for political triumph. We see this expressed particularly clearly at the Sutton Hoo mound cemetery. In the arrangement of its mounds it is tempting to see preserved the genealogy of an East Anglian 'royal' family, with its horse burials representing 'Hengist heroes' to match those of the Kentish royal line.

Because Anglo-Saxon kingdoms and kings claimed their political and genetic legitimacy from twin warhorse-warlord deities, early churchmen were forced to include them in their histories and king lists, albeit appearing as they do through a Christian lens, moderated and taciturn. However, the horse symbolism of the Franks Casket and the Hengist legend illustrates how old heroes died hard. Nevertheless, horse beliefs were certainly at odds with Late Antique Christian thinking, and this is very probably why animal funerary sacrifice, as well as the eating of horse meat, ended in Germanic regions across Europe after Roman conversion. Thus, viewed against the background of Christian consolidation that followed conversion, Bede's caution – "O King, what are you saying? Surely this son of a mare is not dearer to you than the son of God?" – takes on a particularly striking significance.

Acknowledgements

I am grateful to the following for reading and commenting on earlier drafts of this chapter: Martin Carver, Tania Dickinson, Emma Fern, John Hines, Adam Kendry and Sarah Semple. I am also thankful to a number of people for providing information and insightful discussion: Chris Fenton-Thomas, David Moses and Penelope Walton Rogers.

Illustrations are by the author, unless otherwise stated.

References

Primary Sources

Bede, *Historiam Ecclesiasticam Gentis Anglorum*, Trans. C. Plummer, Oxford
Beowulf, Trans. B. Mitchell and F.C. Robinson, Oxford
Homer, *The Iliad*, Trans. P. Jones and D.C.H. Rieu, London
Tacitus, *Germania*, Trans. H.W. Benario, Warminster

Secondary Sources

Åberg, N. (1926) *The Anglo-Saxons in England*, Uppsala: Almqvist & Wiksell
Adams, B. and Jackson, D. (1988/89) The Anglo-Saxon Cemetery at Wakerley, Northamptonshire: Excavations by Mr. D. Jackson, 1968–9, *Northamptonshire Archaeology* 22: 69–178
Arbogast, R-M., Clavel, B., Lepetz, S., Méniel, P. and Yvinec, J-H. (2002) *Archéologie du cheval – des origines à la période moderne en France*, Paris: Errance
Bálint, Cs. (1982) Les tombes à ensevelissement de cheval chez les Hongrois aux IXe-XIe siècles, *Archivum eurasiae medii aevi* II: 5–32
Barber, B. and Bowsher, D. (2000) *The Eastern Cemetery of Roman London. Excavations 1983–1990*, Museum of London Archaeological Services Monograph 4, London: MoLAS
Behr, C. (2000) The Origins of Kingship in Early Medieval Kent, *Early Medieval Europe* 9: 25–52
Benario, H.W. (trans) (1999) *Germany = Germania/Tacitus*, Warminster: Aris and Phillips
Bierbrauer, V. (2003) The Cross Goes North: From Late Antiquity to Merovingian Times South and North of The Alps. In M.O.H. Carver (ed.), *The Cross Goes North: Processes of Conversion in Northern Europe, AD 300–1300*, 429–42, Woodbridge: Boydell
Birley, R. (1988) *The People of Roman Britain*, London: Batsford
Blair, J. (1995) Anglo-Saxon Pagan Shrines and their Prototypes, *Anglo-Saxon Studies in Archaeology and History* 8: 1–28
Bode, M-J. (1998) Schmalstede: Ein Urnengräberfeld der Kaiser- und Völkerwanderungszeit, *Urnenfriedhöfe Schleswig-Holstein* 14, Offa-Bücher 78, Neumünster
Bökönyi, S. (1974) *History of Domestic Mammals in Central and Eastern Europe*, Budapest: Akadémiai Kiadó
Bóna, I. (2002) *Les Huns. Le grand empire barbare d'Europe, IVe-Ve siècles*, Paris: Errance
Bond, J. (1994) Appendix 1: The Cremated Animal Bone. In J.I. Mckinley (ed.), *The Anglo-Saxon Cemetery at Spong Hill, North Elmham, Part VIII: The Cremations, East Anglian Archaeology Report* 69, 121–35, Dereham, Field Archaeology Division, Norfolk Museum Service
Bond, J. (1996) Burnt offerings: Animal Bone in Anglo-Saxon Cremations, *World Archaeology* 28.1: 76–88
Boyle, A., Dodd, A., Miles, D. and Mudd, A. (1995) *Two Oxfordshire Anglo-Saxon Cemeteries: Berinsfield and Didcot, Thames Valley Landscapes Monographs* 8, Oxford: Oxford Committee for Archaeology
Bradley, S.A.J. (1997) *Anglo-Saxon Poetry*, London: Everyman
Briscoe, T. (1983) A Classification of Anglo-Saxon Pot Stamp Motifs and Proposed Terminology, *Studien zur Saschenforschung* 4: 57–71
Briscoe, T. (1985) The Use of Brooches and Other Jewellery as Dies on Pagan Anglo-Saxon Pottery, *Medieval Archaeology* 29: 136–41
Brooks, N. (1989) The Creation and Early Structure of The Kingdom of Kent. In S. Bassett (ed.) *Origins of Anglo-Saxon Kingdoms*, 55–74, London: Leicester University Press
Bruce-Mitford, R.L.S. (1978) *The Sutton Hoo Ship Burial II: Arms, Armour and Regalia*, London: British Museum Press

Burket, W. (1985) *Greek Religion*, Cambridge: Cambridge University Press

Campbell, J. (1986) Bede's *Reges* and *Principes*. In J. Campbell (ed.), *Essays in Anglo-Saxon History*, 85–98, London: Hambledon Press

Carver, M.O.H. (1993) The Anglo-Saxon Cemetery: An Interim Report, *Bulletin of the Sutton Hoo Research Committee* 8, 11–9, Woodbridge: Boydell

Carver, M.O.H. (2005) *Sutton Hoo. A Seventh-Century Princely Burial Ground and its Context*, London: British Museum Press

Carver, M.O.H. and Fern, C. (2005) The Seventh-Century Burial Rites and their Sequence. In M.O.H. Carver (ed.), *Sutton Hoo. A Seventh-Century Princely Burial Ground and its Context*, 283–313, London: British Museum

Cessford, C. (1993) Cavalry in Bernicia: A Reply, *Northern History* 29: 185–7

Collins, A.E.P. (1952/3) Excavations on Blewburton Hill, 1948 and 1949, *The Berkshire Archaeological Journal* 53: 21–64

Collins, D.C. (1959) Kenning in Anglo-Saxon Poetry, *Essays and Studies* 12: 1–17

Clark, G. The Fathers and The Animals: The Rule of Reason? In A. Linzey and D. Yamamoto (eds), *Animals on the Agenda: Questions about Animals for Theology and Ethics*, 67–79, Illinois: Illinois University Press

Clark Hall, J.R. (1960) *A Concise Anglo-Saxon Dictionary*, Fourth Edition, Cambridge: Cambridge University Press

Crabtree, P.J. (1989) West Stow, Suffolk: Early Anglo-Saxon Animal Husbandry, *East Anglian Archaeology Report* 47, Bury St Edmunds: Sufflok County Planning Dept

Crabtree, P.J. (1996) Production and Consumption in an Early Complex Society: Animal Use in Middle Saxon East Anglia, *World Archaeology* 28.1: 58–75

Davis, S. (2001) The Horse Head from Grave 47. In W. Filmer-Sankey and T. Pestell, *Snape Anglo-Saxon Cemetery*, 231–232, Ipswich, Suffolk: Environment and Trsnport, Suffolk County Council

Demarrais, E., Castillo, L.J. and Earle, T. (1996) Ideology, Materialization, and Power Strategies, *Current Anthropology* 37: 15–32

Dickinson, T.M. (2005) Symbols of Protection: The Significance of Animal-Ornamented Shields in Early Anglo-Saxon England, *Medieval Archaeology* 49: 109–63

Dickinson, T.M., Fern, C. and Hall, M.A. (2006) An Early Anglo-Saxon Bridle-Fitting from South Leckaway, Forfar, Angus, Scotland, *Medieval Archaeology* 50: 249–60

Dixon, K.R. and Southern, P. (1992) *The Roman Cavalry. From the First to the Third Century AD*, London: Batsford

Down, A. and Welch, M. (1990) *Chichester Excavations 7: Apple Down and the Mardens*, Chichester: Chichester District Council

Duczko, W. (1996) Uppsalahögarna som symboler och arkeologiska källor. In W. Duczko (ed.) *Arkeologi och miljögeologi i Gamla Uppsala*, 59–93. Uppsala

Earle, T. (1990) Style and Iconography as Legitimation in Complex Chieftains. In M. Conkey and C. Hastorf (eds), *The Uses of Style in Archaeology*, 73–81, Cambridge: Cambridge University Press

Emerton, E. (trans.) (1973) *The Letters of Saint Boniface*, New York: Octagon Books

Ellis Davidson, H. (1964) *Gods and Myths of Northern Europe*, Harmondsworth: Penguin Books

Evison, V.I. (1994) An Anglo-Saxon Cemetery at Great Chesterford, Essex, *Council for British Archaeology Research Report* 91, York: CBA

Fenton-Thomas, C. (Forthcoming) Where Sky and Yorkshire and Water Meet: The Story of the Melton Landscape from Prehistory to the Present, On-Site Archaeology, *Osa Monograph Series* 2, York

Fern, C. (2005) The Archaeological Evidence for Equestrianism in Early Anglo-Saxon England, c.450–700. In A. Pluskowski (ed.) *Just Skin and Bones? New Perspectives on Human-Animal Relations in the Historical Past*, 41–71, BAR International Series 1410, Oxford

Fern, C. (2007) Early Anglo-Saxon Horse Burial of the Fifth to Seventh Centuries AD, *Anglo-Saxon Studies in Archaeology and History* 14: 92–109

Filmer-Sankey, W. and Pestell, T. (2001) *Snape Anglo-Saxon Cemetery: Excavations and Surveys 1824–1992*, East Anglian Archaeology Report 95, Iswich, Suffolk: Environment & Transport, Suffolk County Council

Fletcher, R. (1997) *The Conversion of Europe: From Paganism to Christianity 371–1386AD*, London: Harper Collins

Frye, R.N. (2005) *Ibn Fadlan's Journey to Russia: A Tenth-Century Traveller from Baghdad to the Bulger River*, Princeton: Markus Wiener Publishers

Gaimster, M. (1998) Vendel Period Bracteates on Gotland. On the Significance of Germanic Art, *Acta archaeologica Lundensia* 8.27, Lund

Geake, H. (1997) *The Use of Grave-Goods in Conversion-Period England, c.600–c.850*, BAR British Series. 261, Oxford

Gilhus, I.S. (2006) *Animals, Gods and Humans: Changing Attitudes to Animals in Greek, Roman and Early Christian Ideas*, London: Routledge

Green, B., Rogerson, A. and White, S.G. (1987) *The Anglo-Saxon Cemetery at Morning Thorpe, Norfolk*, East Anglian Archaeology Report 36, Dereham, Norfolk: Norfolk Museums Service

Haddan, A.W. and Stubbs, W. (1869) *Councils and Ecclesiastical Documents Relating to Great Britain and Ireland*, Vol. 3, Oxford: Clarendon Press

Hagberg, U.E. (1967) *The Archaeology of Skedemosse II: The Votive Deposits in the Skedemosse Fen and their Relation to the Iron Age Settlement on Öland, Sweden*, Stockholm: Almqvist & Wiksell

Hamerow, H. (2006) Special Deposits in Anglo-Saxon Settlements, *Medieval Archaeology* 50: 1–30

Härke, H. (2001) Cemeteries as Places of Power. *In* M. De Jong, F. Theuws and C. Van Rhijn (eds) *Topographies of Power in the Early Middle Ages*, 9–30, Leiden: Brill

Haseloff, G. (1974) Salin's Style I, *Medieval Archaeology* 18: 1–15

Haseloff, G. (1984) Stand der Forschung Stilgeschichte Völkervanderungs- und Merowingerzeit. *In* M. Høgestøl, J.H. Larsen, E. Straume, and B. Weber (eds), *Festskrift til Thorleif Sjøvold på 70–årsdagen*, 109–124. Oslo

Hauck, K. (1972) Metamorphosen Odins nach dem Wissen von Snorri und von Amulettmeistern der Völkerwanderungszeit (Zur Ikonologie der Goldbrakteaten IV). *In* O. Bandle, H. Klingenberg and F. Maurer (eds), *Festschrift für Siegfried Gutenbrunner*, Heidelberg

Haughton, C. and Powlesland, D. (1999) *West Heslerton. The Anglian Cemetery*, Landscape Research Centre Archaeological Monograph Series, No. 1, Vol. 1, Yedingham: WRC

Hawkes, J. (1997) Symbolic Lives: The Visual Evidence. *In* J. Hines (ed.), *The Anglo-Saxons from the Migration Period to the Eighth Century: An Ethnographic Perspective*, 311–44, Woodbridge: Boydell

Hawkes, S.C. and Dunning, G.C. (1961) Soldiers and Settlers in Britain, Fourth to Fifth Century: With a Catalogue of Animal-Ornamented Buckles and Related Belt-Fittings, *Medieval Archaeology* 5: 1–70

Hawkes, S.C. (2000) The Anglo-Saxon Cemetery of Bifrons, in the Parish of Patrixbourne, East Kent, *Anglo-Saxon Studies in Archaeology and History* 11: 1–94

Hedeager, L. (1992) Kingdoms, Ethnicity and Material Culture: Denmark in a European Perspective. *In* M.O.H. Carver (ed.), *The Age of Sutton Hoo: The Seventh Century in North-West Europe*, 279–300, Woodbridge: Boydell

Hedeager, L. (2000) Migration Period Europe: The Formation of a Political Mentality. *In* F. Theuws and J.L. Nelson (eds), *Rituals of Power. from Late Antiquity to the Early Middle Ages*, 15–57, Leiden: Brill

Hedeager, L. (2007) Scandinavia and the Huns: An Interdisciplinary Approach to the Migration Era, *Norwegian Archaeological Review* 40.1: 42–58

Hen, Y. (1995) *Culture and Religion in Merovingian Gaul AD 481–751*, New York: Brill

Hey, G. (2004) *Yarnton: Saxon and Medieval Settlement and Landscape. Results of Excavations 1990–96*,

Oxford Archaeology Thames Valley Landscapes Monograph 20, Oxford: Oxford University School for Archaeology

Hill, J.D. (1996) The Identification of Ritual Deposits of Animals. A General Perspective from a Specific Study of 'Special Animal Deposits' from the Southern English Iron Age. *In* S. Anderson and K. Boyle (eds), *Ritual Treatment of Human and Animal Remains, Proceedings of The First Meeting of the Osteoarchaeological Research Group*, 17–32, Oxford: Oxbow Books

Hills, C. (1977) The Anglo-Saxon Cemetery at Spong Hill, North Elmham, Part I: Catalogue of Inhumations, *East Anglian Archaeology Report* 6, Dereham, Norfolk: Field Archaeology Division, Norfolk Museum Service

Hills, C. (1983) Animal Stamps on Anglo-Saxon Pottery in East Anglia, *Studien zur Sachsenforschung* 4: 93–110

Hills, C. (1998) Did the People of Spong Hill come from Schleswig-Holstein?, *Studien zur Sachsenforschung* 11: 145–54

Hills, C., Penn, K. and Rickett, R. (1984) The Anglo-Saxon Cemetery at Spong Hill, North Elmham, Part III: Catalogue of Inhumations, *East Anglian Archaeology Report* 21, Dereham, Norfolk: Field Archaeology Division, Norfolk Museum Service

Høilund Nielsen, K. (1997) Animal Art and the Weapon Burial Rite: A Political Badge?. *In* C.K. Jensen and K. Høilund Nielsen (eds), *Burial and Society. The Chronological and Social Analysis of Archaeological Burial Data*, 129–48, Aarhus: Aarhus University Press

Høilund Nielsen, K. (1998) Animal Style – A Symbol of Might and Myth: Salin's Style II in A European Context, *Acta archaeologica* 69: 1–52

Høilund Nielsen, K. (1999) Style II and The Anglo-Saxon Elite. *In* T.M. Dickinson and D. Griffiths (eds), *The Making of Kingdoms. Anglo-Saxon Studies in Archaeology and History* 10: 185–202

Høilund Nielsen, K. (2002) Ulv, hest og drage. Ikonografisk analyse af dyrene i stil II–III, *Hikuin* 29: 187– 218

Hyland, A. (1990) *Equus. The Horse in the Roman World*, London: Batsford

Kerth, V-K. (2000) Die Tierbeigaben aus vier frühmittelalterlichen Gräberfeldern in Unterfranken, *Germania* 78.1: 125–138

Kiss, A. (2001) Das awarenzeitliche Gräberfeld in Kölked-Feketekapu B, *Monumenta Avarorum Archaeologica* 6, Budapest

Klumbach, H. (1952) Pferde mit Brandmarken, *Festschrift des römisch-germanischen Zentralmuseums in Mainz zur Feier seiner hundertjährigen Bestehens* Band III, 1–12

Kuzmina, E.E. (2006) Mythological Treatment of the Horse in Indo-European Culture. *In* S.L. Olsen, S. Grant, A.M. Choyke and L. Bartosiewicz (eds), *Horses and Humans: The Evolution of Human-Equine Relationships*, 263–70, BAR International Series 1560, Oxford

László, G. (1943) Der Grabfund von Koroncó und der altungarische Sattel, *Archaeologica Hungarica* 27: 107–91

Leahy, K. (2007) Soldiers and Settlers in Britain, Fourth to Fifth Century – Revisited. *In* M. Henig and T.J. Smith (eds), *Collectanea Antiqua: Essays in Memory of Sonia Chadwick Hawkes*, 133–43, BAR International Series 1673, Oxford

Leigh, D. (1984) Ambiguity in Anglo-Saxon Style I Art, *Antiquaries Journal* 64: 34–42

Lepp, T. (2004) Horses. *In* M.N. Walter and E.J.N. Fridman (eds), *Shamanism: An Encyclopedia of World Beliefs, Practices and Culture*, 147–48, Santa Barbara: ABC-Clio

Lindstrøm, T.C. and Kristoffersen, S. (2001) 'Figure it Out! Psychological Perspectives on Perception of Migration Period Animal Art, *Norwegian Archaeological Review* 34.2: 65–84

Mackintosh, M. (1986) The Sources of the Horseman and Fallen Enemy Motif on the Tombstones of the Western Roman Empire, *Journal of the British Archaeological Association* 139: 1–21

Mackreth, D.F. (1996) *Orton Hall Farm: A Roman and Early Anglo-Saxon Farmstead*, East Anglian Archaeology Report 76, Manchester: University of Manchester

Magnus, B. (2003) Krigerens insignier: En parafrase over gravene II og V fra Snartemo i Vest-agder. *In* P. Rolfsen and F.-A. Stylegar (eds), *Snartemofunnene i nytt lys*, Oslo: Universitets Kulturhistor Museer

McClure, J. and Collins, R. (Trans. and eds) (1994) *Bede: The Ecclesiastical History of the English People*, Oxford

McKinley, J.I. (1994) *The Anglo-Saxon Cemetery at Spong Hill, North Elmham, Part VIII: The Cremations*, East Anglian Archaeology Report 69, Dereham, Norfolk: FAD, Norfolk Museum Service

McNeil, J.T. and Gamer, H.M. (1990) *Medieval Handbooks of Penance: A Translation of the Principal Libri Poenitentiales and Selections from Related Documents*, New York: Columbia University Press

Meens, R. (1995) Pollution in the Early Middle Ages: The Case of the Food Regulations in the Penitentials, *Early Medieval Europe* 4.1: 3–19

Miles, D., Palmer, S., Lock, G., Gosden, C. and Cromarty, A-M. (2004) *Uffington White Horse and its Landscape: Investigations at White Horse Hill Uffington, 1989–95, and Tower Hill Ashbury, 1993–4*, Thames Valley Landscapes Monograph 18, Oxford: Oxford School for Archaeology

Mitchell, B. and Robinson, F.C. (eds) (1998) *Beowulf: An Edition with Relevant Shorter Texts*, Oxford: Blackwell Publishers

Moisl, H. (1981) Anglo-Saxon Royal Genealogies and Germanic Oral Tradition, *Journal of Medieval History* 7: 215–48

Morphy, H. (1989) Introduction. *In* H. Morphy (ed.), *Animals Into Art*, London: Unwin Hyman

Moore-Coleyer, R.J. (1994) The Horse in British Prehistory: Some Speculations, *Archaeological Journal* 151; 1–15

Müller, H-H. (1980) Zur Kenntnis der Haustiere aus Völkerwanderungszeit im Mittelelbe-Saale-Gebiet, *Zeitschrift für Archäologie* 14: 145–72

Müller-Wille, M. (1970/71) Pferdegrab und Pferdeopfer im frühen Mittelalter, *Berichten van de Rijksdienst voor het Oudheidkundig* Bodemonderzeok Jaargang 20/21

Müller-Wille, M. (1998) Zwei religiöse Welten: Bestattungen der fränkischen Könige Childerich und Chlodwig, *Abhandlungen der Akademie der Wissenschaften und Literatur*, 3–45, Mainz-Stuttgart

Nylén, E. (1980/2) Vendelryttaren, en länk mellan öst och vöst – forntid och medeltid, *Tor* 19; 163–88

Oaks, L.S. (1986) The Goddess Epona: Concepts of Sovereignty in a Changing Landscape. *In* M. Henig and A. King (eds), *Pagan Gods and Shrines of the Roman Empire*, University Committee For Archaeology Monograph 8, 77–84, Oxford: Oxford Committee for Archaeology

O'Connor, T. (Unpublished) Animal Bones from Lakenheath, Suffolk (ERL046, 104, 114), *Archive Report to Suffolk CC Archaeology Unit*

Oexle, J. (1984) Merowingerzeitliche Pferdebestattungen – Opfer oder Beigaben?, *Frühmittelalterliche Studien* 18: 122–72

Olsén, P. (1945) Die Saxe von Valsgärde, *Valsgärdestudien* 2, Uppsala

Olsen, S.L. (2006) Introduction. *In* S.L. Olsen, S. Grant, A.M. Choyke and L. Bartosiewicz (eds), *Horses and Humans: The Evolution of Human-Equine Relationships*, 1–8, BAR International Series 1560, Oxford

Olsen, S.L., Grant, S. Choyke, A.M. and Bartosiewicz, L. (eds) (2006) *Horses and Humans: The Evolution of Human-Equine Relationships*, BAR International Series 1560, Oxford

Piggott, S. (1962) Heads and Hoofs, *Antiquity* 36: 110–8

Plummer, C. (1896) *Venerabilis Baedae Opera Historica*, 2 Vols, Oxford: Clarendon Press

Pluskowski, A. (ed.) (2007) *Breaking and Shaping Beastly Bodies: Animals as Material Culture in the Middle Ages*, Oxford: Oxbow Books

Richards, J.D. (1992) Anglo-Saxon Symbolism. *In* M.O.H. Carver (ed.), *The Age of Sutton Hoo. The Seventh Century in North-Western Europe*, 131–47, Woodbridge: Boydell

Richards, J.D. (2004) Excavations at the Viking Barrow Cemetery at Heath Wood, Ingleby, Derbyshire, *Antiquaries Journal* 84: 23–116

Rivers, T.J. (1977) *Laws of the Alamans and Bavarians,* Pennsylvania: Pennsylvania University Press

Seaby, W.A. and Woodfield, P. Viking Stirrups from England and their Background, *Medieval Archaeology* 24: 87–122

Speake, G. (1980) *Anglo-Saxon Animal Art and its Germanic Background,* Oxford: Clarendon Press

Talbot Rice, T. (1957) *The Scythians,* London: Thames and Hudson

Tar, (2004) *Treasure Annual Report 2004,* Department of Culture, Media and Sport, London

Thompson, E.A. (1996) *The Huns,* Oxford: Blackwell

Turville-Petre, J.E. (1957) Hengest and Horsa, *Saga Book* 14: 273–90

Tyler, S. and Major, H. (2005) *The Early Anglo-Saxon Cemetery and Later Saxon Settlement at Springfield Lyons, Essex,* East Anglian Archaeology Report 111, Chelmsford: Essex County Council

Vierck, H. (1979/71) Pferdegräber im Angelsächsischen England. *In* M. Müller-Wille, *Pferdegrab und Pferdeopfer im frühen Mittelalter, Berichten van de Rijksdienst voor het Oudheidkundig Bodemonderzoek* Jaargang 20/21, 189–99

Walton Rogers, P. (2007) *Cloth and Clothing in Early Anglo-Saxon England,* Council for British Archaeology Research Report 145, York: CBA

Webster, L. (1998) Archaeology and Beowulf. *In* B. Mitchell and F.C. Robinson (eds), *Beowulf: An Edition with Relevant Shorter Texts,* 183–94, Oxford: Blackwells

Webster, L. (1999) The Iconographic Programme of the Franks Casket. *In* J. Hawkes and S. Mills (eds), *Northumbria's Golden Age,* 227–46, Stroud: Sutton Publishing Ltd

Wicker, N. (2003) The Scandinavian Animal Styles in Response to Mediterranean and Christian Narrative Art. *In* M.O.H. Carver (ed.) *The Cross Goes North: Processes of Conversion in Northern Europe, AD 300–1300,* 531–50, Woodbridge: Boydell

Williams, H. (2001) An Ideology of Transformation: Cremation Rites and Animal Sacrifice in Early Anglo-Saxon England. *In* N. Price (ed.), *The Archaeology of Shamanism,* 193–212, London: Routledge

Wilson, D. (1992) *Anglo-Saxon Paganism,* London: Routledge

Wright, T. (1844) An Account of the Opening of Barrows in Bourne Park, Near Canterbury, *Archaeological Journal* 1: 253–6

York, B. (1993) Fact or Fiction? The Written Evidence for the Fifth and Sixth Centuries AD, *Anglo-Saxon Studies in Archaeology and History* 6: 45–50

Chapter 8

Living On: Ancestors and the Soul

Alexandra Sanmark

Introduction

The written evidence for pre-Christian belief among the Anglo-Saxons is extremely sparse (Wilson 1992, chapter 2) and its character remains elusive. Compared with Norse religion, Anglo-Saxon pre-Christian religion has been subject to few in-depth studies, and only a vague image has been pieced together from the scattered written sources and archaeological material (see *e.g.* Wilson 1992; Herbert 1994; Davidson 1964 and 1982). One of the few scholars who have provided a more detailed view of Anglo-Saxon religion is Stephen O. Glosecki (1989). Through his examination of written sources and some archaeological material, he has argued that motifs in Anglo-Saxon poetry, charms and artefacts contain 'reflexes of shamanism' identifiable from a number of universal traits, such as animism, ecstasy, therapy (healing), shamanic initiation and assistance (from shamanic guardians). Glosecki argued that the "widespread nature of this belief [shamanism] … makes it less difficult to credit its presence in Old English than in its absence" (Glosecki 1989: 79). Shamanism, like a number of other aspects of religion in the pre-Christian north, is more graphically illustrated in the evidence from Norse culture, including early material culture and later writing. It is now clear that great similarities existed between Norse and Sámi religions, particularly regarding sorcery (*seiðr*), and within this, shamanism (Strömbäck 2000: 196–206; Price 2002: chapter 3; Sanmark 2004: chapter 4.1).

This chapter makes use of later Norse religion as an echo or an analogy of Anglo-Saxon religious thinking, but focussing on a particular aspect that could be productive, namely the cult of ancestors. I intend to show that an ancestor cult was a highly significant and fully integrated part of pre-Christian religion in Scandinavia and Iceland, and from this point of departure, to demonstrate that it must have been an important feature in the pre-Christian religion of the Anglo-Saxons too. To this end, I shall employ written sources, archaeological evidence and comparative anthropological and ethnographical evidence. As will be shown below, there are clear similarities between the Anglo-Saxon and the Norse concept of the soul, implying that both had an ancestor cult and also strengthening the link between them.

Structure of Norse religious thinking

Influenced by ideas of evolution, early scholars argued that religions developed from 'primitive' to more 'advanced' stages. Belief in spirits and ancestors was seen to represent religions at an early stage of the evolutionary ladder, while religions that focused on gods, such as Christianity, were seen as more sophisticated (see *e.g.* Klare 1933–4: 1). Thus deities such as Odin, Thor, Frey and Freya would form the most significant part of the more developed Norse religion. Although in theory superseded, this evolutionary perspective has continued to colour scholars' views. A prevailing theme is that Norse religion was constituted in two main strands. One consisted of myths and cults connected to individual and personal deities who were seen as 'ruling and reigning'. The other strand consisted of more 'animistic' cults connected to a wide variety of beings, such as norns, trolls, elves, giants, and dwarves. Many of these were connected to home and nature and played important roles in people's everyday lives and contributed to their general survival (Ljungberg 1980: 117; Hellström 1996: 229).

Thus, during the first half of the twentieth century, scholars who had based their ideas primarily on Snorri Sturlusson's *Edda* and *The Poetic Edda* saw the cult of the gods as the most important religious aspect. This strand was named 'higher religion', while the cult connected to other beings was termed 'lower religion'. Although the *Poetic Edda* also contains many references to gods, this work mentions a larger number of other supernatural beings (Faulkes 1987; Larrington 1996; Ljungberg 1938: 282; Hellström 1996: 229–30). Scholars now mostly avoid weighting the two strands, but distinctions may still be found between 'major' gods, 'divinities of lesser importance' and 'spirits, giants and ancestors' (Brink 2001: 85, 88).

One way of approaching the general theatre of religion, whether involving higher gods or not, is in the study of ancestors and its implied belief in what becomes of us. Many scholars of religion such as Herbert Spencer, Émile Durkheim and Fustel de Coulanges have stressed the centrality of the ancestor cult in religious systems (Artelius 2000: 178; Spencer 1877; Durkheim 1915; Fustel de Coulanges 1874). Very little attention was initially paid to it in Norse religion, yet, as Torsten Blomkvist has pointed out (2002: 136), excluding an ancestor cult from Viking Age Scandinavia and Iceland, would make these peoples the unique exception. Emil Birkeli (1938; 1943) was the first scholar who studied the ancestor cult, separating it from the cult of the gods (Ellis 1943: chapters IVff.) and since then, it has been increasingly emphasised (A.-S. Gräslund 2001; Sognnes 2000; Brink 2001; Artelius 2000: 176–80; Kaliff 1997; Blomkvist 2002: chapter 4; Badou 1989; Gurevich 1969). However, despite studies of this kind, there are many major works, in which the ancestor cult is still not described as a significant part of Norse religion (Näsström 2001; Graham-Campbell 2001; Branston 1980; Steinsland 1992).

Written sources from Iceland and Scandinavia contain a large number of references to the ancestor cult, but we must keep in mind that all these sources are Christian, and written down some time after the introduction of Christianity. One reason why the ancestor cult may seem prominent in these sources is that while the cults of the gods seem to have disappeared rather quickly after the 'official' introduction of Christianity, belief in supernatural beings of various kinds appears to have survived long after the beginnings of the Christianization (Sanmark 2004: chapter 4.1).

Scholars have suggested various definitions of ancestor cult over the years. One of the most useful reads as follows:

> "continuous worship of dead family members, which presupposes that death is only a transition to another form of existence; it usually means a continuous feeling of solidarity and community with deceased ancestors, as well as dependence on and care of these past family members" (after Anne-Sofie Gräslund, 2001: 224).

It is important to point out that an ancestor cult may not be motivated in the same way a cult of the dead would be, as manifested in mortuary rituals, *i.e.* rites performed before and during the burial (Hardacre 1993: 263–4; Ranke *et al.* 1973: 112–15; Williams this vol.). But the two may be difficult to distinguish in practice.

In general, pre-Christian Norse religion consisted of three strands: the cult of the gods, the animistic strand, and magic (Sanmark 2004: 147–50). By looking at other types of evidence, archaeological and anthropological, it is clear that magic and animism must have formed a large part of the religion. The ancestor cult fits into the second strand, as animism can be defined as belief in the existence of spirits (Sanmark 2004: 147–50). The complex concept of animism has been widely discussed (see for example: Bowie 2000: 14–15), and in this regard it is important to maintain the distinction between gods and ancestors (*cf.* Blomkvist 2002: 137).

In recent research Norse religion is seen as most similar to so-called *indigenous religions* (*cf.* B. Gräslund 1994: 16–17; Sanmark 2004: 178–9; Brink 2001; Hultgård 1996: 28). An indigenous religion can be defined as belief in the existence of a supernatural world and supernatural powers, which include 'gods' and spirits of various kinds. The spirits are however seen as more important than the gods, since they play more significant roles in people's daily life. The spirits of the ancestors play a central part, and are contacted through 'medicine men'/shamans (Hultkrantz 1968).

The relationship between the ancestral spirits and the living is often very close and 'characterised by a combination of love, respect and fear' (B. Gräslund 1994: 17). The ancestral spirits are seen as potent and at times also malicious, and incessantly demanding support from the living. They must therefore be treated with reverence. Despite the fact that they are often supposed to dwell in some remote otherworld, they continue to appear among the living, as well as in or close to their graves (B. Gräslund 1994: 17 with references; Brendalsmo *et al.* 1992: 101–111). As a consequence of this, death becomes nothing but a 'temporary exclusion from society' (quote from R. Hertz in Taylor 2002: 164).

Character of the soul

The belief in the enduring presence of ancestors as animated and active spirits is rooted in a belief in a soul that survives after death. Indigenous religions often feature a pluralistic soul, which means that the soul is seen to represent several spirits and spiritual entities (B. Gräslund 1994: 17–18). This concept can be simplified into a duality, consisting of the 'breath soul' (also called the body soul) and the 'free soul' (or the dream soul). The breath soul is seen to leave the body at the time of death ('with the last breath'). The free soul, on the other hand, is believed to stay until the corpse has 'collapsed completely', *e.g.* through decomposition or cremation. After this has taken place, the free soul can begin its new life. It is this soul that is thought to represent the dead in the next life. During life, the free soul is active in the various states of the unconscious mind, such as dreams and trances. As long as a person is conscious, this soul is passive. When a person enters a state of unconsciousness, the free soul becomes active and leaves the body, and when it returns, the person wakes up (B. Gräslund 1994: 18 with references).

The ancestor cult described in the Norse sources is to a large extent connected to a pluralistic soul. The concept has been discussed by many scholars from the end of the 19th century and onwards, and a number of different souls have been identified in the primary sources: *hugr*, *hamr*, *fylgja* and *hamingjur*. It is important to point out that these various souls were in many ways separate beings who could lead their own autonomous existences (Turville-Petre 1975: 227–30; Price 2002: 59–60).

The *hugr*, which can be translated as 'soul', 'thought' or 'mind', could leave the body either in the shape of a human or an animal. A person could control her/his own *hugr*. It is possible that Odin's two ravens, Hugin and Munin, who every day flew across the world, were concrete forms of his *hugr*, *i.e.* his 'thought' and 'mind'. The *hamr* can be translated as 'shell', 'shape', or 'coat', and can be seen as the form that the *hugr* took through shape-shifting (*hamhleypa*). During this phase, the *hugr* most often appeared as a bird, but at times also as *e.g.* a bear, a wolf or a whale. The aim of shape-shifting was temporarily to *become* an animal. In this way, it was possible to enter the otherworld and visit the spirits of the ancestors. While this lasted, the body was in a state of unconsciousness (Ellis 1943: 127; Turville-Petre 1975: 229–30; Hedeager 2004: 235–6; Price 2002: 59–60).

The *fylgja* can be described as a 'follower' or '*doppelganger*', and appeared in either human or animal form. The etymology of this word has been interpreted in different ways (see Glosecki 1989: 186; De Vries 1977: 147f; Price 2002: 59; Hedeager 2004: 235). It is important to distinguish between the animal *fylgja* and the animal shape taken on by a spirit. The latter was active only while the body was unconscious and seems to have been enlightened by the person's conscious mind. The *fylgja* on the other hand was the active follower of the human. At the person's death, the *fylgja* could start leading her own independent existence. Another interesting point is that the *fylgjur* could be inherited and 'belonged' to one family line. They have thus been seen as some kind of dead ancestors (Hedeager 2004: 235; Ellis 1943: 127ff.; Price 2002: 59). The *hamingjur* could also be passed on after death and usually stayed within the same family. The *hamingjur* can be seen as a personification of a person's luck, or luck-spirit (Price 2002: 59–60; Ellis 1943: 13ff.).

The Norse migration of the soul

After it leaves the body, the pre-Christian soul is often said in literature to take the form of an animal. Icelandic sagas contain many examples of this shape-shifting (Ellis 1943: 122ff.), especially in association with Odin, who was the master of this art. According to the *Ynglinga saga*, Odin's body seemed dead or asleep, while he himself took the shape of a winged creature, a quadruped animal, a fish or a snake. In this shape, he then travelled to 'far-off lands' (*Ynglinga saga*, chapter 7, see Hollander 1964: 10–11; Ellis 1943: 122; Ström 1958: 435; Price 2002: 93–107; Hedeager 1997 and 2004: 234–5). It is also interesting to note that Odin, on at least one occasion, is described as the lord of the undead (*drauga dróttin*) (*Ynglinga saga*, chapter 7, see Hollander 1964: 11; Price 2002: 104). In *Hávamál* it is stated that Odin could make hanged corpses walk and talk to him (Larrington 1996: 37, stanza 157; *cf.* Ström 1958: 434). Odin thus had an important function in connection with the dead.

Birds were often the chosen vehicles of shape-shifting. In the *Poetic Edda*, birds were the bringers of prophetic advice. One such example is the eagle in *Völuspá* who was seen as an omen of the New Age (Larrington 1996: 12). Sigurd Fafnisbani was guided by birds after accidentally having consumed some of the dragon's blood (Faulkes 1987: 101–2; Larrington 1996: 162–4). Other examples include *The List of Rig* where Kon was advised by a bird, and *The Poem of Helgi Hiorvardsson*, where Atli made a compact with a bird (Larrington 1996: 123–4 and 252). The significance of birds in the Norse religion also seems to have survived in various forms of Nordic folklore. In southern Sweden, people talked of the 'night ravens', which were evil or unhappy dead who left their graves at night. Birds must moreover be well treated; to kill a small bird, or even imitate one, could be dangerous as they could then take their revenge (Schön 1998: 58).

Intimations of the Anglo-Saxon soul

In contexts that could be pre-Christian, the Anglo-Saxons too appear to have had wandering souls, often showing a strong connection with birds. Bird imagery is clearly seen in the poems *The Wanderer* and *The Seafarer*, in which the speaker refers to 'the flight of his soul'. Glosecki argued that this reflects a pre-Christian tradition of shamanic travel in the form of winged creatures (Glosecki 1989: 78–83).

The Seafarer contains several examples of 'the flight of the soul':

> And so now my mind (hyge) moves out beyond the spirit-locker,
> my soul with the sea flood
> over the whale's country soars widely–
> over the surfaces of the earth – then comes back again to me,
> hungry and greedy; the lone-flier (anfloga) yells,
> whets for the whale-road my spirit; irresistibly
> urges it out over the stretches of seas.
> (*The Seafarer*, lines 58–64a, cited in Glosecki 1989: 78).

This passage refers to the *hyge* which crosses over to another world, screaming like a bird. According to Glosecki, this points to a lingering belief in the existence of a 'free soul' in Anglo-Saxon England. The Old English word *hyge*, 'mind' is a cognate to the Old Norse *hugr*, which was discussed above (Glosecki 1989: 78–9). In another passage from *The Seafarer*, traits of Old English *hama* meaning 'coat' or 'covering' is found. This word is a cognate of the Old Norse *hamr*.

> Therefore now compel
> heart thoughts that I high streams
> salt waves' rolling, should try for myself;
> my heart's desire urges on every occasion

> my spirit to travel, to seek far from here
> the land of strangers.
> (*The Seafarer*, lines 33a-38, Glosecki 1989: 79).

Glosecki interpreted this passage as a reference to the flight of a dissociated soul, which has a life of its own and a capability to compel the body, its 'flesh-coat', *i.e.* *flæschama*. Compounds with *hama* occur frequently in Anglo-Saxon poetry, which demonstrates that the soul was seen as a separate entity surrounded by a coat of flesh. Another such example is *feþerhama*, *i.e.* feather-coat. The Old Norse equivalent is *fjaðrhamr*, which signifies that when someone, *e.g.* Odin, put on this feather coat, he/she can fly to other worlds (Glosecki 1989: 79–80).

Elsewhere the poem suggests that in the minds of the population, the ancestors could at times provide comfort for the human soul. Also in this passage, the ancestral spirits were reached through ecstatic flight, where the soul took the shape of a bird (Glosecki 1989: 80).

> At times the song of the wild swan
> I made do for my entertainment, the cry of the gannet
> and music of the curlew for the laughter of men,
> the singing mew for a drink of mead.
> Storms there beat stone-cliffs, where the tern answered them,
> icy-feathered; full often the eagle screamed,
> dewy-feathered; nor could any protector-kinsman
> comfort my destitute spirit.
> (*The Seafarer*, 19b-26, Glosecki 1989: 80).

Another interesting Anglo-Saxon example where the soul takes the shape of a bird comes from Bede's *Ecclesiastical History*. The chapter which describes how King Edwin and his High Priest Coifi accepted Christianity contains the well-known passage comparing human life to the flight of a sparrow through the hall (Sherley-Price 1968: II.13). According to this description, the bird entering the hall through one door and leaving through another is capable of going between the different worlds.

On at least two instances in the sources, there are possible references to the Anglo-Saxon version of the Old Norse *fylgja*. One such example is the Old English charm *Wið Dweorh*:

> Here came walking in, in here, a spider-creature –
> he had his coat (hama) in hand, said that you were his horse,
> laid his reins on your neck. They began to travel from the land;
> once they came from the land, then the limbs began to feel cold.
> (Glosecki 1989: 186)

Glosecki's interpretation of this is that the 'spider-creature' (*spiderwiht*) is a version of a *fylgja*, carrying its coat/skin (*hama*). The rider may thus be a shape-shifter (Glosecki 1989: 187). Another possible example of a *fylgja* is seen in the term *anfloga* (*i.e.* 'the lone-flier'), which is found in a passage of *The Seafarer* quoted above. The lone-flier and the *fylgja* share some similarities: they leave from and return to the same 'corporeal home', they travel through the same otherworldly medium, and they both resemble winged creatures more than humans (Glosecki 1989: 187).

The evidence of images

Lotte Hedeager has argued that the metamorphosis of animals and humans described in the written sources may be seen in the animal ornament on objects of the 5th to the 7th centuries (Hedeager 2004: 246). For example, the C-type bracteates, which portray human beings surrounded by various kinds of animals have been seen to depict a shaman's journeys to the otherworld. The heads of the humans, often shaped like birds, have been interpreted as the 'free soul'. The large animal that is frequently present (depicted as a hybrid between a horse and an elk) is seen as escorting the shaman to the world of the dead. By the animal's mouth there is often a sign, which has been seen to indicate that the animal is 'ensouled'. Other animals escorting the shamans are birds and snakes. This type of iconography also appears on several of the B-type bracteates (Hedeager 1997: 274–5 and 2004: 227–32; Hauck 1983). The decorations thus include the three animals that are significant as guiding spirits within the shamanic worldview. The snake procures knowledge from the otherworld, the bird flies to different parts of the world and is therefore knowledgeable, and the large animal serves as a protector on the journey (Hedeager 2004: 228–32). Other interesting animal images, probably intended as shape-shifters, are the birds and boars represented on Vendel-period helmets, such as Valsgärde 7 (Uppland) (Figure 8.1) and Torslunda (Öland).

Anglo-Saxon artefacts have similar ornamentation to the Norse, which in turn suggests similarities in belief. A wild boar decorates the crest of the helmet from Benty Grange (Derbyshire). On the Sutton Hoo helmet, a dragon forms the crest from the neck to the forehead, a bird covers the forehead and eyebrows and upper mouth with its beak, wings and tail, while the boars are placed by the temples, at the very edges of the bird's wings (Figure 8.2) (Hedeager 2004: 228–32; Bruce-Mitford 1979: 35). Further Anglo-Saxon examples include the Sutton Hoo purse and shield. The purse-lid is decorated with a pair of plaques depicting a man between two raging animals, an image strikingly similar to the Torslunda dies, and another representing a bird of prey lunging on a duck (Figure 8.3) (Bruce-Mitford 1979: 104 and 110–11). Winged creatures – a bird of prey and a winged dragon – moreover feature on the fittings for the front of the shield (Bruce-Mitford 1979: 32 and 38).

Figure 8.1. The Valsgärde 7 helmet. Photography: Annika Larsson

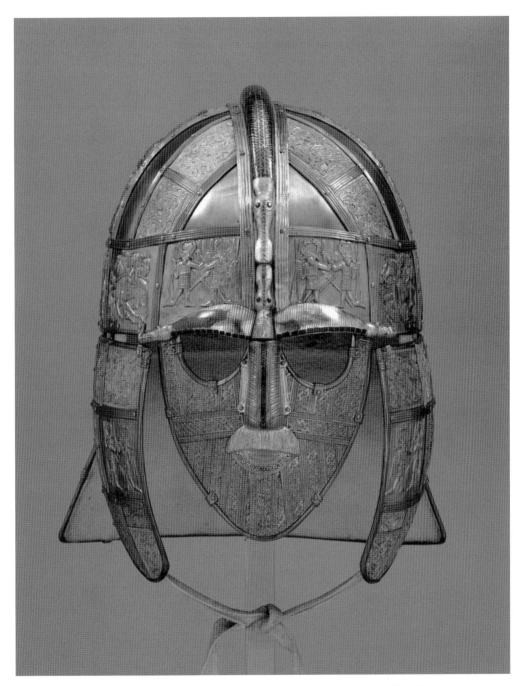

Figure 8.2. Replica of the Sutton Hoo Helmet. © Trustees of the British Museum

Through her detailed study of early Anglo-Saxon animal-ornamented shields, Tania Dickinson concluded that the shields decorated with Salin's Style I frequently include references to 'monstrous, underworld embodiments of evil or death and to gods or sorcerers who can defeat or offer salvation from them'. The interrelationship between the motifs in Style I, the figural mounts, and Scandinavian bracteates suggests that the cult of Odin was at the heart of the iconography (Dickinson 2005: 160).

Stephen Glosecki strengthens the arguments put forward by Hedeager and Dickinson. Glosecki felt that the aggression of the wild boar made it a symbol of 'manly power': 'We can visualize the boar on Beowulf's helmet – especially when we look slantwise at the Benty Grange, Sutton Hoo, or Torslunda analogues – but we can hardly imagine the highly charged resonance the boar image had for men who could recall the last time they were a spear's length way from a quarter ton of animated anger intent on their destruction'(1989: 53). He used the word *nigouimes* to describe the boar, finding English terms, such as 'follower' and 'guardian spirit' to be misleading. *Nigouimes* simply means 'shamanic personal guardian', a term also used by Lévi-Strauss (Glosecki 1989: 31–2 and 55–8). Shamanic peoples believe that such guardians are needed in order to stop shamans and spirits from stealing other people's souls. Since the *nigouimes* is the most effective guardian of the soul, it plays a significant role for the warrior. Glosecki thus concluded that the wearers of the Sutton Hoo and the Benty Grange helmets ascribed the boar images with the animistic power that these spirit guardians were seen to have. An important concept in shamanic societies is that of sympathetic magic: 'the image equals the object represented'. This means that the boar image provided the power of a boar to the

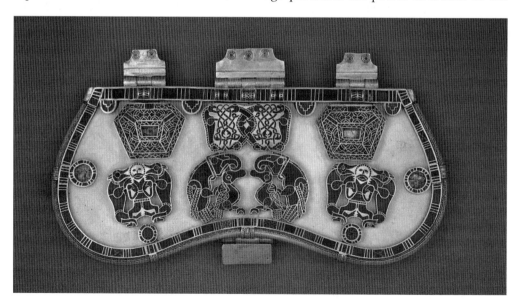

Figure 8.3. The Sutton Hoo purse lid. © Trustees of the British Museum

wearer, and was thus seen as alive, and as a 'power source capable of independent action' (Glosecki 1989: 53–7).

Ancestors and burial

The treatment of burial mounds should provide an important point of entry to the cult of ancestors as these monuments functioned as places for communication between the dead and the living. The rituals performed at burial mounds seem to have had at least two different functions: to honour the dead through offerings, or to wake the dead in order to gain esoteric knowledge (*cf.* Brendalsmo *et al.* 1992: 96). One of the most famous examples of offerings to the dead comes from the *Saga of King Hákon Hákonson*, a Christian king in 10th-century Norway. According to this saga, Hákon had unsuccessfully tried to turn Norway into a Christian country. At one point the farmers of the kingdom demanded that the king should participate in their annual ritual feast, where the participants drank to the gods as well as 'in memory of departed kinsfolk' (Hollander 1964: 107–11).

The waking of the dead appears to be referred to in some Norwegian runic inscriptions, such as that on the stone from Eggja, Sogndal i Sogn, which has been archaeologically dated to AD 650–700 (Brendalsmo *et al.* 1992, 92). According to Ottar Grønvik's interpretation, part of this inscription states that one should "not seek the man who howls over the naked dead". Grønvik argued that this was a prohibition against necromantic practices, which was carried out under ecstatic forms. He saw this kind of necromancy in opposition to the 'traditional' part of the ancestor cult, *i.e.* to sit on the grave of an ancestor (Brendalsmo *et al.* 1992: 92; Grønvik 1985: 154–5, 163). This practice of 'sitting outside' (*útiseta*) had traditionally been connected to *seiðr* (Ström 1961: 227; Brendalsmo *et al.* 1992: 92). Sitting on a mound is connected to the cult of the dead (Ellis 1943: 105ff.). According to Folke Ström, there were two kinds of *útiseta*, one active and one passive. The active form included the waking of the dead, who were then more or less forced to reveal their secrets (Ström 1961: 227). Brendalsmo and Røthe argued that this could be described as necromancy and that it was most likely performed at burial mounds (Brendalsmo *et al.* 1992: 92–3). The eddaic poems also contain several references to the waking of the dead (Brendalsmo *et al.* 1992: 93–6). One such example is *Grogalder*, which tells us about a son who wakes up his mother from the dead in order to get her help (Brendalsmo *et al.* 1992: 93–4). Another example is found in the *Second Poem of Helgi Hundingsbani*, in which a man called Helgi who had died and gone to Valhalla was called back to his burial mound to comfort his mourning widow (Larrington 1996: 139–40; *cf.* DuBois, 1999: 77–8).

Practices connected to the ancestor cult are more evident in the medieval provincial laws of Norway and Sweden. 'Sitting outside' was prohibited in the Law of the Borgarthing (BL I: 16). The Older Law of the Gulathing outlawed the making of sacrifices to mounds (*hauga*) (GL 29: *hauga* most likely refers to burial mounds. *Cf.* Brendalsmo *et al.* 1992: 96). According to the Older Laws of the Gulathing and the Borgarthing, it was illegal to 'wake up trolls'. In line with Grønvik's arguments quoted above, this has been interpreted as the waking of the dead who were buried in mounds (GL 32; BL I: 16; Brendalsmo *et al.* 1992: 97). The Later Law of the Gulathing also prescribed strict punishments for those who 'tried to wake up ghosts or those who lived in the mounds'. This law moreover made it illegal to believe that mounds were inhabited by *landvættir* (Keyser *et al.* 1848: 308). Furthermore, *Gutalagen* (the Law of Gotland) made it illegal to invoke mounds (Holmbäck *et al.* 1979).

For Anglo-Saxon England, Sarah Semple has reviewed secondary uses of prehistoric burial mounds, for burial, ritual deposition, and cult, concluding that burial mounds must have played an important part in a variety of Anglo-Saxon religious practices (Semple 2002: chapters 2, 3, 6). Semple also reviewed the perceptions of burial mounds and barrows in Anglo-Saxon written sources, showing how they changed over time. In the 8th century, burial mounds symbolised "death, terror, sorrow and imprisonment" (*e.g. The Life of Guthlac* and *The Life of Wilfrid*, see Semple 2002: 228–242; this vol.). She saw this perception as due to a "concerted attempt" by ecclesiastics to discourage the population "both from barrow-burial and from using traditional ancestral locations for funerary rites, and ultimately to sever ancestral links with their pagan forefathers and heathen past" (Semple 2002: 246–47). It is well-known that priests made use of local legends during the conversion period in order to explain Christianity to the population. There are many examples from Scandinavia, where priests used figures from the Norse mythology in order to achieve this aim (Sanmark 2004: 95–99).

By the 10th century, two new sets of perceptions had evolved. The barrows were now either seen as places inhabited by 'supernatural agencies' described as criminals or murderers, or as places inhabited by monstrous mythical creatures. Examples of the former are *Andreas, The Wife's Lament* and *Guthlac A*, while examples of the latter type are *Wið Færstice, Maxims II* and the 10th-century account of Cedd's foundation at Lastingham (Semple 2002: 242–47). According to Semple, the reason for the 10th-century perceptions was the increasing use of these monuments as execution cemeteries between the 8th and the 11th centuries. The use of prehistoric remains as places for execution cemeteries formed part of judicial practice particularly from the 8th century onwards. Two thirds of the excavated execution sites are associated with prehistoric or Anglo-Saxon barrows (Reynolds 1999: 105–10; Semple 2002: 318–23).

Semple's analysis implies that an ancestor cult had formed a central part of the Anglo-Saxon pre-Christian religion. Ancestors were not always good-natured: when not properly looked after, they were seen to become angry and dangerous, and were thus often feared. It would not be surprising if horror stories regarding burial mounds were spread in Christian times. Where the belief in ancestral spirits was strong this unrest could be transferred to Christian burial grounds. After the introduction of Christianity in Finland, when the population had to bury their dead in the churchyards, the dead ancestors could no longer be cared for in line with the old traditions. As a result, the churchyards came to be seen as 'frightful places, full of dissatisfied dead' (Lehtosalo-Hilander 1987: 34).

The Wife's Lament from the 10th-century *Exeter Book* has traditionally been seen as a description of a woman who after the death of her lord lived in a 'friendless exile' in an 'earthen dugout' (*eorðscræfe*) or 'earth chamber' (*eorðsele*). Semple has pointed out that these same words were also used in *Beowulf* in the description of the burial mound. She has moreover drawn the attention to the use of the term *leger* in the poem, which is generally associated with the dead and their graves. Semple's interpretation of this poem is therefore that the woman was not exiled, but rather 'a restless ghost confined to the place of her burial, the *eorðscræfe* or *eorðsele*' (Semple 2002: 225–27; Bradley 1982: 382–85).

A well-known scene on the 8th-century Franks Casket has long been seen as representing a burial mound (Becker 1973; Webster 1999; Fern, this vol.; Figure 8.4). The right-hand scene depicts three cloaked figures. The central scene portrays a horse, a bird, a burial mound with a person inside it, and a cloaked figure with a staff. The left-hand scene shows a winged horse sitting on a 'mound' with a snake round its nose. Opposite this creature there is a warrior. The central and left-hand scenes, in contrast to the right-hand one, are set in a forest. The accompanying text reads:

> "Here Hos sits on the sorrow-mound; she suffers distress in that Ertae had decreed for her [had imposed it upon her], a wretched den of sorrows and torments of mind" (Semple 2002: 228; Becker 1973: 27–40 and 275).

Leslie Webster has convincingly argued that the central and the left-hand panels signify a world of terror, similar to that found in Felix's description of Guthlac's fenland. This consisted of woods and rushes, "a world of spiritual dangers, of demons and evil spirits, at least as much as physical ones" (Webster 1999: 241–46; Colgrave 1956: 86–89, 116–19). In this context, it must be of significance that the body inside the mound (in the central scene) is depicted wearing a cloak, and not as a skeleton or a pile of bones, as this implies that the body is neither cremated nor decomposed. The figure standing to the right of the mound seems to be wearing a similar piece of

Figure 8.4. The Franks Casket. © Trustees of the British Museum

clothing. This in turn suggests that the tale set out here is based on a story with pre-Christian origins about a woman whose free soul has not been released. She would thus be trapped in a liminal place, between the world of the living and the world of the dead. The horse, the bird, the winged horse and the snake suggest the animals that Hedeager (above) saw as acting as guiding spirits in a shamanic worldview. The presence of these animals thus further strengthens the idea that the left and the middle scenes represent a liminal phase between the world of the living and the world of the dead (see also Fern, this vol.).

Ancestors and drinking

That burial mounds also served as locations of feasts for the dead has already been mentioned in the story of King Hákon (above). Drinking rituals have been seen as one of the most important elements in the ceremonies that served to strengthen the link between the living and deceased ancestors (Ström 1960a: 120; Sundqvist 2002: 259–66; Sanmark 2004: chapter 5). Chapter 23 of the Older Law of the Gulathing deals with ale feasts that were held for the dead, called 'inheritance ale' or 'soul's ale'. These feasts could be held on 'the seventh or the thirtieth morning' after the death of a person, 'or even later'. The law required a priest to be present at such feasts, presumably to make sure that they were carried out according to Christian rituals (GL 23). In the *Capitula Synodica* (for the year 852) Hincmar of Rheims stated that priests must not get drunk at the annual feasts for a dead person, nor consecrate the devotional bowl at the feasts. It was moreover not allowed to drink to the soul of the dead (Sundqvist 2002: 263; *cf.* A.-S. Gräslund 2001: 226).

That food and drink were offered by pre-Christians not only at the time of death, but also at regular intervals, *e.g.* the anniversary of the death, is strongly suggested by much later evidence from Estonia and Latvia, areas officially christianized in the first quarter of the 13th century. According to the Riga Provincial Council of 1428, the Livonians organised meals in cemeteries and churches, and brought food to their dead ancestors in order to console them. This statement is supported by the pottery fragments found in churchyards, and also by the traditions present in the isolated area of Setomaa in south-eastern Estonia. Here, the population hold commemorative meals on the graves of their dead ancestors, both on church holidays and at commemorative days for the dead (*e.g.* 40 days, 6 months, 1, 3, 6 and 9 years after the death). As part of this tradition, vodka can also be poured on the grave. According to popular belief, the commemorative meal is a way of communicating and reconnecting with the deceased, who are believed to take part in the meal. The reasoning behind the current practices may not be the same as in pre-Christian times, but echoes a similar expression of the human need to be near their loved ones. It should also be noted that food offerings to the honour of the dead are part of Orthodox Christianity. There seems to be no reason to doubt that the population has had a continuous tradition of offering food to the dead from early Christian times onwards. These rituals in themselves most likely derive from pre-Christian religious practice (Valk 2001: 7, 81–4). The tradition of leaving food offerings on graves was also present in Sweden as late as the twentieth century (A.-S. Gräslund 1992: 142; A.-S. Gräslund 1969).

Another interesting example from the present day comes from the Khanties, a Finno-Ugrian people living in Western Siberia. In the Khanty burial grounds, small house-like constructions are erected on the graves. These 'houses' have small windows that lead straight into the grave chamber. When the people visit the grave of a dead relative, they open the window and knock three times. They then have a memorial meal on the grave and put a serving of food and drink close to the window of the house-like construction (A.-S. Gräslund 2001: 222–23).

Anne-Sofie Gräslund has linked these rituals to archaeological finds from Sweden, in particular to the external cists found at the edges of some Viking Age burial mounds. These cists are *c.* 1.5 x 1.2 metres in size. Some are square and others have three sides, with the open end towards the mound. The contents of these cists varied. Some contained very few finds, such as cremated bones or potsherds. Among the most interesting finds were however a horse skull, and a set of horse's teeth (A.-S. Gräslund 2001: 227–31; A.-S. Gräslund 1969). Gräslund has argued that these cists were used for food and drink offerings to the dead (A.-S. Gräslund 2001: 227–31; A.-S. Gräslund 1969).

Another possible example of this tradition comes from the island of Gotland. On the southern side of some graves from the early Iron Age, there are large, often flat, stones. These have been interpreted as a kind of sacrificial stone or table (Blomkvist 2002: 144; Nylén 1958: 80–81). It is interesting to note that these stones, as well as the external cists discussed above are located on the south or southwest side of the grave. (*cf.* A.-S. Gräslund 2001: 227ff.).

In Anglo-Saxon England evidence of drinking and feasting associated with burial has been noted in a few cemeteries. At Sutton Hoo, a cattle feast was inferred immediately following the construction of the first mound in the princely cemetery, Mound 5 (Carver 2005: 83–4, 187–99). At the mixed cemetery at Snape (Suffolk) seven pits of early Anglo-Saxon date were interpreted as cooking pits used for ritual feasting or cooking at the time of the burial. Pestell pointed to other possible examples of such pits at a number of cemeteries including Norton (Cleveland), Flixton (Suffolk) and Nettleton Top (Lincolnshire) (Pestell 2001: 260). A similar interpretation was offered for two features identified within a Bronze Age round barrow at Cossington (Leicestershire), re-used for burial in the early Anglo-Saxon period (Thomas 2008: 63–65). In this context it is naturally important to note that post-burial feasting would in most cases not leave any traces or may not be dated conclusively as contemporary with the use of the site. Pestell's findings however led him to conclude that features of this type may well prove 'to have been far more common in Anglo-Saxon cemeteries and to have played a regular part in the ritual associated with burial' (Pestell 2001: 260). A late reference to the practice is found in the 10th-century writings of Ælfric, who advised priests not to 'eat or drink in the place where the corpse lies, lest you are imitators of the heathenism which they practise there' (Whitelock *et al.* 1981: 218; Morris 1989: 61).

Ancestors and landscape

Ancestors were connected to natural features in the landscape, such as mountains and hills. In the *Landnámabók* and *Eyrbryggja saga*, we are told about a father and a son (Thorolf Mostur-Beard and Thorstein Cod-Biter) who after their deaths retired to their 'familial mountain', where they feasted together with their ancestors. This mountain was called *Helgafell*, *i.e.* the holy mountain (Chapter 11, Pálsson *et al.* 1989: 38; Pálsson *et al.* 1972: chapter 85, 45–46)

Another interesting example is found in *Landnámabók*. Here it is stated that the descendants of the Christian settler Auðr Djúpúgða (Aud the Deep-minded), began to worship the hills where she used to pray during her lifetime. The descendants are also reported to have sacrificed to her/the mountain and to have built a 'temple' there. It is moreover stated that they 'believed they would go into the hills when they died' (Pálsson *et al.* 1972: chapter 97, 52). The connection between ancestor cult and natural landscape features is supported by evidence from both Sámi and indigenous religions, where the ancestor cult is often combined with the concept of transmigration. This means that the deceased can reappear in animals, plants, stones or other objects. This also includes the concepts of rebirth and reincarnation into another person. (B. Gräslund 1994: 17; Price 2002: 244–47). We are told that when the brothers Haukr and Gaukr drowned together with their father, they were transformed into dragons (Klare 1933–34: 24).

The fact that ancestors seem to have been connected to features in the landscape also fits in with the arguments that the pre-Christians believed in an 'ensouled' landscape. Stefan Brink has argued that to the people of pre-Christian Scandinavia, the landscape was metaphysically charged, and that they thus lived in a 'numinous environment' (Brink 2001: 81–82). He compared this to the religion of the Greeks where "all nature must be described as a sacred landscape, created by the gods and inhabited by gods, and especially demons, spirits or 'powers'" (Brink 2001: 84). In Roman religion, similarly, supernatural powers, named *numen* or *genius loci*, were believed to be present in particular places. Brink associated these concepts to the Polynesian *mana*, which both people and places were seen to possess, and thus became taboo in various degrees (Brink 2001: 84–85; for the ensouled world of the Siberian peoples, see Price 2002: 293–96). The aspect of taboo is particularly interesting in connection to the description of *Helgafell* in *Landnámabók*, as it is stated that "no one was allowed even to look at it [the holy mountain] unless he'd washed himself first" (Pálsson *et al.* 1972: chapter 85, 45.)

It seems very likely that the ancestor cult formed a large, if not the major part, of the ideology behind these practices. In Anglo-Saxon England the same ideas may be implied by placenames connected to the gods, such as Wenslow (Bedfordshire), *i.e.* Woden's mound (*hlāw*), Thunderlow, (Essex), *i.e.* Thunor's mound. (Meaney 1995: 36).

Malevolent ancestors: the laying of ghosts

In Icelandic sagas ghosts are often said to cause illnesses, madness or death. One such example concerns the story of Thorolf Twist-Foot in *Eyrbryggja saga*. After his death, Thorolf began to terrorise the area around his old home. Animals that came too close to his grave were driven mad and died. Soon afterwards, humans started dying from strange illnesses. In the end, all the farms in the valley were abandoned. The people had either been killed, or driven away, by the spirit of Thorolf (Pálsson *et al.* 1989: chapter 34). The descriptions of the ghosts' physical appearance in the sagas are particularly interesting in this context. The most crucial point is that the ghosts have retained their human body. The suggested term 'corpse ghosts' thus seems rather fitting (Ström 1960b: 253). An example of a 'corpse ghost' is found in the *Second Poem of Helgi Hundingsbani* mentioned above. When Helgi returned from the dead, he had blood streaming from his wounds, and his hands were ice cold (Larrington 1996: 139f). There were various methods to stop the corpse from haunting the world of the living. The body could be decapitated, staked, or its spine could be broken. Another alternative was cremation, followed by the scattering of the ashes into the sea (Ström 1958: 432–34). Thorolf's body was removed from his grave, and reburied in a new grave. On top of this grave, a wall was erected that was so high that only birds could fly over it. This stopped Thorolf temporarily. When he again started to haunt the living, his body was exhumed and then cremated, and the ashes were scattered in the wind (Pálsson *et al.* 1989: chapters 34 and 63). In Medieval Greenland, hunters are reported to have boiled two corpses to rid them of the flesh and prevent them haunting, then buried the bones in the churchyard at Garðar (Nedkvitne 2004: 146–48).

It seems likely that stories of this kind indicate behaviour from pre-Christian times. The presence of this type of belief is also indicated by burial practices at Valsgärde, Sweden. Frands Herschend has pointed out that the boat burials were "open, or at least easily accessible" until some time after the funeral. According to Herschend, this suggests that "the living considered the deceased gone, rather than dead. Eventually they declared him dead and closed the grave" (Herschend 2001: 71).

Evidence of belief in 'corpse ghosts' is found also in Anglo-Saxon England. In the writings of Ælfric it is stated that "Witches still go to cross-roads and heathen burials with their delusive magic; and call to the devil; and he comes to them in the likeness of the man who is buried there, as if he arise from death; but she cannot bring it about that the dead arise through her magic" (Pope 1968: 796, lines 118–23; Meaney 1984–5: 130–31). The words 'in the likeness of the man who is buried there' is significant in this respect and can be seen as evidence of a belief in ghosts in the shape of 'corpse ghosts'. Ælfric's statement that the witches could not raise the dead, suggests necromantic practices, as was discussed above in relation to the Norse religion (*cf.* Meaney 1984–85).

The Life of St Modwenna (Chapter 47) tells the story of two peasants who had wrongfully left the abbot of Burton in order to live under the jurisdiction of Count Roger the Poitevin (Bartlett 2002: 193–99). The peasants brought false charges against the abbot, which caused the count to seize and destroy the monastery's crop. The next day, the two peasants suddenly died. They were placed in coffins and buried in the churchyard. However, the same evening, they reappeared carrying their coffins. This happened also the following evening, when they walked through the paths and fields of the village, now in the shape of men carrying coffins on their shoulders, now in the likeness of bears or dogs or other animals. When these astonishing events had taken place every evening and every night for some time, such a disease afflicted the village that all the peasants fell into desperate straits and within a few days all except three perished by sudden death in a remarkable way. In order to stop the two ghosts, the bishop gave his permission for the exhumation of their corpses. When the graves were opened, the bodies were found to be intact. The villagers decapitated them and placed their heads between their legs. They also tore out their hearts and placed them on a fire, where they eventually "cracked with a great sound and everyone there saw an evil spirit in the form of a crow fly from the flames. Soon after this was done, both the disease and the phantoms ceased". Despite this, the village was abandoned, and for a long time, no one dared to live there.

Some of the best evidence for the treatment of the potentially malevolent dead comes from the Anglo-Saxon execution cemeteries recently collected and studied by Andrew Reynolds (Reynolds 1999: 105–10; Reynolds 2009). The execution sites were often located on the borders of the hundreds, *i.e.* in the physically liminal place of society, and, not least, in places where the 'dissatisfied' ancestors were seen to dwell. In the case of Sutton Hoo the execution cemetery was founded by the Christian authorities on a seventh century princely burial ground, presumably in living memory (Carver 2005: Ch 9). Andrew Reynolds argued that the reason why these places were used for this purpose was that they were seen as 'evil and and haunted and outside of normal society' (Reynolds 1997; Semple 2002: 244). The bodies were often decapitated or in other ways mutilated, presumably to stop them from haunting the living. The executed were also denied burial in consecrated ground, and would therefore not be received into Paradise on Judgement Day (Reynolds 1999: 105–10). Consequently, they would also have been trapped between the world of the living and the world of the dead. This may well have been visibly demonstrated by the gallows where the dead were left hanging 'between heaven and earth being deemed unworthy of both' (Reynolds 1999: 109).

Ancestors and the church

On Christianization, the concept of the soul and thus the attitude to ancestors was modified. One of the few aspects of eschatology on which the Scriptures are clear is the separation of body and soul at the time of death: the soul departed once and for all (Cross *et al.* 1974: 1292; *cf.* MacGregor 2005). Like pagans, Christians made a connection between breath and soul, the soul being seen as an exhalation or a breeze. This originated from Genesis where it is stated that God created man and 'breathed into his nostrils the breath of life; and man became a living soul' (Genesis 2: 7; Cross *et al.* 1974: 1292). This idea is also clearly seen in the Latin words for 'soul' and 'breath', *animus* and *anima*. A further parallel is the Latin *spiritus*, which denotes both 'breath' and 'spirit' (Hellquist 1999: vol. 1: 20). The Old Norse word *önd* is derived from the Old Saxon word *ando*, which can be traced back to the Indo-European root *an*, 'to blow', 'to breath'. Old English *anda* was used for anger (*i.e.* snorting). Moreover, the Gothic word *usanan* denoted both to exhale and to die (Hellquist 1999: vol. 1: 20). On some occasions in the Norse sources the verb *andast/ændast* was used for 'to meet one's end'/'to breath'. A particularly striking use of the verb occurs in *andadiz i hvítavaðum*, which presumably refers to people who were baptised on their deathbeds, and thus 'met his/her end in white clothes' (*i.e.* in their baptismal robes). It is also interesting to note that *andalauss* denoted 'soulless', as well as 'without breath' (Heggstad 1930: 19–20; Fritzner 1893: 53). Significantly, the verb *andast/ændast* also appears on rune stones, most frequently in reference to people who died in the east. Ingmar Jansson has pointed out that the use of this particular word seems to have come from Byzantium. In this area the expression 'to die' was avoided in favour of 'to meet one's end' (Jansson 2005: 48–9 See *e.g.* Sö 40, Sö 345, Sö 148, U 518 and U 136. Brate *et al.* 1924–36; Wessén *et al.* 1940–43). Two such inscriptions from the province of Småland commemorate people who died in England (Sm 27 and Sm 29. Kinander 1935–61).

The above examples suggest that the use of *andast/ændast* was Christian. The same idea of dying is expressed by the Old Swedish *siælas*, Old Icelandic *sálast* and Anglo-Saxon *sáwlian* (Hellquist 1999, vol. 2: 918), suggesting that the Old Norse word for 'soul' *sál* (and its variants) was a Germanic word introduced by Christian writers for Christian concepts only (Hellquist 1999, vol. 2: 917–18; Turville-Petre 1975: 229).

It is also interesting to note that in older translations of the Bible death is described as 'surrendering the spirit' or 'giving up the ghost' (Parrinder 1993: 548). Further evidence of this idea is also found on rune stones, where the frequently occurring expression 'may God help her/his soul', always contains the word soul (*sál*) in the singular (see *e.g.* U 440, U 940, Sö 66, Sö 195, Sö 289 and Sö 382: Brate *et al.* 1924–36; Wessén *et al.* 1940–43). The introduction of the Christian concept of the soul thus also entailed a new concept of death; that the one and only soul was seen to leave the body with the last breath.

The Christian idea of ghosts thus also differs from that found in the sagas. According to the Gospel of Luke, the disciples were terrified by the resurrection of Christ, as they believed that they were seeing a ghost. Christ however assured them this was not the case since he, unlike a ghost, was made of flesh and blood (Parrinder 1993: 548; Luke 24: 37–40). Over time, the Christian attitude to ghosts was rather divided, and the existence of ghosts was neither rejected nor accepted. All Souls' Day has been celebrated since the 10th century in the Western church. Exorcism has been practised in order to put drifting souls to rest. In the *Dialogues* of Gregory the Great, which were widely read among the Norse, there are several stories about ghosts. Augustine of Hippo, on the other hand, had rejected the existence of ghosts (Parrinder 1993: 548; Nedkvitne 2004: 142). Another difference is that in the sagas that relate to pre-Christian times it was not a punishment to become a ghost: it was a voluntary decision taken by the dead. The damage caused by the ghosts was a result of their evil minds (Nedkvitne 2004: 38–43). By contrast, clerics explained the appearance of ghosts as due to burial in unconsecrated ground. This laid the foundations among the population that burial in consecrated ground was a necessity in order to give peace to the dead. This must have strengthened people's belief that access to Paradise was dependent on churchyard burial. Thus, the ecclesiastical legislation and the ghost stories worked in the same direction (Nedkvitne 2004: 148–51; Sanmark 2004: 264–68).

Clerics presumably used the ancestor cult for their own purposes, as they wished to take the dead away from the communal feeling of kin and farm, and instead bring them together in the community of the churchyards. Christian burial was clearly a high priority in early Christian times, as it was one of the five major Christian practices that were required by law, the other four major practices being the observance of fast and feast days, baptism, and Christian marriage regulations (Sanmark 2004: chapters 5–7).

Conclusion

As scholarship moves away from traditional views of religion, the importance of the ancestor cult, both for the Anglo-Saxons and the Norse, becomes increasingly clear and further evidence of this will most likely come to light in future research. This may apply particularly to archaeological evidence as awareness of features possibly related to this cult develops among excavators.

Acknowledgements

I would like to offer my thanks to Howard Williams for discussing feasting associated with burials with me and for providing references. I am also indebted to Tania Dickinson who kindly provided her article on animal-ornamented shields prior to publication.

References

[The alphabetical order including the Scandinavian and Icelandic characters is: aábcdðeéfghiíjklmnoópqrstuúüvwxyzþåäæöø]

Artelius, T. (2000) *Bortglömda föreställningar. Begravningsritual och begravningsplats i halländsk yngre järnålder.* Riksantikvarieämbetet arkeologiska undersökningar skrifter 36, Gotarc. Series B. Gothenburg Archaeological Theses 15: Göteborg
Badou, E. (1989) Hög – gård – helgedom i mellannorrland under den äldre järnåldern, *Arkeologi i norr* 2: 9–43
Bartlett, R. (ed. and tr.) (2002) Geoffrey of Burton, *Life and Miracles of St Modwenna*, Oxford: OUP
Becker, A. (1973) *Franks Casket. Zu den Bildern und Inschriften des Runenkästechens von Auzon,* Regensburg: H. Carl
The Bible. n.d., *The Holy Bible Containing the Old and New Testaments.* Translated out of the Original Tongues: And with the former Translations Diligently Compared and Revised, By His Majesty's Special Command, Authorized King James Version, Cambridge
Birkeli, E. (1938) *Fedrekult i Norge. Et forsøk på en systematisk-deskriptiv fremstilling,* Oslo: Dybwad
Birkeli, E. (1943) *Fedrekult fra norsk folkeliv i hedensk og kristen tid,* Oslo: Dybwad
BL – 'The Law of the Borgarthing', Meissner, R. (ed.) (1942) *Bruchstücke der Rechtsbücher des Borgarthings und des Eidsivathings,* 2–73, Germanenrechte, Neue Folge, Weimar, H. Böhlau Nachf
Blomkvist, T. (2002) *Från ritualiserad tradition till institutionaliserad Religion. Strategier för maktlegitimering på Gotland under järnålder och medeltid,* Uppsala: University Press
Bowie, F. (2000) *The Anthropology of Religion. An Introduction,* Oxford: Blackwells
Bradley, S.A.J., (ed. and tr.) (1982) *Anglo-Saxon Poetry: An Anthology of Old English Poems in Prose Translation with Introduction and Headnotes,* London: Everyman
Branston, B. (1980) *Gods of the North,* London: Thames and Hudson
Brate, E., and Wessén, E. (eds) (1924–36) *Södermanlands runinskrifter,* Stockholm: Almqvist & Wiksell
Brendalsmo, J. and Røthe, G. (1992) Haugbrot eller de levendes forhold til de døde – en komparativ analyse, *Meta* No. 1–2: 84–119
Brink, S. (2001) Mythologizing Landscape. Place and Space of Cult and Myth. *In* Michael Stausberg (ed.) *Kontinuitäten und Brüche in der Religionsgechichte. Festschrift für Anders Hultgård*

zu Seinem 65. Geburtstag am 23. 12. 2001, 76–112, Berlin: W. de Gruyter

Bruce-Mitford, R. (1979) *The Sutton Hoo Ship Burial. A Handbook*, London: British Museum Press

Carver, M. (2005) *Sutton Hoo: A Seventh-Century Princely Burial Ground and its Context*, London: British Museum Press

Colgrave B. (ed. and tr.) (1956) *Felix's Life of Saint Guthlac*, Cambridge: CUP

Cross, F.L., and E.A. Livingstone (eds) (1974) *The Oxford Dictionary of the Christian Church*, Second Edition, Oxford: OUP

Davidson, H.R.E. (1964) *Gods and Myths of Northern Europe*, Harmondsworth: Penguin Books

Davidson, H.R.E. (1982) *Scandinavian Mythology*, London: Hamlyn

De Vries, J. (1977) *Altnordisches etymologisches Wörterbuch*, Second Edition, Leiden: Brill

Dickinson, T.M. (2005) Symbols of Protection: The Significance of Animal-Ornamented Shields in Early Anglo-Saxon England, *Medieval Archaeology* 49: 109–63

Dubois, T.A. (1999) *Nordic Religions in the Viking Age*, Philadelphia: University of Pennsylvania Press

Durkheim É. (1912) *Elementary forms of Religious Life*, Paris

EL – The Law of the Eidsivathing, Meissner, R. (ed.) (1942) *Bruchstücke der Rechtsbücher des Borgarthings und des Eidsivathings*, Germanenrechte, Neue Folge, 74–133, Weimar: H. Böhlau

Ellis, H.R. (1943) *The Road to Hel. A Study of the Conception of the Dead in Old Norse Literature*, Cambridge: CUP

Faulkes, A. (tr.) (1987) Snorri Sturluson, *Edda*, London: Dent

Fritzner, J. (1893) *Ordbog over det gamle norske Sprog*, Kristiania: Feilberg & Landmark

Fustel De Coulanges, N.D. (1874) *The Ancient City. A Study of Religion, Laws and Institutions of Greece and Rome*, Boston: Lee & Shepard

Gennep, A., Van. (1960) *The Rites of Passage*, Chicago: University of Chicago Press

GL – The Law of The Gulathing, Larson. L.M. (ed. and tr.) (1935) *The Earliest Norwegian Laws. Being the Gulathing Law and the Frostathing Law*, 35–210, New York: Columbia University Press

Glosecki, S.O. (1989) *Shamanism and Old English Poetry*, New York and London: Garland

Graham-Campbell, J. (2001) *The Viking World*, Third Edition, London: Francis Lincoln

Gräslund, A.-S. (1969) Särdrag inom vikingatidens gravskick, *Nordsvensk forntid, Kungl. skytteanska samfundets handlingar* 6, 133–50, Umeå

Gräslund, A.-S. (1992) Kultkontinuitet – myt eller verklighet? *In* Bertil Nilsson (ed.) *Kontinuitet i kult och tro från vikingatid till medeltid*, Projektet Sveriges kristnande, publikationer 1, 129–50, Uppsala: University Press

Gräslund, A.-S. (2001) Living with the Dead. Reflections on Food Offerings on Graves. *In* Michael Stausberg (ed.) *Kontinuitäten und Brüche in der Religionsgeschichte. Festschrift für Anders Hultgård zu Seinem 65. Geburtstag am 23. 12. 2001*, 222–35, Berlin

Gräslund, B. (1994) Prehistoric Soul Beliefs in Northern Europe, *Proceedings of the Prehistoric Society* 60: 15–26

Grønvik, O. (1985) *Runene på Eggjastenen. En hedensk gravinnskrift fra slutten av 600–tallet*, Oslo: Universitetsforlaget

Gurevich, A. (1969) Space and Time in the *Weltmodell* of the Old Scandinavian Peoples, *Mediaeval Scandinavia* 2: 42–53

Hardacre, H. (1993) Ancestor Worship, *The Encyclopedia of Religon*, (ed.) Mircea Eliade, 263–68, New York: Macmillan

Hauck, K. (1983) Text und Bild in einer Oralen Kultur. Antworten auf die zeugniskritische Frage nach der Erreichbarkeit mündlicher Überlieferungen im frühen Mittelalter. *In* Karl Hauck (ed.) *Frühmittelalterliche Studien*, Jahrbuch des Instituts für Frühmittelalterforschung der Universität Münster, Vol. 17, 510–645, Berlin, Muünster: Münster University

Hedeager, L. (1997) Odins offer. Skygger af en shamanistisk tradition i nordisk folkevandringstid, *Tor* 29: 265–78

Hedeager, L. (2004) Dyr og andre mennesker – mennesker og andre dyr, *Ordning mot kaos. Studier av nordisk förkristen kosmologi*, 219–52, Lund: Norsk Academisk Press

Heggstad, L. (1930) *Gamalnorsk ordbok med nynorsk tyding. Ny umvølt og auka utgåve av 'Gamalnorsk ordbok' ved Hægstad og Torp*, Oslo: Det Norske Samlaget

Hellquist, E. (1999) *Svensk etymologisk ordbok*. 2 Vols. Third Edition, Malmö: Gleerups

Hellström, J.A. (1996) *Vägar till Sveriges kristnande*, Stockholm: Atlantis

Herbert, K. (1994) *Looking for the Lost Gods of England*, Pinner: Anglo-Saxon Books

Herschend, F. (2001) *Journey of Civilization. The Later Iron Age View of the Human World*. Opia 24, Uppsala: Dept of Archaeology and Ancient History

Hollander, L.M. (tr.) (1962) Sturluson, Snorri. *Heimskringla. History of the Kings of Norway*, Austin, Texas: University of Texas Press

Holmbäck, Å., and Wessén, E. (eds) (1979) *Skånelagen och Gutalagen, Svenska landskapslagar. Tolkade och förklarade för nutidens svenskar*, fjärde serien, second edition, Stockholm: A W R / Geber

Hultgård, A. (1996) Fornskandinavisk kult – finns det skriftliga källor? *In* Kerstin Engdahl and Anders Kaliff (eds) *Religion från stenålder till medeltid. Artiklar baserade på religionsarkeologiska nätverksgruppens konferens på Lövstadbruk den 1–3 december 1995*, Riksantikvarieämbetet arkeologiska undersökningar, skrifter 19, 25–57, Linköping: Riksantikvarieämbetet

Hultkrantz, Å. (1968) Naturfolkens religion. *In* Åke Hultkrantz (ed.) *Primitiv religion och magi. Naturfolkens trosliv i regional belysning*, Second Edition, 1–18, Stockholm: Läromedelsförlaget

Jansson, I. (2005) Situationen i Norden och Östeuropa för 1000 år sedan – en arkeologs synpunkter på frågan om östkristna inflytanden under missionstiden'. *In* H. Jansson (ed.) *Från Bysans till Norden. Östliga kyrkoinfluenser under vikingatid och tidig medeltid*, 37–95, Skellefteå: Artos

Kaliff, A. (1997) *Grav och kultplats. Eskatologiska föreställningar under yngre bronsålder och äldre järnålder i Östergötland*. Aun 24, Uppsala: University Press

Keyser, R., and P.A. Munch (eds) (1848) *Norges gamle love indtil 1387*. Ifölge offentlig foranstaltning og tillige med understöttelse af det Kongelige norske videnskabers selskab, andet bind, lovgivningen under Kong Magnus Haakonssöns regjeringstid fra 1263 til 1280, tilligemed et supplement til förste bind, Christiania: Gröndahl

Kinander, R. (1935–61) *Smålands runinskrifter*, Stockholm: Almquist & Wiksell

Klare H.-J. (1933–4) Die Toten in der altnordischen Literatur, *Acta Philologica Scandinavica* 8: 1–56

Larrington, C. (tr.) (1996) *The Poetic Edda*, Oxford: OUP

Lehtosalo-Hilander, P.-L. (1987) The Conversion of the Finns in Western Finland. *In* B. Sawyer *et al.* (eds) *The Christianization of Scandinavia*, 31–5, Alingsås: Vikrosia Bokföslag

Ljungberg, H. (1938) *Den nordiska religionen och kristendomen: studier över det nordiska religionsskiftet under vikingatiden*. Nordiska texter och undersökningar 11, Uppsala: University Press

Ljungberg, H. (1980) *Röde orm och vite krist: studier till Sveriges kristnande*, Stockholm: Proprius

Macgregor, G. (2005) Soul: Christian Concepts. *In* Lindsay Jones (ed.) *The Encyclopedia of Religon*, Second Edition, 8561–6, Detroit: Macmillan

Meaney, A.L. (1984–5) Ælfric and Idolatry, *Journal of Religious History* 13: 119–35

Meaney, A.L. (1995) Pagan English Sanctuaries, Place-Names and Hundred Meeting-Places. *In* David Griffiths (ed.) *Anglo-Saxon Studies in Archaeology and History* 8: 29–42

Morris, R. (1989) *Churches in the Landscape*, London: Dent

Nedkvitne, A. (2004) *Mötet med döden i norrön medeltid*, Stockholm: Atlantis

Nylén, E. (1958) Gotländska gravformer och deras betydelse för kronologien, *Tor* 4: 64–86

Näsström, B-M. (2001) *Fornskandinavisk religion: en grundbok*, Lund: Studentlitteratus

Parrinder, G. (1993) Ghosts. *In* Mircea Eliade (ed.) *The Encyclopedia of Religon*, Vol. 5, 547–50, New York: Macmillan

Pálsson, H., and P. Edwards (tr.) (1972) *The Book of Settlements: Landnámabók,* Winnipeg: Univeristy of Manitoba

Pálsson, H., and P. Edwards (tr.) (1989) *Eyrbryggja Saga,* Harmondsworth: Penguin Ltd

Pestell, T. (2001) Burnt Stone Features. *In* W. Filmer-Sankey, W. Pestell and T. Pestell (eds) *Snape Anglo-Saxon Cemetery: Excavations and Surveys 1824–1992,* East Anglian Archaeology Report, 259–61, Ipswich, Suffolk: Environment & Industry, Suffolk County Council

Pope, J.C. (ed.) (1968) *Homilies of Ælfric. A Supplementary Collection Being Twenty-one Full Homilies of his Middle and Later Career for the Most Part not Previously Edited with some Shorter Pieces Mainly Added to the Second and Third Series.* Published for the Early English Text Society Oxford, Vol. II, Oxford: OUP

Price, N. (2002) *The Viking Way.* AUN 31, Uppsala: University Press

Ranke, K. and Kuhn, H. (1973) Ahnenglaube und Ahnenkult. *In* H. Beck *et al.* (eds) *Reallexikon der germanischen Altertumskunde, zweite, völlig neu bearbeitete und stark erweiterte Auflage unter Mitwirkung zahlreicher Fachgelehrter,* Vol. 1, 112–15, Berlin and New York: W. de Gruyter

Reynolds, A. (1997) The Definition and Ideology of Anglo-Saxon Execution Sites and Cemeteries, G. De Boe and F. Verhaege (eds) *Death and Burial in Medieval Europe,* II, 33–41, Zelik: Instituut voor het Archeologisch Patrimonium

Reynolds, A. (1999) *Later Anglo-Saxon England. Life and Landscape,* Stroud: Tempus

Reynolds A (2009) *Anglo-Saxon Deviant Burial Customs,* Oxford: OUP

Sanmark, A. (2004) *Power and Conversion. A Comparative Study of Christianization in Scandinavia,* Opia 34, Uppsala: Uppsala University Press

Schön, E. (1998) *Svensk folktro A-Ö: hur vi tänkt, trott och trollat,* Stockholm: Prisma

Semple, S. (2002) *Anglo-Saxon Attitudes to the Past: A Landscape Perspective. A Study of the Secondary Uses and Perceptions of Prehistoric Monuments in Anglo-Saxon Society,* Unpublished D. Phil Thesis. Oxford

Sherley-Price, L. (tr.) (1968) *Bede. The Ecclesiastical History of The English People, A History of the English Church and People,* Revised Edition, 33–347, Harmondsworth: Penguin Ltd

Sognnes, K. (2000) Det hellige landskapet: religiøse og rituelle landskapselementer i et langtidsperspektiv, *Viking* LXIII: 87–121

Spencer, H. (1877) *Principles of Sociology,* London: Macmillan

Steinsland, G. (1992) Nordisk hedendom, *Viking og Hvidekrist. Norden og Europa 800–1200,* (ed.) E. Roesdahl, 144–51, København: Gyldendal

Ström, F. (1958) Döden och de döda, *KL* 3, 432–8

Ström, F. (1960a) Förfäderskult, *KL* 5, 119–121

Ström, F. (1960b) Gengångare, *KL* 5, 252–3

Ström, F. (1961) *Nordisk hedendom. Tro och sed i förkristen tid,* Göteborg: Akademiförlaget – Gumpert

Strömbäck, D. (2000) *Sejd och andra studier i nordisk själsuppfattning,* Second Edition, med bidrag av Bo Almqvist, Gertrud Gidlund, Hans Mebius (ed.), Gertrud Gidlund, Hedemora

Sundqvist, O. (2002) *Freyr's offspring. Rulers and Religion in Ancient Svea Society,* Uppsala: University Press

Taylor, T. (2002) *The Buried Soul. How Humans Invented Death,* London: Fourth Estate

Thomas, J. (2008) *Monument, Memory and Myth: Use and Re-Use of Three Bronze Age Round Barrows at Cossington, Leicestershire with Contributions by Carol Allen [et al.]; Based on Excavations Directed by Tim Higgins, Colm O'Brien and Joanna Sturgess; Illustrations by Matthew Beamish. [et al.],* Leicester: Leicester Archaeological Services

Turville-Petre, E.O.G. (1975) *Myth and Religion of the North. The Religion of Ancient Scandinavia,* Westport: Greenwood

Valk, H. (2001) *Rural Cemeteries in Southern Estonia 1225–1800,* Tartu: University of Tartu, Estonia

Webb, J.F. (Tr.) (1983) Bede: Life of Cuthbert, *The Age of Bede*, 41–102, Harmondsworth: Penguin

Webster, L. (1999) The Iconographic Programme of the Franks Casket. *In* J. Hawkes and S. Mills (eds) *Northumbria's Golden Age*, 227–46, Stroud: Sutton

Wessén, E., and S.B.F. Jansson (1940–43) *Upplands runinskrifter*, Stockholm: Almquist & Wiksell

Whitelock, D., Brett, M. and Brooke, C.N.L. (eds) (1979) *Councils & Synods: With Other Documents Relating to the English Church; 1, AD 871–1204*, Oxford: OUP

Wikander, S. (ed. and tr.) (1978) *Araber, vikingar väringar*, Svenska humanistiska förbundet 90, Norrtälje, Lund: Svenska Humanistiska Förbundet

Wilson, D. (1992) *Anglo-Saxon Paganism*, London and New York: Routledge

Chapter 9

Creating the Pagan English

From the Tudors to the Present Day

Sue Content and Howard Williams

Introduction

From the late eighteenth century onwards the ascription of furnished graves to the early Middle Ages has given archaeology a special but ambivalent role in shedding light on the pagan Anglo-Saxons. Drawing on this material, historians and archaeologists have interpreted the pagan ancestors of the English in different ways, reflecting the shifting socio-political, religious and intellectual climates of the day. These attitudes have stretched from denial of the barbarian and pagan roots of the Anglo-Saxons through to a celebration of the noble Teutonic civilization from which the values and ideals of the English people, nation and church were believed to stem. Between these extremes is a widespread and persistent objective: to narrate the story of the Anglo-Saxons from their origins as pagan migrants to their 'redemption' through conversion and nation-building. To locate the understanding of paganism in the interpretations of Anglo-Saxon archaeology, it will be necessary to review, however briefly, its role in our discipline's historiography.

The historiography of Anglo-Saxon archaeology

The history of archaeology is a burgeoning sub-discipline in its own right (Murray and Evans 2008). For its part, British archaeology has received recent assessments of the origins and development of the discipline from its antiquarian roots (*e.g.* Levine 1986; papers in Pearce 2007) including dedicated studies of the invention of Prehistory (*e.g.* Briggs 2007; Rowley-Conwy 2007), the development of Roman archaeology (*e.g.* Hingley 2008) and the history of medieval archaeology after the Norman conquest (Gerrard 2003). By contrast, the origins and development of Anglo-Saxon archaeology have received relatively little scholarly attention, although this is now being addressed. Our brief analysis defines three main phases of historiography, which we have chosen to term 'prehistoric', 'protohistoric' and 'historic'.

The 'prehistory' of Anglo-Saxon archaeological thinking emerges in the sixteenth century following the Dissolution of the monasteries and the Reformation of the Church of England. The Saxons began to be celebrated in earnest as progenitors of the English church and nation, with Anglo-Saxon manuscripts as the focus of sustained research. Coins and graves were afforded only brief examination and burials were not yet attributed categorically to the Anglo-Saxons (Parry 1995). Even so, early medieval archaeology began its development during this period (Content forthcoming). The initial reluctance to attribute graves and artefacts to the pagan Anglo-Saxons may reflect more than a lack of chronological expertise. As Philip Schwyzer has argued in relation to Thomas Browne's *Hydriotaphia* of 1658 (in which early Anglo-Saxon urns are described but given a Roman date), the Saxons may often have been seen as too much of a political 'hot potato' to risk recognition by antiquaries (Schwyzer 2007).

The eighteenth century, which saw the rise of antiquarian interest in Anglo-Saxon and other 'northern antiquities' (Sweet 2004), might be described as the 'protohistory' of Anglo-Saxon archaeology. The earliest barrow-diggers explored and recorded numerous early medieval graves although they still frequently failed to attribute them to the Saxons. The antiquary Bryan Faussett excavated over seven hundred early medieval graves but regarded them as 'Romans Britonised or Britons Romanised' (*e.g.* Smith 1856: 102, 136). Furthermore, Faussett's notebooks and discoveries were only made public with Charles Roach Smith's publication of *Inventorium Sepulchrale* in 1856: close to a century after their discovery (Hawkes 1990; Hingley 2008). Up to the last decade of the eighteenth century the Romans were often regarded as a safer bet until Douglas' 1793 *Nenia Britannica* saw early medieval graves first ascribed to the Saxons.

With the early nineteenth century, we move from the 'prehistory' and 'protohistory' into the 'early history' of Anglo-Saxon archaeology, associated with the overall rise in popularity of the discipline, including the Victorian pastime of barrow-digging. Although there is a sizeable literature of antiquarian, historical and philological studies from the nineteenth century, its modern historiography has so far seen only a minor focus on the rationale of Anglo-Saxon archaeology itself and the excavations and collections of individual antiquaries (*e.g.* Hawkes 1990; Kidd 1978; 1979; Rhodes 1990; White 1988; Wiley 1979; Wilson 1984). In terms of the wider context of the history of archaeology, Anglo-Saxon scholars like John Yonge Akerman, Charles Roach Smith and Thomas Wright have been primarily noticed because of their resistance to the adoption of the Three Age System (Briggs 2007; Rowley-Conwy 2007: 114–118; 126–38; 288–89).

However, other recent overviews have illuminated the historical and intellectual context of nineteenth century Anglo-Saxon archaeology (Lucy 1998; 2000; 2002; Rhodes 1990) and the broader role of Anglo-Saxonism in early Victorian culture (Content 1995; Frantzen and Niles 1997; Young 2008). There have been more detailed explorations of how philological and historical ideas informed, and became embedded within, the archaeological work of individual early Anglo-Saxon archaeologists (Williams 2006a; 2006b; 2008 and see below). The international context of dialogue between English antiquaries and Continental and Scandinavian scholarship has also received attention (Kidd 1978; Williams 2006a; Williams 2007a). Meanwhile, a consideration of early Victorian Anglo-Saxonism as an intellectual programme and socio-political discourse has highlighted the role of archaeology in constituting the social 'forgetting' of the sub-Roman Britons (Williams 2007b).

Less attention has been afforded so far to the history of Anglo-Saxon archaeology in the twentieth century. Useful overviews are available in the form of introductions to studies of the early Anglo-Saxon period (*e.g.* Arnold 1997; Lucy 2000; 2002; Wickham-Crowley 1999), and Catherine Hills (2007) has recently provided the most extensive critical appraisal of the twentieth century development of Anglo-Saxon archaeology. Also, in a recent paper, Arthur MacGregor (2007) has presented the first-ever assessment of the archaeology of E.T. Leeds. Yet the later history of Anglo-Saxon archaeology remains less well-studied than its early history.

For the last forty years, changing theoretical approaches, new methods and evolving discoveries have yet to be fully and adequately charted in relation to the history of studying the pre-Christian beliefs and practices of the Anglo-Saxons, although some valuable reviews of the evidence have been conducted (*e.g.* Wilson 1992). Within the post-processual climate of the last thirty years, in which self-reflexivity has been championed, early Anglo-Saxon archaeology has seen some detailed attempts to critique its terminologies, theories and methods (*e.g.* Lucy 1998). However, while some scholars, notably Tania Dickinson (2002), have called for studies that critique the ideas underpinning current as well as past research, there appears to have been little appetite for this to be put into action. Therefore, while there remains an ongoing theoretical debate over the interpretation of early Anglo-Saxon graves in terms of migration, ethnicity, religion, social structure, identity, ideology and social memory (see Williams 2007c for a recent summary), Anglo-Saxon archaeology still faces the challenge of opening itself to self-critique and genuine dialogue over both its history and its future.

This brief review teaches us three things. First, that the importance of the pagan Saxons in the cultural imagination of the English has been recognised by those studies that have explored the history of Anglo-Saxon archaeology. Second, that detailed research on this topic has only recently begun, and it is not yet evident that the critical history of research is fully recognised as a stand-alone study. Third, any current or future study of the archaeology of Anglo-Saxon paganism must take heed of this history of research and its influence upon current labels, concepts and ideas. This background aims to justify the need for this paper and simultaneously it illustrates the inevitability of its partial and sketchy nature. We will now review the perception of the pagan Anglo-Saxons from the Reformation to the twentieth century.

Proto-protestants

Among early modern historians it is commonly accepted that the 'Saxons' enter into English consciousness only during the Reformation in Tudor England (B Scott Robinson 2002: 54; McDougall 1982: 2; Murphy 1982: 1). Prior to this they held a wholly negative role as primitive and heathen aggressors given that, for the previous four hundred years, Geoffrey of Monmouth's *History of the Kings of Britain*, written *c.* 1136 had provided a satisfactory origin story for English kings and had inspired subsequent medieval accounts (Thorpe 1966: 29). By the fifteenth century, the Tudor monarchy, anxious to justify its rule, after the final defeat of the Yorkists in 1485, promoted the authenticity of Geoffrey's *History*. Indeed, its appeal was to last through the sixteenth and even into the seventeenth century. Yet as Reformation controversies plagued England throughout the sixteenth century, so the Saxons emerged in a political and religious discourse of defining the antiquity and authenticity of the Protestant religion as well as Catholic reactions to this history.

Following Henry VIII's break with Rome, Polydore Vergil (1470–1555), an Italian humanist and papal appointee as the collector of Peter's Pence, was given permission by Thomas Cromwell to publish his *Anglica Historia* (Hay 1952: 82). Published in 1533, this work drew upon classical ancient writers as well as Gildas, Bede and Paul the Deacon. It rejected Geoffrey of Monmouth's narrative and served to portray a continuity from the British and Roman past through the inheritance of the Saxon kings, regarding the Tudor monarch as the direct descendant of Constantine the Great. With an increasing number of Old English manuscripts in circulation following the Dissolution of the monasteries, the *Great Bible* of 1540 introduced the 'Saxon tonge', which was perceived as the 'mother tonge' of contemporary English (Cranmer 1540: 1). The Saxons came to be regarded as the true and primitive Protestant Christians. This formed the basis for a Protestant ideology through the publication of the *Actes and Monuments* (*The Book of Martyrs*: Foxe 1570) authored by John Bale and John Foxe, amongst many others, with the backing of William Cecil and Matthew Parker). The text of *Actes and Monuments* drew explicitly on the role of the Saxon language as evidence of the antiquity of the Protestant English faith.

Building on this new Protestant history, William Camden first published his *Britannia* in Latin in 1586 and is widely purported to have disseminated a view of the British past that had a wide and unifying appeal, as propagated by the Protestant agenda of William Cecil in the reign of Elizabeth. Drawing upon German propagandists and classical references, instead of the usual reliance upon British sources only, Camden melded a religious and national story of origin. In contrast to his discussion of the British and Roman past, Camden's section on the Anglo-Saxons was purely based on written sources rather than material culture and landscape (see Hingley 2008: 24–43). It was small but significant because it served to link Camden's narrative of the British and Roman past with that of Camden's present. Consisting of seven pages (55–62) Camden envisaged the Saxons as "a most warlike people very much feared by the Romans, terrible in valour and dexterity and with great strength of mind" (Camden 1587: 58). In later editions, he raised the profile of the Saxons, recognising their importance and their reception of Christianity. Camden commented on the origins and characteristics of the Saxons, but said little of their religion, although he noted that Hengist and Horsa worshipped the god Mercury "whom they call Woden, to whom they sacrificed human victims and dedicated to him the fourth day of the week" (Camden 1587: 60). This is taken from a passage in Tacitus *Germania* 9, which refers to Germans as a whole. The pagan origins of 'Eoster month' reported by Bede are mentioned. However, Camden's focus is upon the conversion, which the Saxons embraced "with eager zeal" and erected sacred buildings and spread the word of Christ. Thus Camden perceived the paganism of the Saxons as an essential corollary to their wholesale conversion to a proto-Protestant faith.

Catholic resistance

If the paganism of the Saxons was recognised but sidelined in Protestant discourse, the paganism of the Saxons was exaggerated by writers with Catholic sympathies, possibly to disparage Protestant propaganda. The earliest example appears to be Humfrey Lluyd's *Commentariol Brittanicae descriptionis fragmentum* (1573). This historical geography, or chorography, the first of its kind in Britain, portrayed the Saxons as the ancient ancestors of the Protestants and in wholly negative terms. As a Welshman and a probable Catholic who certainly had many close Catholic friends, Lluyd regarded the Saxons as treacherous and violent primitives who burned churches, monasteries and libraries (Lluyd 1573: folio 13).

The paganism of the Saxons received an alternative treatment by Richard (Rowlands) Verstegan (*c.* 1550–*c.* 1640). As a Catholic who was staunchly critical of Elizabeth's regime, Verstegan lived in exile in Antwerp for much of his life having fled England in 1582 for printing illegal Catholic pamphlets and propaganda. *The Restitution of Decayed Intelligence in Antiquities* (1605) was dedicated to James I, possibly to demonstrate loyalty to the crown as a Catholic to a sympathetic ruler, an aspiration that was dashed with the Gunpowder Plot later that year (Parry 1995: 51). The book was published in English and staunchly advocated the Germanic characteristics of the English using history, philology and legend: "Englishmen are descended of German race" (Verstegan 1605: 1) and, together with other Teutons, built the nations of Europe. He explored Saxon origins in the post-diluvial diaspora of nations following Babel and the origins of the Saxons through Japhet's son Gomer and his grandson Tuisco, the patriarch of the Germans. Following Tacitus he outlined the customs of the Saxons including their funerary practices, religious worship and gods (Parry 1995: 59) as well as the inheritance of their 'English-Saxon' tongue (Parry 1995: 64).

According to Parry (1995: 52), Verstegan's favouring of English origins, including his dismissal of the traditional British and Roman origin myths and his reliance on the pseudo-Berosus manuscript, suggest that *Restitution* was originally formulated in the 1570s when Verstegan was a student of Anglo-Saxon at Oxford. Yet the motivations for Verstegan's account can be further discerned in his text and images. It can be argued that *Restitution* was Verstegan's attempt to dismiss the Protestant histories of the previous half-century as myths by means of parody. With this agenda in mind, Verstegan appears to celebrate England's Saxon roots while simultaneously mocking the idea of the Saxons as Protestant ancestors. It is possible to suppose that Verstegan's illustrations of Germanic pagan gods were intended to parody Elizabeth's reign. For instance, his image of the moon as a powerful female divinity might have been intended to mock Elizabeth (Hamilton 1999: 10) and his depiction of Thor might be seen as a parody of William Cecil. Therefore, Verstegan's text was a highly charged but subtle piece of anti-Protestant propaganda by an exiled Catholic. What is certainly clear is that such subtle messages implicit in the *Restitution* – which would have been appreciated by an informed reader of the early seventeenth century – were undoubtedly lost when his text was resurrected in the writing of Anglo-Saxon history during the later eighteenth century!

Therefore, the portrayal of the Saxons as heathen aggressors or as proto-Protestants shows their propagandistic use in religious and political conflicts of the sixteenth and early seventeenth centuries. Yet their advocates had not drawn upon archaeology. Sir Thomas Browne's *Hydriotaphia* of 1658 provides the first detailed recording of early Anglo-Saxon graves, but he attributed them to the Roman period and used them to demonstrate the futility of pagan religion in attempting to preserve memory through material things. Hence, the urns were pagan and this defined their significance while their precise date and cultural affiliation were then unknown or perhaps avoided (Schwyzer 2007). This may be resultant from the widespread use of the Saxons in political discourse against the perceived despotism of the Stuarts.

Hanoverian heathens

With the ascent of the Hanoverian regime, the Saxon origins of the English came increasingly to the fore. Manuscript studies of Old English continued to provide a means by which the Saxons legitimised the Church of England. Yet equally important was the perception that English liberties, institutions and law were also derived from the Saxons. For both religious and socio-political dimensions of the Saxon legacy, it was the later Christian Anglo-Saxon period that was the focus of interest (Sweet 2004: 194). Consequently, the barbarous origins and the paganism of the Saxons were eschewed in favour of their civility. Furthermore, the Saxon legacy was increasingly linked to an overall passion for the shared northern features of Saxon, Norse and 'Gothic' antiquities (Sweet 2004: 215).

At the beginning of this period, Edmund Gibson's revised edition of Camden's *Britannia* in 1695, reissued in 1722, referred to the language, laws, customs and names of persons and places as 'Saxon Original' (Mayhew 2000; Sweet 2004: 189). By the century's end, volume 1 of Sharon Turner's *The History of the Anglo-Saxons* published in 1799, chronicled the Saxons' progress from barbarity to civilization. In positive terms, Turner celebrated the ancient origins of the Saxons, their Continental homelands, migrations, conquests, conversion and apogee with Alfred's reign. Notably, Turner did not discuss the paganism of the Saxons at all and adeptly avoids mention of the pagan affiliation of any Saxon king (*e.g.* Turner 1807: 142–43; see Sweet 2004: 217–18). Moreover, Turner offered a narrative based on texts alone and appears oblivious to the potential of archaeology or landscape to inform knowledge of the Saxons of the pre-Christian period. For example, he regarded the fifth century as a: "barbarous age... unfriendly to human fame. When the clods of his hillock are scattered, or his funereal stones are thrown down, the glory of a savage perishes for ever; nor can fancy be admitted to supply the loss" (Turner 1807: 125).

While text-based narratives were the norm and the material culture of the Saxons had yet to be discerned clearly in earthworks or graves, the Saxons were increasingly afforded a material form in their coins, place-names and in the topography and counties of England (Sweet 2004: 209–213). Moreover, Joseph Strutt (1749–1802) popularised the Saxons in a series of illustrated books on their dress, manners and customs in an explicit attempt to create a patriotic English equivalent visual history to Montfaucon's *Monarchie Francoise*. Based upon late Saxon manuscript illustrations of weaponry and costume, Strutt provided a faux-material culture for the Saxons (Sweet 2004: 214). Almost by happenstance, it was Strutt – ironically an engraver and publisher of popular histories rather than a 'serious' antiquary – who first attributed a sixth-century artefact to the 'Saxons'. Aware of the jewellery uncovered from Childeric's grave and keen to assert an English parallel to this 'ancestor' of the French monarchy, Strutt included an illustration of a silver gilt jewelled disc brooch of Kentish Class 6.1 (assigned by modern scholarship to the sixth century AD: Avent 1975: 35–6), in his *Horda Angelcynnan*, thereby proclaiming its Anglo-Saxon origin. Strutt noted that this artefact "... [that] was lately dug up in Kent, I have now in my possession, the representation of which is in Plate 23, the exact size of the original." (Strutt 1774: 46).

Strutt's attribution opened the door to the materialisation of the Anglo-Saxons, and it fell to the antiquary James Douglas (1753–1819) to first assign clusters of small barrows at Chatham Lines, Greenwich Park and elsewhere to the 'Saxons' (Jessup 1975). Douglas was inspired by Strutt's illustrations of the disc brooch (see above) and of supposed similarity between grave-finds and the weapons redrawn by Strutt from Anglo-Saxon manuscripts (Douglas 1793: 116, 128). Notably, when Douglas first met Strutt, he was already over half-way through the composition of his *Nenia Britannica* which was originally produced for sale in twelve parts (Jessup 1975: 102). In the first seven of the instalments of the text published from 1786 to 1790, Douglas was still unclear as to the date and tribal affiliation of the furnished graves and attributed them to 'Romans', 'Britons', 'Pagan Gauls' (Douglas 1793: 43) or 'Danes' (Douglas 1793: 108). Only having met Strutt did Douglas attribute the graves to 'Saxons'.

Douglas on burial and belief

With this context set out, let us explore how Douglas discussed these furnished graves in relation to the religious beliefs of those interred. Certainly discussions of magic and superstition were already prevalent in Douglas' view of the grave goods when he still thought they were the graves of Romans or Britons. He drew extensively on classical texts and early medieval magical treatise in interpreting graves. Some grave goods were regarded as having been made especially for the funeral for example glass vessels (Douglas 1793: 14). Meanwhile other containers were regarded as containing 'lustral water' for pagan rituals. Further artefacts were seen as having amuletic or divinatory properties such as amber (Douglas 1793: 9), crystal balls (Douglas 1793: 15–19), gemstones (Douglas 1793: 34), glass beads (Douglas 1793: 60), fossils (Douglas 1793: 65), cowrie shells (Douglas 1793: 73), brass boxes (Douglas 1793: 74), gold pendants (Douglas 1793: 86), re-used Roman coin-pendants (Douglas 1793: 96) and even an axe (Douglas 1793: 50). He likewise perceived a re-used ancient stone celt as an amulet that had been "preserved with a superstitious veneration"(Douglas 1793: 92). For the overall practice of providing grave goods, Douglas uses ethnographic analogy and Norse mythology in combination to come to a conclusion that the practice was one ubiquitous among the 'Northern nations':

> "The Laplanders, to this day, inter with the dead *their bows* and arrows, hatchets, swords, &c. Which they conceive will be useful to them in a future state... This appears to have been the custom of most of the Northern nations from the earliest period of time. See the *Eddae Mythol. c. v. Saxo. lib. 8.* where the ancient Northern people threw money and other things of value into the funeral pile, as a certain

means of conducting the dead to the sacred Valhalla, or the hall of the slain, where they believed their great deity Odin presided" (Douglas 1793: 29).

Elsewhere, Douglas highlights that placing vessels with the dead was not exclusive to one people, citing the Romans and many ethnographic examples to show its ubiquity as a primitive pagan trait. They were 'superstitious customs' shared by all the 'ancients' (Douglas 1793: 45). Douglas cited Shakespeare's *Hamlet* to sustain his explanation for the observed scattering of pottery within graves (Douglas 1793: 10). He also considers the location of barrows beside roads "so as to receive the benediction of the passenger"(Douglas 1793: 94).

Importantly, Douglas shied away from labelling the graves 'pagan' once he began to realise they were likely to be 'Saxon' (Douglas 1793: 94), a fact that has been repeatedly ignored by commentators on the *Nenia Britannica* (*e.g.* Jessup 1974: 108). While informed and inspired by Chiflet's report and subsequently Montfaucon's discussion of Childeric's grave (Jessup 1975: 110–11), he questioned their reliability, noting that the date of the coins interred do not date the grave itself (Douglas 1793: 123). He admitted them to have been of 'barbaric or Pagan origin' (Douglas 1793: 177) but noted that many early Christians would have retained pagan customs such as providing grave goods and burying away from churchyards (Douglas 1793: 50). Interestingly, prior to assigning them to the Saxons, Douglas recognised that some were sixth-century in date, but he subsequently assigns them to between AD 582 and AD 742, regarding them as 'early Christian' (Douglas 1793: 131). He supported this view by evoking Tertullian who refers to the embalming and entombment of the early Christian dead with: "perfumes, odours, drugs and ointments" (Douglas 1793: 97):

> "It may admit of a favourable conjecture, that these places of sepulture were affixed to the neighbouring villages before cemeteries were annexed to churches; it will therefore be concluded they must belong to the primitive Christians..." (Douglas 1793: 96).

Subsequently he used the law of Charlemagne to illustrate how Pagan and early Christian burials were 'promiscuously blended' (Douglas 1793: 120, also 178). Douglas' low opinion of the pagan Saxons was clear. He regarded them as: "...illiterate Saxons, who were Pagans, on their first descent into Britain, had not the art of producing works of such ingenuity as are obviously defined on the *fibulae*, gems, and other costly trinkets, found in these graves..." (Douglas 1793: 129). Douglas speculated that pagan Saxons were interred elsewhere, probably by cremation. Douglas asserts that Stukeley's excavations of barrows near Stonehenge produced just such evidence; an urn containing the "relics of an unconverted Saxon female" (Douglas 1793: 177). Likewise, the urns of Thomas Browne from Walsingham were implicitly seen as pagan Saxons (Douglas 1973: 177 & 178).

Douglas noticed the influence of Romans upon the graves he uncovered, for which "history has sufficiently warranted", presumably referring to Christian influence rather than cultural continuity (Douglas 1793: 178). In his Kentish graves, he noted the 'Eastern customs' of many of the artefacts showing links with the Greek (Byzantine) world that he considered had been imported with Archbishop Theodore in AD 668. Therefore, Douglas regarded the shared affinity with "magical superstitious ceremonies" found in the Greek isles (Douglas 1793: 129–130) and a "commixture of customs" as purely a Christian and imported fascination. Such artefacts were even regarded by Douglas as a strategy for converting the pagan Saxons:

> "Imposing arts of such influence among an unlettered and ignorant people would readily find their value in fascinating their minds, and rendering them the more open to the Christian conversion" (Douglas 1793: 131).

In summary, Douglas' *Nenia Britannica* interpreted early medieval furnished graves in relation to early Christian superstition while steering clear of directly discussing Anglo-Saxon paganism. Indeed, Douglas emphasised the Christian and imported nature of these superstitions upon his interpretation of the furnished graves as those of Saxons. In doing so, Douglas set a trend of regarding early medieval furnished graves of what later became known as the 'final phase' (Leeds 1936) as resulting in the blending of Roman Christian and pagan Saxon traditions on the slow road to Christianity. In any case, the *Nenia Britannica* received a poor reception (Jessup 1975: 113) and, as we have seen, the first volume of Sharon Turner's influential *History* published six years later in 1799 did not recognise the potential contribution of archaeology to the study of the Anglo-Saxons. Indeed, Douglas' work was to lie dormant for a further fifty years before its resurrection in the early Victorian era. By the time it was rediscovered, the paganism of the Saxons had risen in importance and the magical interpretations of the early sections of *Nenia* were subsumed into his later ascription of the graves to the Saxons.

Saxon pagandom

Evans has regarded the rise of 'archaeology' as comprising only two overlapping generations of scholars (Evans 2007: 270–71) yet for Anglo-Saxonism it really only effectively comprised the first of these: a cluster of scholars associated with the period from *c.* 1845 to 1860. Key figures in this period include Thomas Wright, Charles Roach Smith and John Yonge Akerman who excavated and collected Anglo-Saxon antiquities found during both barrow-digging and cemetery excavations. This generation affirmed their racial and nationalistic association with the Anglo-Saxons (see also Levine 1986; Hingley 2007). For example, Roach Smith lobbied for the creation of a national museum of archaeology, albeit unsuccessfully, and published Faussett's *Inventorium Sepulchrale* (Smith 1856). Eschewing many of Douglas' 'magical' interpretations of artefacts and his Christian attribution of the burials (*e.g.* Smith 1856: xix, xxvii, 68), Roach Smith and his contemporaries advocated the 'scientific' description, illustration and comparison of artefacts to write a material history of the Saxon settlement. As well as the detailed description and illustration of artefacts from graves, increasingly, bones were employed in defining the Saxon people and their inheritance of the British and Roman past through the examination of stature and craniology (Davis and Thurnam 1865). With differing degrees of emphasis, this generation of scholars defined graves in relation to the contemporary trend of racial theories. Archaeologists employed these poorly defined concepts of race that incorporated ideas from philology, history, ethnology and biology to explore the relationships and succession of Celt, Roman and Saxon

(Wright 1852; see also Morse 1999; 2005; Young 2008: 42). Rather than attempting to review the extensive literature of this period, we can focus upon two individuals with related, but distinctive, approaches to the paganism of the Anglo-Saxons: John Yonge Akerman and John Mitchell Kemble.

John Yonge Akerman, a long-serving secretary of the Society of Antiquaries, was a prolific writer with many interests in archaeology, numismatics and medieval history. He oversaw the excavation of a number of early Anglo-Saxon burial grounds in the Upper Thames region and Wessex and reported upon the discoveries in *Archaeologia*. Akerman also produced two books that embodied the preoccupations of the day and reported discoveries of Anglo-Saxon antiquities from across the country: his *Archaeological Index* (Akerman 1847) and his lavishly illustrated *Remains of Pagan Saxondom* (Akerman 1855a). He reviewed the study of Anglo-Saxon graves prior to his generation, deploring the disregard afforded to Douglas' *Nenia* and the 'sad confusion' of Colt Hoare's *Ancient Wiltshire*. He regarded cemeteries as indicators of his 'Saxon forefathers' and 'our Pagan-Saxon ancestors' (Akerman 1855c: 477). The graves were those of settlers and farmers, providing: "proofs beyond all question of the occupation of the various sites by a people in undisturbed possession of the land" (Akerman 1860b: 327). They are repeatedly referred to as 'national antiquities' (Akerman 1855a: viii). The value of cemeteries offered considerable potential: "sufficient to show how extensive a population must have occupied this valley in Saxon times, and suggests that much light might be thrown on the habits, manners, and history of our ancestors by investigating the antiquities of the district" (Akerman 1860b: 328). Akerman's archaeology followed the lead of the existing historical narrative, defining the paganism of the Saxons in terms of an absence of evidence of surviving temples and a panoply of written sources for their existence from 'Upsala' (Akerman 1855a: xxiii) and 'Irminsul' (Akerman 1855a: xxi) to Goodmanham (Akerman 1855a: xxiv) and preserved place-names (Akerman 1855a: xxv). Moreover, paganism never did die completely, but was preserved fossilised in the peasant class: "Even at this day there yet linger among the peasantry of this country superstitions, from which even the educated classes are scarcely emancipated" (Akerman 1855a: xxviii).

Cremation for Akerman embodied an earlier settlement of Germanic groups, possibly during the time of the rebel Carausius (the later third century AD). Meanwhile *Beowulf* afforded historical evidence of the practice of cremation among the Angles (Akerman 1855a: xv). Individual burial practices were also interpreted in terms of pagan beliefs. Like Douglas, Akerman evoked Shakespeare's Hamlet to discuss the scattering of flints and pottery in grave-fills (Akerman 1855a: xvi; 1855b: 265) and regarded fragments of Roman and Saxon pottery found in grave 53 at Brighthampton as a deliberate burial rite (Akerman 1860a: 90). Meanwhile, the knuckle-bone of a sheep in grave 28 at Harnham Hill was seen as one of a number of *tali* that possibly represented a pagan 'superstition' (Akerman 1855b). Furthermore, the teeth of oxen, sheep and goats were seen as evidence of feasting: 'which our pagan forefathers were accustomed to celebrate over the graves of their dead'. Akerman interpreted the presence of only teeth as evidence that the heads of animals were left displayed on poles as offerings to the gods (Akerman 1855b). Some objects were afforded a pagan significance following Douglas, such as certain glass vessels deemed "objects of an unusual and sacred character" (Akerman 1855a: 4). Meanwhile, the deposition of grave goods of high value was "costly to their owners" and offered "an illustration of the inveterate superstition of our heathen forefathers in their sepulchral observances" (Akerman 1855a: 60). Even human sacrifice received a mention. In the first report on excavations at Brightampton, Oxfordshire, a male skeleton was found lain prone over a female skeleton. The synchronous deaths were suggested by the fact that the tibiae of the male pressed on the skull of women. He speculated as to whether this represented a voluntary sacrifice (Akerman 1857c).

However, grave goods were often regarded as reflecting social roles rather than religious rites, with the dead man "clothed as he lived" (Akerman 1855c: 477) and the women interred with "articles of housewifery" (Akerman 1855a: xi). The discovery of a wealthy weapon-burial at Brighthampton, Oxfordshire, allowed Akerman to suggest a social hierarchy was present because it: "... strongly favours the conjecture that this cemetery contained the remains of the individual from whom the village derives its name, his kindred, dependents, and bread-eaters." (Akerman 1860a: 90).

Paganism is implicit when Akerman interpreted the location of cemeteries, the association with water courses is regarded as indicative that these sites were "so highly venerated by our heathen forefathers" (Akerman 1857b: 145). Likewise he regarded the site selected for the cemetery at Kemble, Gloucestershire, as chosen "by the ancient inhabitants for their cemetery" that commanded "a view of the source of the stream (the River Thames), whose onward course may be likened to that of the race to which these early remains must be ascribed" (Akerman 1857a: 113). In other words, the relationship of burial ground to river was seen as a poignant metaphor for the pagan and sacred origins of England, the English and the 'Anglo-Saxon' Empire (see also Young 2008: 177–95).

The conversion to Christianity was also perceived by Akerman in the graves he excavated. For example, in the second Brighthampton (Oxfordshire) report Akerman debated whether the abandonment of cremation was due to the influence of surviving Roman-Britons or the conversion to Christianity. Either way, cremation was recognised as the older rite but co-existed in the same cemeteries with inhumation (Akerman 1860a: 85). The end of pagan burial was marked by the historical conversion of the Anglo-Saxon kingdoms (Akerman 1855b: 270). At one cemetery, Long Wittenham (now in Oxfordshire), Akerman explained the poorer furnished graves as those of converts (Akerman 1863: 137); likewise, at Harnham Hill those graves without relics were seen as later in date (Akerman 1855a). Yet grave goods could themselves be Christian, since Akerman found a bucket in a grave at Long Wittenham with explicit Christian symbolism. While many vessels were interpreted as porringers (porridge bowls) (Akerman 1855a: 56), others were seen as holy water stoups made by priests (Akerman 1855a: 28; Akerman 1860b: 336–7; Akerman 1863: 136).

Akerman's reports reveal the use of the rich cemetery data to infer the history of the Saxon settlement and pagan customs. The pagan status of the graves was an implicit assumption and it surfaced repeatedly to explain distinctive elements of the burial rite and burial location. Meanwhile the conversion to Christianity could also be charted in the decline in grave goods and the eventual abandonment of these field cemeteries.

Burnt Germans

By way of contrast with Akerman we have a more explicit Germanist stance of John Mitchell Kemble's archaeology in which the paganism of the Saxons gained a further significance (Williams 2006; for a slightly different perspective see Carver 2009). Kemble not only was inspired by the German Romantic Movement and built upon the ideas of the Teutonic race, language and material culture of the Enlightenment philosophers Johann Gottfried Herder and Johann Gottlieb Fichte, which were also employed in the folklore, philology and mythology of the Grimm brothers. This approach melded a common heritage, law, language and folk-memory, family ties and love of ancestors with the idea of a shared racial origin (Barnard 2003: 20). Kemble was a follower of Jacob and Wilhelm Grimms' work from the 1830s and befriended them through correspondences and visits. He shared their affinity with Germany, having a Swiss-German mother and marrying a German woman. When he later turned to archaeology, Kemble brought to the study of burial customs and grave-finds his historical and philological pan-Germanic emphasis but also the Grimms' passion for pagan folklore. Kemble's *The Saxons in England* was as much a compliment to Jacob Grimm's *Deutsche Mythologie* (1844) as it was a history of the Anglo-Saxons following upon the tradition of Sharon Turner.

The Saxons in England had a long lasting effect on historical and archaeological thought concerning early medieval England. His chapter on pre-Christian belief was an important element of its significance and was written to explicitly complement Grimm's *Mythologie*. Kemble questioned the historical account of the Saxon migrations as a post-Roman invasion. He suggested that the 'extensive migrations of Germans to the shores of England' of the fifth century were founded on fact (Kemble 1849: 7) but followed earlier Germanic migrations of the pre-Roman and Roman periods (Kemble 1847; 7–13; see also Williams 2006: 6). These settling Teutons made 'slow and gradual progress' in conquering Britain and its native people who 'probably suffered little by a change of masters' and who persisted and mingled with the ruling Germans (Kemble 1849: 20). Kemble's concern was with pagan Teutonic racial expansion and succession. He focused less upon the history of the Germanic invasions but instead upon the inalienable institutions and customs that the Saxons shared with the other branches of the Teutonic peoples (Kemble 1849: 35–71).

In a detailed chapter, he isolates 'Heathendom' as one of these pan-Germanic elements and regards 'Paganism' as like a 'twilight' before the dawn of Christianity. The pagan Anglo-Saxons already had a clearly-defined moral and spiritual character (Kemble 1849: 328). Kemble did not doubt that the Anglo-Saxon religion had close and direct connections with Continental and Scandinavian German religion which could be used to fill in the gaps in knowledge of Anglo-Saxon pagan cosmology, from the pantheon of gods to views about the beginning and end of the world: "... in the main it cannot be doubted that the heathendom of both races was the same" (Kemble 1849: 405). Kemble outlines two overlapping types of ancient Teutonic religion, the sacerdotal and the heroic (Kemble 1849: 440). The same religion would have been found across 'Teutonic Europe' had Christianity not 'deprived us of the mythological records which the North supplies' (Kemble 1849: 442). This was a moral faith as clear and strict as

Christianity itself (Kemble 1849: 443) and laid the foundations for conversion: 'Those who had believed in runes and incantations were satisfied with the efficacy of the mass...' (Kemble 1849: 444). 'How should Christianity fail to obtain access where Paganism stepped half way to meet it...?' (Kemble 1849: 444). This became the stock-in-trade of some later popular histories of England; namely that: "The religion of the English was the same as that of the whole German family" (Green 1915: 4). Paganism enters the account as a primordial pan-Germanic mythology and backdrop to history.

When in later life Kemble turned to archaeology, his excavations and research in the Kingdom of Hanover and extensive reading of the British archaeological literature on 'Anglo-Saxon' cinerary urns like those from Eye in Suffolk (see Akerman 1855a: 7–8; 43–44), widely regarded as an 'ancient pagan practice' of the Germans (*e.g.*; Smith 1856: xiv-xv), allowed him to forge a material correlation to his Teutonic heathendom. In particular, the paganism of the cremation custom was integral to Kemble's narrative of the origins of the Anglo-Saxons and the material testimony of their migration to England and their confirmation by 'scientific' methods (Kemble 1855: 309). Memorably he defined cinerary urns as containing the "Burnt Germans of the Age of Iron" while inhumations were the Christianised 'Unburnt Germans'.

Likewise, Kemble elsewhere ascribed a wide range of customs to pagan rites drawing upon literary and historical sources for support. These included the use of runes, the sacrifice of animals, barrow-burial and the location of graves upon the boundaries of territories (Kemble 1863; see Williams 2006b). Inhumation by way of contrast, showed the influence of Christianity and hence the erosion of these primitive Teutonic traits. Linking gods, folklore and funerary customs, the historical, philological and archaeological evidence all pointed to the Germanic forefathers of the Anglo-Saxons.

Akerman and Kemble display alternative explorations of contemporary early Victorian racial theories in which 'race' was rooted in shared language, history, institutions and customs, as much as biological descent (Young 2008: 32–70). Their archaeological studies show how these theories were applied and developed through the study of burial customs and the light graves shed on the paganism of the Anglo-Saxons. Yet even this generation varied in its approach to the evidence. For instance, some contemporaries used 'Saxon' and 'Anglo-Saxon' as little more than a chronological label without explicit interpretation (Williams 2006a). Furthermore, few followed Kemble's views directly, although his approach was emulated by William Wylie (Wylie 1852; 1857; see Williams 2007a; 2008). Indeed, even among the early Victorian generation of Anglo-Saxonists there was a clear perception that the custom of furnishing graves with artefacts showed similarities between Roman and Saxon customs rather than defining a uniquely Teutonic pagan religion (Williams 2007b). Kemble's early death and the passing of his contemporaries left few interested in developing a racial and mythological archaeology. Henceforth, Anglo-Saxon history developed upon traditional and anti-archaeological grounds based upon early medieval written accounts with a dose of place-name evidence in support, very much along the lines established by Sharon Turner (McDougall 1982: 92–93).

Therefore, the heyday of the archaeological manifestation of Victorian Anglo-Saxonism was short-lived and the attention afforded to the paganism of the Anglo-Saxons suffered the same fate. Subsequently, the period from *c.* 1870 to 1910 saw a stagnation in Anglo-Saxon archaeology and little discussion of Anglo-Saxon paganism. The nationalist perspectives of Roach Smith, Wright and Akerman and the more pan-Germanic emphasises of Kemble and Wylie found little purchase in this era as Teutonism slowly fell from intellectual favour (Young 2008: 140–176). In terms of archaeological research, the period saw the shift of emphasis abroad to the exploration of ancient civilizations of the Mediterranean and Near East. Meanwhile at home, Roman Britain provided a clear predecessor and parallel for the British Empire (Hingley 2008).

Twentieth-century pagans

With the approach to World War I and between the two world wars, a new if muted passion for the early medieval origins of the English can be recognised. Most notable are the works of E.T. Leeds and J.N.L Myres in their compilation of nineteenth century data to create typologies, chronologies and distributions for brooches and pottery respectively to chart Saxon settlement. What is notable in their work is the virtual absence of any detailed discussions of Anglo-Saxon paganism; it appears that the Saxons were back on the agenda but their paganism was perhaps too closely connected to pan-Germanic Aryan fantasies to tolerate close attention (*e.g.* Leeds 1913; Myres 1942). For example, Myres had travelled extensively on the Continent and his studies continued after the Second World War (*e.g.* Myres 1948). Yet only for rare anecdotes does Myres entertain pagan religion as affecting the material he studied (Myres & Green, 1973: 118). Likewise, Lethbridge noted an interpretation of artefacts placed in cremation urns as indicating pagan magical practices, but this is broached in terms of cross-cultural analogies from societies in south-east Asia rather than in relation to Continental or Scandinavian evidence (Lethbridge 1951: 12–13). It is again with regard to Christian conversion and E.T. Leeds' definition of the 'final-phase' that the religious identity of those interred comes to the fore in discussions (Leeds 1936). The 'heathen' ascription of furnished burial and cremation was itself never doubted (see MacGregor 2007).

   This trend was to persist until the 1980s, with paganism providing a background context to the various burial rites involving inhumation and cremation compiled in Audrey Meaney's *Gazetteer* (Meaney 1964). Again an exception is found in discussions of the 'final-phase' (Meaney & Hawkes 1970) and amulets and other 'special' artefacts (Hawkes *et al.* 1965; Meaney 1981; Reynolds 1980). Likewise, before Martin Carver's re-interpretation (eg Carver 2000, and this vol.), Sutton Hoo's Mound 1 was widely perceived as shedding light on the Anglo-Saxon kingdoms during the conversion process rather than as a window onto local cosmology and belief (Bruce-Mitford 1974; Wilson 1992). Moreover, with the advent of 'processual' or 'new archaeology' and its detailed criticism of culture-historic approaches, the emphasis shifted away from studies of belief and culture to studies of economy and society (*e.g.* Arnold 1997). In such a context, the study of Anglo-Saxon paganism fell from favour (see Hines 1997) and this reluctance to explore Anglo-Saxon religion has likewise affected many post-processual studies that retain a focus upon the social interpretation of burial data (*e.g.* Lucy 1998). This shying away from religion and belief in the study of the early Anglo-Saxon period is a natural response to earlier generations' uncritical use of paganism as a normative cultural label (see Williams 2002). For early medieval archaeology it is also an after-effect of attempts to break the strangle-hold of Christian discourse in medieval history that has dominated attitudes towards early medieval societies and their pre-Christian origins. However, it can also be situated in relation to broader shifts in British society in the later twentieth century, when the separation of church and state was finally accomplished, with the disengagement of religion from daily life and from mortuary behaviour in particular.

But this is not the whole story, for while the last forty years of scholarship has prioritised the social and political over the cultural and religious in studying the Anglo-Saxons, the study of Anglo-Saxon paganism in archaeology has found new avenues for investigation through the combination of new discoveries, post-processual theories and increasing interdisciplinary dialogue (Williams 2007c; Wilson 1992). Hence, while the culture-historic paradigm has been successfully critiqued and challenged, David Wilson's valuable summary of early Anglo-Saxon archaeology can be criticised for using paganism as a catch-all for all pre-Christian practice (Wilson 1992). Certainly there exist summaries of the 'pagan Anglo-Saxons' that afford the term with little qualification (*e.g.* Meaney 2003) and studies by historians of religion who have drawn upon archaeological evidence in their broad narratives (Ellis Davidson 1993). Yet the most fruitful studies that have explored Anglo-Saxon paganism have persisted down specialist and narrow trajectories, in the study of animal art (Dickinson 2005), mortuary symbolism (Richards 1992), unusual and distinctive grave-types (Dickinson 1993) and even in shrines (Blair 1995) and settlement archaeology (Hamerow 2006).

Therefore, ironically it has been the shedding of the shackles of paganism as a cultural and chronological label within a broader context of a secularised and multi-cultural society that has finally facilitated the detailed contextual analysis of paganism in early Anglo-Saxon England. A further context for this invigoration of studies of Anglo-Saxon paganism can be found in the increasing popularity of fantasy literature such as Tolkien's *The Hobbit* and *The Lord of the Rings* as well as innumerable literary and media portrayals of the pagan Saxons inspired by literature and archaeology as with the recent films *Beowulf* and *Beowulf and Grendel*.

As well as this secular interest in the Anglo-Saxons, there are both ongoing and new religious interests in British society. The last quarter-century has witnessed the rising popularity of modern 'heathenry'. These beliefs and practices mesh together diverse aspects of Norse and Anglo-Saxon material culture from runes to grave-finds and adopt sites like Gamla Uppsala and Sutton Hoo as well as museum collections as places of pilgrimage (Blain and Wallis 2006; 2009; Wallis and Blain 2009: 592, 599). Calls by some modern pagans for the reburial of human bones and 'sacred' artefacts are beginning to extend from prehistoric and Roman remains to 'British Saxon culture' (Honouring the Ancient Dead 2009 http://www.honour.org.uk; Wallis and Blain 2009: 604). Yet this is but one response to early Anglo-Saxon graves by pagans. In contrast, for the site of the rich chamber grave of the 'Prittlewell Prince', paganism and environmental campaigners have joined forces to protect the Anglo-Saxon cemetery site against planned road developments (Williams 2007c: 8; Wallis and Blain 2009: 601–02).

Modern pagans do not hold an exclusive interest in early Anglo-Saxon graves. For modern British Christians too, the story of conversion of the pagan English to Christian continues to appeal. For example, in the recently commissioned television series 'Christianity: A History' (episode 3: the 'Dark Ages') theologian Robert Beckford presents pagan sanctuaries and the Sutton Hoo cemetery in a popular re-telling of the established narrative; Christianity created both a unifying faith and multi-cultural inclusivity following a post-Roman regression into paganism and ethnic division (Channel Four 2009).

Against this popular background, studies have begun to re-engage with early Anglo-Saxon material culture and mortuary practices at a new theoretical level as well as considering the varied, complex and layered significances the relationships between belief and practice, as testified by the contributions to this volume.

Conclusion

This review illustrates that the paganism of the Anglo-Saxons has had a minor and intermittant presence in the antiquarian and archaeological narratives of English origins and Englishness. The careful negotiation and management of this ambivalent aspect of the customs and beliefs of the early Anglo-Saxons has meant that only in the heady context of early Victorian Anglo-Saxonism have archaeologists felt able to fully explore pagan beliefs in the archaeological record. For much of the 'prehistory', 'proto-history' and 'history' of Anglo-Saxon archaeology, the paganism of the Saxons has been a silent partner to – sometimes almost an apparition hovering behind – the migration myth. Likewise, the paganism of the Anglo-Saxons has been widely juxtaposed beside Christian conversion and an historical narrative of national origins and nation-building. It therefore remains to be seen whether the resurgent interest in the pagan English by archaeologists and cognate disciplines reflects the development of more sophisticated theories and methods of enquiry, free from the shackles of outmoded dogma, or simply yet another phase in the socio-politics of English identity.

Acknowledgements

The authors thank Martin Carver, Sarah Semple and Robert Wallis for comments on earlier drafts of this paper.

References

Akerman, J.Y. (1847a) *An Archaeological Index to the Remains of Antiquity in the Celtic, Romano-British and Anglo-Saxon Periods,* London: J.R. Smith

Akerman, J.Y. (1855a) *Remains of Pagan Saxondom,* London: Privately Printed

Akerman, J.Y. (1855b) An Account of Excavations in an Anglo-Saxon Burial-Ground at Harnham Hill Near Salisbury, *Archaeologia* 35: 259–78

Akerman, J.Y. (1855c) Note on Some Further Discoveries in the Anglo-Saxon Burial-Ground at Harnham Hill, Near Salisbury, *Archaeologia* 35: 475–8

AkerMan, J.Y. (1857) An Account of the Discovery of Anglo-Saxon Remains at Kemble, in North Wiltshire, *Archaeologia* 37: 113–21

Akerman, J.Y. (1857b) An Account on Researches in Anglo-Saxon Cemeteries at Filkins, and at Broughton Piggs, Oxon, *Archaeologia* 37: 140–6

Akerman, J.Y. (1857c) Report on Researches in a Cemetery of the Anglo-Saxon Period at Brighthampton, Co. Oxford, *Archaeologia* 37: 391–98

Akerman, J.Y. (1860a) Second Report of Researches in a Cemetery of the Anglo-Saxon Period at Brighthampton, Oxon, *Archaeologia* 38: 84–97

Akerman, J.Y. (1860b) Report on Researches in an Anglo-Saxon Cemetery at Long Wittenham, Berkshire, in 1859, *Archaeologia* 38: 327–52

Akerman, J.Y. (1863) Report on Further Researches in an Anglo-Saxon Burial-Ground at Long Wittenham, in the Summer of 1860, *Archaeologia* 39: 135–42

Arnold, C.J. (1997) *An Archaeology of the Early Anglo-Saxon Kingdoms*, 2nd Edition. London: Routledge

Avent, R. (1975) *Anglo-Saxon Disc and Composite Brooches*, BAR British Series 11, Oxford

Barnard, F.M. (2003) *Herder on Nationality, Humanity and History*, Montreal and Kingston: Mcgill-Queen's University Press

Blain, J. and Wallis, R.J. (2006) Re-Presenting Spirit: Heathenry, New-Indigenes, and the Imaged Past. *In* I.A. Russell (ed.) *Image, Simulation and Meaning in Archaeology in Archaeology and the Industrialisation and Marketing of Heritage and Tourism*, 89–118, London and New York: Springer

Blain, J. and Wallis, R.J. (2009) Heathenry and its Development. *In* J. Lewis & M. Pizza (eds) *Handbook of Contemporary Paganism*, 413–31, Handbooks on Contemporary Religion, Leiden and Boston: Brill

Blair, J. (1995) Anglo-Saxon Pagan Shrines and their Prototypes. *In* D.Griffiths (ed.) *Anglo-Saxon Studies in Archaeology and History 8*, 1–28, Oxford: Oxford Committee for Archaeology

Briggs, C.S. (2007) Prehistory in the Nineteenth Century. *In* S. Pearce (ed.) *Visions of Antiquity: the Society of Antiquaries of London 1707–2007*, 227–266, London: Society of Antiquaries of London

Bruce-Mitford, R. (1975). *The Sutton Hoo Ship-Burial Volume 1: Excavations, Background, the Ship, Dating and Inventory*, London: British Museum

Browne, T. (1658) *Hydriotaphia, Urne-Burial, Or, A Discourse on the Supulchrall Urnes Lately Found in Norfolk*, London: Brome

Camden, W. (1587) *Britannia*, London

Carver, M.O.H. (2000) Burial as Poetry: the Context of Treasure in Anglo-Saxon Graves. *In* E.M. Tyler (ed.) *Treasure in the Early Medieval West*, 25-48, Woodbridge: York Medieval Press

Carver, M.O.H. (2009) *On Reading Anglo-Saxon Graves*, J.M.Kemble Lecture for 2008, Trinity College Dublin

Channel Four (2009) Christianity: A History. Episode 3: The Dark Ages. Broadcast 25th January 2009. Http: //www.channel4.com/programmes/christianity-a-history/episode-guide/series-1/episode-3. Retrieved 13th February 2009

Content, S. (1995) The Text as Culture: The Making of the English, *Scottish Archaeological Review* 9 & 10: 36–40

Content, S. (Forthcoming) *Anglo-Saxons: Fact or Fiction? A Historiography of the Literature from the Sixteenth to the Twenty-First Century*, Unpublished Doctoral Thesis: University of Chester

Cranmer, T. (1540) *The Great Bible*, London

Davis, J.B. and Thurnam, J. (1865) *Crania Britannica*, London: Privately printed

Dickinson, T. (1993) An Anglo-Saxon 'Cunning Woman' from Bidford-upon-Avon. *In* M. Carver (ed.) *In Search of Cult: Archaeological Investigations in Honour of Philip Rahtz*, 45–54, Woodbridge: Boydell

Dickinson, T. (2002) Review Article: What's New in Early Medieval Burial Archaeology? *Early Medieval Europe* 11: 71–87

Dickinson, T. (2005) Symbols of Protection: The Significance of Animal-Ornamented Shields in Early Anglo-Saxon England, *Medieval Archaeology* 49: 109–63

Douglas, J. (1793) *Nenia Britannica*, London: Nichols

Ellis Davidson, H. (1993) *The Lost Beliefs of Northern Europe*, London: Routledge

Evans, C. (2007) 'Delineating Objects': Nineteenth-Century Antiquarian Culture and the Project of Archaeology. *In* S. Pearce (ed.) *Visions of Antiquity: The Society of Antiquaries of London 1707–2007*, 267–305, London: Society of Antiquaries of London

Foxe, J. (1570). *Actes and Monuments of these Latter and Perilous Days, Touching Matters of the Church*, 2 Volumes

Frantzen, A. and Niles, J.D. (1997) Introduction: Anglo-Saxonism and Medievalism. *In* J.D. Niles and A. Frantzen (eds), *Anglo-Saxonism and the Construction of Social Identity*, 1–14, Gainsville: University of Florida Press

Gerrard, C. (2003) *Medieval Archaeology*, London: Routledge

Green, J.R. (1915) *A Short History of the English People*, Volume One. London: Dent

Grimm, J. (1844) *Teutonic Mythology* (Translated by James S. Stallybrass, 1883), 1999 Edition. London: Routledge

Hamerow, H. (2006) 'Special Deposits' in Anglo-Saxon Settlements, *Medieval Archaeology* 50: 1–30

Hamilton, D. (1999) Richard Verstegan's A Restitution of Decayed Intelligence 1605: A Catholic Antiquarian Replies to John Foxe, Thomas Cooper, and Jean Bodin, *Prose Studies* 2: 1–38

Hawkes, S.C. (1990) Bryan Faussett and the Faussett Collection: an Assessment. *In* E. Southworth (ed.) *Anglo-Saxon Cemeteries: A Reappraisal*, 1–24, Stroud: Sutton

Hawkes, S.C., Ellis Davidson, H.R. and Hawkes, C. (1965) The Finglesham Man, *Antiquity* 39: 17–32

Hay, D. (1952) *Polydore Vergil: Renaissance Historian and Man of Letters*, Oxford: Clarendon Press

Hills, C. (2007) Anglo-Saxon Attitudes. *In* N. Higham (ed.) *Britons in Anglo-Saxon England*, 16–26, Woodbridge: Boydell

Hines, J. (1997) Religion: The Limits of Knowledge. *In* J. Hines (ed.) *The Anglo-Saxons From the Migration Period to the Eighth Century*, 375–400, Woodbridge: Boydell

Hingley, R. (2007) The Society, its Council the Membership and Publications, 1820–50. *In* S. Pearce (ed.) *Visions of Antiquity: The Society of Antiquaries of London 1707–2007*, 173–97, London: Society of Antiquaries of London

Hingley, R. (2008) *The Recovery of Roman Britain: 1586–1906*, Oxford: Oxford University Press.

Honouring The Ancient Dead (2009). http://www.honour.org.uk/faq. Retrieved 13th February 2009

Jessup, R. (1975) *Man of Many Talents: an Informal Biography of James Douglas 1752–1819*, London: Phillimore

Kemble, J.M. (1849) *The Saxons in England. A History of the English Commonwealth till the Period of the Norman Conquest*, Volume 1. London: Longman

Kemble, J.M. (1855) Burial and Cremation, *Archaeological Journal* 12: 309–37

Kemble, J.M. (1856) On Mortuary Urns Found at Stade-on-the-Elbe, and Other Parts of North Germany, Now in the Museum of the Historical Society of Hannover, *Archaeologia* 36: 270–283

Kemble, J.M. (1863) *Horae Ferales; or, Studies in the Archaeology of the Northern Nations, Edited by R.G. Latham & A.W. Franks*, London

Kidd, D. (1977) Charles Roach Smith and his Museum of London Antiquities. *In* R. Camber (ed.) *Collectors and Collections*, 105–35, London: British Museum Yearbook 2

Kidd, D. (1978) Charles Roach Smith and the Abbe Cochet, *Centenaire de l'Abbe Cochet – 1975. Actes du colloque international d'archaeologie*, 63–77, Rouen

Leeds, E.T. (1913) *The Archaeology of the Anglo-Saxon Settlements*, Oxford: Clarendon Press

Leeds, E.T. (1936) *Early Anglo-Saxon Art and Archaeology*, Oxford: Clarendon Press

Lethbridge, T.C. (1951) *A Cemetery at Lackford, Suffolk*, Cambridge: Cambridge University Press

Levine, P. (1986) *The Amateur and the Professional: Antiquarians, Historians and Archaeologists in Victorian England. 1838–1886*, Cambridge: Cambridge University Press

Lluyd, H. (1573) *The Breviary of Britain*, Translated by Thomas Twyne, London

Lucy, S. (1998) *The Early Anglo-Saxon Cemeteries of East Yorkshire: An Analysis and Reinterpretation*, BAR British Series 272, Oxford

Lucy, S. (2000) *The Anglo-Saxon Way of Death*, Stroud: Sutton

Lucy, S. (2002) From Pots to People: Two Hundred Years of Anglo-Saxon Archaeology. *In* C. Hough & K.A. Lowe (eds) *'Lastworda Betst' Essays in Memory of Christine E. Fell With Her Unpublished Writings*, 144–169, Donnington: Shaun Tyas

Macdougall, H.A. (1982) *Racial Myth in English History – Trojans, Teutons, and Anglo-Saxons*, Montreal: Harvest

Macgregor, A. (2007) E.T. Leeds and the Formation of an Anglo-Saxon Archaeology of England. *In* M. Henig and T.J. Smith (eds) *Collectanea Antiqua: Essays in Memory of Sonia Chadwick Hawkes*, 27–44, BAR International Series 1673, Oxford

Mayhew, R. (2000) Edmund Gibson's Editions of *Britannia*: Dynastic Chorography and the Particularist Politics of Precedent, *Historical Research* 73: 239–61

Meaney, A. (1964) *A Gazetteer of Early Anglo-Saxon Burial Sites*, Oxford: Allen and Unwin

Meaney, A. (1981) *Anglo-Saxon Amulets and Curing Stones*, BAR British Series 96, Oxford

Meaney, A. (2003) Anglo-Saxon Pagan and Early Christian Attitudes to the Dead. *In* M. Carver (ed.) *The Cross Goes North*, 229–42, Woodbridge: Boydell

Meaney, A.L. and Hawkes, S.C. (1970) *Two Anglo-Saxon Cemeteries at Winnall*, London: Society for Medieval Archaeology Monograph Series No. 4

Montfaucon, B. (1750) *A Collection of Regal and Ecclesiastical Antiquities of France*, London: Privately Printed

Morse, M. (1999) Craniology and the Adoption of the Three-Age System in Britain, *Proceedings of the Prehistoric Society* 65: 1–16

Morse, M. (2005) *How the Celts Came to Britain: Druids, Ancient Skulls and the Birth of Archaeology*, Stroud: Tempus

Murphy, M. (1982) Antiquary to Academic: The Progress of Anglo-Saxon Scholarship. *In* C.T. Berkhout and M.M. Gatch (eds) *Anglo-Saxon Scholarship: The First Three Centuries*, 1–18, Boston: G.K. Hall

Murray, T. and Evans, C. (eds) (2008) *Histories of Archaeology: A Reading in the History of Archaeology*, Oxford: Oxford University Press

Myres, J.N.L. (1942) Cremation and Inhumation in the Anglo-Saxon Cemeteries, *Antiquity* 16: 330–41

Myres, J.N.L. (1948) Some English Parallels to the Anglo-Saxon Pottery of Holland and Belgium in the Migration Period, *L'antiquité Classique* 17: 453–72

Parry, G. (1995) *The Trophies of Time: English Antiquarians of the Seventeenth Century*. Oxford: Oxford University Press

Pearce, S. (ed.) (2007) *Visions of Antiquity: The Society of Antiquaries of London 1707–2007*, London: Society of Antiquaries of London

Reynolds, N. (1980) The King's Whetstone: A Footnote, *Antiquity* 54: 232–7

Rhodes, M. (1990) Faussett Rediscovered: Charles Roach Smith, Joseph Mayer, and the Publication of *Inventorium Sepulchrale*. *In* E. Southworth (ed.) *Anglo-Saxon Cemeteries: A Reappraisal*, 25–64, Stroud: Sutton

Richards, J.D. (1992) Anglo-Saxon Symbolism. *In* M. Carver (ed.) *The Age of Sutton Hoo*, 131–48, Woodbridge: Boydell

Rowley-Conwy, P. (2007) *From Genesis to Prehistory: The Archaeological Three Age Syustem and its Contested Reception in Denmark, Britain, and Ireland*, Oxford: Oxford University Press

Schwyzer, P. (2007) *Archaeologies of English Renaissance Literature*, Oxford: Oxford University Press.

Scott Robinson, B. (2002) John Foxe and the Anglo-Saxons. *In* C. Highley and J. King (eds) *John Foxe and His World*, 54–72, Aldershot: Ashgate

Smith, C.R. (1856). *Inventorium Sepulchrale: An Account of Some Antiquities Dug up at Gilton, Kingston, Sibertswold, Barfriston, Beaksbourne, Chartham, and Crundale, in the County of Kent From AD 1757 to AD 1773 by the Reverend Bryan Faussett*, London: Privately printed

Strutt, J. (1774) *Horda Angel-Cynnan*, London: Benjamin White

Sweet, R. (2004) *Antiquaries: The Discovery of the Past in Eighteenth-Century Britain*, London: Hambledon and London.

Thorpe, L. (Trans.) (1966) *Geoffrey of Monmouth: The History of the Kings of Britain*, London: Penguin

Turner, S. (1807) *History of the Anglo-Saxons*, Volume 1, 2nd Edition, London: Luke Hansard.

Verstegan, R. (1605) *A Restitution of Decayed Intelligence in Antiquities*, Antwerp

Wallis, R.J. and Blain, J. (2009) 'Sacred' Sites, Artefacts and Museum Collections: Pagan Engagements with Archaeology in Britain. *In* J. Lewis and M. Pizza (eds) *Handbook of Contemporary Paganism*, 591–609, Brill Handbooks on Contemporary Religion 2, Leiden and Boston: Brill

White, R.H. (1988) Mayer and British Archaeology. *In* M. Gibson and S.M. Wright (eds) *Joseph Mayer of Liverpool 1803–1886*, 118–36, London: Society of Antiquaries of London.

Wickham-Crowley, L. (1999) Looking forward, Looking Back: Excavating the Field of Anglo-Saxon Archaeology. *In* C. Karkov (ed.) *The Archaeology of Anglo-Saxon England – Basic Readings*, 1–25, London: Garland

Wiley, R.A. (1979) Anglo-Saxon Kemble: The Life and Works of John Mitchell Kemble 1807–1857, Philologist, Historian, Archaeologist. *In* S.C. Hawkes, D. Brown, and J. Campbell (eds), *Anglo-Saxon Studies in Archaeology and History* 1, 165–273, BAR British Series 72, Oxford

Williams, H. (2002) "The Remains of Pagan Saxondom"? Studying Anglo-Saxon Cremation Practices. *In* S. Lucy and A. Reynolds (eds) *Burial in Early Medieval England and Wales*, 47–71, Society of Medieval Archaeology Monograph Series 17, London: Maney

Williams, H. (2006a) Digging Saxon Graves in Victorian Britain. *In* R. Pearson (ed.) *The Victorians and the Ancient World: Archaeology and Classicism in Nineteenth-Century Culture*, 61–80, Cambridge: Cambridge Scholars Press

Williams, H. (2006b) Heathen Graves and Victorian Anglo-Saxonism: Assessing the Archaeology of John Mitchell Kemble. *In* S. Semple (ed.). *Anglo-Saxon Studies in Archaeology & History 13*, 1–18. Oxford: Oxford University School of Archaeology

Williams, H. (2007a) "Burnt Germans", Alemannic Graves and the Origins of Anglo-Saxon Archaeology. *In* S. Burmeister, H. Derks and J. Von Richthofen (eds), *Zweiundvierzig. Festschrift für Michael Gebühr zum 65. Geburtstag*, 229–238, Internationale Archäologie – Studia honoraria 25. Rahden: Westf.

Williams, H. (2007b) Forgetting the Britons in Victorian Anglo-Saxon Archaeology. *In* N. Higham (ed.) *Britons in Anglo-Saxon England*, 27–41, Woodbridge: Boydell

Williams, H. (2007c) Introduction: Themes in the Archaeology of Early Medieval Death and Burial. *In* S. Semple & H. Williams (eds) *Early Medieval Mortuary Practices: Anglo-Saxon Studies in Archaeology & History 14*, 1–11, Oxford: Oxford University School of Archaeology

Williams, H. (2008) Anglo-Saxonism and Victorian Archaeology: William Wylie's *Fairford Graves*. *Early Medieval Europe* 16(1): 49–88

Wilson, D.M. (1984) *The Forgotten Collector. Augustus Wollaston Franks of the British Museum*, London: Thames and Hudson

Wilson, D. (1992) *Anglo-Saxon Paganism*, London: Routledge

Wright, T.M. 1852. *The Celt, the Roman, and the Saxon: A History of the Early Inhabitants of Britain Down to the Anglo-Saxon Conversion to Christianity*, London: Trübner

Wylie, W.M. (1852) *Fairford Graves*, Oxford: Parker

Wylie, W.M. (1857) The Burning and Burial of the Dead, *Archaeologia* 37(2): 455–78

Young, R.J.C. (2008) *The Idea of English Ethnicity*, Oxford: Blackwell

Afterword

Caveats and Cutures

Ronald Hutton

This is the best kind of edited collection of scholarly essays, with a firm focus on a subject, a common purpose in tackling it, and a clear division of the material according to theme, between authors with a proven expertise in each area and comparable ability. It deserves to carry the study of Anglo-Saxon paganism forward into the new decade with renewed momentum and a new framework equipped with a useful set of comparisons and insights. If the thoughts that follow focus more on the problems of the exercise than its achievements, that is simply because every contributor has worked well enough to focus a reader's mind, immediately, upon what more can now be done.

What the whole book seems to reveal, and Martin Carver specifically and fluently depicts, is a world of fluid religious identities, between which individuals and communities can move and which indeed they are largely free to construct according to their own tastes. Although zealots may characterise it in terms of cohesive and competing kinds of faith, the reality is actually one in which belief and practice are both profoundly variable. Not only do people pick and mix between religious systems, but they develop their own idiomatic and personal manifestations of each. Institutional structures exist, above all within Christianity, but have only very limited impact on the way in which the supernatural is represented and understood, and in which humans engage with it, at any particular time and place. Christianity itself, so often treated by less sensitive commentators as a single phenomenon, appears on closer inspection to take forms as various and as localised as any other tradition. The European continent is divided into different polities, which have their own importance, but in cultural matters, including those of religion, it is far better now to take a view of it which transcends political boundaries, and above all those of the traditional and familiar modern nation states, which now provide some of the worst limitations to productive insights. In particular, this transcontinental culture possesses an acute awareness of the general importance of the natural environment, partly as a source of sustenance and comfort but also as one of disquiet and concern, loaded with both actual and potential problems. As part of this outlook, animals are regarded not as mere sources of food or sport but as beings with their own independent importance and significance, worthy of respect and taking their place in a complex set of relationships with each other and with humanity. In every sense, it is a time of newly opened horizons and opportunities, in which the fall of long-accustomed frontiers and cultural barriers have permitted a novel degree of mobility, opportunity and change. Nobody can fail to see which world is being described here: it is that of Europe in the early twenty-first century.

This does not, of course, mean that it was not also that of Anglo-Saxon paganism and early Christianity. If, however, one of the intentions of this collection is to raise the study of both to a new level – and I have agreed that it is worthy of that enterprise – then it might need to show a stronger focus on scholarly reflexivity. In practice, historians and prehistorians have for a long time managed both to emphasise that every age views the past through the prism of its own preoccupations, prejudices and ideals, and to imply that in some fashion they are less prone to this tendency than their predecessors. The present collection continues this tradition: Sue Content and Howard Williams make an admirable job of showing how Anglo-Saxon studies developed out of previous cultural changes, but stop short of showing how close the fit is between its own conclusions and the circumstances and ideals of the current decade.

This pattern, of seeing the past – and I stress again that we may indeed be seeing it better – through the prism of our own time, is the more important because of the particular nature of the evidence for early Anglo-Saxon religion. Professor Carver has faced the problems of it candidly, and in some detail, but they deserve additional emphasis. We are effectively in the position of people who are trying to analyse the contents of a sealed can for which they have no opener. This does not mean that we know nothing about the contents: the fact that they are in a can, of a particular design, tells us something about them in general terms, and we can read some labelling on the exterior, put there by early medieval Christians, though we may suspect that they did not know much about what is really inside either. None the less, we cannot get in, and should beware that, in giving the impression of genuine advances in understanding, we are not just changing the labels. When Sarah Semple tells us that the whole landscape was to a greater or lesser extent sacred to the pagan Anglo-Saxons; or Julie Lund that watery features in it seem to have been particularly numinous; or Howard Williams that burial rites are performances to transform the living as well as the dead by the promotion of ideologies; or Jenny Walker that ideology was built into the architectural components of sites; or Aleks Pluskowski and Chris Fern that animals played a key part in social and cosmological organisation; or Alexandra Sanmark that there was fairly clearly a strong belief in the survival of the soul; what is actually happening is that the exterior of the can is being described with more care than before.

Let's go back into Julie Lund's wetlands. We can accept that pagan Europeans regarded watery places as the haunt of spirits and deities, and certain waters as especially numinous, because all the evidence of literature, folklore and epigraphy indicates that they did. The analysis of material finds in watery contexts suggests convincingly that many if not most of them were placed there in deliberate acts of deposition, and the manner in which such deposits increase, notably in particular places and times, argues fairly conclusively for cult activity. The ancient Greek geographer Strabo quotes a description by the traveller Posidonius of just such a cult as it was carried on at sacred lakes by the native Gallic people of what is now Toulouse, 'by way of invoking and propitiating their god' (*Geographia* 4.1.13). Our problem is that so many different intentions may have been served by the same kind of action. To lay an object in water may have been a means of worshipping a deity or group of deities whose home that water happened to be. Or the water may have been regarded as a gateway to a larger otherworld, inhabited by such beings. Conversely, it could have been the location which mattered rather than the water in particular: at Posidonius' Toulouse, treasure was both cast into the pools and heaped up in enclosures on dry land nearby, both being within the same area demarcated as sacred. The spoils in the enclosures were easily looted when the Romans conquered the area, but those in the water were naturally much harder to remove. Alternatively, the gesture of deposition could be intended to propitiate the forces that controlled the waters in order to ensure a safe journey for particular humans across or along them, or to prevent the waters concerned from spreading, or going into flood. If water on the land was related in some fashion to that from the sky, such gifts may have related to increasing or diminishing the wetness of a season. On the other hand, the wetland in question may have been viewed as a boundary rather than a focus in itself, and the placement of the object designed to hold back human enemies on the far side. These are very different ways of structuring landscape, which can all be comprehended within the material evidence. They are part of that lost interiority of religious experience.

Such exercises could, of course, be reproduced for each of the areas of activity considered in the other chapters. To choose just one other, and more briefly, when Howard Williams suggests that we should regard Anglo-Saxon funerals as contexts for the production and reproduction of social memories and cosmologies, he is making sound intuitive sense. On the other hand, it is by no means clear that we are any closer to recovering the memories and cosmologies involved in those funerals. We seem to have no idea, for example, whether cremation and inhumation were regarded as two functional means to the same spiritual destination, or whether they were based on two very different conceptions of the relationship between body and soul, and of the fate of the latter. Likewise, grave goods may have been deposited as gifts for the dead to take into the next world, or to comfort them in this one, while they waited to make the journey, or as items too intimately associated with the deceased to be retained by the living without a fear of being troubled by the dead person's spirit; to name but three possible options among several. Dr Williams demonstrates very well the complexity of the mortuary rites detectable in the Anglo-Saxon context, and the variety and mutability of practices present within it, reflecting diverse traditions; but we have no sure idea of what any of those traditions were. This is, of course, where comparative archaeological data, literary sources and anthropology are usually deployed to provide suggestions. Professor Carver has dealt directly with the inherent problems of all, as used in the Anglo-Saxon context, but there are others that directly affect the essays in this volume.

When the historical evidence for the Roman and Norman conquests and the Viking settlements of England is compared with the archaeological, it makes a pretty good fit, in religious as in military, social, economic and political contexts. To be sure, argument and doubt can arise over particular events and figures, and the extent of particular developments, but in general the data is compatible. In their record, the Anglo-Saxons now present a striking, and troubling, anomaly. All of the historical evidence, whether that left by contemporaries or near-contemporaries such as Gildas and the fifth-century Gallic authors, or retrospective sources such as Bede, the *Anglo-Saxon Chronicle* and the *Historia Brittonum*, portrays an intensely traumatic experience of invasion, conflict, slaughter and dispossession. This is also in apparent harmony with the linguistic and place-name evidence, and the creation of Brittany itself presupposes mass migration provoked by danger at home. The material evidence of settlement, however, has been powerfully and commonly argued of late to refute all this, and so the two bodies of data are at apparent odds to an unusual extent.

This chasm extends to religion. As is repeatedly noted in these essays, the literary sources, notably Pope Gregory, Bede and Aldhelm, are united in speaking of pagan temples, shrines, altars, images and pillars in Anglo-Saxon England, and Bede alludes to a designated priesthood bound by taboos. Gregory and Aldhelm may be counted as contemporary to the phenomena that they describe, and the latter should have been within living memory when Bede was young. As this collection also emphasises, however, archaeology has so far been unable to find undisputable evidence for any of these religious trappings. This is not business as usual, but an exceptional situation.

There is, fortunately, plenty of material evidence to support the argument of this book for the diversity and mutability of Anglo-Saxon paganism, and indeed of early English Christianity. Here the material data are easier to reconcile with the literary; but even so some slight doubts linger. The missionary effort in southern Britain during the seventh was much more cohesive and centrally directed than that in the same region in the fifth. None the less, the latter seems to have packed enough punch to finish off Romano-British paganism and enough theological uniformity to confront and defeat a major heresy, in Pelagianism. It may be that the diversity and localism are more apparent in the material record than they were to contemporaries: and it should never be forgotten that the issues discussed at the synod of Whitby divided Christians right across the archipelago though they appear now rather trivial in scale, in comparison to the huge number of beliefs and practices that British and Irish Christians held in common.

The greatest achievement of this book is to open the discussion of Anglo-Saxon paganism to continental Europe, or at least to Scandinavia. This should certainly be the place in which to start, with a good ethic and cultural match for the early English, great archaeology and dynamic scholarship, and a growing tendency for its academic community to publish in English. Only two cautions need be entered. The first is the obvious one: that we now need to repeat the exercise with other continental comparisons. Germany is a clear example, from Schleswig-Holstein southward, being more of an exact homeland for Anglo-Saxon culture than Scandinavia proper. The Franks are another, being the nearest Germanic people to undergo a parallel experience of conquest and settlement of Roman territory. Both make guest appearances in this volume, but few compared with the amount of material from further north.

The other concern is rather less obvious: that religion can manifest itself in very different ways in neighbouring peoples with apparently similar social, political, cultural and economic attributes. In the late pre-Roman Iron Age, for example, the inhabitants of what is now northern France were celebrating rites in large rectangular enclosures of earth and timber decorated with human bones and weapons. Those of Ireland were constructing similarly impressive ritual monuments, but circular, and apparently composed largely of freestanding posts. Those of southern Britain, between, were making small shrines, mostly square or rectangular in shape and better fitted for individuals or small groups than mass rituals. That is why we should perhaps expect to find important differences as well as similarities between the physical manifestations of Scandinavian and Anglo-Saxon paganism; which is what indeed we seem to do.

One place at which some of the contributors to this book clearly need to look harder is Siberia. Anthropological concepts have been fruitful sources of comparative insight for archaeologists, ever since the latter first began to emerge as a discipline, but they need to be used as tools and not as cloaks. This has become especially true of the one which is the honoured guest in parts of this collection: shamanism. There are two problems with its usage here. The first was highlighted by Graham Harvey in his reader on the subject, when he declared that the word 'shamanism' has ceased to be a term and become a semantic field, lacking any common deployment and significance (Harvey 2003: 1–25). This degree of confusion means that it is crucially important that any scholar who uses it is careful to define and defend its exact meaning to her or him, and the relationship of that meaning to others circulating within and between different disciplines. This is clearly not happening in the present book. The second difficulty is geographical. The term itself was coined by Western scholars to describe a phenomenon that they had encountered amongst native Siberians, in which relations between humans and a spirit world were mediated by an expert who engaged in a dramatic public performance in the course of which she or he went into an ecstatic trance. 'Classical' shamanism, in this sense, is not an umbrella term for dealings with a spirit world by specialists among indigenous peoples, but, to adopt the terminology of one prominent author upon it, Anna-Leena Siikala, a particular 'rite technique' (Siikala 1987). European travellers who encountered it were fascinated by it, and European scholars coined an expression to characterise it, precisely because it seemed so unfamiliar to them (Flaherty 1992).

In fact there is no doubt that the classical Siberian shamanic rite was found (at least until early modern times) among one European people, the Sámi or Saami of northern Scandinavia. Furthermore, Neil Price and I converge, from different starting-points, on an agreement that there are definite expressions of it in medieval Scandinavian culture, almost wholly recorded in Icelandic literature (Price 2002; Hutton 2001). What is by no means clear is whether this was because either ancient northern Europe had itself possessed shamanism of the Siberian kind, which died out at the beginning of history, or because the Norse had absorbed it from the Sámi. I incline to the latter view, partly because the sagas actually distinguish Sámi sorcerers as experts in a powerful magic which employed trances, and partly because medieval Norse culture does seem to be a hybrid in which shamanic elements were mixed with others more generally characteristic of northern European religion and magic. This is where comparative exercises are valuable again, this time with magical techniques as represented in other medieval literatures that draw on pre-Christian tradition such as the Irish, and with later collections of folklore across Europe. When these are considered, it does seem that the Norse were very unusual in clearly having elements of Siberian-style shamanism and that they had absorbed them from the Sámi. This makes a simple projection of them from the Norse to the Anglo-Saxons rather unwise, and the matter cannot be settled by scanning ambiguous passages of early English literature and arguing that they might refer to shamanic trance-states of the Siberian and Sámi kind. A better starting-point would be to compare the latter in detail with the quite extensive records of Anglo-Saxon magical practices: and to my eyes, at least, they seem substantially different.

A final word should be said in praise of Martin Carver's instinctive desire to bring Christianity into a discussion of Anglo-Saxon paganism. Here there is indeed rich potential for building up a picture of early medieval religious behaviour which crosses confessional boundaries and adds to our understanding of the nature of conversion. It may be proposed that, in many ways, at a popular level ancient paganism and medieval Christianity were parallel systems. Both depended on human relationships, for different purposes, with a wide range of supernatural beings – in the Christian case saints – in which female figures were as prominent and potent as male. For most people, dealings with these beings were concentrated at a few major seasonal festivals and ad-hoc moments of acute needs, although a few manifested a need for more continuous contact. The central act for both was sacrifice, in the Christian context embodied in the mass. These correspondences may enable us better to understand what ancient and medieval Europeans expected from religion in general.

The stronger the light that is cast, the more pronounced the shadows that it produces. If I have devoted a lot of space to those thrown by this book, then that is a consequence of its success in revealing a landscape of research so clearly. It is, in my opinion, the best single work on its subject at the present, and should be a stimulus to many more.

References

Flaherty, G. (1992) *Shamanism and the Eighteenth Century*, Princeton: University Press
Harvey, G. (ed.) (2003) *Shamanism: A Reader*, London: Routledge
Hutton, R. (2001) *Shamans: Siberian Spirituality and the Western Imagination*, London: Hambledon and London
Price, N. (2002) *The Viking Way: Religion and War in Late Iron Age Scandinavia*, AUN 31, Uppsala
Siikala, A.-L. (1987) *The Rite Technique of the Siberian Shaman*, Helsinki: Academia Scientarum Fennica

Index

Index of Place-Names

Gosforth, Newcastle upon Tyne, North-
 umberland, 121
Great Chesterford, Essex, 141, *142*
Greencroft, Lancaster, 53
Grimes Graves, Norfolk, 29
Grimeshole, Berkshire, 29
Guilden Morden, Hertfordshire 113
Hanbury, Worcestershire, 33, 38
Harford Farm, Norfolk, 35, 40
Harnham Hill, Wiltshire, 190, 191
Harrow Fields, Cheshire, 40
Harrow Hill, Sussex, 27, *28*, 29
Harrow-on-the-Hill, Middlesex, 27
Heath Wood, Ingleby, Derbyshire, 121
Highborough Hill, Eastry, Kent, 140
Howletts, Kent, 140
High Wycombe, Berkshire, 38
'Hundred tree', Buckinghamshire, 41
Hurbuck, Durham, 58
Jarrow, Durham, 96
Knowlton, Dorset, 36
Lastingham, Yorkshire, 168
Lackford, Suffolk, 75
Loxton, Somerset, *133*
Long Wittenham, Oxfordshire, 96, 191
Lowbury, Berkshire, 27
Marlcliffe, Worcestershire, 29
Melton, East Yorkshire, 150
Merlewood Cave, Lancashire, 29
Monkwearmouth, Durham, 96
Milfield in Northumberland, 96
Minster-in-Thanet, Kent, 29
Morning Thorpe, Norfolk, 141
Mucking, Essex, 135
Nazeing, Essex, 58
Nettleton Top, Lincolnshire, 171
Newark, Nottinghamshire, 72
Nikerpole, Mildenhall, Wiltshire, 30
Northampton, Nottinghamshire, 113
Norton, Cleveland, Durham, 171
Ogbourne St Andrew, Wiltshire, 38
Ovingham, Northumberland, 121
Poukeput, Harting, Sussex, 29
Prittlewell, Essex, 16, 195
Rivers, Adur, 32, Arun, 32, Avon, 53, Boyle,
 59, Cherwell, 31, 53, 54, Cuckmere, 32,
 Deben, 32, Dee, 32, *32*, Glen, 89, Kennet,

53, Lark, 113, Lea, 53, 58, 60, Lung, 59,
 Nene, 53, Ouse, 32, Rhine, 9, 130, 131,
 138, 149, Thames, 30, 31, 53, 54, 55, 60,
 111, 112, 190, 191, Wey, 53, 55, Witham,
 15, 30, 31, 33, 53, 55, 60
Rudston, Yorkshire, 33, 36, *37*
Scutchmer Knob, Berkshire, 25, *34*
Sheffield's Hill, Lincolnshire, 110
Silbury Hill, Wiltshire, 38
Slonk Hill, Sussex, 33, 40
Spong Hill, Norfolk, 72, 73, 74–5, 110,
 114–15, 131, 134, *137*, 141, *142*
Sancton, East Yorkshire, 72, 114, 141
Skipwith, Yorkshire, 121
Sockburn, Durham, 121
Skerne, East Yorkshire, 55
St. Mary the Virgin, Stanton Drew, Somerset,
 33
St. Paul-in-the-Bail, Lincolnshire, 34
Springfield Lyons, Essex, 131, 134
Stanton Drew, Somerset, 33, 36
Snape, Suffolk, 77–8, 131, 171
Sutton Courtenay, Berkshire, 84, 135
Sutton Hoo, Suffolk, 5, 8, 16, 145, 194, 195
 Cemetery, 6, 8, 9, 10, 32, 68, 76, 77–9, 108,
  112, 114–15, 118–9, 131, *132*, 134–5, *135*,
  147, 149, 151, 171, 173, 194, 196
 Helmet, 112, 116–7, 140–1, *140*, 164, *165*,
  166–7
 Purse, 117, *139*, 166, *166*
 Sceptre, 13
 Shield, 108–10, *109*, 111, 113, *139*, 166
Taplow, Berkshire, 38
Thunresfelda, Wiltshire, 25
Thunderlow, Essex, 172
Thursley, Surrey, 26
Thurstaple, Kent, 41
Thurstaston, Wirral, Cheshire, 42, *43*
Tyesmere, Worcestershire, 57–8
Thyrspit, Usselby, Lincolnshire, 29
Tishoe, Surrey, 27
Tislea, Hampshire, 25
Uffington, Wiltshire, 130
Uley, Gloucestershire, 12
Vindolanda, Northumberland, 34
Waden Hill, Wiltshire, 38
Wakerley, Northamptonshire, *137*